STUARTS AND ROMANOVS

T0353123

Peter I and William III, Medal struck for 'friendly interview' at Utrecht, 1697, *A Summary of Mr Rapin de Thoyras's History of England*, 1751, University of Aberdeen [*A Summary*, p. 38, medal no. 4].

Front: The King's bust crowned with laurel, and this legend round it: GULIELMUS III, DEI GRATIA, MAGNAE BRITANNIAE, FRANCIAE, ET HIBERNIAE REX, FIDEI DEFENSOR, PIUS, AUGUSTUS; *William III, by the grace of God, King of Great Britain, defender of the faith, pious, august.*

Reverse: The King receiving the Czar at the gate of his palace, with these words in the rim: SIC OLIM HEROES; *Thus acted the ancient heroes.* The city of Utrecht is seen in the offings. In the exergue is the following inscription: PETRI ALEXIEWICZ CZAR MAGNIQUE GULIELMI REGIS AMICITIA TRAJECTI AD RHENUM, XI SEPTEMBRIS, MDCXCVII; *The friendly interview between the Czar Peter Alexiewicz and King William the Great, at Utrecht, 11 September 1697.*

STUARTS AND ROMANOVS

The Rise and Fall of a Special Relationship

Paul Dukes
Graeme P. Herd
Jarmo Kotilaine

DUNDEE UNIVERSITY PRESS

First published in Great Britain in 2009 by
Dundee University Press

University of Dundee
Dundee DD1 4HN

http://www.dup.dundee.ac.uk/

ISBN: 978 1 84586 055 4

British Library Cataloguing-in-Publication Data
A catalogue record for this book is available on request from the British Library

Typeset by IDSUK (DataConnection) Ltd.
Printed and bound by CPI Group (UK) Ltd, Croydon, CR0 4YY

Contents

Illustrations

Maps

Preface

The Stuarts and the Romanovs are two of the most famous dynasties in history. There have been many books about both. Yet this is the first to discuss a full range of contacts between them. While it aims not to repeat what has already been said, it does throw some fresh light on both dynasties and encourages comparisons, especially concerning their attempts to establish variants of absolutist government within the framework of international relations.

Most of the seventeenth century was dominated by the Stuarts in Britain and the Romanovs in Russia. Through their actions and policies, they came to define much of what happened in and between the two countries. However, the story is about much more than the two dynasties, not least because the initial contact between both England and Scotland on the one hand and Russia on the other took place during the reigns of their predecessors, the Tudors and Riurikovichi, but also because the Stuart dynasty in the paternalist, would-be absolutist male line was removed from the throne at a time when the tsar who came to be known as Peter the Great embarked on the expansion of the Russian empire.

Moreover, Stuart–Romanov contacts marked the genesis of regular interaction between Muscovite Russia and Britain, never before systematically analysed. This interaction is not only of interest in its own right, but also of critical importance for the development of the two countries as well as for Europe and the wider world. Much of the previous writing on the Anglo-Russian, that is to say Brito-Russian, relationship is misinformed and fails to appreciate the full complexity and significance of the encounter between the two geographical extremes of early modern Europe. In fact, the relationship went through a number of different phases which reflected the evolution of the two countries and their responses to the increasingly rapid pace of change in Europe, which was in the throes of major commercial, diplomatic and military transformations, even revolutions.

In our book, we concentrate on three important dimensions of the contacts between the two countries, namely commerce, diplomacy and war. These three areas are related, but in many ways different. They also varied a great deal over time. While the first encounter was above all diplomatic in nature, it was concerned to a considerable extent with trade, and the relationship was driven forward by merchants organised in the Muscovy Company. In its turn, the *modus operandi* of the company continued to be circumscribed by the diplomatic objectives of the Stuarts in the wake of the Tudors. If their Dutch rivals were aggressively commercial in their approach to the Russian market, the merchants of the Muscovy Company in concert with their royal patrons insisted on upholding privileges that became increasingly outdated and difficult to justify in view of the operations of the Dutch and other rivals.

Meanwhile, Russia under the Romanovs was a power recovering from a profound Time of Troubles, craving recognition and seeking strategic advantage. Reluctant to make binding commitments, the Stuarts nevertheless gave some support to the activities of mostly Scottish soldiers playing a key role in the modernisation and growth of the Russian army. As the diplomatic relationship reached a crisis with the onset of Civil War in England, Scotland and Ireland, the role of soldiers and merchants was critical in ensuring continued interaction between the two countries, and ultimately decisive in reviving Anglo-Russian relations on a more realistic and sustainable basis. Many of the English and Scottish residents in Russia came to understand the country and its needs in a manner that visiting British diplomats quite simply failed to appreciate. Some of these individuals eventually became drivers of diplomacy as well. Moreover, the takeover and transformation of the Muscovy Company by people more focused on profits than privileges created the basis for exploiting commercial opportunities in a way that initially emulated and ultimately outshone the Dutch. By this time, however, the absolutist pretensions of the Stuarts had been crushed.

All these developments have to be considered in the context of seventeenth-century wars. Although both Stuarts and Romanovs had a peripheral relationship to the Thirty Years' War that dominated most of the first half of the century, they were nevertheless subject to its influence, especially in the pan-European crisis that immediately followed it. Subsequently, while the Stuarts were at war in the West, especially with the Dutch Republic, the Romanovs were in conflict with their immediate neighbours, especially the Poles and the Ottoman Turks, to a lesser extent the Swedes. Before the end of the century, however, wars at both ends of the continent converged, in particular at the time of the removal from the throne of James VII and II, who was suspected of attempting to install a Roman Catholic absolutism reminiscent of that of Louis XIV of France.

Stuarts and Romanovs includes not only the kings and tsars but also includes their subjects pursuing both peaceful and warlike ends. There was a clear division of labour here. Nearly all the merchants from the British Isles were English, while most of the soldiers were Scots. Stuart diplomats were predominantly English, but there were outstanding Scots among them, too. As for the

Romanovs, they were dependent on their advisers to varying extents. Even Peter I, the future Peter the Great, relied heavily in the earlier days of his ascendancy on such individuals as the Scot Patrick Gordon as well as other foreigners and Russians. A whole range of merchants, statesmen and soldiers is discussed in the book, as well as the kings and tsars.

The emphasis of the book varies from chapter to chapter, depending on the balance between commerce, diplomacy and war. Chapters 1 and 8 constitute an introduction and conclusion. Chapters 2 to 7 are predominantly narrative. Chapter 1 introduces the subject with a comparison of the predecessors to the Stuarts and Romanovs, the Tudors and Riurikovichi. It looks at the relations developing from 1553 onwards, with some discussion of commerce, diplomacy and war. It then introduces the Stuarts and Romanovs before a description of the first meeting of Stuart and Russian representatives in 1600. Chapter 2 stretches from the accession of James VI of Scotland as James I of England in 1603 to his death in 1625. It takes in the accession of Mikhail Fedorovich Romanov in 1613, which helped to bring to an end the Time of Troubles and led to the formal beginning of the relationship between the two dynasties. Chapter 3 considers a break in diplomatic contact between 1623 and 1646 during the turbulent reign of Charles I. It includes the accession of Aleksei Mikhailovich as well as bringing in the origins of the Civil War in England, Scotland and Ireland and aspects of the Thirty Years' War. Chapter 4 describes serious social disturbances facing Aleksei Mikhailovich, and introduces the problem of a mid-century crisis with the execution of Charles I as an event of key significance. It continues with a description of relations during the years of the Interregnum up to the first years of the Restoration. Chapter 5 continues the story of the Restoration of Charles II and the resumption of official Stuart–Romanov relations up to the death of Aleksei Mikhailovich in 1676, with a more detailed description of some of the embassies. Chapter 6 contains similar description as it proceeds through the reign of Alexei's son Fedor and the Regency of his daughter Sophia to the eve of the assumption of power by another son, the future Peter the Great, in 1689. Just before that, 1688 saw the removal from the throne of the male Stuarts in the person of James VII and II soon after his accession in 1685. Chapter 7 focuses on the end of the paternalistic Stuarts with special reference to the birth of Jacobitism in Russia, and on the consolidation of the Romanovs. Chapter 8 begins with the meeting of the future Peter the Great with William III in Utrecht at the beginning of the 'Great Embassy' of 1697–8. Observations follow on war and diplomacy, then commerce, in the seventeenth century and some reference to the historiographical problems encountered in the approach to the subject of Stuarts and Romanovs, including the failure of the Stuarts to establish an absolutist government while the Romanovs succeeded. The book ends with a brief epilogue on the last meeting of representatives of the two dynasties.

We have approached our joint project like the fictional contemporaries of its subject, the Three Musketeers: 'All for one: one for all.' Certainly, none of us could have produced this work by himself. In the first instance, Jarmo Kotilaine was responsible for commerce, Graeme P. Herd for diplomacy and Paul Dukes for war. Dukes assumed responsibility for overall editing, but the agreed final version includes further emendations by Herd and Kotilaine.

A few words are necessary about weights, measures, money and dates. A *pud* or *pood* is 16.38 kilograms. A *chetvert'* varied between 4 and 8 *pud*, tending towards 4 at the beginning of the seventeenth century and more normally 8 at the end. A *chetvert'* was also a measurement of land, usually half a *desiatina*, that is to say half of 11,197.44 square metres. A *versta* or *verst* was 1.067 kilometres in length. A rouble, abbreviated as R, and reichsthaler, abbreviated as Rtl, were the most common monetary units apart from the pound sterling. Throughout the seventeenth century, the Julian calendar was observed in most of Protestant Europe, including Britain. In 1700, it was adopted in Russia, where the years had previously been counted from the alleged date of the Creation. Catholic Europe adhered to the Gregorian calendar, ten days in advance of the Julian in the seventeenth century.

Illustrations are provided of people and places. While pictures may indeed be worth thousands of words, they must also be viewed with care. For example, portraits of tsars were usually made for Orthodox ceremonial purposes, drawings of cities normally conveyed little of their hustle, bustle and smell. The cover is taken from the Blaeu map of Russia in 1614. The three figures symbolise the diplomat, the soldier and the merchant. The Bibliography lists full titles for the wide, multilingual (Danish, Dutch, English, Estonian, Finnish, French, German, Polish, Russian, Swedish as well as Latin) range of primary and secondary sources indicated in the Notes. We have drawn heavily on the work of scholars such as Sergei Konovalov and Anna Liubimenko (as variously spelled) from older generations, Maria Salomon Arel and Geraldine Phipps from newer. We owe a debt of gratitude to these and other scholars, and to Geraldine Phipps in addition for reading an earlier version of the whole work and making many useful suggestions.

We acknowledge with sincere thanks the help and advice that we have received from many other colleagues. The late Professor Lindsey Hughes, two anonymous readers for Dundee University Press and John Tuckwell made a thorough appraisal of the penultimate version. John Tuckwell first accepted the work for Dundee University Press. Mairi Sutherland and other associates of Birlinn Ltd saw the book through to publication. Three former PhD students at Aberdeen

University – Alexeia Grosjean, Steve Murdoch and David Worthington – rendered assistance on Sweden, Denmark and the Habsburg Empire respectively. David Worthington also made a useful reading. Jan Willem Veluwenkamp and others at Groningen University were most supportive. Ingrid Maijer of Uppsala corrected and supplemented our analysis of the *vesti-kuranty* 'newspapers'. Dmitry Fedosov of Moscow, who is translating and editing the Diary of Patrick Gordon, suggested some emendations. Mr John Reid Hebden (author and publisher of *Sir John Hebdon Kt, 1612–1670: His history and family*, 2003) gave advice on the career of his illustrious ancestor as well as helping us to locate Sir John's Portrait. Without Jill Golden of the Library of the George C. Marshall European Center for Security Studies, Garmisch-Partenkirchen, Christina Schori-Lang of the Geneva Centre for Security Policy and Ray Scrivens of Cambridge University Library, we would never have completed the bibliography. Professor Daniel Waugh of the University of Washington has allowed us to make use of his photographic collection. Colleagues in Historic Collections, King's College, Old Aberdeen, could not have been more assiduous in locating and copying illustrations. Owen Logan applied his expertise to technical aspects of the illustrations. Cathryn Dukes helped with the proofs. Linda Sutherland produced the index. There are many others, too numerous to name, who have answered importunate questions, and made constructive suggestions. Of course, we ourselves take full responsibility for the book, errors, inadequacies and all.

We dedicate the book to the memory of our dear friend Lindsey Hughes.

Abbreviations

APC	Acts of the Privy Council
ARA	Algemeen Rijksarchief, The Hague
AUL	Aberdeen University Library
BL	British Library
CASS	Canadian-American Slavic Studies
CSP CO D F V	Calendar of State Papers, Colonial, Domestic, Foreign, Venetian
EAA	Eesti Ajalooarhiv
EEBO	Early English Books Online
EHR	English Historical Review
GAA NA	Gemeeente Archief Amsterdam, Notariële Archieven
GHL	Guildhall Library
GKEL	Goldsmith'-Kress Library of Economic Literature
HMC	Historical Manuscripts Commission
HU BBL	Harvard University Baker Business Library
JHC	Journal of the House of Commons
NA	Notariële Archieven
OSP	Oxford Slavonic Papers
PC	Privy Council
PRO SPD SPF	Public Record Office, State Papers Domestic, State Papers Foreign
RA	Riksarkivet, Stockholm
RSL	Royal Society Library
RGADA	Rossiiskii Gosudarstvennyi Arkhiv Drevnikh Aktov
RGVIA	Rossiiskii Gosudarstvennyi Voenno-Istoricheski Arkhiv
SEER	Slavonic and East European Review
TKMG	Tamozhennye knigi moskovskogo gosudarstva
TRHS	Transactions of the Royal Historical Society

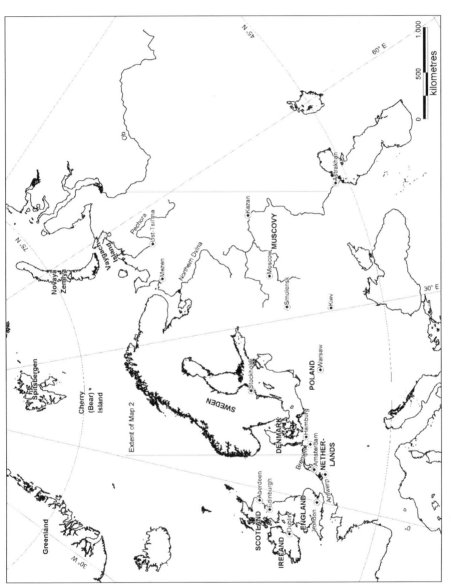

Map 1: Northern Europe

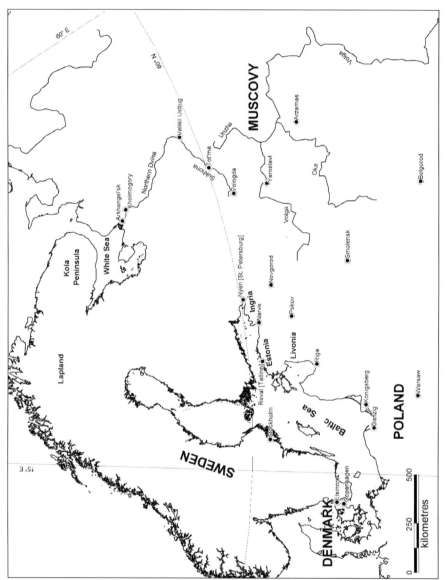

Map 2: Muscovy

ONE

Introduction: The Sixteenth-Century Legacy

Tudors and Riurikovichi

In the sixteenth century, European monarchies found their justification not only from God but also from time. The upstart Welsh Tudors, who had seized the throne in 1485, had no difficulty in constructing a respectable genealogy for themselves based on title, marriage and conquest. However, while Henry VII was vague about his inheritance and postponed his marriage until he was firmly on the throne, he insisted that God's will had been revealed in his victory over Richard III. Contrasting the claim of Henry's house with that of its successor, Geoffrey Elton wrote of opposite views of divine right: 'The Tudors appealed to fact – God spoke through the arbitrament of war. The Stuarts believed in an indefeasible right which no amount of adverse circumstances could lessen or destroy.'[1] This would be a fateful distinction. Meanwhile, the Russian tsars drew a line stretching back to the ninth century. 'Let us seek a prince who may rule over us, and judge us according to the Law', said the warring peoples of ancient Russia to each other in 862, as quoted in the *Primary Chronicle*, which continues: 'They accordingly went overseas to the Varangian Russes: these particular Varangians were known as Russes, just as some are called Swedes, and others Normans, English and Gottlanders.'[2] Three brothers in particular were chosen, and the eldest of them, Riurik, founded a princely dynasty allegedly leading in an unbroken manner to Ivan the Terrible in the sixteeenth century.

In that century, Varangian connections between the British and the Russians were alleged to be supplemented by early expansion: 'Arthur which was sometimes the most renowned king of the Britains, was a mightie, and valiant man, and a famous warrior. This kingdome was too little for him, and his mind was not contented with it. He therefore valiantly subdued all Scantia, which is now called Norway, and all the Islands beyond Norway, . . . and all the other lands and Islands of the East Sea even unto Russia'[3] Other early connections with

---

1 Elton, *England under the Tudors*, p. 9. Full publication details in Bibliography.
2 Cross, *The Russian Primary Chronicle*, p. 59.
3 William Lambard, *Archaionomia sive de priscis anglorum legibus libri*, London, 1568, fol. 137, p. 2, as in Hakluyt, *The Principall Navigations*, p. 245.

Russia were ascribed to Scotland. For example, the world view of the Gaelic bard Ossian was said to extend as far east as the River Ob in Siberia. A further affiliation is suggested by the Declaration of Arbroath of 1320, which begins by saying that the Scots originated in the land of the Scythians, that is by the Black Sea, before travelling to their present home via the Mediterranean Sea. Back near the Black Sea, of course, the patron saint of both Russians and Scots, Andrew, is believed to have carried on his principal mission.

Certainly, in medieval times, there were connections between England and Russia before the Norman Conquest of 1066.[4] Both English and Scottish knights participated in the Northern Crusade from the eleventh to the sixteenth century: a Prussian chronicler's description of a fracas in Königsberg in 1391 includes the observation 'that there was dissension on the part of the English and Scots'. Among those undergoing the defeat of the Teutonic Knights at the battle of Tannenberg in 1410 was a certain 'bastard d'Escoce, qui se appelloit comte de Hembe': conceivably, members of both the families at the centre of this book's attention fought on opposite sides.[5] Meanwhile, throughout much of the medieval period, there were commercial connections between the offshore islands and the east of the continent via the Hanseatic League.

But, more certainly, we begin our introduction in the sixteenth century, or, to be precise, in 1553. There may have been connections between the newly arrived Tudors and the ancient Riurikovichi during the reigns of Henry VII and VIII, but, in any detail, we know much more about a connection made accidentally at the end of the reign of their immediate successor. In 1552, the 'Mystery Company and Fellowship of Merchant Adventurers for the discovery of unknown lands' was founded in London with Sebastian Cabot at its head. Royal patronage supplied what the chronicler Richard Hakluyt was to call 'The copie of the letters missive, which the right noble Prince Edward the Sixt, sent to the Kings, Princes, and other Potentates, inhabiting the Northeast partes of the world, towards the mighty Empire of Cathay, at such time as Sir Hugh Willoughby knight, and Richard Chancelor, with their companie, attempted their voyage thither in the yeere of Christ, 1553. and the seventh and last yeere of his raigne.' The original was in Latin, but the letter was also written in Greek and 'divers other languages' unspecified. It sets the scene for England's 'discovery' of Russia, as well as capturing aspects of the theme of this book in its assertion that:

For the God of heaven and earth, greatly providing for mankinde, would not that all things should be founde in one region, to the ende that one shoulde

---

4 Franklin and Shepherd, *The Emergence*, pp. 202–3.
5 Macquarrie, *Scotland and the Crusades*, pp. 83–8.

have neede of another, that by this meanes friendshippe might be established among all men, and every one seeke to gratifie all, as well to seeke such things as we lacke, as also to cary unto them from our regions, such things as they lacke. So that hereby not onely commoditie may ensue both to them and us, but also an indissoluble and perpetuall league of friendship be established betweene us both, while they permit us to take of their things, such whereof they have abundance in their regions, and we againe grant them such things of ours, whereof they are destitute.[6]

Addressed 'toward the Empire of Cathay' or China, Edward VI's letter actually reached Ivan IV, the Terrible, of Muscovy, as the English called Russia at the time. For Willoughby perished in the White Sea in a vain attempt to reach China by the North-East Passage, and Chancellor travelled with the survivors to Moscow. Ivan's response to his brother monarch's missive, translated into English as 'The copie of the Duke of Moscovie and Emperour of Russia his letters, sent to King Edward the Sixt, by the hands of Richard Chanceler', included the following passage:

And we with christian beliefe and faithfulnesse, and according to your honourable request, and my honourable commandement will not leave it undone, and are furthermore willing that you send unto us your ships and vessels, when and as often as they may have passage, with good assurance on our part to see them harmelesse. And if you send one of your majesties counsell to treate with us whereby your countrey merchaunts may with all kindes of wares, and where they will make their market in our dominions, they shall have their free Marte with all free liberties through my whole dominions with all kindes of wares, to come and goe at ther pleasure, without any let, damage, or impediment. . .

Hakluyt comments:

This letter was written in the Moscovian tongue, in letters much like to the Greeke letters, very faire written in paper, with a broad seale hanging at the same, sealed in paper upon waxe. This seale was much like the broad seale of England, having on the one side the image of a man on horsebacke in complete harnesse fighting with a dragon. Under this letter was another paper

---

6 Hakluyt, *The Principall Navigations*, pp. 264–5.

written in the Dutch tongue, which was the interpretation of the other written in the Moscovian letters.[7]

Hakluyt's note, like the letters of Edward and Ivan themselves, clearly demonstrates both the closeness and the apartness of English and Russian culture. The two cultures were Christian, and shared veneration of St. George. But one was Protestant and the other was Orthodox. One was styled 'king', the other 'emperor'. A further division was that Edward dated 1553 as the year 5515 from creation, Ivan the year 1554 as the year 7063 from that dawn of time. Both languages were members of the family that came to be known as Indo-European, but one was of German-French origin and used the Latin alphabet, the other was Slavonic adapted to the Greek alphabet. Edward, who wanted to address rulers via the North-East Passage as far over as China, used Greek, Latin and other languages.

Emphasis was given in both letters to commerce, but again, we must remember that Ivan's was in response to Edward's, that the English king did not know that his letter was to be read by his Russian counterpart, and that neither ruler could be certain about the items that would be involved in any commerce. Probably, Edward was in the first instance hoping for the luxuries of the East, and Ivan for necessities as well as luxuries from the West. However, as Hakluyt made abundantly clear in *The Principall Navigations*, the whole world was opening up to English commerce in the second half of the sixteenth century, as the small island kingdom began the rise that would make it a major world power. Trade with Muscovy in particular, although small in comparison to that with western Europe, was to become significant in cordage and other naval stores. According to one authority, 'the fleet that defeated the Spanish Armada was largely rigged with Russian cordage and cables'.[8] From the Russian point of view, now that the Hansa was in steep decline, new markets were necessary for not only its naval stores but also its furs, tallow, wax and other items. Moreover, normally excluded from the Christian community of nations not only for its Orthodoxy but also because of its remote vastness, Russia sought recognition via alliances between its tsars and sibling monarchs to the west.

Thus, as the relationship developed between the Tudors and Riurikovichi, a political element entered into it, too. As ever, another important part was played by the wars in which both dynasties were involved, although never against each other.

7 Ibid., pp. 292–3.
8 Wretts-Smith, 'The English in Russia', p. 95.

Commerce

Neither Sir Hugh Willoughby nor Richard Chancellor was to survive Muscovy Company expeditions led by them: Willoughby was frozen to death in Lapland on the outward journey at the beginning of the attempt to find the North-East Passage to the Indies; Chancellor was drowned in Pitsligo Bay in north-east Scotland on the way home from a second mission to Moscow in a shipwreck which also accounted for many of the precious gifts being brought by Ivan the Terrible's ambassador, Osip Nepea, for Edward VI's successors, Philip and Mary. Nepea survived the shipwreck, and finally reached London in April 1557.[9]

In spite of such unpromising beginnings, the 'discovery' of Russia via the White Sea in 1553 enabled the Muscovy Company to exploit this new trade outlet. Confirmation of this activity was given in the Charter of February 1555 giving the Muscovy Company a monopoly over all trade with Russia. The Muscovy Company was a new departure in English corporate history, a joint-stock company whose members could trade only as a body and not privately or individually.[10] The Company was controlled by one or two governors, four consuls and 24 assistants, who together could make acts and ordinances 'for the government, good condition, and laudable rule' of the company and punish those who offended such ordinances.[11] The Company had 191 members in 1555, although the figure appears to have risen to 400 within the ensuing decade. A perhaps incomplete figure of 80 is recorded for 1595, since the total at the turn of the century was 160. The starting capital of the company, £6,000 provided by 240 shareholders, rose to £48,000 by 1564. A further increase undoubtedly ensued three years later when interlopers active in Narva in the Baltic were allowed to join the Company. Following several augmentations of the company stock, the par value of a share rose from the initial £25 to £450 by 1572.[12]

The Company's structure was revised in 1586, when the old stock was replaced by a 'terminable' joint-stock, under which members invested for limited, so-called 'adventures' of one to three trading seasons. At the end of each adventure, the capital, as well as any accrued profits, were distributed among the investors. There was no obligation on members to participate in all adventures. The restructuring led to a concentration of capital in the hands of a limited number of members and there is some evidence to suggest that it may have constituted a deliberate takeover of the company by some of its wealthier directors.[13]

---

9 Willan, *The Early History*, pp. 15–18. Willan incorrectly refers to 'Napea'.
10 Willan, *The Muscovy Merchants*, p. 7. Muscovy or Russia Company.
11 Ibid., p. 9.
12 Ibid., pp. 6, 41–7; Lyubimenko, *Les relations*, pp. 79, 86, 88.
13 Willan, *The Early History*, pp. 208–16, 272.

In 1555 the first Muscovy Company traders opened a 'factory' or warehouse within the foreign quarter of Moscow. The English received a general authorisation to enter and leave White Sea ports as well as travel to the Muscovy interior in addition to exemption from the heavy commercial customs duties that other foreigners were to be charged. As one well-informed seventeenth-century source recounts: 'The English in their adventures at sea having found out the Sea Port at the mouth of the River Dwina had for their losses and paines great Priviledges conferred on them by the Tzaar, especially to Trade without paying of Toll or Custome, whereby encouraged they had erected a considerable trade and kept an agent, which continued many yeares with considerable advantage.'[14]

Ivan IV granted the English merchants the privilege of relocating their factory in the vicinity of the Kremlin in Moscow in 1567. This relocation was a valuable concession as it placed the factory nearer to its protector's presence. This physical proximity to the source of power also aided the English agents in their petitioning for the redress of grievances. Added to these privileges, the English were also to be exempt from having to trade in the foreign goods market. The location of the English Factory within Moscow, as well as the trade concessions and privileges, allowed the English an advantage over all their rivals.

The Muscovy Company created a trading system within Russia, centred upon the use of agents in the major cities which studded the trade route between Moscow and the White Sea. Rose Island, dominating the mouth of the Dvina and lying opposite to the monastery of St Nicholas, was first used as the White Sea port, and only later, towards the very end of the century – probably between 1596 and 1597 – was Russia's White Sea trade centred upon the new town of Archangel,[15] where a factory storing Russian and English imports and exports was situated. Ships arriving in May would complete the loading and offloading operations by August at the latest, for fear of the Russian winters.

English imports to Russia included copper, lead and munitions for the army; jewels, rich silks, velvets and damask for the court; cloth, pewter and paper for industry. They were loaded onto heavy, flat-bottomed barges and transported 70 miles down the River Dvina to Kholmogory. Here the Company had a second factory warehouse. Kholmogory served as the major market in northern Russia; Samoyeds, Lapps, Russians Tartars and Karelians all bought and sold their goods – fish, fur, feathers, oil – at this market. From Kholmogory the journey continued for several hundred miles along the river to the town of Vologda. During the Time of Troubles, 1598–1613, we find a contemporary description of the living conditions of merchants under siege in 1609: 'All the merchants who regularly do business in

---

14 Gordon, Diary, 23 June 1666, vol. 2, p. 490.
15 Wretts-Smith, 'The English in Russia', p. 76, n. 4. In Russian, Arkhangel'sk.

this county had gathered in Vologda, taking refuge in the house of the English – their factory, which is very large, and like a castle. There, with a good guard around them, they passed the winter in perpetual fear and anxiety.'[16]

From Vologda to Moscow, the merchants faced the choice of either travelling by land or by water. In winter, the journey by sledge was comfortable and fast, with hostelries and staging posts for those whom the tsar favoured. By contrast, the summer land journey was slow and frustrating due to impassable roads. If the river was followed then the route lay through the city of Yaroslavl, the site of another Muscovy Company factory-warehouse.

In the sixteenth century, the Moscow-stationed Muscovy Company agent co-ordinated the efforts of the other Company agents in cities and towns throughout Russia: he became the Company's chief agent in Russia, responsible for all economic transactions with the Russian Government. (By the seventeenth century, in fact, the Moscow agent appears to have become the sole formal representative of the Company.)[17] Agents had absolute control over all the English associated with the Company. They had the privilege of trying the English under their own law whilst in Russia.[18]

The other Muscovy Company employees were categorised as either apprentices or stipendiaries, and these employees could and did marry Polish and Russian women. Apprentice was the lowest grade, and consisted of the latest and therefore the youngest employees sent from England. The stipendiaries had served the Muscovy Company for a greater length of time, and were employed as accounts clerks. They assisted with the buying and selling of goods within their own district and, when the agents were visiting other cities, they could be deputised to run the day-to-day business which the agent would normally attend to. The Muscovy Company agents were allowed to employ two or three Russians as domestic servants, but were forbidden to employ Russians in any sort of trading capacity. These restrictions could be a means of ensuring that Russians were not inculcated with ideas and concepts of Western civilisation.[19]

However, if this were the real reason, it seems likely to have back-fired; employment within the household of the most educated, learned and 'civilised' of all Englishmen in Russia would have indoctrinated the Russian domestics far

---

16   Massa, *A Short History*, p. 178.
17   Arel, *The Muscovy Company*, p. 20.
18   *CSPD*, 1547–1580, no. 39, p. 695 [undated 1580?]: Petition of Tho. Wynington, to Sir Fr. Walsyngham: 'That having come from Moscow to London, about certain disorders there committed by one Northern, a merchant, he had been imprisoned at the instance of the Master and Governors of the Company of Moscovia. Desires that he will proceed to the hearing of the matter.'
19   Wretts-Smith, 'The English in Russia', pp. 72–102.

more with ideas of Western civilisation than ever would haggling with Lapps or Tatars in the local market place for skins, furs or feathers. Should personal relations go as far as marriage to a Russian, however, the English had to renounce their faith, be baptised Orthodox and reapply for Muscovy Company membership.[20]

During the sixteenth century, both English and Russian merchants were to accuse each other of fraudulent and illegal behaviour; Muscovy Company privileges were hated by the Russian mercantile community and jealously guarded by the Company itself. The Russians at Archangel were accustomed to selling their goods to the French and the Flemish, and resented the loss of profits which resulted from the granting of the privileges allowing the English to trade with the interior. Accusations and counter-accusations might be accepted as normal trading practice and so perhaps they should not be taken too seriously.[21] However, as some of the accusations against English trading conduct emanated from within the wider English community in Russia, as well as from some of the English merchants themselves, there are grounds for supposing that there was some truth in the Russian accusations.

Temptation might well have been encouraged by the circumstance that Muscovy Company employees were to find it difficult to leave their place of employment, and had no legal means of acquiring wealth on their own account while in Russia. Moreover, in an effort to protect themselves from Muscovy Company punishment for their illegal behaviour, crooked employees wined and dined Russian courtiers, so hoping to gain their favour. One Muscovy Company agent, Thomas Glover, had 'used the Company's purse like a prince'. Christopher Burrough, one of the Muscovy Company merchants, complained about the meagreness of their allowances, the licentious and corrupting nature of Muscovite society and the Muscovy Company's frugality in not providing a preacher.[22] With no warning from men of the cloth against the pitfalls of temptation, a possible reflection of consequent illegal activities could be found in the comment of a Dutch observer that after the death of Boris Godunov in 1605 'most were convinced that the English merchants had taken him with rich treasures to their own country'.[23]

---

20 *CSPD*, 1581–1590, p. 667, 26 May 1590: 'Order for re-admission for Francis Pope into the Company of Merchants Adventurers, having lost his freedom by marrying a wife born beyond the seas.' It is possible that this readmission policy was widely enforced. Some Muscovy Company servants were to die in the course of their placements. See *CSPD*, 1547–1580, no. 106, p. 701 [undated, 1580?], 'Petition of Wm. Copland and Anthony Greene (orphan of Tho. Greene, who died in Muscovia), to the Queen.'
21 For similar problems in a later period, see Kahan, 'Observations', p. 225.
22 Wretts-Smith, 'The English in Russia', pp. 89–90.
23 Massa, *A Short History*, p. 106.

Ivan IV had acquired the port of Narva through conquest in 1558. It appears that a minority of merchants from within the Muscovy Company traded privately to this port, from 1564 until it was closed to the Russians in 1584.[24] Non-Muscovy Company merchants from the ports of Hull, York, Yarmouth, Harwich and London also traded to Narva.[25] When Narva was closed, the interlopers took their ships to the northern shores of Lapland, and traded with Kholmogory, thus breaking the Muscovy Company monopoly.[26]

In 1567, the newly acquired towns of Kazan on the Volga and Astrakhan at its mouth were now open to the Company's sphere of operations. A new grant in 1569 allowed transit trade with Bukhara, Qazvin and 'other states' and the right to retail trade, as well as permission to build bases in Vologda, Kholmogory and other towns 'as necessary'. The Company was allowed to prospect for iron along the Vychegda River, a tributary of the Northern Dvina, and, perhaps most importantly, was given a monopoly on the northern sea passage.[27]

The Company's operations could be highly profitable, with a general rate of 20 per cent. We know that the Persia expedition of 1568–73 netted £40,000. The dividend for the last voyage of the expedition attained 108 per cent.[28]

Diplomacy

By the mid-sixteenth century, international diplomacy had developed a complex ritual on a basis allegedly stretching back over hundreds of years. One Russian claim was of a protocol stretching back not only to Byzantium, but even to Babylon.[29] Relations between monarchs were well-established, including the practices of calling each other 'brother' and 'sister', and informing each other about their accession. However, complaints frequently occurred about the manner in which the monarchs themselves should be styled and their ambassadors received. By no means capable of escaping old norms or alleged

---

24 *CSPD*, 1581–1590, no. 44, p. 323, 28 April 1585: 'Letters Patents by the Queen to the Governor and Company of the Merchants Adventurers of England, confirming all their former privileges; and prohibiting interlopers within the limits of the same.'

25 For example, William Bond was accused of being an interloper. *CSPD*, 1547–1580, no. 20, p. 246, 20 November 1564: 'Memorial of the Merchant Adventurers to the Council . . . Request that William Bond and his partners be restrained from trading to the Narve.' Ibid., no. 22, p. 246, 25 November 1564: Bond denied the charge, arguing 'that the traffic of the said Bond and Foxall to the Narve is in no way prejudicial to the company.'

26 See Willan, 'The Russia Company', pp. 405–19; Zins, *England and the Baltic*, pp. 35–53; Kirchner, *Commercial Relations*, pp. 59–77; Zordanija, 'Les premiers marchands', pp. 7–30.

27 Ivanov, *Anglo-gollandskoe torgovoe sopernichestvo*, pp. 83–4.

28 Lyubimenko, *Les relations*, pp. 88–9.

29 Iuzefovich, *Kak v posol'skikh obychaiakh*, pp. 9–10.

infringements of them, the agents of the Muscovy Company could nevertheless also make use of their professional skills.

They had language expertise, understood local customs and laws, and had been granted privileges and rights of residence in various Russian cities. With their knowledge of the contemporary Russian commercial environment, they were able to advise the governors in London how and when to press for greater trade privileges. For example, in 1602, Lord Buckhurst wrote to Cecil, Secretary of State, describing a 'long debate' held with the merchants of the Muscovy Company in London, where he 'gathered from them as much understanding as we could for the better managing of this ambassade'.[30] They were also ideally placed to aid envoys and ambassadors within Russia.

Peers, Privy Councillors and holders of high office all appeared as signatories to the list of Charter members of the Muscovy Company. Willan argues that: 'the presence of so many peers and holders of high office was quite unprecedented . . . whether these men did much more than adorn the company it is difficult to say, but they may well have proved useful friends at court'.[31]

The Charter members, as well as enjoying influence at court, were themselves customs administrators and thus were capable of framing commercial treaties in a competent manner; their specialism may help account for the expertise with which trading privileges were to be sought and the persistency with which every embassy was to deal with this matter. For example, Sir Jerome Bowes' embassy of 1583–4 was sent in response to the Russian embassy to England of 1581–2, in which the questions of a political alliance between England and Russia, and a marriage alliance between Mary Hastings (a cousin of Queen Elizabeth) and Ivan IV, were broached. Fedor Pisemskii and Neudacha Khorvalev were also sent to England in 1581:

> to find out how the Queen of England deals with the French king, the Lithuanian, the Pope, and the Emperor? And why the Pope and the Queen are unfriendly toward one another? And how are the Emperor's relations with the Turks and the French? And, to find out everything about their affairs and customs and how they are conducting their affairs, and how large was English territory, and whether many military people live there?[32]

Special ambassador Bowes was instructed to forestall the marriage and other questions raised in England and instead attempt to secure for the English a

---

30 Lord Buckhurst to Mr Secretary Cecil, 5 August 1602, *HMC*, Salisbury, xii, pp. 383–4.
31 Willan, *Muscovy Merchants*, pp. 10–11.
32 Grabar, *The History*, p. 27.

monopoly on the White Sea trade and to deal with specific Muscovy Company grievances against the Russian government (as well as concessions concerning private English individuals).

Furthermore, Muscovy Company influence was used to select envoys and ambassadors for diplomatic missions. It has been argued that: 'Received wisdom suggests that the men who served as ambassadors overseas were haphazardly chosen and at best a randomly prepared lot.'[33] This argument fails to describe accurately the considerations that governed the selection of diplomatic personnel for missions to Russia. For example, Sir Jerome Horsey began life as an apprentice in the Muscovy Company, rising to the rank of stipendiary at the Moscow warehouse, second in rank only to the Muscovy Company Moscow agent. Horsey developed a friendship with Boris Godunov and was to serve as a Russian envoy. Another example of how the appointment of diplomatic personnel was contingent upon Muscovy Company support is revealed by the career of Francis Cherry. He had spent ten years of his boyhood at the Russian court, and later joined the Muscovy Company, gaining special trading privileges from Boris Godunov who 'permitted all the company's servants to trade in all places in his Kingdom while no other stranger may'.[34]

In general, the Muscovy Company was able to influence the content of diplomatic exchanges and to make recommendations for the appointment of ambassadors. It also provided the mechanisms through which the diplomacy took place – Muscovy Company ships provided all the transport, the Muscovy Company purse often underwrote the costs.

An apt further example comes at the end of Elizabeth's reign. In a letter of 24 June 1599, the queen promised to send 'an expresse ambassador' to deliver formal congratulations to Tsar Boris Godunov on his accession. But she did not keep her promise until nearly a year later, when she appointed Richard Lee as 'our true and undoupted Atturney, Procurator, Legit and Ambassador'. Illegitimate half-brother to the Master of the Ordnance, Sir Henry Lee, Richard had no diplomatic experience. This occasioned little concern, perhaps, since his mission was deemed to be 'more of complement than such of more importance'. Knighted on 1 June 1601, and supplied with written instructions by the queen's advisers and the Muscovy Company, Lee arrived in Archangel on 29 July. According to a contemporary Dutchman Isaac Massa, he was 'a worthy and respectable old man' with 'a suite of 40 young gentlemen, all wearing scarlet cloaks'. They arrived 'on a ship belonging to the English merchant

33 Bell, *A Handlist*, p. 11.
34 *HMC*, Salisbury, xii, p. 505.

company trading with this land'. Massa tells us of Lee's audience with the Tsar Boris Godunov and of his attempt in particular to secure a trading monopoly for English merchants in addition to the privileges that they already possessed. The ambassador failed in this attempt, but was well received, apparently, Massa observing that 'expenses of his stay were borne by the Muscovite treasury, and in addition he received rich presents of furs'.[35]

As N. E. Evans correctly points out, 'The basic principle of English policy towards Russia, consistent for nearly half a century, had been to avoid any kind of political entanglement with Moscow.' The emphasis was on trade rather than alliance through marriage or any other means. However, to maintain commercial privileges, something had to be done to forestall matrimonial proposals being put to Tsar Boris by the Austrian Habsburgs. As Evans also suggests, 'With ruin or riches at stake the risk involved in an immediate pledge of English marriage partners for the tsar's children, to be honoured or evaded at some future date, assumed acceptable proportions.' Asked by the tsar 'who they were that her majestie would make an honnorable choyse for them', Sir Richard Lee replied encouragingly, although he said that 'he cold not particularlye name the parteyse'.[36]

The imbroglio was complicated by the fact that, while Lee was talking to the tsar in Moscow, a Russian ambassador was already in London. We shall follow this story below as the question arose not only of an English, but also of a Scottish marriage.

War

On 2 August 1560, the Northern Crusade came to an end with the defeat by the Muscovite Russians of an outnumbered force of a few hundred members of the Livonian Order of the Knights of the Sword. Robert Frost evocatively describes the subsequent fate of those who were captured: 'Dragged to Moscow, these proud dignitaries were executed on the Orders of Tsar Ivan IV; their bodies were left to rot in the street. It was a miserable end to a great ideal.'[37] However, a great ideal for Roman Catholics was anathema to both Russian Orthodox and Protestants. Undoubtedly, religious affiliations as well as commercial concerns played a significant part in the Livonian or First Northern War, 1558–83. From

35 Evans, 'The Anglo-Russian Royal Marriage Negotiations', pp. 366–70; Massa, *A Short History*, pp. 50–1.
36 Evans, 'The Anglo-Russian Royal Marriage Negotiations', pp. 373–5.
37 Frost, *The Northern Wars*, p. 1. See also Christiansen, *The Northern Crusades*, pp. 219–53.

the point of view of Ivan the Terrible, the opportunity was presented for Muscovy to fill a sizeable part of the vacuum left by the decline of the Livonian Order and the Hanseatic League at the same time as taking lands which he considered to be integral parts of 'Holy Russia' and establishing a firm foothold on the Baltic Sea. At the end of the war, however, Ivan was forced to give up considerable gains to his greatest enemy, the King of Poland-Lithuania.

We know little of individual English or Scots involved in this war.[38] However, more generally, according to Sir Jerome Horsey, in 1581: 'The emperor's [Ivan's] soldiers and army, far greater in number ranged far into the Swedes' country and did much spoil and rapine, brought many captives away to remote places in his land, Livonians, French, Scots, Dutchmen, and some English. The emperor settling and seating a great many of them in the city of Moscow to inhabit by themselves without the city.'[39] Here were some of the beginnings of the Foreign Settlement or German Quarter in which many Scots and English were to live along with other immigrants and visitors down to the end of the seventeenth century. Horsey relates how, 'among other nations, there were four score and five poor Scots soldiers left of seven hundred sent from Stockholm, and three Englishmen in their company, brought among other captives in most miserable manner piteous to behold'. Horsey claims that he interceded with Ivan on behalf of the Scots to find useful employment for them on the campaigns which usually took place each summer against the Crimean Tatars. This is how he describes their contribution along with that of other prisoners from Sweden, Poland–Lithuania and Livonia:

They were a nation strangers, remote, adventurous, and warlike people, ready to serve any Christian prince for maintenance and pay, as they would appear and prove if it pleased his majesty to employ and spare them such mainte-nance, now out of heart and clothes and arms, as they may show themselves and valor against his mortal enemy the Krym Tatar. It seems some use was made of this advice, for shortly the best soldiers and men-at-arms of these strangers were spared and put apart, and captains of each nation appointed to govern the rest – Jamy Lingett for the Scottish men, a valiant honest man. Money, clothes and daily allowance for meat and drink was given them, horse, hay and oats; swords, piece and pistols were they armed with. Poor snakes

---

38 Steuart, *Scottish Influences*, p. 20, suggests that a General Carmichael was made commander of 5,000 men in 1570 and later became Governor of the strategically important town of Pskov. But there is no evidence for this.

39 This and subsequent Horsey quotations are from Berry and Crummey, *Rude and Barbarous Kingdom*, pp. 288–9.

afore, look now cheerfully. Twelve hundred of them did better service against the Tatar than twelve thousand Russes with their short bow and arrows. The Krym, not knowing then the use of piece and pistols, struck dead off their horses with shot they saw not, cried, 'Away with those new devils with their thundering puffs', whereat the emperor made good sport. Then had they pensions and lands allowed them to live upon, married and matched with the fair Livonian women, increased into families and live in favor of the prince and people.

The identity of 'Jamy Lingett' remains elusive, and we know the names of none of his comrades. However, Horsey also mentions one Gabriel Elphinstone, 'a valiant Scottish captain' who came to Muscovy with six other Scots on the recommendation of a Colonel Steward who had served the King of Denmark. Possibly, this group was among those involved in an incident at Ivan the Terrible's court described by Dr Samuel Collins in the seventeenth century: 'Some foreigners, English and Scots, had laughed at certain things the tsar had done during a drinking bout. The tsar when he heard this had them stripped naked and forced them to pick up, one by one, five or six bushels of peas which had been poured into his room. Then he gave them drink and sent them away.'[40]

After the death of Ivan the Terrible in 1584, Boris Godunov began his ascent to the highest power as adviser to his brother-in-law, Tsar Fedor Ivanovich (1584–98), corresponding with his counterpart Lord Burghley, as Fedor wrote to Elizabeth. The Queen of England also received letters from the King of Scotland. On 26 November 1591, George Barne, one of the Governors of the Russia Company, wrote to Burghley saying that he understood that the queen, at the request of James VI, was about to intercede with the tsar for the release of a Scottish captain who was a prisoner in Moscow. The queen, according to Barne, had already acted so often on behalf of individual men and for minor reasons that Russian officials had said that 'the Queen of Englandes letters are good cheape'. Barne therefore asked Burghley if it would be more appropriate for the queen to write twice, once on behalf of the captain and once on Company business, or to include both matters in one communication. Although James had asked 'our dearest sister' to secure the release of 'a Scottis capitane callit James . . . deteined captive in Moscovia . . . ane idolatrous countrey', Elizabeth does not appear to have interceded on the captain's behalf.[41]

---

40 This quotation, as well as information on Captain Elphinstone and General Carmichael, is from Steuart, *Scottish Influences*, pp. 17–20.
41 *CSPD*, Elizabeth, ccxl, no. 70 and *HMC* Portland, ii. 18, as quoted by Willan, *The Early History*, pp. 221–2.

This little episode illustrates the manner in which commercial, diplomatic and military affairs often interacted, as well as indicating how James VI had no direct contact with a tsar of Russia before his accession as James I. Before that occurred, Muscovy was to begin to undergo the horrendous experience known as the Time of Troubles, normally said to have commenced with the accession of Tsar Boris Godunov in 1598 and to have ended with the election of Mikhail Romanov in 1613. The Time of Troubles was to involve the activities of Scottish and other mercenaries and interfered with the activities of English and other merchants.

Stuarts and Romanovs: Introduction

At first glance, to compare the destinies, describe the connections and then assess the relationship of the two dynasties might appear as a twentieth-century superimposition upon an earlier period where Russia and the British Isles were far apart in any conceptual framework. On the other hand, the argument could be put forward that later centuries including the twentieth are responsible for the breakdown of an association that was made in the seventeenth century itself, as well as at earlier times. For example, in *A Brief History of Moscovia and other less-known Countries lying Eastward of Russia as far as Cathay*, first published posthumously in 1682, John Milton, who had died in 1674, wrote as follows:

> The study of Geography is both profitable and delightful: but the Writers thereof, though some of them exact enough in setting down Longitudes and Latitudes, yet in those other relations of Manners, Religions, Government and such like, accounted Geographical, have missed their proportions ... [This circumstance] perhaps brought into the mind of some men, more learned and judicious, who had not the leisure or purpose to write an entire Geography, yet at least to assay something in the description of one or two Countreys, which might serve as a Pattern or Example, to render others more cautious hereafter, who intended to make the whole work.

And so Milton decided to follow a predecessor, Paolo Giovio, in concentrating upon Muscovy and England, explaining that he 'began with Muscovy, as being the most northern Region of Europe reputed civil'. Let us be clear then, one of the greatest English writers of the seventeenth century believed that Muscovite Russia was an integral part of Europe, and that, furthermore, it bore comparison with England from the point of view of 'Manners, Religions, Government and such like'. Perhaps the obvious point needs to be added that, in the seventeenth century, boundaries between academic disciplines were not as rigid as they later became, and that geography and history could overlap to the point of interchangeability.[42]

Not everybody today would agree with John Milton, but the task of continuing that comparison is made easier by published as well as archival sources. We have at our disposal a considerable range of records of the diplomatic and other contacts made between Stuarts and Romanovs. There is also a variety of pertinent interpretation. We will bring in this wealth of primary and secondary material as we make use of it.

In 1613, nobody could have predicted that, while the Romanov dynasty would last for more than 300 years, Stuarts would soon be ejected from the throne twice, first in less than 40 years, and again another 40 years later. For, while Mikhail became tsar when the catastrophic Time of Troubles was still raging, James VI of Scotland had become James I of England in 1603 on the death of Elizabeth in a completely peaceful manner.

The whole subject has to be considered within the context set at the beginning of the relationship, commerce. Here questions arise not only of different rates of internal development but also of patterns of international trade. For example, to what extent were the fortunes of the Muscovy Company bound up with the relations between the two monarchies? We must also recall that we are dealing with two embryonic empires, the British more seaborne, the Russian more landward. Ideas of monarchy have to be examined, as well as its practice. Is it possible to consider both Stuarts and Romanovs under the heading of absolutism? Was Charles I executed and James VII and II ejected because of a failure to establish the kind of monarchy that Aleksei Mikhailovich and Peter the Great would succeed in establishing? Light is thrown on this important subject by the nature and content of the diplomatic interchange. Further illumination is afforded by the study of the military activity of the period, especially that of Scottish mercenaries.

So let us take a preliminary glance at aspects of the provenance and ideology of the Stuarts and Romanovs. Scottish monarchy was deemed to originate far back in the mists of time. But the Stuarts were comparative newcomers, not even by origin Scottish. Descended from a Breton immigrant to Norfolk, England, Walter Stewart gained his surname from the fact that he served as high steward to the Scottish king in the twelfth century. A descendant, the seventh steward, became King Robert II in the fourteenth century owing to his

---

42 *The Works of John Milton*, vol. 10, pp. 327–8. Milton may be said to have anticipated the arguments of Lucien Febvre, founder of the *Annales* school, in his merger of geography and history.

father's marriage to Marjory, daughter of Robert the Bruce. His descendant, James VI, had already been a reigning monarch in Scotland for more than 30 years when he became James I of England in 1603 as great-grandson of the Scottish King James IV's English wife, the Princess Margaret, eldest daughter of Henry VII.

James VI's mother was Mary Stuart (to give the French and now more normal version of the name, encouraged no doubt by her French mother, Mary of Lorraine, wife to James V). Mary Stuart was, of course, famous throughout Europe, at first because of her marriage to Francis II of France, after whose early death she returned to Scotland. There she married Lord Darnley, and produced her only son, the future James VI and I, in 1566. The following year, the baby's father was assassinated, his mother forced to abdicate and he himself proclaimed king of Scotland. Imprisoned in England, Mary remained an object of attention on the continent. For example, in 1574, a Russian ambassador to Austria discussed her support for the Catholic cause and claim to the throne of England that were to contribute to her execution in 1587.[43] Two years later, James VI went to Denmark where he married Princess Anne. Their son Charles was born in the royal burgh of Dunfermline in 1600, becoming heir to the two thrones on the death of his elder brother Henry in 1612.[44]

So much for the genealogy, what about the ideas that James took with him from Edinburgh to London, and then passed on to Charles? Among other tribulations, he had been exposed to the full force of the Scottish Reformation. Andrew Melville, who had preached boldly against absolute authority before the General Assembly of the Presbyterian Church in 1582, headed a deputation to 'remonstrate' with James in 1596. Melville told the king that, in the kingdom of Christ, he was only 'God's sillie vassal', and that in this kingdom, embodied in the Kirk, 'King James the Saxt is . . . nocht a King, nor a lord, nor a heid, but a member!'[45] James was in no mind to accept Melville's concept of the 'two kingdoms', and went on to express his own ideas of monarchy in *The True Lawe of Free Monarchies* and the *Basilikon Doron* in 1597 and 1598. In *The True Lawe*, for example, he declared, 'a good king will frame all his actions to be according to the law; yet is hee not bound thereto but of his good will, and for good example-giving to his subjects.' He regarded Parliament as 'nothing else but the head court of the King, and his vassals', and to be held seldom when new laws were necessary 'for few laws and well put in execution, are best in a well-ruled commonwealth'. He believed in the old institution of three estates in

43 Rogozhin, *U gosudarevykh del*, p. 45.
44 Dunbar, *Scottish Kings*. Not all Scottish historians write 'Stuart', some preferring 'Stewart'.
45 James Melville, *The Autobiography and Diary*, p. 370, quoted in Burns, *The True Law*, p. 225.

Parliament, and, in 1597, he managed to have legislation adopted for the royal nomination of bishops who would have seats in Parliament, thus reinforcing one of the central pillars of his constitutional edifice.[46]

The essential ideas of James VI were modified when he became James I. They were further developed by his son Charles I, who spoke just before his execution in 1649 of his deep conviction (shared with his father) that the ultimate authority on earth was that of the monarch. His own strong belief in the episcopacy was to be the main reason for the outbreak of civil war in 1638. We will examine Stuart ideology further in Chapter 2.

For the moment, let us follow this brief account of the Stuarts before 1603 with another – of the Romanovs before 1613. Like its Scottish counterpart, the family stemmed from an immigrant, in this case from Prussia in the fourteenth century, Andrei Ivanovich Kobyla. From his fifth son Fedor stemmed the Koshkin family who occupied prominent places at the Muscovite court. Fedor's great grandsons Iakov and Iurii were outstanding military leaders under Vasilii III, who deemed them 'his boyars for ever' and asked them to give their firm support to his son, the future Ivan the Terrible. The daughter of their brother Roman became Ivan's wife, the Tsaritsa Anastasia, and was held in high esteem by many of her contemporaries after her early death. Anastasia's brother, Nikita Romanovich, was also popular as a leading statesman. There was a popular song about him telling how he protected the Tsarevich Fedor from the anger of Ivan the Terrible. Nikita Romanovich had seven sons and six daughters, several of whom became related through marriage to some of the most outstanding families of the time such as the Mstislavskiis, Golovins, Morozovs, Cherkasskiis, Sitskiis and Godunovs. Nikita's eldest son Fedor became the Patriarch Filaret and the father of Mikhail.

No doubt, Mikhail's connections helped him to become tsar. Undoubtedly, too, he exaggerated them after his election, calling himself in official documents the grandson of Ivan the Terrible, although, of course, Anastasia was not his grandmother. This arrogation enabled him to declare his succession to the throne legitimate, rather than a consequence of election alone, and was used to assure everybody, especially fellow monarchs, that he continued the lawful line of Muscovite princes.[47]

The awesome power of Holy Writ in print had been exploited by Ivan, who claimed through this medium the further joint inheritance of God and Rome, a 'Caesaropapist' combination transcending divine right. Thus, the Romanovs were to claim their appointment from God as well as descent from Caesar

---

46 Burgess, *Absolute Monarchy*, p. 41. See also essays by Jenny Wormald and J. P. Somerville in Peck, *The Mental World*.
47 Chakshov, 'Romanovy: kto oni?', pp. 167–76.

Augustus and Constantine via the Riurikovichi, and thus they reasserted the claim of Moscow to be a new Jerusalem and another Rome.[48] On this firm basis, the new dynasty could drive from Russian soil the last vestiges of heresy.[49]

We need to reiterate that, for at least some other authorities in the seventeenth century in addition to John Milton, to discuss British and Russian systems of government in the same context was completely justified, both Stuarts and Romanovs being addressed under the heading of kingship and empire by, for example, John Selden in his *Titles of Honor*.[50] Moreover, some of the discussion among the Stuarts and Romanovs themselves was well informed, as we shall see in later chapters. For the moment, we will move on to the first meeting between a diplomatic representative of James VI of Scotland with a Russian counterpart, the ambassador of Tsar Boris Godunov. Although this meeting took place a couple of years before the accession of James to the throne of England and a dozen years before Mikhail Romanov became Russian tsar, it pointed the way towards later encounters after both dynasties had come to power.

First meeting

On 14 October 1600, at Richmond Palace, Grigory Ivanovich Mikulin was the first Russian ambassador to be received in a well-attended audience at the English Court. While the Great Chamber was 'most richly hanged', Mikulin himself was dressed in a gown of cloth of gold, a great fur cap and high-heeled buskins of red leather and accompanied by 'very great fatte men', his attendants.[51] According to a contemporary account: 'The Embassador read the great titles of his master [Tsar Boris Godunov], delivered her Majestie his Lettre of Audience and presented unto her, in open sort, a timber of sables and one sengle pair of excellent goodness: at this time there passed only many compliments. When he had done with her Majestie he was brought to a great banquett and had his belly full of garowses [grouse]'.[52] Unfortunately, partly because of his own ineptness, partly because of the strictness of his instructions, Mikulin was unable to make the most

---

48 Pavlov and Perrie, *Ivan the Terrible*, p. 36, downplay the fact that the second wife of Ivan III was the niece of the last Byzantine Emperor: 'The title of tsar was presented not as a recent borrowing from Constantinople, but as a traditional appellation of the dynasty' traced back to 'the caesars of ancient Rome'.

49 Pozdeeva, 'Pervye Romanovy', pp. 41–52.

50 Selden, *Titles of Honor*, London, 1614.

51 'A full narrative or description of the reception and entertainment of the Muscovite Ambassador . . .', with an appendix on the audience of 14 October 1600, published in 'Manuscripts of His Grace the Duke of Northumberland', *HMC* 3rd Report, 51b.

52 'De L'isle and Dudley' Ms, vol. II, *HMC*, London, 1934, p. 488.

of his time in London. For example, because of protocol, he could neither dine with the Lord Mayor nor attend the first performance of Shakespeare's *Twelfth Night*. According to N. E. Evans, who has given the fullest description of the embassy, the greater part of Mikulin's time was spent 'in haughty isolation, punctuated at intervals by empty if impressive ceremonial.'[53] Much of what he was able to learn about the situation in England came through contact with escorts and liaison officers appointed by the government from the Muscovy Company, Francis Cherry, John Merrick and Sir Jerome Bowes.

One problem needing diplomatic tact more than most was that of the English succession. Who would ascend the throne on the death of the 'Virgin Queen'? Probably it was this question more than most that prompted the visit to Mikulin of three strangers who, with all due decorum and deference, announced that they had been commanded to propose an interview with him by their master, the Scottish ambassador in London. Soon after this meeting, Mikulin was informed by Francis Cherry and John Merrick that one of his recent visitors had been none other than the Scottish ambassador passing himself off as a member of his own suite. The 'cloak and dagger' aspect of this whole episode is given emphasis by the fact that, in the Russian Report,[54] the Scottish ambassador is referred to throughout as 'Erl Bodvel Garr', a figure who cannot be positively identified. Quite possibly, of course, difficulties of mutual understanding played their part here. After all, there had never been any previous official contact between Russia and Scotland, and Mikulin was most unlikely to have possessed any more than the dimmest awareness of the northern kingdom remote from London.

However, at a meeting with Sir Jerome Bowes on 22 April, he attempted to rectify this deficiency by asking, among other questions on international politics, what was the reason for the presence of a Scottish embassy in London? Bowes replied that Queen Elizabeth alone knew the purpose of this mission from King James, but that the Scottish king was rumoured to be seeking formal acknowledgement of his right by closeness of blood to the throne of England before the death of its present occupant.[55] Two weeks later, on 4 May, John Merrick came to Mikulin to announce that 'Erl Bodvel' sent his request for a further meeting along with apologies for the anonymous nature of that taking place earlier. With appropriate observations about the improper nature of the first encounter, Mikulin agreed to the second.[56]

---

53 Evans, 'The Meeting', p. 519.
54 Bestuzhev-Riumin, 'Pamiatniki', pp. 340–52. An edited version is to be found in Likhachev, *Puteshestviia*.
55 Bestuzhev-Riumin, 'Pamiatniki', p. 340; Likhachev, *Puteshestviia*, pp. 181–2.
56 Bestuzhev-Riumin, 'Pamiatniki', p. 348; Likhachev, *Puteshestviia*, p. 189.

On 7 May 1601, there duly took place the first formal negotiations between representatives of the Russian and Scottish Crowns, even if Mikulin's counterpart was 'no longer in menial guise but still secure in the anonymity of a bogus title which could not be traced to any living person'.[57] But who was this emissary attended by a suite numbering over fifty and including six Gentlemen of the Household? 'Erl Bodvel Garr' could not be Francis Stewart Hepburn, Earl of Bothwell, as has sometimes been alleged, since that disgraced nobleman was in exile on the continent of Europe at the time. Almost certainly, this was John Erskine, Earl of Mar. A close associate for some years of James VII, Mar had come to London in March 1601 along with Edward Bruce, titular Abbot of Kinloss, to make as certain as possible that their royal master would become James I.[58]

The first Russo-Scottish exchanges are described verbatim in the Russian Report. Mar spoke first, doffing his hat and asserting that he had come 'for the sake of affection' and to apologise for his first appearance incognito. He excused his conduct by his wish to hear privately about Tsar Boris and his intention to keep his identity secret. Still no doubt not that much the wiser as to Mar's true motives, Mikulin and his secretary expressed their regrets that they had not been able originally to receive him with the honours due to him. Nevertheless, Mar insisted on sitting on a joint-stool, yielding the pride of place of the principal chair to Mikulin.

The preliminaries over, the session got down to something like business. After regretting that their friendship had not yet led to any significant relations between Russian tsars and Scottish kings, Mar suggested that God might ordain such contacts between Tsar Boris and King James. Mikulin responded that his sovereign desired friendship with all Christian peoples as well as the peace of Christendom in general. More specifically, the tsar aspired to a united front of Christian Princes against the Muslim Infidel. Avoiding any hint of commitment, Mar asked about the current situation regarding Russian relations with the Tartars and received a long, detailed reply. Mikulin then asked about the Scottish king's foreign relations both amicable and hostile, and was told that James was at peace with all Christian princes and had no enemies, except those of England. Persisting with his initial line of enquiry, Mikulin asked if the Scottish king gave any military or financial support to the Holy Roman Emperor, and if any other Christian princes rendered such help. Mar gave a negative if somewhat tortuous answer, then asked in turn about the tsar's relations with the sultan. Mikulin went to some lengths to blame hostilities on the Turks.

---

57 Bestuzhev-Riumin, 'Pamiatniki', pp. 348–52; Evans, 'The Meeting', p.523.
58 Ibid., pp. 522–3.

After some refreshments, the diplomatic conversation came to an end. What had been achieved beyond a fuller appreciation of Russian and Scottish foreign policy priorities? Possibly, following the wish of King James to assert his title to the English throne in both an open and a secret manner, Mar had made some progress in this direction. A potentially more substantial link between the House of Stuart and the family of Tsar Boris was the marriage projected in the summer of 1601 between John, the youngest brother of James VI's queen, Anne of Denmark, and Godunov's daughter Kseniya, but John died in Moscow in October 1602.

In his concluding assessment on the first meeting between Stuart and Romanov representatives, Robert Evans asserts that:

> The price of Russia's moral and diplomatic support for King James's claim to the English crown might well be a pledge of future Anglo-Scottish military and financial aid to Russia and the reversal of the uncooperative Tudor policy which had so long frustrated Ivan IV and his successors. In 1601 no one knew how long Queen Elizabeth would survive or whether King James's ambitions would ultimately be fulfilled. In the circumstances the adoption of pseudonym, allowing the King of Scots the adoption of total repudiation in the last resort, had solid advantage. Retribution could fall only on the English.

As Evans also points out, as far as the associates of the intermediaries Cherry, Merrick and Bowes were concerned, 'the choice for the Muscovy Company must have lain between possible reprisals in Russia and certain official hostility in England'.[59] This choice was to constitute a dilemma for the Muscovy Company at several junctures throughout the seventeenth century.

On 9 February 1602, John Merrick arrived in Moscow with a secret letter and verbal message from Queen Elizabeth. Regarding the question of an English marriage, Merrick emphasised that the naming of candidates had to be restricted out of respect for the tsar's 'divinitie'. The queen herself had insisted that any prospective English marriage partner should be of royal blood. Merrick went on to produce an elaborate pedigree to the evident satisfaction of Tsar Boris. Conversation on other topics followed, for example the tsar talking of the pope as 'a bloudy infidell'. Merrick was then dismissed with a daily allowance 'very greet and extraordinary for her Majesties sake'. In a final audience on 22 June, the tsar commended Queen Elizabeth's deference to his position as demonstrated in her refusal 'to propose unto him any of her owne kyndred farre remote in blood from her roiall person'. He stood to give Merrick

---

59 Ibid., pp. 527–8.

a letter to the queen with the declaration that he was 'more beholding to her Majesty then unto any prince in the world besides' and the assurance that her merchants would receive precedence over all others with favours shown to them 'increased many ways hereafter'.

The immediate danger of a rival Danish marriage to the tsar's daughter averted by the death in Moscow of Prince John in October 1602, the elaborate charade of English pedigrees and prospective brides for the tsar's son came to an end with the death of Queen Elizabeth on 24 March 1603. Just over two years later, Tsar Boris was also to die during the turbulent period of Russian history known as the Time of Troubles. His son was murdered, while his daughter lived on, after taking the veil, until 1622.[60]

Conclusion

Regime change in Russia was violent, in England peaceful. Yet the sixteenth century had provided a basis for the development of the special relationship between the Stuarts and Romanovs in the shape of the privileges granted to English merchants by Ivan the Terrible, and the early seventeenth century offered the promise that a transition was possible to more regulated commercial relations, stronger diplomatic ties and a clearer understanding of state interests in peace and war. Could this promise be fulfilled? And how would the relationship between Russia and Great Britain affect the nature of the Stuart and Romanov systems of government?

Of course, there was more to the sixteenth-century relationship of Tudors and Riurikovichi than the linkages through commerce, diplomacy and war. In addition, deep-rooted beliefs and patterns of behaviour shaped evolving state interests and identities. So did elite and popular ideas of power, its role, purpose and place within the emerging international system. Indeed, culture in the narrower and wider sense was of significance for the relationship of the dynasties and their subjects in the sixteenth century, and in the seventeenth century, too. As J. H. Burns observes, ideas in late medieval and early modern Europe were 'preponderantly, and inevitably, about kings and kingship'.[61]

In Britain, with a new monarch, royal house and Union of Crowns, political culture in particular was on the move, as interests and identities were both subject to change. Moreover, it was not only the British monarchs and their subjects who were thinking in terms of their influence in the wider world. As

60 Evans, 'The Anglo-Russian Royal Marriage Negotiations', pp. 379–87.
61 Burns, *The True Law*, p. 1.

Valerie Kivelson makes clear, for example, the religious vision of the Russians was soon to mould 'a unique sort of imperial mission, based on a tangibly territorial sense of the meaning of expansion, which involved a divinely dictated destiny of spreading Russianness throughout the land and rivers of the Far North and Far East'.[62]

62 Kivelson, *Cartographies*, p. 12.

TWO

New Beginnings, 1603–1625

War – The Time of Troubles, 1598–1613

James VII of Scotland was to become James I of Great Britain with little or no disturbance. Mikhail Romanov, on the other hand, was not to become tsar until the end of one of the most turbulent periods in the whole of Russian history.

The Time of Troubles was both a civil war and a war of foreign intervention. It is usually said to have commenced at the extinction of the Riurikovichi with the death of the last of the line, Fedor Ivanovich, in 1598, and to have ended with the election of the first Romanov, Mikhail, in 1613. The period as a whole forms an important backdrop to the early negotiations of Stuarts and Romanovs and to the continuation of commercial activity.

In Platonov's 'classical' formulation, the Time of Troubles is divided into three parts: dynastic, 1598–1606, as Godunovs and other great families struggled among themselves; social, 1606–10, as the Cossacks became the focus of widespread discontent; and national, 1611–13, the fight for nationhood against foreign intervention. More recently, Chester Dunning has expressed strong reservations about the manner in which, following Platonov, Soviet and other scholars have given emphasis to 'class war' aspects of the Cossack movement. Undoubtedly, however, Russian society was visibly shaken by years of infighting exacerbated by the incursions of foreigners.[1]

Those familiar with Mussorgsky's operatic adaptation of Pushkin's verse drama *Boris Godunov* will recall how the dying tsar was tortured by the ghost of the Tsarevich Dmitry, and how the first impostor 'False Dmitry' came to claim his 'rightful inheritance' with the support of Polish interventionists. A contemporary, Henry Brereton, tells us how the second such impostor was driven back in 1609 and the Russians 'gave great praises and giftes to the French, English and Scottish for their paines taken, and valours shewne'. Soon afterwards, however, Zygmunt King of Poland–Lithuania prepared for another attack by raising 'a mighty Army, compounded of many Nations, as Tartars, Leiflanders, Coerlanders, together with some Companies of English, Scottish and Dutch, and many numbers of Cossakes, which be a people drawne from all partes, following onely for spoyle and prey'. To counter this threat, the Russian

---

1 Platonov, *The Time of Troubles*, pp. 43–4; Dunning, *Russia's First Civil War*, p. 6.

'Vansusce' [V. I. Shuisky] asked for help from King Charles of Sweden, who sent messengers to Western Europe. In response to this appeal: 'There were taken up in England of Voluntaries, English, and Scottish, two thousand under the commaund of Captain Caluine a Scottishman, lieutenant Coronel to my Lord of Wormston, and of Captaine Coborne a valiant Souldier Coronell of the horse.' English and Scottish, French and Dutch mustered in Sweden before moving into Russia via Finland. Later on in the narrative, Captain 'Crale' an Englishman and Captain 'Creton' a Scotsman also receive mention.

However, among the many acts of treachery described by Brereton, a campaign launched by the Swedes in 1610 is among the more harrowing:

> Now must the miseries of Russia be augmented by the coming of this Army compounded of so many Nations, English, French and Scots. For though they came as a friend, and for their aid, yet who can stay an Army from spoil and rapine, which the unhappy Russian found true in the pursuit of this bloody war, not only on their goods and chattels, but even in their wives and daughters which in all places were made a prostituted prey to the lustful appetite of the soldiers.[2]

No wonder a national movement arose to drive all the foreigners from Russia and elect a new tsar. However, peace was not agreed with Sweden until 1617, and with Poland until 1619.[3]

The Accession of the Stuarts

For James, the question of the implications of his policy towards Russia was posed less hypothetically than during the Mikulin embassy when he succeeded Elizabeth in 1603 to become King of Great Britain, France and Ireland. Of these titles, the second was an archaic aspiration and the third less of a reality than the first, and even the first title was not as firm as James would have liked.[4] As he himself put the point to the House of Commons soon after his accession in March 1604:

> Do we not remember, that this little Kingdom was divided into seven little kingdoms, besides Wales? And is it not now the stronger by their Union? And hath not the Union of Wales to England added a greater strength thereto?

2 Brereton, *Newes*, pp. 37, 42–3, 46, 50, 53–4.
3 Frost, *The Northern Wars*, p. 47.
4 Murdoch, 'Diplomacy in Transition', pp. 93–5.

Which, tho' it was a great Principality, was nothing comparable, in greatness and power, to the ancient and famous Kingdom of Scotland . . . Hath not God united these Two Kingdoms [Scotland and England] both in language, religion, and similitude of manners? Yea, hath he not made us all in one island, encompassed with one sea, and of itself by nature so indivisible, as almost those that were borderers themselves on the late borders, cannot distinguish, nor know or discern their own limits? These two countries being separated neither by sea nor by great river, mountain, nor the strength of nature, but only by little small brooks, or demolished little walls; so as rather they were divided in apprehension, than in effect, and now, in the end and fullness of time, united, and right and title of both in My person alike lineally descended of both the Crowns . . . What God hath conjoined then, let no man separate. I am the husband, and the whole isle is my lawful wife: I am the head, and it is my body: I am the shepherd, and it my flock . . .[5]

However, the hopes of James for political and commercial integration of England and Scotland were wrecked by the House of Commons in 1607.[6]

Nevertheless, in 1610, he made clear to the English Parliament his view that 'the King takes himself to be beholding to no elective powers, depends upon no popular applause, that he derives the lines of his fortune and greatness from the loins of his ancestors'.[7] John Selden echoed this sentiment in 1614 with a quotation from 'a long since ordained' act of the Parliament of Scotland indicating that 'our Souerain Lord has full iurisdiction and Free Empire within this Realme'. To be sure, Selden might on occasion let his patriotism run away with him, in one instance observing that Constantine the Great was born in Britain.[8] In our present study of the relationship between the Stuarts and the Romanovs, we also must avoid distortion, resisting any temptation to simplify our analysis by equating Great Britain with England, since Scotland continued to play an important part through to the rise and fall of Jacobitism.

We must also remember that, like his Tudor predecessors, the first Stuart had wider, imperial interests. As far as Russia was concerned, soon after his accession James VI and I sent Thomas Smith as ambassador to establish friendly relations with the tsar. (*En route* for Moscow, incidentally, he stayed at Iaroslavl' with G.I. Mikulin, formerly Russian ambassador to England.) Among the precious

---

5 Tanner, *Constitutional Documents*, p. 26.
6 Macinnes, *The British Revolution*, p. 40.
7 Burns, *The True Law*, pp. 247, 225; Foster, *Proceedings in Parliament 1610*, vol. 2, Oxford, 1983, p. 49.
8 Selden, *Titles of Honor*, London, 1614, pp. 18, 27.

presents brought by him was a carriage [*povozka*] decorated with the lion and the unicorn and the two-headed eagle, and scenes of the Russian struggle against the Turks. Smith was to make clear that the British relationship with the Turks was no more than commercial, and would never approach political alliance. As with his predecessors, he was to represent the interests of the members of the Muscovy Company and other merchants in addition to those of the monarch.[9]

Some years later, as the Time of Troubles was coming to an end, under the influence of the Muscovy Company, King James went so far as to contemplate the acquisition of a large part of Russia. In 1611, a Scottish mercenary James Hill wrote to Lord Salisbury that such an acquisition 'would be a thousand times more profitable unto England as Virginia'.[10] A 'Proposition' to this effect appears to have been drawn up in 1612. It begins by observing that 'the safety and wealth of this island dependeth principally upon the shipping thereof'. Anything that promoted navigation and the commerce that flowed from it was appropriate, therefore, and such a scheme had been devised in consultation with Sir Thomas Smith, Governor of the Muscovy Company and formerly ambassador to Muscovy. Noting the manner in which this country had been invaded and despoiled by the Poles and the Swedes for several years past, the 'Proposition' went on to draw the conclusion that:

> yf his Magestie may have an offer of that part of Moscovia, which lyeth betweene the Archangell and the river Volga, with the tract along that river to the Caspian or Persian sea, or at least the commaunds and protection of yt, with libertie and assurance of that trade, yt will be the greatest and happiest ouverture that ever was made to any King of this realme, since Columbus offered King Henry VII the discovery of the West Indies.

Diplomatic negotiations might well lead to such a treaty which could 'put into the Englishe companies hands there so much treasure and commodities, as will defray the charge of the arming and transporting the number of men that they desire'. There was talk of sending the king's son Charles, later Charles I, as a candidate for the position of tsar or a least as 'protector' of North Russia. Moreover, the Archbishop of Canterbury was attracted by the possibility of reducing Roman Catholic influence in Russia. However, having learned from

---

9 Arel and Bogatyrev, 'Anglichane v Moskve', pp. 439–40, 444–5. *Sir Thomas Smithes voyage*, [p. 18].

10 Quoted by Bushkovitch and Jansson in their 'Introduction' to Jansson and Rogozhin, *England and the North*, pp. 64–5.

the experience of his predecessor Queen Elizabeth that dealings with the Muscovites should always be cautious, and a man of peace in any case, James VI and I did not press his claim for part of Muscovy against Polish and Swedish rivals. And by the time his ambassadors arrived there in 1613, the election had taken place of a new, Russian tsar, Mikhail.[11] In any case, there is force in I. I. Lubimenko's argument that the proposed protectorate reflected the desire of the English merchants to assert their interests in the Russian market at a time of great uncertainty. After all, the 'protectorate' comprised essentially the entire sphere of activity of the Muscovy Company.[12]

The Accession of the Romanovs

In 1612, Prince Dmitri Pozharsky from Nizhnii Novgorod is said to have declared: 'We do not now need hired people from other states . . . We ourselves, boyars and nobles . . . serve and fight for the holy, godly churches, and for our Orthodox Christian faith and for our fatherland without pay.'[13] In concert with a merchant named Kuzma Minin from the same region, Pozharsky is tradition-ally believed to have led the movement of national revival that brought to an end the Time of Troubles.

Along with the expulsion of the Roman Catholic Polish and other heretics, a further necessity was the election of new tsar. Mikhail Romanov, a youth of sixteen, seemed young and malleable enough to fill the bill, as well as sufficiently qualified with a family pedigree extending way back over the centuries along with a tradition of service and experience of the ways of the court. To be sure, there was some suspicion that he was the creature of the Cossacks. But to quote Platonov again, 'The tsar's election, which pacified the Troubles and quieted the country, seemed to the popular side the special beneficence of the Lord, and to ascribe to the Cossacks the election of him whom "God himself had revealed" was in their eyes an unseemly absurdity.'[14]

Thus, there was a further element of the new tsar's power, reinforcing its derivation from man as well as God. Here, we continue to follow the 'classical' interpretation of Platonov who observed that Mikhail was 'the single figure around whom both sides of the still not finally reconciled segments of Muscovite society – the service class of the countryside and the Cossacks – could unite'. An important conduit of the general agreement was the *zemskii*

11 Lubimenko, 'A Project', pp. 248, 252–3; Dunning, 'A Letter' pp. 94–8; Dunning, *Russia's First Civil War*, pp. 421–3.
12 Liubimenko, 'Torgovye snosheniia', p. 8. See also Virginskii, 'Proekty prevrashcheniia'.
13 Borodin, *Inozemtsy*, p. 7.
14 Platonov, *The Time of Troubles*, p. 162.

sobor or Assembly of the Land first convened in the reign of Ivan the Terrible. To quote Platonov at greater length on the relations between Mikhail and the Assembly that elected him in 1613:

> The tsar elected by the 'land' and the popular assembly not only did not dispute each other's rights and primacy, but firmly supported one another in the same concern for their common safety and security. Consciousness of a common weal and mutual dependence led the central authority and its council of 'all the land' to the fullest agreement, and converted the tsar and 'all the land' into one indivisible political force, which struggled with currents hostile to it within and without the state. Thus the circumstances of the Troubled Time gave a complex structure to the Muscovite constitution; it was composed of the personal authority of an unlimited sovereign and the collective authority of a *sobor* of 'all the land'. Every 'affair of the great sovereign and of the land' was resolved at the time 'by the decree of the great sovereign and by the compact of all the land'. The sovereign's decree, moreover, willingly relied upon the 'compact of the land', whereas the 'compact of the land' received force only by the sovereign's order. No charters existed that might have defined this interrelationship of the central authority and the popular representation, and there is no possibility of speaking about a 'limitation' of Mikhail Fedorovich's authority. Nevertheless, the close connection between the tsar and 'all the land' and the collective character of the state authority under Tsar Mikhail stand beyond doubt.

However, while the Assembly of the Land functioned apparently without interruption for the first decade of Mikhail's reign, it then met less frequently. Later, under his son Aleksei Mikhailovich, ' "all the land" gradually became not the administrator but an administered ward of the state'.[15] At a time that the English centuries-old representative assembly was moving into the ascendancy, therefore, its more recent Russian counterpart was already losing its influence. But of course, we must be careful about pushing the comparison too close: we must not be misled by the fact that early-seventeenth-century Russians had no difficulty in translating parliament as *zemskii sobor*.[16] The English House of

---

15 Platonov, *The Time of Troubles*, pp. 159, 173–4. Dunning, *Russia's First Civil War*, p. 449, criticises the view of the state distinct from the person of the tsar as 'hopelessly anachronistic and inaccurate'. However, as we have just seen, Platonov wrote 'there is no possibility of speaking of a "limitation" of Mikhail Fedorovich's authority'.

16 Bushkovitch and Jansson, intro., Jansson and Rogozhin, *England and the North*, p. xii: 'Curiously, the one English institution which presented no difficulty in translation was parliament. That was simply "Assembly of the Land" (*Zemskii sobor*), a usage which may well tell us much about their understanding of both institutions.'

Commons had evolved through many reigns before it was poised to assert its authority, a process that is well documented, at least in comparison with the Russian Assembly, whose composition and procedure are far less clear, and appear to have varied considerably throughout the short period of its existence according to the reasons for which the government summoned it.

To spread the good news of the Romanov accession abroad, Embassies asserting the legitimacy of the new tsar and the authority of his government were sent off to Austria, Denmark and Poland, to the Crimean Tatars, Persia, Ottoman Turkey and the Patriarch of Constantinople. In November 1613, Aleksei Ivanovich Ziuzin came to Great Britain for this purpose, assisted by Aleksei Vitovtov. The ambassadors left Moscow on 7 July 1613, arrived in London on 26 October and were received by James VI and I a day later. An announcement of the accession and the presentation of gifts was formally made before James VI and I on 7 November 1613.

Although it was customary European diplomatic practice to send out ambassadors to announce the accession of one monarch after the death of another, the heavy emphasis of this embassy's instructions was on the profound problems arising from the Time of Troubles. To be sure, the ambassadors were instructed to inform James VI and I that Mikhail was prepared to enter an alliance with the pope, the emperor, the Spanish and French kings, and the Venetian doge against the Moslem infidel, but the same heads of state were urged to reprove 'the wicked Polish King'.[17] Moreover, one well-informed contemporary observer noted that 'affairs of state and of commerce' were jointly under discussion, and that the Russian ambassador was 'always surrounded by merchants' and 'in the matter of commerce he has given the greatest satisfaction'. Certainly, English merchants were to be guaranteed toll-free access to Archangel and most-favoured nation status.[18] However, the ambassadors were specifically to ask for help against the Polish and Swedish interventionists in the shape of 'treasure, money and gold, and goods and all sorts of artillery supplies, as much as will be possible'. Military assistance in the shape of several thousand troops at the king's own expense would also be welcome.[19] And, when necessary, the English would be expected to sell or exchange Russian Treasury goods abroad.[20]

17 Jansson and Rogozhin, *England and the North*, pp. 100, 102, 112.
18 *CSPV*, 1613–1615, no. 137, p. 65; no. 166, p. 81; no. 174, p. 84; Jansson and Rogozhin, *England and the North*, pp. 109–10.
19 Ibid., pp. 100, 102.
20 Solov'ev, *Istoriia Rossii*, V/9, p. 69; Martens, 'Rossiia i Angliia', II, pp. 18–19; Demkin, *Zapadnoevropeiskoe kupechestvo*, I, p. 45.

Diplomacy

Before the Muscovite embassy of 1613 arrived, the Muscovy Company's trading privileges had been reconfirmed by the Stuart government.[21] In this manner, a political role was added to the economic function of the Muscovy Company agent. The dual position of chief agent for the Muscovy Company and Royal Representative had been for the first time invested in Fabian Smith. As such, he supplied the government with advice concerning forthcoming diplomatic negotiations and furnished any diplomatic mission with translators and interpreters. He helped in dealings with Russian diplomatic bureaucracy and protocol. The conflation of the two roles provided the framework through which diplomacy was to be conducted for the rest of the century.

Thenceforth, the two royal houses were engaged in further negotiations towards a closer relationship. But with what priorities? Sergei Konovalov suggests that the Russians were 'looking for moral, political and financial support in their desperate struggle against the Polish Pretender to the Russian crown', while the 'English' were ready to give 'some measure of support, in the hope of seeing more stable conditions in Russia and of securing exclusive and exceptional trade privileges in return for their help'.[22] Paul Bushkovitch and Maija Jansson, however, give new emphasis to British political motives. Foreshadowed by the Stuart king's peace-seeking policy as James VI of Scotland, they argue, his first actions as James I of England included an agreement with the Netherlands and peace with Spain. In their view:

> Although commerce was important, other issues hinging on the configurations of continental alliance dominated politics at Whitehall from two decades before the Spanish Armada to the years immediately preceding England's involvement with the Thirty Years' War. Well outside the narrow confines of Muscovy Company business, the crown was rapidly becoming absorbed with the larger problems of alignment between the Habsburgs and their enemies and the crisscrossing alliances among the Catholic and Protestant states. In short, religious and political issues were instrumental in molding England's diplomacy with the Scandinavian states, Poland, and Russia at this time to a much greater extent than is generally realized.[23]

21 *CSPD*, 1611–1618, no. 98, p. 178, 30 March 1613: 'Confirmation of the liberties granted to the Company of English Merchants for discovery of new trades in Russia and Muscovy, and prohibiting all, not of that Company, to trade in Cherry Island, Greenland, or other Islands discovered by the said Company, &c; also granting new liberties.'
22 Konovalov, 'Anglo-Russian Relations', 1617–1618, p. 64.
23 Paul Bushkovitch and Maija Jansson, in Jansson and Rogozhin (eds), *England and the North*, pp. vii–viii, 47–8.

After the Gunpowder Plot of 1605, James adopted 'a more aggressive pro-Protestant stance', and his fear of radical Catholicism drove him towards the Protestant Union of 1608.[24] Moreover, he also pursued a wider, more ecumenical policy involving the highly unlikely possibility of union between the Church of England and the Greek Orthodox Church.[25]

By far the best way of giving a further perspective on the question of strategic, political and economic priorities is to subject successive embassies in both directions to close scrutiny. One consequence of the Time of Troubles had been economic dislocation leading to a dramatic reduction of trade between Russia and England. As the Dutchman Isaac Massa described the situation in the year 1609, the merchants from Vologda went downriver to Archangel: 'There they found ships from Holland and England, which they had despaired of ever seeing again. But since there was no trade, and they had suffered great losses, the vessels left almost empty after they had waited for some merchants who had still not returned from the interior of the country'.[26] In response, the Muscovy Company attempted to open up new markets and new trade routes, which it then sought to monopolise. This initiative included the idea already described and later dropped, to capture Archangel and the North, the principal zone of Muscovy Company influence in Russia, for James VI and I. Spitsbergen, Greenland and places even more remote were investigated, as we shall see later.

In this period, Dutch commercial competition first began to undermine England's predominant economic position in the Russian markets, with bases at the mouth of the Dvina and on the Kola peninsula. However, in their relations with the English merchants, the Russians had to deal only with one principal agent who 'could be made responsible for the actions of all the other factors' and a united company which was better able to pay the cost of diplomatic embassies as well as present a united front at court.[27] These points may be illustrated through reference to episodes in the career of Sir John Merrick, who was ideally suited for the job of representing Stuart interests to the Romanovs. He was the son of William Merrick, who had been one of the founding members of the Muscovy Company, and had grown up in the Foreign Quarter of Moscow. John himself had served the company since 1584 in various capacities.

In his dealings with the first False Dmitrii in 1605, Merrick was able to meet the goal of restoring the right to trade with Persia, a feat he reported in a letter to Lord Salisbury. Somewhat more problematically, however, the new rights did

24 Ibid., p. 49.
25 Patterson, *James VI and I*, pp. 217–19.
26 Massa, *A Short History*, p. 179. See also *CSPV*, 1607–1610, no. 700, p. 380.
27 Lubimenko, 'The Struggle of the Early Dutch', p. 33.

not necessarily restore the comparative advantage of the English, since the Dutch also received a grant of privileges from the pretender.[28] In essence, the Russians were eager and determined to get any help they could find.

Playing this game of diplomacy entailed considerable risks at a time of exceptional political instability. Relations with the Russians may have suffered from an intervention by King Zygmunt III of Poland–Lithuania. Hoping to gain British support for the conquest of Russia, the king, in February 1611, wrote to James VI and I asking him to ensure that English merchants would not get involved in the political developments ongoing in Russia and, in particular, that they would not support the opposing side. Failure to comply, Zygmunt implied, might lead to a loss of privileges.[29]

The end of the Time of Troubles naturally provided the English with an opportunity to try to establish their commercial ties with Russia on a new footing. After the Ziuzin mission to England in 1613–14, Sir John Merrick led an embassy to Russia between June 1614 and November 1617.[30] Newly knighted, Merrick left for Russia in June 1614. He was instructed to pursue a set of privileges that would again permit English trade with Persia. The Dutch suspected as much and Massa even claimed in a letter to the States General that the 'English create more worries and trouble for us than the Spanish ever did.'[31] Merrick was also instructed to intercede and conclude a peace between Russia and Sweden, and was involved in the Russo-Swedish peace negotiations held in Narva and Novgorod. The peace resulted in the Treaty of Stolbovo in 1617.[32] Sweden relinquished attempts to gain control of Muscovite trade through the Baltic (Pskov) and White Sea (Archangel) trade routes. As Artur Attman has observed: 'The Peace of Stolbovo marked a watershed in Swedish policy. The Arctic programme was completely abandoned and instead it was Sweden's policy during the seventeenth century to concentrate on trying to channel the Arctic trade through the Baltic sea.'[33]

The next embassy from Russia was sent in response to a letter from James VI and I to Mikhail dated 1 June 1617. The Venetian ambassador in London wrote of 'the present Muscovite ambassador, who in point of fact made his appearance at this Court rather on account of the commercial interests of his nation with the

---

28 Ivanov, *Anglo-gollandskoe torgovoe sopernichestvo*, pp. 108-9; Kordt, *Ocherk snoshenii*, p. LXXIX. A detailed description of the privileges granted by False Dmitrii to the English in December 1605 can be found in: Demkin, *Zapadnoevropeiskoe kupechestvo*, I, p. 44.

29 Jasnowski, *England and Poland*, p. 29.

30 *CSPV*, 1615-1617, no. 18, p. 12: 'September 15, 1615. Antonio Foscarini, Venetian Ambassador in England, to the Doge and Senate'; ibid., no. 28, p. 18; Phipps, *Sir John Merrick*, Chapter IV, *passim*.

31 Ivanov, *Anglo-gollandskoe torgovoe sopernichestvo*, pp. 146-50.

32 A contemporary copy of this treaty in French can be found in *PRO*, SP 103/61, fols 15-9.

33 Attman, *The Struggle*, p. 214.

London merchants than for any other purpose, although his mission is understood to be with the King.'[34] The ambassadors Stepan Ivanovich Volynsky and Marko Ivanovich Pozdeyev arrived in London on 5 November 1617 and were at audience on 14 November. On or about 10 January 1618, they dined with the king. Noting that the king was most pleased with the hawks that they gave him, among other presents, a contemporary asserted that the ambassadors had come 'to renew the trade.'[35] The ambassadors wished 'to make a league with England' and requested a loan of £60,000 'which the merchants will furnish.'[36] And in return for substantial Stuart military support and assistance in the Russo-Polish conflict which would manifest itself in a 'general and invyolable league', they alluded to a new 'Charter of Priviledges', 'which never the like hath been given to any' and which operated 'to the utter exclusion of the Dutch.'[37] The trade privileges included free transit of English merchandise from Persia through Russia to Archangel, and also the possibility of opening up a direct trade route to China via Siberia and following the line of the River Ob. The Muscovy Company agreed to pay the loan, which was shared with the East India Company, 'on condition of sharing of their profits for eight years.'[38] The Company also paid the 'heavy' expenses incurred by the Russian ambassador and his 'numerous retinue.'[39]

King James sent Sir Dudley Digges as ambassador to Russia in 1618 to follow up the possibilities offered for negotiation. However, according to Konovalov, this Embassy ended in 'complete failure'.[40] Isaac Massa, the contemporary Dutch observer, described Digges' progress: how he was welcomed 'rapturously by a salvo of musketry', but 'did not go further than Kholomogory, despite the pleas of the governors'; how the Russian 'bailiffs' attempted to halt his escape back to Archangel, and how Russian 'nobles' and the English agent tried to dissuade the English ambassador. But he did not heed them, and, on 2 September, he departed on two ships that fired broadsides. One shot went straight through one of the houses. Massa reported the Dutch reaction to this embassy:

34   *CSPV*, 1617–1619, no. 218, p. 136.
35   *CSPD*, 1611–1618, no. 11, p. 512; no. 23, p. 495; no. 28, p. 497.
36   *CSPD*, 1611–1618, no. 83, p. 530.
37   *CSPV*, 1617–1619, no. 402, p. 235. For a contemporary translation of the Russian ambassador's speech, see *PRO*, SP 91/2, fol. 38r-v. It is more than likely that this poor English translation was done by a Muscovy Company employee. A contemporary noted: 'the interpreterr, whether abashed or imperfaict in the language, or not so well comprehendinge, was not so readie or facound in his interpretation, but made shift to goe through to the end'. See Sir Gerard Herbert to Carleton, 14 November 1617, *CSP* (*Col*), East India, 1617–21, p. lxi.
38   *CSPD*, 1611–1618, no. 2, p. 532; ibid., no. 9, p. 533.
39   *CSPV*, 1617–1619, no. 107, p. 65.
40   Konovalov, 'Anglo-Russian Relations, 1617–1618', p. 64.

This is at least true; the English are embarrassed, and our credit is good. Finally, the Princes in Moscow will realize the truth about trade with England, from which the tsar has derived no benefit in the course of fifty years, whereas a significant sum has accrued annually from the customs duty paid by the Dutch. Now they will realize who has better served Russia's interests throughout the world. The Russians will note that nobody has offered the Muscovite state an insult such as the English have offered, not even the Turks in the course of all their wars against Russia. Never have they been so insulted. As highly as the English were regarded before, so now are they despised. As much as they exalted themselves, so now they hang their heads and are notably ingratiating to us. Henceforth they cannot do otherwise, and unless something unforeseen occurs, their company will dissolve within a year; for only three of their ships have come this year, whereas we have had more than thirty, selling every kind of merchandise.

Massa attempted to find the reason for Digges' disastrous embassy:

The Russians were astounded and greatly perturbed. They sent the Englishman's compatriot and secretary to Moscow in disgrace. I cannot rightly guess the cause of this commotion. Some say it was caused by ill tidings from upriver, others that it was caused by my arrival, for there is a rumour current that we had come with a huge subsidy, together with many other things the English did not have. It is also said that the ambassador found this country unpleasant, and that the East India Company in England had deceived the Muscovy Company. In short, everyone has his own version, and it is hard to distinguish the truth.[41]

On 26 October, the Venetian ambassador reported that Digges had returned 'without being able to effect anything, as he found the country overrun with Polish troops which had advanced under Moscow, and he therefore deemed it advisable to come back without waiting.' However, his nephew, Thomas Finch went on to Moscow and had an audience with the tsar on 16 March 1619.[42]

Sir John Merrick's embassy to Moscow from June 1620 to October 1621[43] attempted to rebuild Stuart–Romanov relations and secure the 'clearing of any

---

41 *Massa's Short History*, pp. 186–8, 'Letter of Isaac Massa to the States-General, written at Archangel on 4 September and received on 17 November 1618'. For Massa's diplomatic instructions, see *APC*, 1616–1618, pp. 101–3, 151–2.

42 *CSPV*, 1617–1619, no. 570, p. 340.

43 *CSPD*, 1619–1623, no. 112, p. 96, 28 June 1620: Chamberlain to Carleton: 'Sir John Merrick has taken leave, and had a tablet given him with portraits of the king and his children.'

difficultie that may disturbe or interrupt their free commerce, as allsoe for the enlardgeing of Trade into Persia by way of the Volga'.[44] Mikhail would only agree to the renewal of the trading privileges if there were also military and political compensations, in the form of a 'Perpetuall League of Allyance' sufficient to merit the financial losses which Muscovy would incur. In order to gain the privileges, Merrick promised an alliance, but persuaded the Russian negotiators that according to his commission he was not empowered to ratify it. Konovalov comments:

> One again, Merrick gave evidence of his skill as a negotiator. In fact, he not merely succeeded in concealing his government's true intentions from his Russian contemporaries, inducing in them an "outward satisffaction", but even misled later Russian historians, who have relied on Russian documents recording Merrick's declarations in Moscow without taking into consideration the material in the Public Record Office.[45]

It seems that, on the strength of Merrick's promise, the general trade privileges of the Muscovy Company were renewed on 11 May 1621: 'the great Duke and the Patriarch graunted them newe priveleges under their golden Seale to continew the trade in joynte stocke, a matter of greatest advantage for the marchantes affairs in Russia at Present'.[46] In order that the alliance be properly sealed, Mikhail sent ambassador Isaak Samoilovich Pogozhevo[47] with Merrick to London, which he reached in October 1621. An audience with James VI and I ensued on 1 November 1621, the ambassador presenting the king with 'rich furs, carpets, cloths of gold and silver, a Persian mat, &c.' The Muscovy Company continued to orchestrate the observance of diplomatic protocol in London, as is evidenced by the 'Order in Council, at the request of the Russia Company, that the ambassador just arrived from Russia with Sir John Merrick, be received by the Lord Mayor of London, as has usually been done, and that, on the company's security, a fitting proportion of the King's plate be delivered for his use.'[48]

On 4 January 1622 Pogozhevo delivered a document to the Privy Council which attempted to declare the reasons for his embassy, especially a 'perpetuall league'.

---

44 Konovalov, 'Anglo-Russian Relations, 1620-1624', pp. 99–100, Appendix I.
45 Ibid., p. 75. See also Phipps, *Sir John Merrick*, pp. 154–64.
46 *PRO*, SP 103/61, fol. 26: 'Relation of his Maties Embassadors proceedings with the great Duke, 1621'.
47 The Russian ambassador was described by a contemporary witness as 'a handsome young man with goode and confident behaviour'. John Chamberlain to Dudley Carleton, 10 November 1621 in Chamberlain, *Letters of John Chamberlain*, vol. II, p. 406.
48 *CSPD*, 1619–1623, no. 100, p. 308; ibid., no. 11, p. 295.

On 29 March 1622, Sir John Merrick supplied the Privy Council with a supplementary account of his negotiations with Russian diplomats in Moscow while on his last embassy to Russia. This enabled the Privy Councillors to fully grasp the complexity of the British diplomatic position over the question of 'trade concessions for political-military alliance', Konovalov suggests.[49] With some exaggeration, the Venetian ambassador in London stated that Great Britain possessed 'fleets of hundreds and thousands of ships together with all the material for building and arming them, except pitch, flax, tow and rope, which comes in quantities from Mouscovy and Danzig'.[50] Before his departure, Pogozhevo was lavishly feasted at the expense of the Muscovy Company, while James VI and I wrote to Mikhail: 'Wee maie not omit to give you thanks for your Majie and great favours to Our marchauntes and to Our Agent Fabian Smith, now residing there, whom Wee doe earnestly recommend unto you, praying you to hold them still under the protection of your grace and favour'.[51] However, the king would sign no alliance, promising the tsar no more than 'as strict and correspondant Amitie with your Majestie, as hath been between anie our Progenitors . . .'[52]

The four Embassies sent from England to Russia between 1613 and 1623 were paid for by the Muscovy Company, and the heavy expenses were to place the Company in financial difficulties. For example, in November 1618 the Muscovy Company was pleading 'losses' as the reason why it could not fulfil a promise to contribute 'towards suppressing pirates'.[53] The Muscovy Company in this period was suffering from a slump in trade due partly to general economic depression which took place between 1620 and 1624.[54] In 1621, according to a contemporary source, 'The Muscovy traders declare themselves disabled, by the extraordinary charges of the Ambassadors to and from Russia, from paying the additional impost of one per cent'.[55] For this reason Sir John Merrick, on behalf of the Muscovy Company, asked King James if the Embassies could cease; to this end he submitted a report suggesting 'the best way of paying the debts of the Company'.[56] It was agreed that diplomatic transactions between the two monarchs would now be conducted by a Royal Representative permanently stationed in Russia.[57]

---

49 Konovalov, 'Anglo-Russian Relations, 1620–1624', pp. 105–11; Phipps, *Sir John Merrick*, p. 166.
50 *CSPV*, 1617-1619, no. 603, p. 431, 21 September 1622.
51 *RGADA*, fond 35, op. 2, no. 32: James VI and I to Filaret Nikitich, 1 June 1622
52 *Acts of the Privy Council*, quoted by Phipps, *Sir John Merrick*, p. 168.
53 *CSPD*, 1619–1623, no. 27, p. 96.
54 Supple, *Commercial Crisis*, pp. 103, 264, Appendix A, Table 4.
55 *CSPD*, 1619–1623, no. 57, p. 302.
56 *PRO*, SP/14/124, fol. 50, Muscovy Company to James VI and I, 17 December 1621; *CSPD*, 1619–1623, no. 4150, p. 300.
57 *PRO*, SP 103/61, fols 26r–27v, Sir John Merrick's Report on his embassy.

The next British embassy to Russia confirmed this arrangement. In April 1623, Secretary of State Conway recommended Christopher Cocks for the post of king's 'Agent or Consul', and as a replacement of Fabian Smith as the Muscovy Company's official agent in Muscovy.[58] Cocks was empowered to negotiate 'such other things as he shall receave comand from Us, whch also maybe negotiated wthout ye trouble & hazard of Ambassadors betweene two such remote kingdomes'.[59] James wrote of 'some other person of quality and discretion to reside and remain there ... Our trusty welbeloved subject and servant Christopher Cocks gentleman to remayne with in Your Mat.s Dominions as Our Agent'.[60] The Privy Council, in a letter to Cocks, referred to him as having been 'honoured with the title of his Majesties Minister'.[61] Konovalov, in his assessment of the changed function of the Muscovy Company agent, states: 'In this way the new agent of the Muscovy Company in Russia became a kind of diplomatic representative of the King, enjoying powers of an envoy or ambassador.'[62] This point has not been fully appreciated by other historians, one of whom wrote: 'There was no official exchange of permanent ambassadors between Russia and foreign powers until Peter I's reign, but from the 1660s, several countries (Sweden, Denmark, Poland and Holland) maintained accredited agents, termed *rezidenty* (residents) in Russia. Russia's major permanent representative abroad was the resident in Poland. Business with other countries was conducted by means of ad hoc missions.'[63] Because of its significance for commerce as well as diplomacy, we shall examine the Cocks mission more closely below.

In 1624, on Cocks' return to London bearing a letter from Mikhail,[64] he was debriefed firstly on behalf of the king's business, and then in his capacity as Muscovy Company agent, as the following state paper makes clear:

58 *CSPD*, 1619–1623, p. 565, 21 April 1623: 'The Same to the Muscovy Company. Recommends Chris Cocks for employment as their agent in Russia'; Ibid., p. 573, 30 April 1623: 'Sec. Conway to the Governor of the Muscovy Company. On behalf of Mr. Cocks to be their agent in Russia'.

59 *RGADA*, fond 35, opis 2, no. 31, James VI and I to Tsar Mikhail, 30 May 1623.

60 Konovalov, 'Anglo-Russian relations, 1620–1624', pp. 111–13. *PRO*, SP 91/2, fols 91–2, a copy of the *RGADA* original, reveals difference in spelling and, on occasion, in emphasis.

61 *APC*, 1623–1625, p. 237, 12 June 1624: A Letter from the Board of the Council to Christopher Cocks in Moscow.

62 Konovalov, 'Anglo-Russian Relations, 1620–1624', p. 85.

63 Soloviev, *History of Russia*, vol. 25, p. 239, n. 32. See also Leitsch, 'Kliuchevskii's Study', p. 299: 'resident diplomats were admitted to Moscow only in exceptional situations, and this only from the 1630s onwards.'

64 *RGADA*, fond 35, opis 2, no. 35: Christopher Cocks 'To the Right Hon. Evan Terafuche Lord Highe Chancelor of Russia and one of his Imperial Maiestes most honourable privie Councell, 1624' Sir John Merrick received the letter for translation by 24 October 1624, and the translated letter was sent to James VI and I by 6 November. *CSPD*, 1623–1625, no. 87, p. 361; no. 21, p. 372.

also a letter from the Emperor of Muscovy to the King, brought by Mr. Cocks, who went thither as agent last year. Suggests that Cocks should open to the Council his mission about a league with the Muscovite, to save the King trouble, it being of no great weight, and that meanwhile he should be permitted to give the Russia Company an account of their business, which he has foreborne to do, until his duty to his Majesty be first discharged.[65]

The conflation of the two roles of Muscovy Company agent and resident ambassador represented an effective response on behalf of King James and the Muscovy Company to both the economic (including the expense of such Embassies) and the geopolitical facts of life in early-seventeenth-century Europe. For all its commercial significance, Russia was situated on the periphery of Europe, and was therefore neither of great interest nor of much use as a political ally to Great Britain, even if the two powers shared an antipathy to Roman Catholicism.

Reviewing diplomatic missions from Elizabethan times to the 'Glorious Revolution' of 1688, Bell has stated that:

> it is abundantly clear where the foci of English interest lay during the entirety of the period under review. France and the Low Countries were dominant military and economic concerns. Here, in these areas that were also most proximate to England, the need for observation was unceasing. Here, England's leaders maintained the diplomatic web most consistently. In point of fact, more missions, of longer duration, were served in these two regions than in all other areas of diplomatic activity combined.[66]

Thus, while Spain, the Netherlands, France, the Holy Roman and Ottoman Empires received regular accredited British agents, Russia was not considered to be a major European power.[67] However, as the Muscovy Company agent had been upgraded to the position of Royal Representative, a more continuous acquisition of intelligence from Russia would now be forthcoming.

To sum up so far, Russia attempted throughout the first quarter of the seventeenth century, as she had attempted in the second half of the sixteenth century, to gain a closer military and political alliance with Great Britain. But, especially after the fading of the dreams of universal peace entertained by King James, British interest in Russia concentrated on maximising the opportunities for trade exploitation: the combination of Royal Representative with that of

---

65 *CSPD*, 1623–1625, no. 65, p. 358: Sec. Calvert to [Sec. Conway].
66 Bell, *Handlist of Diplomatic Representatives*, p. 11.
67 Aylmer, *The King's Servants*, p. 26; Lachs, *The Diplomatic Corps*, p. 14..

Muscovy Company agent signalled that the Romanovs were to expect no firm political or military commitment from the Stuarts, but rather the pursuit of an economic relationship, albeit in the context of a wider sympathy. The tension created by this conflict of inter-state interests, aims and objectives helps to explain many of the diplomatic manoeuvres and political manipulations and machinations of the period. But of course, commercial activity was significant enough for it to deserve closer attention in its own right.

Commerce

The Muscovy Company embarked on the new century with its *de iure* status in Muscovy somewhat eroded, but still extremely strong. The Dutch merchants, who had established themselves in the Dvina estuary in the closing decades of the sixteenth century and eventually successfully challenged the English supremacy of the northern route, could only view their rivals' status with considerable envy. In March 1605, Boris Godunov reaffirmed the privileges of the Muscovy Company, although, to the great disappointment of the English, no concessions were made regarding trade with Persia.[68] The English could, in theory, look forward to at least maintaining their positions on the Muscovite market; in particular, their special status offered lucrative opportunities for trade, even with their rivals.

A more important challenge to the status of the Company was domestic, in the shape of the free-trade debate of 1604. The vocal opposition to the Muscovy Company may have been due to 'the anger of the outport merchants at its recent forays into and monopoly claims to Spitzbergen whaling'.[69] In a report submitted to the Commons by the free-traders, the Muscovy Company was described as a 'Strong and shamefull monopoly, a monopoly in a monopoly', apparently because of the tight control exerted by the Company's 15-member court of assistants.[70] The Company defended itself against these charges in a special memorandum 'Concerning the State of the Russia trade'.[71] It claimed that a minimum of £30,000, as well as many lives, had been spent on establishing regular trade with Muscovy, while the various Embassies and trips to Russia had demanded another £30,000. The Muscovy merchants further pleaded that the company's productive operations required an organisational structure based on several agents, as did the commercial operations in the

---

68 Ivanov, *Anglo-gollandskoe torgovoe sopernichestvo*, p. 108.
69 Arel, *The Muscovy Company*, p. 26.
70 *JHC*, I, pp. 218–20.
71 *PRO* SPD 14/8, fol. 59.

Russian interior. Liberalising this trade, the argument went, would jeopardise its profitability, since the terms of trade would inevitable shift markedly against the English. Moreover, the small scale of the export trade to Russia promised limited gains from such a move. In the end, the impact of the free-trade debate on the Company is likely to have been small. The 1604 free-trade bill lowered the entry fees ('fines') to established companies, including in all probability the Muscovy Company. However, there is no evidence of any significant organisational changes.[72]

During the first decades of the century, business in Russia was strong and the profitability of the Company good. Nevertheless, during the first decade of the century, while the number of English ships typically rose to at least ten a year, this appears to have been normally no more than a half of the total number of Dutch vessels. Thereafter, the numbers began to diverge increasingly. An English account of the 'Expansion of Trade' in 1615 claimed that the Dutch annually sent 35 ships to Russia. Isaac Massa, writing in March 1618, similarly put the annual average number of Dutch vessels at close to 30. However, the surviving Amsterdam notarial records suggest that there were at least some years with significantly smaller totals.[73]

Overall profits of the Muscovy Company reached 40 per cent in 1608 and 27 per cent in 1617. A 1618 report stated that the highest profit between 1608 and 1615 was 90 per cent in 1611–12 and the lowest 11 per cent in 1614. The annual sale of English wares during this period has been estimated at £40,000.[74] The one reasonably complete source of comparative data on Anglo-Russian trade in the opening years of the seventeenth century is a 1604 list of Russian imports. At the time, English imports amounted to R60,104 [roubles], compared with R81,078 for the Dutch. The English 'market share' was still a highly respectable 40.25 per cent of the total Muscovite imports of R148,849. The Muscovy Company accounted for R59,072 of the total with an interloper 'Tomos Ivanov' providing R1,028 worth of goods.[75] At the time, English exports to Russia were to a significant degree dominated by cloth, with textiles accounting for 55 per cent of the known total value, R60,468, of Muscovy Company and interloper exports to Archangel in 1604. In contrast, the English exported relatively little specie, compared with the Dutch, whose commercial operation relied to a significant degree on cash-based transactions.

72 Arel, *The Muscovy Company*, pp. 30–1, 33–4.
73 Wijnroks, 'Mezhdunarodnaia konkurentsiia', p. 24; Lipson, *The Economic History*, II, p. 330; *RGADA* fond 35, 1604, opis 1, No. 41; *ARA* Liassen Moscoviën 7361, 1618; *GAA NA.*
74 Willan, *The Early History*, pp. 214–15; Liubimenko, 'Torgovye snoshenii', p. 142; Arel, *The Muscovy Company*, p. 29; Ivanov, *Anglo-gollandskoe torgovoe sopernichestvo*, pp. 120–1.
75 Floria, 'Torgovlia Rossii', pp. 142, 144.

The share of bullion in the English export bundle in 1604 was 17.6 per cent. The dominance of cloth appears to have been great even in subsequent years, even if complete data are no longer available.[76] The importance of Russia for English cloth trade in general was secondary, but still of some, and perhaps even growing, importance. Barry Supple put Russia's share of the total English cloth exports at just under 2 per cent in 1598–1620. However, this figure rose to 3.3 per cent in 1628, 3.9 per cent in 1632, and 5.4 per cent in 1640.[77] In 1604, the Company also exported 34,812 lb of gunpowder to Russia.[78]

As its once unassailable position was steadily eroded, the Muscovy Company embarked on some new ventures north of the Russian mainland to diversify its portfolio and to improve profits. An expedition to Cherry Island was undertaken in 1603 with a 50-ton vessel. Two years later, a new expedition devoted itself to walrus hunting and discovered a lead mine. In 1605, the company acquired 11 tons of train (whale) oil, followed by 22 tons the year after. By 1608, the total had risen to 31 tons, which fell to a mere 500 lb in 1609. In 1606, the English killed a total of 1,000 walruses and even shipped some live ones home as a present to the king. These operations attracted the interest of the Hull Company and prompted the Muscovy merchants in 1609 to take formal control of the island. While an important departure, the Cherry Island shipping in fact grew out of a more long-standing interest in the northern waters. An initial whale-hunting monopoly of 1577 had come to be of greater importance during the Company's financial crisis in the 1580s. It was made all the more urgent by the evident concern over the Company's health in 1593–4.[79]

The Company also sponsored a longer expedition to Novaia Zemlia and the Vaigach Isles in 1608 but it apparently reached a negative conclusion about the utility of continuing further afield.[80]

As a consequence of John Merrick's diplomatic activities already described, and of the end of the Time of Troubles in 1613, in July 1617 Mikhail Fedorovich granted a letter of privilege to 23 members of the Muscovy Company. The charter was identical to that received in 1586. The privileges were subsequently renewed in 1621, 1625, 1628, and 1645. However, the English failed to regain their right to trade with Persia first established in 1567. In 1617, this privilege was denied on the

---

76 Floria, 'Torgovlia Rossii', pp. 142, 145–6; Arel, *The Muscovy Company*, pp. 319, 323, 326; *RGADA* fond 35, opis 1, No 41.
77 Supple, *Commercial Crisis*, p. 258.
78 Arel, *The Muscovy Company*, p. 350; *RGADA* fond 35, opis 1, No 41.
79 Scott, *The Constitution*, II, pp. 49, 53; Purchas, *Hakluytus Pusthumus*, XIII, pp. 260, 270, 276, 293.
80 Liubimenko, *Les relations*, p. 223.

pretext of the Russian-Polish war and troubles in Persia. The Russians never delivered on their promise to revisit the issue in calmer times.[81]

However, contrary to its own commercial interests, the Russian government even lent its support to the Muscovy Company's efforts to prevent English inter-lopers from undercutting their monopoly. In 1616, the Russians issued a decree banning all trade by English merchants not associated with the company. If the Dutch had the backing of several high-ranking members of the Russian govern-ment, the English were not without supporters either. Duma Secretary Petr Tretiakov headed a pro-English faction in the Muscovite court.[82]

The collapse of the arms trade and the increasingly evident failure to main-tain parity with the Dutch meant that the situation of the Company was far from secure. Profitability declined to a relatively modest level. A figure of 28 per cent is cited for 1617. At the same time, the Company had trouble attracting new capital. The total at the time of £64,687 marked an increase of merely £17,000 on the level attained already half a century earlier in 1564. In 1618, the Company was forced to borrow £1,000, which it had difficulty repaying two years later. The Privy Council ordered in 1623–4 that the principal should be paid, albeit not any interest.[83]

The precarious financial situation forced the Company to continue with its search for new ventures. The focus of operations shifted in 1610 to Spitsbergen, another important source of walruses and whales. However, success there was far more difficult to attain than the fellows had expected. Two Company vessels sank in 1611, their equipment rescued by rivals from Hull. Two more ships were sent the year after, although they were now challenged by a Dutch and a Spanish vessel. This prompted the English to deploy a squadron of seven ships, one of them equipped with 21 cannon, in 1613. The Dutch responded in kind and sent an impressive fleet of 18 ships, 14 of them with 30 cannon each, in 1614. This now compared to three large English ships and two fishing smacks. There were repeated sea battles between the two rivals in 1611–16. Even with the resources of the East India Company, which helped dispatch a flotilla of 16 ships in 1618, the English were unable to overwhelm their rivals, who regrouped under the auspices of the *Noordsche Compagnie*. Increasingly, the Muscovy Company had to face competition from English interlopers as well, most notably the Hull Company.[84]

81 Ibid., pp. 176–7.
82 Demkin, *Zapadnoevropeiskoe kupechestvo*, I, pp. 36–7.
83 Liubimenko, *Les relations*, pp. 89, 183.
84 Scott, *The Constitution*, II, p. 54; Liubimenko, *Les relations*, p. 224. For a survey of the activities of the Dutch, see: Muller, *Geschiedenis der Noordsche Compagnie*.

The highly variable whale catch meant that there were years with a yield of 3,000–4,000 tons of whale oil, which was far beyond the capacity of the Muscovy Company to transport home. The Company's resistance to the interlopers eventually waned, although it still claimed the best locations of Bell Sound and Horn Sound for its exclusive use. To look briefly at the sequel, in 1645, the Company petitioned the Parliament to order other English ports to help the Company guard Spitsbergen from foreigners in return for annual catch quotas for the outports. Instead, the Naval Committee authorised all those arming vessels to whale around the islands. The necessary tonnage required to defend English interests was put at 3,000 tons, of which the Company would furnish 1,600, Hull and York 500 each, Yarmouth 300, and other merchants the remaining 200. The committee chosen to regulate this trade was heavily dominated by the Muscovy Company, which in 1658 renewed its efforts to gain exclusive control of Bell Sound and Horn Sound. Eventually, in 1672, the House of Commons deregulated whaling in the northern waters altogether, 27 years after a similar move by the Dutch.[85]

Another area where the English sought to pre-empt the Dutch was in the fur trade. One of the long-standing objectives of the Muscovy Company had been to gain more direct access to the Siberian fur markets, an idea that was revived during and after the Time of Troubles. The first attempts to establish contact with areas to the east of Archangel had been made by Stephen Burroughs (Borrow) who, in 1556, reached the Vaigach Isles, Novaia Zemlia, and the Pechora estuary, the centre of an important fur-producing area, as part of his efforts to locate the north-east passage. However, further interaction was undermined by the tsar in the 1580s.[86] The Muscovy Company made its first attempt to exploit direct trade with Siberia in 1611 when the *Amitie* was sent on an expedition to the delta of the River Ob. Josias Logan, William Pursglove and Marmaduke Wilson chose to spend the winter in the area, while the *Amitie* took on bird feathers and fox skins for its return trip to England. In the spring of 1612, Logan sailed up the Pechora to Ust'-Tsil'ma, while Pursglove had some months earlier gone west to the Mezen, where the Lampozhnia Island fair took place twice every winter. In January 1612, after a trip to Kholmogory, Pursglove returned to Pechora.[87] It appears that local tribal warfare and the opposition of the Russian merchants made any serious fur purchases impossible, however, and the three Englishmen spent their money mainly on salted fish and whale oil. They sailed on a small Russian vessel to Archangel in 1612 and spent the following winter in Kholmogory. However,

85 Liubimenko, *Les relations*, pp. 226–8.
86 Liubimenko, *Les relations*, p. 220; Dalgård, *Det Petsoriske Kompagni*, pp. 13–14.
87 Purchas, *Hakluytus posthumus*, I, pp. 200, 231, 241, 244–6; Platonov, *Proshloe russkogo severa*, pp. 70–1; Bol'shukhin, *Anglo-russkie otnosheniia*, pp. 211–12.

Wilson, along with William Gordon, returned to Pechora in the winter of 1614–15 and there is evidence to suggest that similar expeditions had been undertaken in the two intervening years. The results of the expedition far exceeded those of the first trip, and several boat trips were required to load Wilson's purchases aboard a Dutch ship that came to fetch the English in 1615 to take them to Dordrecht. British exports to the region consisted of foodstuffs such as flour, groats, meat and butter, as well as more valuable kinds of grain, raisins, figs, liquor and salt. There were different kinds of mainly less valuable cloth, copper, bronze and iron products, as well as tools. Last but not least, significant quantities of ready specie were carried.[88] Ultimately, operations in Pechora appear not to have lasted beyond these rather tentative expeditions.

Neither Spitsbergen nor Pechora was sufficient to restore the Company to fiscal health. The financial crisis prompted the fellows to seek a merger with the East India Company in 1618, a move that was approved in March of the year.[89] This was in many ways a logical step, given an overlap in the membership of the two companies. The East India Company was an important buyer of Muscovy Company cordage and obviously shared the latter's interest in finding the north-east passage. Moreover, the East India Company saw the merger as an opportunity to revive trade with Persia via the Volga route. The merger grew out of the two companies' involvement in Spitsbergen whaling which they appear to have conducted in a loose alliance in the 1610s. George Edmundson even argued in 1910 that the merger was an attempt to pool resources in response to the stiff Dutch competition in the northern fishing grounds. The Muscovy Company reported to the king that the Dutch had caused total losses of £66,000 in a 1618 attack.[90] Theodore Rabb has found that 70 per cent of Muscovy Company members in 1575–1630 were large-scale investors with investments in several companies, while Robert Brenner described the Russia merchants as part of a 'Levant-East India combine'.[91]

Another important development may well have played a role in prompting the merger, as argued by I. I. Liubimenko. After Sir John Merrick's success as a peace mediator at Stolbovo in 1617, the Russian government, anxious to get back on its feet militarily, requested a loan of R40,000–200,000 from the English government. The Muscovy Company was eagerly in favour of financial support for the new Romanov government and drew up a petition to the English authorities to

88 Dalgård, *Det Petsoriske Kompagni*, pp. 14–18.
89 Lubimenko, *Les relations*, p. 224.
90 Phipps, *Sir John Merrick*, p. 148; Arel, *The Muscovy Company*, pp. 33–4, 36–7, 47; Edmundson, *Anglo-Dutch Rivalry*, p. 47.
91 Rabb, *Enterprise*, p. 108; Brenner, *Merchants and Revolution*, p. 79; Arel, *The Muscovy Company*, pp. 78–9.

that effect. Clearly, such a gesture would have given the English an advantage in the struggle against the Dutch at a critical time.[92] The Privy Council, appreciative of the strategic importance of Russia as a potential supplier of naval stores, lent its support to the project. However, the government lacked the requisite financial resources, whereas the Company itself subsequently described its state in 1618 as being 'very weak through many losses in trade.' Total losses during the Time of Troubles due to the destruction of Company property and the impossibility of collecting loans reached £72,000.[93]

The merger did a great deal to replenish the capital resources of the Muscovy Company. The Company stock for various adventures had varied between £11,000 and £27,400 in 1607–16, but now rose to £60,000 shared equally between the two companies. Under the terms of the merger, a group of East India Company members joined the Muscovy Company's court of assistants and were able to participate in the northern trade. The move allowed the companies to grant the Romanov government a loan, although its exact size is unknown. According to Sir Dudley Digges, who was entrusted to deliver the money, the loan amount was £50,000, composed of £27,000 in bullion and the rest in cloth and other goods. However, a 1620 Privy Council memorandum gives the figure of £16,500. In the end, the money was not delivered until March 1619, by which time, following the conclusion of peace with Poland–Lithuania, the fiscal emergency had passed. Moreover, the Russians only received £10,000 in cash.[94] Apparently Digges, having reached Russia, refused to carry such a large sum of money past Kholmogory and, concerned about his safety, returned to England with half the intended loan amount. This behaviour appears to have confused the Russians and may have contributed to the Russian government's reluctance to restore the Company's privileges, especially regarding trade with Persia.[95]

The merger between the Muscovy and East India Companies, intended to last for eight years, was ultimately dissolved after only two. In late 1619, the companies concluded that unforeseen losses suffered in Russia and around Spitsbergen were too great to make the merger profitable. These apparently included a hefty sum due to an alleged Dutch attack on Archangel in 1619, which was supposed to have resulted, among other things, in the destruction of the customs house and the foreign merchants' yard (*gostinyi dvor*). The East India Company put the total losses at £33,000, while the Russians still owed the full £10,000 they had received and the Dutch had not paid the £22,000 they

---

92 *PRO SPF* 91/2, fol 58; Arel, *The Muscovy Company*, pp. 37–8.
93 Arel, *The Muscovy Company*, pp. 42–4; *PRO SPD* 15/42, fol 69.
94 Arel, *The Muscovy Company*, pp. 49–50; *PRO SPD* 15/42: 69.
95 Phipps, *Britons*, pp. 113–15.

owed for the destruction caused in Spitsbergen.[96] The association of the two companies seems to have ended in 1620, at which point Ralph Freeman is said to have bought the stock of the Muscovy Company for £12,000. It is unlikely that he acted entirely alone, however, given unambiguous government opposition to limiting access to the Company. In spite of this, his domination of the new Company was overwhelming. A few years later, Merrick noted that due to 'the bargaine sold Mr. Alderman Freeman . . . [he] was far more ingaged in the Trade than all the Company besides'.[97] All the Company houses in Russia were bought by a 'great merchant', almost certainly Freeman, in the early 1620s following the restructuring. People outside of the Freeman circle were now expected to acquire their own houses. In 1650, there were three Company houses in Archangel, one of them apparently a ropewalk.[98]

The legacy of the disassociation was so devastating that the Privy Council ordered the Company to produce a memorandum indicating '1. whether it planned to continue its trade, and 2. how it planned to do so given its financial woes'.[99] Threatening to 'desert' its trade and claiming debts of £20,000, the Company sought government support for the continuation of its operations. In addition to demanding an embassy to Russia to discuss the losses incurred there, the company sought to concentrate further its operations and to ensure that the members of the revamped Company should not be responsible for old debts. In response, the Council advocated a restructuring as a regulated company. Apparently, the Company had its way, since the Council was forced to note in March 1622 that the Muscovite trade had been in the hands of 'only a few brethren' over the preceding two years. However, the government in March 1620 did agree to exempt new members from old debts. This concession is likely to have been crucial in permitting the Company's continued operation in the early 1620s.[100] In 1621, a report into the Company's affairs found that outstanding debts since 1607 amounted to £24,502, 36 per cent of this figure consisting of ambassadorial charges. In 1622, the Privy Council once again agreed to delay the payment of the Company's debts 'in reason of State and for the publicke good of the kingdome'. However, the Council reversed its position within a month. Following further resistance by the Russian merchants, the Council ordered that the government should collect a minimum of one-third of its debts. Once again, a compromise

96 Arel, *The Muscovy Company*, pp. 44, 51–2.
97 Arel, *The Muscovy Company*, pp. 52–4; Konovalov, 'Anglo-Russian Relations, 1620–24', p. 131.
98 Arel, *The Muscovy Company*, pp. 278–9.
99 Arel, *The Muscovy Company*, p. 54; PRO SPD 15/42: 69.
100 *APC*, 1621–1623, pp. 159, 328; Arel, *The Muscovy Company*, pp. 55–9.

was eventually worked out, however, and in July 1623, the government exempted the Company from all interest payments. The order was repeated the following year.[101]

The ultimately unsuccessful efforts by Merrick at the time (during his 1620–1 embassy) to pay for the restoration of the right to trade in Persia must be viewed against this background of a company increasingly desperate for new sources of revenue. In contrast to the failure of the Persia overture, which nonetheless held considerable attraction to the cash-stripped Muscovite Treasury, Merrick did manage to negotiate the right for Muscovy Company merchants to buy tar directly from the Russian suppliers. Moreover, Merrick gained the Russians' consent for the appointment of a special 'protector' for the 'better proteccion both of themselves and goodes from any violence that might be offered in Russia'. The person selected was Ivan Tarasevich Gramotin, who headed the Diplomatic Chancellery in 1618–26.[102]

Merrick's energetic activity, the Russian government's recognition of the Muscovy Company's old privileges and the expansion of the Company activities to new areas were not sufficient to bring about a renaissance in Anglo-Russian trade. Nor was much done in practice to curb the activities of the interlopers. By the beginning of the 1620s, the English were, according to Telegina, sending annually only seven or eight ships to Archangel.[103] However, surviving British sources suggest that at least the official numbers were in most years even lower. Telegina's figure, if accurate, would have to include all shipping by English inter-lopers, as well. The small totals are all the more astounding when one considers that the onset of the Thirty Years' War was creating serious obstacles to English trade in the Baltic, adversely affecting the country's shipbuilding industry.[104] The overall value of English trade in Russia has been estimated at R60,000 in 1612 and 1626, much as it had been in 1604.[105]

The Muscovy Company responded to the crisis by seeking to reorganise itself. It petitioned the government to accept a change in its status from a joint-stock to a regulated company, which would allow its members to operate independ-ently at their own risk ('every man for himself').[106] The Privy Council accepted this proposal and, in April 1623, selected one of the main advocates of the restructuring, Christopher Cocks, as the English diplomatic envoy to Russia.

---

101 Arel, *The Muscovy Company*, pp. 60, 62–3; PRO SPD 14/124: 50; *APC* 1621–23, pp. 159, 258, 327, 345–6.
102 Arel, *The Muscovy Company*, pp. 159–63. See also Phipps, *Sir John Merrick*, pp. 155, 182.
103 Telegina, 'K voprosu', p. 220.
104 Ibid., pp. 207–10.
105 Liubimenko, 'Torgovye snosheniia', p. 733; Floria, 'Torgovlia Rossii', p. 144.
106 Ibidem, p. 435; Turner, *The Privy Council*, I, pp. 152–3.

The reorganisation applied only to trade with Russia. Thus whaling around Spitsbergen was exempted.[107]

Having assessed the diplomatic significance of the Cocks mission above, we now consider its commercial importance. Even as the British government came to accept the demands for a restructuring, the Company, in fact, was deeply divided on the way forward. A faction headed by John Merrick rejected the regulated-company approach and considered the Cocks mission to Russia to be inappropriate. Merrick dismissed his rival as 'a new man unexperienced in those affaires and unknown to the now State of Russia'.[108] Merrick distrusted Cocks because of his past activities as an interloper and saw his campaign as an expensive way to undermine the Muscovy Company:

> Besides how open wee lye to divers greate inconveniences by the malice of the enimies of our Trade the Hollanders, by the uncivill practises of our owne nacyon the interlopers, by the mischiefe that may befall us for the personall presence of some, to be this yeare in Russia under the Companyes proteccion, which the last yeare and divers yeares before paid their customes to the Russe as Interlopers, and by the sodaine innovacion, soe palpable to the eye of the Russe, especially in this employment of Mr. Cox, a Brother to one of the greatest Interlopers of our Nacyon, allwaies opposite to us in our Trade and reputation with the Russe, and punished by that State as Interlopers.[109]

Not lacking foresight, Merrick was further concerned that the reorganisation might jeopardise the key privilege of the company, its duty-free status. Merrick worried that interlopers would be drawn to join the Company. Then it would be difficult to explain to the Russians why they should no longer be required to pay customs duties.[110]

Cocks arrived in Moscow in November 1623 armed with a draft treaty on a 'Perpetuall League of Amity and Alliance, Entercourse and Commerce'.[111] King James clearly expected that the restructured Muscovy Company would continue to enjoy the generous privileges of the old one. The Russians, however, refused to endorse the English plans, warning that such a grant would only invite increasing numbers of English merchants to Russia. The Russian authorities

107 *PRO* SP 14/214; Arel, *The Muscovy Company*, pp. 63–4.
108 *PRO* SP 91/3, fol. 66.
109 Ibid.
110 Ibid.; Arel, *The Muscovy Company*, p. 66.
111 The 11 clauses of the project reaffirmed all existing previous privileges of the Company. *Foedera*, XVII, pp. 504–7.
112 Demkin, *Zapadnoevropeiskoe kupechestvo*, I, p. 45.

were particularly alarmed by the opportunities for abusing the new arrangement: non-English merchants, as well as English interlopers, of course, would pose as Muscovy Company members and deprive the government of customs receipts.[112] Just as importantly, the Russians clearly felt that the English had abused the privileges they had enjoyed. The Russians had expected the Muscovy Company to reciprocate their favoured status by effectively acting as the tsar's agents. A May 1624 letter to Cocks spelled out the Russian government's position in unambiguous terms:

> ... the English merchants are graced by the Emperors favour in all thinges, which is not don to straingers in any other cuntrye. And therefore the English merchants should shewe their service to the Emperors Majestie and should bring unto him all Royall commodities which are fitt for his Majesties Treasury and to deliver it into the Emperors Treasury according to the true price, and to trade into the Empire of Russia with their owne commodities, and not with other mennes goodes, to bring them as their owne not to sell them.[113]

However, the Russians claimed the English had increasingly failed to hold up their end of the bargain:

> But the Englishe merchants have begunn to doe many thinges contrary to the Emperors priviledge, and they bring not goodes to the Emperors Treasury as they have don heretofore, but give it into the Emperors Treasury at deare rates, the velvets, sattines, and dammaskes which they bring are naught, thynne, soft, and light in weight.[114]

Nor did the English supply arms, gunpowder, or saltpetre in any significant quantities or at reasonable prices, as had once been the case.[115] Low-quality standards were observed in other goods as well. Moreover, the English engaged in retail trade and sold wares belonging to other foreigners. Perhaps most importantly, however, the Russians recognised that the privileges of the Muscovy Company had outlived their usefulness: 'And other straingers which the Emperor Majestie doth allowe to traffique in his Cuntrye doe bringe many more commodities then the English, and upon those their commodities there is Custom taken according to the Emperors Rates, whereby the Emperors Treasury is much replenished.'[116]

---

113 *PRO SP* 91/2, fol. 98v.
114 *PRO SP* 91/2; *RGADA* fond 35, 1616g., No 2.
115 *PRO SP* 91/2; *RGADA* fond 35, 1616 g., No 2.
116 *PRO SP* 91/2, fol. 98v.

This argument also applied to the interlopers, whom the Muscovy Company construed as enemies to be excluded from the Russian market. The Muscovite government, on the other hand, saw the interlopers as valued taxpayers. In I. I. Liubimenko's words, 'the greatest advantage of the English – their duty-free status – had turned into its opposite – the greatest ill afflicting their trade'. The relative failure of Cocks' mission marked the end of an era for English traders in Russia, even if it still took some time for the Russians to take their stance to its logical conclusion.[117] During Cocks' mission, the Russian authorities evidently nonetheless still agreed to continue with the tax exemption of the Muscovy Company.[118]

While the Russian government reluctantly tolerated the Company's machinations, the restructuring quite clearly resulted in considerable confusion. In particular, the Russians were unclear about the number of Englishmen permitted to trade free of duty. The 1621 grant of privilege had enumerated 21 members, but the 1623 shipping season saw the arrival of a number of newcomers who claimed Company membership. In a sign of things to come, the tsar demanded an explanation from King James, threatening that, otherwise, the issues of customs duties would be settled 'as it shall please our great Lord his Imperiall Majestie to determine'.[119] But the ailing king died before he was able to reply, thus ending his relationship with Tsar Mikhail in an inconclusive manner.

Conclusion

James had come to the throne of England in 1603 without strife and with high hopes of establishing a united kingdom of Great Britain under his absolute paternal control. Meanwhile, he aspired to peace throughout Europe although resorting sporadically to war, especially in support of Protestantism. Muscovy, peripheral and weak, was not among his foreign policy priorities, although he was fully conscious of its commercial potential.

In 1613, at the end of the Time of Troubles, Mikhail was elected tsar with the fundamental aim of re-asserting full control over Muscovy. Early Romanov foreign policy partly reflected the existential Russian struggle for survival, but was also aimed at the consolidation of the domestic elite and the state. As the interventionists departed and civil strife diminished, he sought recognition

---

117 Liubimenko, 'Torgovye snosheniia', pp. 747–8.

118 In August 1624, before his departure, Cocks wrote to the tsar thanking him for 'that gracious message of remitting his Customes to all the Englishe merchantes as well those that came to Archangell as those that came to Mosco'. PRO SP 91/2, fol. 113.

119 PRO SP 102/49 (reproduced in: Konovalov, 'Anglo-Russian Relations, 1620–1624', p. 127); Arel, *The Muscovy Company*, pp. 67–8.

from fellow monarchs elsewhere. For his young regime, diplomatic relations brought with them an external legitimacy that strengthened the emergent domestic order. In particular, having been on the receiving end of the anti-Orthodox Northern Crusade, the Russian government now sought a revival of the anti-Moslem Crusade to the south, where repulse of the infidel could also mean security for Muscovy's steppe frontier. Even though the attempt failed, it aligned Russia ever closer to the Christian West as the rhetoric of Muscovite diplomatic negotiations was careful to stress and reinforce. Thus, diplomacy served to underpin Muscovite identity, along with the consolidation of the domestic political, social and economic order. Mikhail and his advisers also hoped for material support from the west, including financial loans.

Commerce furthered the objectives of both the Stuart king and the Romanov tsar. Undoubtedly, its significance was greater than trade figures might suggest. The British government needed naval stores while its Russian counterpart sought revenue. Moreover, the activities and aspirations of James and his entourage were inextricably intermixed with those of the Muscovy Company, which acted as diplomatic intermediary as it searched for profit over a vast area stretching from the Arctic Ocean to beyond the Caspian Sea. Symbiosis was almost complete in 1612, when the prospect of the establishment of a protectorate over a large swathe of Muscovy was proclaimed to be 'the greatest and happiest ouverture that ever was made to any King of this realme, since Columbus offered King Henry VII the discovery of the West Indies', 'a thousand times more profitable unto England as Virginia'. (Later in the seventeenth century, of course, Virginia was to produce one of the most profitable crops in the colonial trade – tobacco.)

Certainly, in 1625, Great Britain appeared more stable than Muscovy. Less than a quarter century later, however, Stuart government was to collapse in civil war while Romanov power was consolidated after a serious, but less critical, systemic shock.

THREE

From Decline to Disruption, 1625–1649

The Russians seized the opportunity to capitalise on the confusion immediately following the death of King James in order to maximise commercial gain. A 1625 decree ordered that customs duties should be levied at half their regular rate on English merchants not listed on the 1621 letter of privilege. This position was modified during negotiations with Fabian Smith and the matter was finally laid to rest following the arrival of a letter from Charles I in the summer of 1625. The Russia Company's privileges were renewed in 1626 and listed 22 members entitled to the duty-free status. The extensive use of agents naturally made the *de facto* number much greater.[1] However, the Russian government's position clearly reflected Moscow's determination not to throw duty-free trade open to all claiming to be members of the Company, while the Muscovy Company's continued privileges were undoubtedly the impetus for a protest by Russian merchants in 1627. Nevertheless, the letter of privilege issued to the Company in 1628 put the number of authorised merchants at 23,[2] although the size of the Company's board of directors was reduced from at least eleven in 1620 to seven in 1630–1.[3]

A Gap in Diplomacy

After 1625, although governmental and diplomatic contacts between Great Britain and Russia were transacted within a familiar framework, the Muscovy Company had come to dominate the relationship fully. Letters from the Governor of the Muscovy Company and its Moscow agent continued to privilege trade matters. For example, in 1629: 'Petition of Kenelm Willoughby, merchant . . . The Merchant Adventurers into Muscovia having employed him to convey letters to the city of Mosco . . . carried the same to Plesco [Pskov], a city in Russia within eleven days of Mosco, where being stayed by soldiers and robbers, he got

---

1 The only restriction in the new letter of privilege was the English could not directly trade with Oriental merchants. Arel, *The Muscovy Company*, pp. 68–9; *AA*, IV, No. 13; Bantysh-Kamenskii, *Obzor*, I, pp. 106–7; Telegina, 'K voprosu', pp. 211–19. A 1646 petition in fact claims that the English claimed their grant of privileged by bribing State Secretary Petr Tret'iakov. *Chteniia v istoricheskom obshchestve Nestora-letopistsa*, XXIII, 1912, 1, p. 5.

2 The charter is reproduced in Muliukin, *Ocherki*, pp. 361–9.

3 Telegina, 'K voprosu', pp. 222–3; Arel, *The Muscovy Company*, p. 93.

his letters safely conveyed to Mosco by a Russian messenger.'[4] These letters continued to be the responsibility of the newly appointed agent. Meanwhile, traditional goods such as cordage were imported from Russia,[5] although it was maintained that the Russian variety was 'not altogether so strong and good as home-made cordage'.[6] Throughout, the Muscovy Company maintained its vigilance over the importation of traditional goods to the exclusion of interlopers into what they saw as their own preserve.[7]

Contact between the courts was maintained through letters carried by Muscovy Company merchants aboard Muscovy Company ships (one such ship was indeed called *The Muscovia Merchant*)[8] and translated and read at Court by Muscovy Company agents in Moscow.[9] The appointment of Muscovy Company agents continued in the early 1630s. In 1631, diplomatic letters refer to 'Our Factor Thomas Wiche' and 'Our Agent Fabian Smith'.[10] In 1632, Wyche was promoted from Muscovy Company Factor to the position of 'Our agent to negotiate the afaires of Us and Our Subjects there, in the place of the late deceased Fabian Smith'.[11] Richard Swift and Simon Digby followed[12] and their tenure in Moscow did not pass unsuccessfully. A New Charter of Privileges was granted by Mikhail on 12 June 1628 in response to a request by King Charles.[13]

4 *CSPD*, 1629–-1631, no. 40, p. 136.

5 *CSPD*, 1634–1635, no. 97, pp. 305–6, 342; *CSPD*, 1633–1634, no. 59, p. 96.

6 *CSPD*, 1633–1634, no. 39, p. 256; *CSPD*, 1637, no. 114, p. 30; *CSPD*, 1637–1638, no. 13, p. 4. Indeed, a measure of the concern at a supposed diminution in quality control is attested by the sending of Robert Atherall, '. . . a master workman for making cordage at Woolich . . . [to] Muscovy for oversight of cordage made there'. *CSPD*, 1634–1635, no. 57, p. 14. On tar, *CSPD*, 1636–1637, no. 112, p. 302; *CSPD*, 1638–1639, no. 66, p. 127. On rye-corn, *CSPD*, 1640, no. 46, p. 354. On hemp, yarn and cables, *CSPD*, 1633–1634, no. 11, p. 515. The exotic was also imported. See *CSPD*, 1635, p. 64 for beaver wool and 'beaver wombs'; *CSPD*, 1637–1638, no. 27, p. 31: 'two Muscovy ducks'.

7 *CSPD*, 1631–1633, no. 40, p. 418; no. 60, p. 483.

8 *CSPD*, 1637-1638, p. 137.

9 The Royal letters of the 1620s tended to be commercial in content. For example, *CSPD*, 1625–1626, no. 2, p. 512. Minutes of the business to be brought before the king: 'letter to the Emperor of Russia that Wm. Rawley may have liberty to trade in those parts'.

10 *RGADA*, fond 35, opis 2, no. 59: 'Charles to Michael, 20 May 1631'.

11 *RGADA*, fond 35, opis 2, no. 61, 18 June 1632: Charles to 'Michael Pheodorowich'. It appears that Thomas Wyche, brother-in-law to another Muscovy Company merchant, 'Job. Harbie', stayed on in Russia – *CSPD*, 1638–1639, no. 66, p. 127.

12 *RGADA*, fond 35, opis 2, no. 75 (copy), 4 June 1641: Charles to Mikhail. Charles acknowledges Mikhail's letter of 12 May 1638 in reply to his of 12 December 1636. As well as complaining about the difficulties John Cartwright was encountering, Charles names 'Simon Digby Esqr. Our Agent now resident with yo.r Imperiall Matie'. See also *CSPD*, 1635, no. 52, p. 87.

13 Lyubimenko, 'Letters', pp. 97–8: Charles to Mikhail, 1 February 1626/27. See also Konovalov, 'Seven Letters', pp. 32–63. The Russian text is printed in Konovalov, 'Twenty Russian Royal Letters', pp. 117–56 and a copy of the charter may be found in *PRO*, SP 91/2, fols 139–45.

The fact that there was no Stuart embassy to Russia between 1623 and the early 1650s attests to how stable and efficient the existing arrangements of the Royal Representative had become.[14] However, Dutch competition from the Time of Troubles onwards had begun to supplant this apparent British domination of Russian relations with the West. The relationship of the Netherlands with Russia was to be exclusively commercial from the beginning, and Dutch Embassies would consider only commercial agreements. The Dutch came to import into Russia a wider variety of goods at cheaper prices than their rivals, and they were able to employ more ships and greater amounts of capital than the Muscovy Company.[15]

For all the aggressive and determined trading practices employed by the Dutch, the Muscovy Company's outstanding mercantile advantage was the Charter of Privileges. However, the Muscovy Company was not entirely satisfied with the terms of the New Charter of Privileges, as many royal letters revealed. For example: 'We have observed in the Priviledges now granted to Our Marchauntes, that they are prohibited to entertain or keepe any of your Majesties Subjects of the Russian Nation to serve them in their ordinary affaires, contrary to that which hath been formerely graunted to them.' More commercially damaging was the complaint that, owing to the shallowness of the Pudozemsk bar on the River Dvina by Arkhangel'sk, merchant ships were 'forced to ride in open sea, and their to lade and unlade their goods in Boates and small vessels, to their great danger, trouble and charges, besides their loss'.[16]

The loss of commercial advantage to the Dutch, and subsequent attempts to regain it, formed the framework within which diplomatic relations between Great Britain and Russia were confined until the expulsion of James VII and II in 1688–9. However, until the execution of Charles I in 1649, the Anglo-Dutch rivalry needs also to be understood in the context of the Thirty Years' War, 1618–48, as well as being viewed as a reflection of internal developments. Moreover, as diplomatic links came to rely increasingly on the expertise, finance and personnel employed by a trading company, the diplomacy itself, the issues and affairs of state discussed, tended to both reflect and promote the mechanism by which the diplomacy took place. Thus, the means by which diplomacy was supposedly facilitated came to dominate and dictate the diplomacy itself. The control of the diplomatic process was co-ordinated by the

14 Russian missions are discussed in Vinogradoff, 'Russian Missions', pp. 43–50.
15 Lubimenko, 'The Struggle', pp. 39–40. See also Attman, *The Russian and Polish Markets*, pp. 84–93; Eekman, 'Muscovy's International Relations', pp. 44–67. Eekman, while lamenting the paucity of sources for the study of Russo-Dutch history, lists the embassies sent before Van Keller in the mid 1670s, somewhat contradicting Lubimenko.
16 *RGADA*, fond 35, opis 2, no. 42, 23 April 1629, Charles to Mikhail.

Muscovy Company's London-based headquarters from which financial and technical aid was afforded to the diplomatic missions of Russian ambassadors to Britain.[17]

When Gerasim Dokhturov's embassy, 1645–6, was sent to inform King Charles of the death of Tsar Mikhail and 'to renew the ancient alliance between these two states which has long been established for navigation and trade',[18] the Muscovy Company financed the reception and living expenses of the Russian ambassador to the sum of £1,500.[19] Dokhturov arrived at Greenwich on 27 November 1645, stepped off the Muscovy Company boat upon which he had travelled from Archangel, and was received by prominent Muscovy Company members, including its Governor, Richard Snelling. A few days after his arrival, *The True Informer* reported that, knowing he was to die, the tsar had 'made and had published a lengthy speech'. Thus, said the newspaper, Mikhail had died 'in print'.[20] Such a story was in evident need of correction. However, the main result of Dokhturov's embassy to an England under parliamentary rule was a devastating blow on the position of trading privileges that the English merchants had hitherto enjoyed in Russia at the expense of both other foreign competitors and native Russian merchants.[21]

Dokhturov entered London and requested an audience with King Charles, but was informed by Parliament that, as the king had opposed the will of his subjects, this was not possible. Moreover, instability brought about by the Civil War had rendered travel outside of London hazardous. Instead of a royal reception and diplomatic negotiations with King Charles, Dokhturov was received by 'the Lords and Commons assembled in Parliament' on 10 March 1646, where, after insisting that the members of both houses stood up and doffed their hats, he accepted a letter. This letter, as well as formally congratulating Aleksei on his accession, explicitly stated Muscovy Company support for Parliament, declaring that: 'those who follow and are now with the king, are no

---

17 'Throughout the seventeenth century the Muscovy Company frequently aided the English government in the preparation of royal letters, the translation of Russian letters and the delivery of letters to both courts.' Phipps, 'The Russian Embassy', p. 260, n.8. This argument could go further, especially as the period from 1646 onwards was concerned.
18 *CSPV*, 1643–1647, no. 320, p. 229, 14 December 1645. *The True Informer* of 29 November–6 December 1645, p. 259, quoted in Frank, *The Beginnings*, p. 112. This news item might have been stimulated by the arrival in London of Dokhturov.
19 *CSPD*, 1653–1654, no. 149, p. 340.
20 Quoted in Frank, *The Beginnings*, p. 259.
21 Phipps, 'The Russian Embassy', p. 259 implicitly makes this argument: 'the attitudes it [Muscovy Company] adopted during the English Civil War . . . may very well have undermined its position in Russia'.

merchants, nor trade in merchandize at all; but that our merchants in general, and especially those who trade to Your Most Excellent Highness' Imperial Dominions, are residing here in the City of London.'[22]

Representation in Moscow would continue through 'Mr Spencer Bretton now Resident there as Agent or Consull, for the negociating of the affaires of the English Nation.'[23] In London, the Muscovy Company merchants successfully persuaded a reluctant ambassador to address both chambers of Parliament on 13 June 1646. The promise of an unlimited supply of troops levied to further Aleksei's military aims in addition to a desire to return to Moscow appears to have prompted this unusual display of personal initiative by a Russian diplomat of this era.[24]

A decree was issued on 1 July 1646, which abrogated the Charter of Privileges by abolishing the Company's duty-free right through the imposition of a 3 per cent fee on goods. But the decree was not a consequence of Parliament's struggle against the king. Phipps argues that: 'This edict was not a punitive action taken against the Muscovy Company for its part in the rebellion in England; it had resulted from the need to increase the Tsar's revenue and to enable the Russian merchants to compete more effectively with the foreign merchants.'[25] As Lyubimenko had suggested earlier: 'The fact that the petition of the Moscovite merchants had preceded the steps taken against the English trade shows clearly that these steps cannot be considered merely as a punishment of the English merchants for their revolutionary sentiments, but were the natural consequences of changes since the sixteenth century in the economic conditions of both countries.'[26]

As a result, all Muscovy Company exemptions from payment duties were revoked. A 'Statement on behalf of the Muscovy Company' describes the effect of the decree and attempts to place it in its historical context: 'The trade has been unquestioned one hundred years, in spite of revolutions of Emperors, till in 1646 Aleksei Michaelowich, the present Emperor, took away our privileges, imposed

---

22 'The Lords and Commons assembled in Parliament' to Tsar Aleksei, 10 March, 1646, *RGADA*, fond 35, opis 2, no. 78; Phipps, 'The Russian Embassy', p. 270.

23 This letter has had all decorative motifs and seals removed. It is badly faded in a third of the left-hand side, top and bottom, and a three-inch band down the right. A longer version of this letter, but one which contained no new material, was later received by the Russian ambassador from Parliament: 'Parliament to Aleksei, June 1646', *PRO*, SP 22/60, fol. 71.

24 'The situation was difficult, as in that period etiquette was most strict for a Russian diplomat, and personal initiative closely proscribed.' Lyubimenko, 'Anglo-Russian Relations', p. 41.

25 Phipps, 'The Russian Embassy', p. 272. However, note comments on p. 272, footnote 47 which support Lyubimenko's argument.

26 Lyubimenko, 'Anglo-Russian Relations', p. 44.

large customs on us, and seized goods of great value by fraud.'[27] Writing on the eve of the restoration of Charles II, John Hebdon noted that the Russians, 'taking aggravation by the unhappie troubles here in England first impose[d] excise duties and customes on English merchants'.[28] The old story was persistent.

Dokhturov left London on 27 June 1646 on a Muscovy Company ship, reaching Moscow on 9 August, where he presented a report outlining the Muscovy Company's relationship with both king and Parliament. This report reflected upon both the integrity and political beliefs of Muscovy Company men in Russia, an issue of particular interest when read alongside a letter from King Charles. This letter was written when Charles was evading capture by Parliamentarians: it called for the destruction of Muscovy Company privileges along with the imposition of customs duties on merchants who were disloyal to him, and requested 300,000 quarters of grain in exchange for English cloth. The king named a loyal royalist, Luke Nightingale, as the purchaser: 'By reason of the late Comotions in Our Kingdome of Ireland, & the yet unsettled and discomposed condition of that Country, the Natives our good subjects have bene so interrupted in their tillage husbandry, as we have cause to fear a scarcity of Corne.'[29]

On capture and confinement to Holdenby House, King Charles was pressurised into reversing his own preferences and instead recommending: 'Our Loving Subject Spencer Bretton, noe residing at your Imperiall Court, as Agent to negociate the affaires of Our said Marchants untill such time as We shall cause to send another fitt person to reside there.' Charles also requested the restoration of Muscovy Company privileges and reiterated the Parliamentary excuses given to Dokhturov in order to explain his inability to meet with him. Charles went on to explain that because of the troubles 'Gerasime Simonove' could not leave London without exposing himself to danger. 'Onecke Evomore Chistova', a Russian official, had informed English merchants at Archangel that customs were not to be paid. Thomas Bond, a physician seeking employment in Muscovy, carried this letter to Aleksei.[30]

Nightingale was to return from Russia, having purchased only 30,000 quarters of grain for the royalist cause.[31] King Charles sent a last letter to Aleksei,

---

27 *CSPD*, 1653–1654, no. 149, p. 340: Aleksei allegedly called the English merchants 'traitors and the servants of traitors, and unfit to lie in any Christian State'.

28 'The Humble Remonstrance of John Hebdon, Resident for his Imperial Majestie', 16 March, 1661, *PRO*, SP 91/3, fols 77r–79v.

29 Charles I to Aleksei, 7 December 1646 – *RGADA*, fond 35, opis 2, no. 79. (Copy: *PRO*, SP, 22/60, fol. 70.)

30 King Charles to Aleksei, 31 March 1647, *RGADA*, fond 35, opis 2, no. 80. (Copy: *PRO*, SP, 22/60, fol. 72.)

31 Lyubimenko, 'Anglo-Russian Relations', p. 45.

and Nightingale made a second visit to Russia, as we shall see. However, before any response was made, the second Stuart monarch of England, Charles I, had been executed.

Commerce

Having weathered the storms of the 1620s, the English merchant community experienced renewed consolidation and growth in the 1630s. Although the size of the Company's board of directors was reduced from at least eleven in 1620 to seven by 1630–1, there was a clear increase in the number of English merchants operating in Russia between 1625 and 1635.[32] This increase was reflected, among other things, in a slight increase in the number of English vessels calling at Archangel. From typical annual totals of three to four in the second half of the 1620s, the numbers rose to six in 1630–2, nine in 1633, and seven in 1634–5.[33] Their renewed strength once again prompted the English to export much more from Russia than they imported into it. In 1633, the English sent eight barges to Vologda, while twenty-one made the return trip. The corresponding numbers in 1635 were five and eleven, respectively.[34] The scale of English trade in the Russian interior remained impressive even as shipping gradually declined. The number of Dutch merchants active in the country appears to have been smaller than that of the authorised Muscovy Company merchants.[35] Towards the middle of the century, the Muscovy Company appears to have owned about 40 large river barges, known as *doshchaniki*, for transportation on the Dvina.[36]

The renaissance of the Company had nothing to do with a lull in the bitter rivalry between its two factions, which was still ongoing. The renewed privileges of the Muscovy Company were issued in 1628 to 23 Company members belonging to the original Merrick faction.[37] Matters were further complicated by the increasingly high-handed ways of the Company agent Fabian Smith. The Smith faction around 1631 declared William Rowley, one of the men listed on the renewed letter of privilege, to be an interloper, and the Russians, consequently, charged him customs. Smith and his associates, moreover, had a habit of bribing Russian customs officials in order to obtain information about the movement of goods. In this way, they were often able to '[forestall] the markets of the rest of the company'. Additional difficulties were caused by Smith's

---

32 Telegina, "K voprosu", pp. 222–3; Arel, *The Muscovy Company*, p. 93.
33 These numbers are compiled from the London Port Books in *PRO* E 190.
34 Telegina, 'K voprosu', pp. 225–6; *TKMG*, I, pp. 104–26, 147–54, 288–96.
35 Lyubimenko, *Les relations*, p. 192.
36 Arel, *The Muscovy Company*, p. 215.
37 Ivanov, *Anglo-gollandskoe torgovoe sopernichestvo*, p. 247; *RGADA* f. 35, 1

hearing problems and advanced age.[38] The feud found its counterpart in Russian bureaucratic politics. The local officials in Ustiug grew increasingly concerned over the shortfall in customs revenues that the passes for duty-free travel issued by the Diplomatic Chancellery were causing. The officials, who controlled customs receipts in Ustiug-Velikii and Tot'ma, enquired in October 1638 about the correct procedure on taxing foreign merchants. The reply, received nearly two years late, in November 1640, stated that only 23 English merchants of the Merrick faction enjoyed a duty-free status.[39] Another instance of internal dissension was a seizure by John Osborne and his nephew of Thomas Wyche's houses in Vologda and Moscow in September 1634. The actions appear to have been part of a larger power struggle which had resulted in Wyche's removal from the position of agent in July 1634.[40]

Even as the Company experienced a period of renewed growth, dark clouds were appearing on the horizon. In 1630, Charles I unsuccessfully petitioned Filaret to appoint a boyar as a special protector of the English merchant community following the earlier example of Boris Godunov. In 1633, the king complained of unfair searches and embezzlement that English merchants were subjected to by Russian officials, probably prompted by illicit tobacco sales. In 1635, Company agent Thomas Wyche lodged a formal complaint about the problem of corruption: 'Contrary to the sovereign's grant, everywhere, in all towns from Moscow to Archangel, the leading merchants known as the *gosti* and their assistants, and appointed people forcibly exact petty customs, and take surety bonds from them for these sums, for their own gain; and because of these arbitrary actions, the English suffer many losses and much hindrance in their trade.'[41]

In 1638, the Muscovy Company turned to the Russian government, complaining of the nuisance caused to English merchants by local customs officials. In several cases, the company claimed, collectors refused to recognise the documents issued to the Company and exacted various duties. Goods belonging to English merchants were often detained on the road if the prescribed customs duties were not paid. Recourse to higher level officials was made difficult because of bribery by the customs officials. The petition met with at least some success and, in 1639, all Vologda townsmen were interrogated by the government.[42] The problem was exacerbated by Russian frustration at the English practice of sometimes writing

---

38 Arel, *The Muscovy Company*, pp. 72–3.
39 Ivanov, *Anglo-gollandskoe torgovoe sopernichestvo*, pp. 247–8.
40 Phipps, *Britons*, pp. 208–10; Arel, *The Muscovy Company*, pp. 275–6.
41 *RGADA*, f. 35, op. 1, No 124, fol. 4ᵛ quoted in Arel, *The Muscovy Company*, p. 252. The complaints were reiterated by Digby annually in 1636–9. See also: ibid., p. 246.
42 Ibid., pp. 250–1. Smirnov, 'Novoe chelobit'e moskovskikh torgovykh liudei o vysylke inozemtsev v 1627 g., pp. 19–20; *PRO* SP 91/2, fols 240–1.

their own travel passes. In 1639, Russian officials were ordered to disregard passes not issued by the government. Apparently, the new practice failed to fully solve the problem, however. Nor was the matter laid to rest after the English tax-exempt status was revoked in 1646. A year later, the Company complained of being charged two to three times the prevailing rate of customs duty. Further tensions were created by the English insistence that duties should be levied on the market price of their cargoes, rather than on the official valuations of the customs administration at Arkhangel'sk.[43]

The English suffered from the Russian insistence that ships approaching Archangel should use exclusively the Pudozemsk channel of the Dvina estuary. The relatively shallow waterway became increasingly risky in the years following the Time of Troubles as the average size of English vessels increased. Two English ships were wrecked and their cargoes lost in 1630–1. In 1637, Digby claimed that three vessels had been lost in 1634–5. This problem was, moreover, by no means confined to the English. Nonetheless, the Russians investigating the matter found that the channel had not become shallower and could merely recommend using smaller ships. Following Dutch petitions, the Russian government in 1637 agreed to authorise the use of the Berezovo and Murmansk channels but required additional payments to cover the cost of new fortifications and guards. Faced with increased costs, foreigners apparently withdrew their demand and unloaded larger vessels on the open water.[44]

The English, like the Dutch and the Germans, developed an interest in Russia as a potential new supplier of grain. English grain prices had risen rapidly since 1628, due to a combination of local factors and supply problems in Poland–Lithuania, and inflation was made worse by a string of bad harvests in 1630–9.[45] Charles I first approached the Russian government in 1628–9 when, in two letters, he described the high grain prices and bad harvests afflicting his dominions.[46] In February 1630, a British envoy, Thomas Wyche, was sent to Russia for the purpose of buying 100,000 *chetvert'* or quarters of grain and his efforts were reinforced by more royal letters in August–September. Another envoy, John Scroop, was sent in October with a royal letter requesting grain sales of 30,000 *chetvert'*. A further three envoys came to Moscow by April 1630 as the Dutch ambassadors Albert Coenraadszoon Burgh and Johan van Veltdriel were conducting their negotiations. One of the envoys, Alexander

43 Arel, *The Muscovy Company*, pp. 263–6, 269, 271–2.
44 Ibid., pp. 192–5, 199–200, 234.
45 Rogers, *A History*, V.
46 Ivanov, *Anglo-gollandskoe torgovoe sopernichestvo*, p. 338; *RGADA* fond 35, opis 2, delo 40, 44.

Stuart, made a concrete offer of British weapons in return for Russian grain. He further sought to establish a British–Swedish–Russian axis to counter Dutch plans. Apparently, the Dutch had, with some success, tried to convince the Russians that any grain sold to the British would be used for speculative purposes instead of feeding the hungry.[47] Two more envoys, Edward Johnson and John Livingston, who arrived in February 1631, may have complicated matters further by raising the issue of an alleged R9,000 debt for the participation of three British officers in the Swedish army during the Time of Troubles. The envoys proposed that the debt could be settled with 100,000 *chetvert'* of wheat. Livingston further hoped to be allowed to buy 14 shiploads of rye.[48]

In spite of these persistent diplomatic efforts, the Russian government agreed to sell only 30,000 *chetvert'* of grain, which was allotted to Wyche, a long-standing member of the Muscovy Company. The tsar's reply emphasised his desire to maintain friendly relations with the English, however, and justified the decision by a bad harvest. Moreover, he permitted the grain to be exported free of duty and at cost. The English reciprocated by giving the Russians 2,000 muskets.[49] Thomas Chamberlain was further authorised to buy 100,000 *chetvert'* [of grain] free of duty, although it is not known if any of this amount was actually exported by the English.[50] As G. M. Phipps has demonstrated, there were a number of reasons that might have caused the Russian government to be this lukewarm towards the British requests.[51] However, it is difficult not to view this decision within the context of the general deterioration of Anglo-Russian relations.

The friction of the 1630s escalated dramatically with Aleksei Mikhailovich's ascent to the throne in 1645. At first, the new tsar promised to renew the Company's privileges and even suggested that the rights might be broadened. In May 1646, a pass was issued to the Company for the Archangel–Moscow route in accordance with the old privileges.[52] An abrupt turnaround ensued less than a

---

47 Lyubimenko, *Les relations*, pp. 107–8; Liubimenko, 'Torgovye snosheniia', p. 96; Ivanov, *Anglo-gollandskoe torgovoe sopernichestvo*, pp. 338–9; *RGADA* fond 35, opis 2, delo 47–9, 52–3; opis 1, delo 104, fols 1–14; 1630 g., delo 103, fols 59, 67–8.

48 The British officers claimed to have been in Russian service, since Shuiskii had used the Swedish troops against the Polish intervention. However, the Russians claimed that their agreement had been with the Swedish king, not with any British officers. Ivanov, *Anglo-gollandskoe torgovoe sopernichestvo*, pp. 341–2; *RGADA* fond 35, 1630 g., delo 103, fols 176–8, 191–2.

49 Ivanov, *Anglo-gollandskoe torgovoe sopernichestvo*, p. 343; Liubimenko, 'Torgovye snosheniia', p. 96; Lyubimenko, 'Letters Illustrating', p. 101; *RGADA* fond 35, 1630 g., delo 103, fols 220–2; *PRO SP* 102/49–25, 26.

50 Lyubimenko, *Les relations*, p. 108.

51 Phipps, *Britons*, pp. 129–34.

52 Arel, *The Muscovy Company*, pp. 438–9.

month later, however. As we have already noted, a June 1646 decree forced the Company, along with all other foreigners, to pay full duty. In essence, the Muscovy Company lost the one institutional comparative advantage it enjoyed over other foreigners. The government's policy put the English merchants on a collision course with the Russian authorities. The Company refused to pay duties; for instance, the company's agent, Spencer Bretton, in addition to verbally abusing the customs officials, offered a mere promissory note in lieu of cash. Members of the Company apparently locked up their wares at their Kholmogory base and refused to resume their business operations in the Russian interior. Bretton twice appealed to the tsar, perhaps encouraged by government backtracking on eliminating tax exemptions to various Russians, threatening in February 1647 that 'if the services of our nation are no longer required by Your Imperial Highness', the English were prepared to quit Russia altogether. John Osborne, another Company agent, finally conceded defeat in July 1647 but petitioned that Bretton's promissory notes be cancelled, since the change of status had caught the English unawares.[53] Bretton, in his petitions to the tsar in December 1646–January 1647, claimed that Company members, in response, again locked up their wares and refused to trade.[54] The English resumed their offensive with two new petitions in 1648, perhaps not coincidentally after the June 1648 uprising in Moscow which, among other things, eliminated one of the Company's main adversaries, Nazarii Chistoi of the Diplomatic Chancellery. The Company warned that the new customs regime was threatening to seriously undermine its operations, which were, moreover, already under attack because of the unrest at home. The end result of the pleas was nil as the Russians stood their ground.[55]

By the 1640s, the Company, and its various members, had created an impressive commercial infrastructure along the Archangel–Moscow axis. Thomas Wyche, active in Russia between the 1620s and 1640s, owned a house in Vologda. Fabian Smith owned two houses in the city in 1627, while Robert Cocks had one. This is spite of the fact that the Moscow government had rejected the English request for the Company to be given 'libertie to stand in severall houses everie one apart, by himself . . . by reason of their trading in severall'. In 1639, Ralph Bladwell, Richard Fowell and John Osborne all had houses in Volgoda. By 1649, Osborne already had two houses, while John White, Richard Duncombe, John Dee and Thomas Steistet had joined the ranks of those with one. Osborne,

53　Demkin, *Zapadnoevropeiskoe kupechestvo*, I, p. 46; Bantysh-Kamenskii, *Obzor*, I, p. 113; Arel, *The Muscovy Company*, pp. 437, 440, 443–4, 465; RGADA fond 35, opis 2, 1647 g., delo 24.
54　Arel, *The Muscovy Company*, pp. 83–4.
55　Ibid., p. 467; Demkin, *Zapadnoevropeiskoe kupechestvo*, I, p. 46.

furthermore, had a house in Kholmogory, and Anthony Tivery owned one in Iaroslavl'. Reason Chapman in 1635 bought a large house in Moscow but sold it to Simon Digby a year later for general Company use.[56]

Anglo-Russian trade, and the status of the Company, were complicated by the ongoing Civil War in England, Scotland and Ireland. Not lacking political acumen, Russian merchants responsible for penning an anti-foreigner petition in 1646 pointed out that the Company's original rights had been issued in response to a request by the King of 'England'. Now, however, 'all the English traders, are not loyal to Him, but have been at war with him for four years'.[57] A particularly striking example of the confusion caused by the troubles in Britain was the so-called Nightingale Affair, already mentioned above. It will be recalled that Luke Nightingale, a member of the Company, arrived in Russia in June 1648 as an envoy of Charles I who requested permission for grain purchases of 300,000 *chetvert'* (to be exchanged for English cloth) in response to shortages at home. Nightingale, however, claimed to have a secret mission to convince the tsar of the disloyalty of the Muscovy Company and to suggest that 'the Russia trade be thrown open to all English merchants on equal terms'.[58] In essence, the king, who was said to approve of the new customs regime, was suggesting the abolition of the Company's nearly century-old monopoly of Russian trade. Charles distrusted the Muscovy Company and, according to Nightingale, 'consider[ed] those merchants to be his enemies'.[59]

As agreeable as Nightingale's agenda might in some ways have appeared to the tsar, there were serious questions as to the envoy's authenticity and credibility. Matters were further complicated by the arrival of Thomas Bond, an English physician seeking employment in the court. Bond also delivered a letter, dated 31 March 1647, allegedly from Charles but, according to G. M. Phipps, almost certainly from the Parliament. The author of the epistle, in a marked departure from the message conveyed by Nightingale, 'expressed "wonderment and grief" at the imposition of customs on the Muscovy Company, and at its harsh treatment by officials at Archangel'.[60] The Russians apparently distrusted Bond, whereas Nightingale initially made a very good impression in Russia and gained the tsar's trust.[61] But he departed with no more than 30,000 *chetvert'* of grain.

56 Arel, *The Muscovy Company*, pp. 101, 106, 174.
57 Quoted in ibid., p. 442.
58 Herd, *General Patrick Gordon*, p. 32; Arel, *The Muscovy Company*, pp. 446, 458–9; *PRO* SP 22/60, fol. 70.
59 Arel, *The Muscovy Company*, p. 456.
60 Arel, *The Muscovy Company*, p. 461; Phipps, 'The Russian Embassy', p. 274.
61 Arel, *The Muscovy Company*, pp. 449, 463.

Nightingale returned to Russia in September 1648, apparently for the main purpose of trying to buy the outstanding 270,000 *chetvert'* of grain he had requested during his previous visit.[62] King Charles had sent a last letter to Aleksei on 1 June 1647, having escaped from parliamentary forces, in which he supported Aleksei in his decision to 'punish' disloyal merchants, and asked that Nightingale be allowed to make up the shortfall in grain, providing Aleksei with a list of those merchants who had remained loyal and could thus carry out the transaction. These merchants included: 'Our said servant Luke Nightingale Esqr John Richardson, Edward Ropur & John Canon, Our Merchantes, their substitutes and factors, to buy and transporte for any use and service the afore-said proportion of three hundred Thousand Chetfords [*chetvert'*].'[63] Prince Charles, exiled to the Hague, also asked that his merchant, Henry Crowe, be allowed to acquire 40,000 quarters of grain.[64]

A month into his stay, however, Nightingale was denounced to the Diplomatic Chancellery as an impostor by one of his servants, Hugh Wainwright. Subsequent interrogations of Wainwright and others ruined Nightingale's credibility. The envoy himself was forced to admit that he had not met with the king, although the letter he delivered had been prepared on the king's behalf. After a month, the Russians declared Nightingale an impostor. In a bid to regain his stature, the disgraced envoy launched a renewed attack on the Company. He alleged that a group of Muscovy merchants were preparing a military raid on Archangel in revenge for the loss of old privileges. The Russians, in response, set Nightingale free. The veracity of Nightingale's claims have been impossible to ascertain. However, we know that Earl of Carlisle, on a diplomatic mission to Russia in 1664, following the Restoration, denounced Nightingale as an impostor unknown to the king.[65]

The position of the Company was further threatened by a 1648 collective petition by Russian merchants and government officials to the Diplomatic Chancellery and the Assembly of the Land. Foreigners were, as usual, charged

---

62 Lyubimenko, 'Anglo-Russian Relations', p. 45; Herd, *General Patrick Gordon*, p. 32; Arel, *The Muscovy Company*, p. 494.

63 King Charles to Aleksei, 1 June 1648, RGADA, fond 35, opis 2, no. 81. (Copy: *PRO*, 22/60, fol. 73.) Phipps, 'The Russian Embassy', p. 271, has argued that these competing recommendations and counter requests, self-contradictory and therefore unfulfillable, must have further discredited the Muscovy Company in Russian eyes.

64 'Charles Prince of great Britaine, Duke of Cornwall, Albany and Rosbery . . . to Aleksei', 16 December 1648, RGADA, fond 35, opis 2, no. 82. (Copy: *PRO*, SP 22/60, fol. 74.) This 'Corne and graine' was for Ireland. Henry Crowe's commission was all embracing. He was ordered 'to buy and provide for Our use 4000 Chetverts of Corne Vologdey measure or tenne shipps lading of Corne of all sorts, as Rye, wheate, buckwheate, barely, pease, oats, oate meale and upsheene.'

65 Arel, *The Muscovy Company*, pp. 449, 495–504.

with distorting the terms of trade in their favour, selling low-quality goods, engaging in dishonest business practices and enslaving their Russian debtors.[66] Apparently in response to the letter, the tsar in December 1648 ordered a review of all letters of privilege issued to foreign merchants and a survey of the services provided by them, thus emphasising the traditional linkage between commercial privileges and service to the tsar.[67] The petitions of 1646 and 1648 made several charges specifically against the English. According to Russian merchants, the Company fellows: came to Russia in much larger numbers than established by the privilege grant of 1628; bought and built themselves many houses in Russia and established themselves there permanently; employed indebted Russians as factors who bought up Russian goods for them in towns and in the countryside, and so they had no need to trade with Russian merchants; sold Russian goods to Dutch and German merchants at Archangel, thus robbing the Treasury of customs and seizing the trade of Russian merchants; coloured the goods of Dutch and German merchants, to the harm of the Treasury.[68]

The fourth of these charges was particularly serious because it posed a major challenge to the government's customs revenues. There is other evidence to suggest that the Russian claim may have been fully accurate. We know that the scale of Muscovy Company shipping declined to very low levels during the first half of the century. However, the English were able to sustain a large commercial operation in Russian and the combined number of their merchants and agents appears to have been at least comparable to that of the Dutch. Indeed, according to A.V. Demkin, the 1630s and 1640s marked the peak of English commercial activity in Russia, at least in terms of the number of merchants and agents.[69] The inevitable conclusion seems to be that not all English goods were exported on English ships. Thus the Company clearly made a large share of their profits by selling goods free of duty to Dutch and German merchants who otherwise would have incurred higher transaction costs.[70]

The English also managed to gain control of some government monopolies. At the beginning of the century, they initially enjoyed a monopoly right, renewed in 1614, as a tar exporter. Yet the Muscovy Company had sought to ban all tar exportation from Archangel already by the following year and John Merrick in 1620 had advised the Russians to restrict tar exports so as to promote domestic cordage

---

66 Ibid., p. 471; Hellie, 'The Stratification', pp. 165–8.
67 Arel, *The Muscovy Company*, p. 475.
68 Ibid., p. 481.
69 Ibid., p. 27.
70 Arkhangel'skii, 'Anglo-gollandskaia torgovlia', p. 13.

production. However, by 1633, tar was made a Russian Treasury monopoly.[71] A more important breakthrough came in potash production. Following the pioneering efforts of the Dutch merchant Karel du Moulin since 1630, Simon Digby was in 1643 able to outbid his rivals and take control of the potash monopoly. After an initial two-year tax-exempt period, Digby was to hold the farm for a decade. Digby's enterprise was taken over after his death (1645) by a relative, John White. Jointly with colleagues Francis Ash and John Dought, White in 1648 acquired extensive rights for production in central Russia, in the Arzamas, Nizhnii Novgorod, Iaroslavl' and Vologda regions. Persistent difficulties notwithstanding, a total of 200 barrels was produced for export on the Digby lands in 1647. Moreover, Alexander Crawford gained a seven-year grant for potash production in Murom district in 1644. The English privileges came to end in 1649 when White's newly built potash mills in the Arzamas region were 'nationalised' by the Treasury.[72]

The Muscovy Company appears to have controlled the Russian caviar monopoly in the early part of the century, until the Dutch took over around 1630. In 1636, the English under their factor John Osborne regained the monopoly for five years at the cost of R12,600 a year. Annual exports may have totalled 540,000 lb a year, a figure that rose to 810,000 lb by 1644.[73] Writing to the Diplomatic Chancellery in 1644, Spencer Bretton claimed that the Company had two types of vessels on the White Sea route: 'large' ships that supplied caviar to Italy and 'smaller' vessels for the London route.[74]

The Company was finally expelled from the Russian interior on 1 June 1649, since 'the English people committed great evil in killing their king, and for such an evil deed [the Muscovy Company] was ordered out of Russia'.[75] Even as John Osborne, as the *de facto* agent of the Company, accepted the Russian decision, he challenged the Russians' excuse for the move by claiming that the Company had not betrayed the king. Bowing to the inevitable, however, the Company presented the first inventory of Company assets and outstanding debts to the Investigations Chancellery just over a month later.[76] At the time, Russian merchants owed a total of R21,487 to the Company: 55.2 per cent of this sum was accounted for by Moscow merchants, followed by Iaroslavl' (18.6 per cent)

71 Smirnov, *Ekonomicheskaia politika*, pp. 7–8; Demkin, 'Zapadnoevropeiskie kapitaly', pp. 22–3; Arel, *The Muscovy Company*, pp. 373–6, 378–80.
72 Demkin, 'Zapadnoevropeiskie kapitaly', pp. 26–7; Arel, *The Muscovy Company*, pp. 416–17; *RGADA* fond 35, 1649–1652 gg., delo 173, fol. 48.
73 Arel, *The Muscovy Company*, pp. 369–72.
74 Ibid., p. 235.
75 *Sobranie gosudarstvennykh gramot i dogovorov*, III, p. 456.
76 Arel, *The Muscovy Company*, pp. 508, 511.

and Vologda (13.4 per cent) traders. Debts owed by other Russians amounted to R4,911, while the total of other foreigners was R2,573.[77]

To conclude, the first half of the seventeenth century was marked by a steady descent into a long-lasting crisis by the once-mighty Muscovy Company. A central problem was its failure to adjust to the dramatic changes that the Russian export market had undergone since the sixteenth century. The Company remained a relatively close-knit clique of merchants with, consequently, limited capital. Although M. S. Arel has located the names of 319 Company members for the period 1600–49, the distribution of wealth and importance became increasingly uneven over time. Moreover, the number of members steadily declined in this period, from around 160 at the beginning to an average of 60–70.[78] The Company's *modus operandi* was allowed to become highly dependent on privileges, most notably its duty-free status, which by 1649 could no longer be deemed to serve the purpose that had prompted their issue nearly a century earlier. And it is quite possible that the Company's profits came to depend increasingly heavily on illegal activity, namely supplying other foreigners with goods free of duty.

Available data on the scale of English shipping in the first half of the century is scarce and typically fragmentary. Initially, the Muscovy Company focused on a rather narrow selection of goods with relatively high value:weight ratios. The best-selling Russian imports to England during the early part of the century were hides, furs, wax, tallow, train oil and cordage. The London Port Books shed light on the relatively limited import bundle in the first half of the seventeenth century. In the last quarter of 1604, the combined imports by English merchants from Archangel to London were valued at £7,247. The leading categories were hides (29.6 per cent), cordage (19.2 per cent), cable yarn (17.9 per cent), wax (13.7 per cent) and tallow (12.9 per cent). In 1621, English merchants brought £7,207 worth of goods from the White Sea to London. The share of furs was 38.4 per cent, that of various types of yarn 28 per cent and that of hides 13.9 per cent. In 1633, imports by English merchants to London from Archangel reached £7,359, of which skins and furs accounted for 28.7 per cent and hides for 28.4 per cent. Imports by 'alien and denizen merchants' reached £15,813, of which the share of cable yarn was 39.5 per cent and that of tallow, 22.6 per cent. In 1634, 'alien and denizen' imports from Russia totalled £11,883, of which cable yarn accounted for 34 per cent, hemp for 25.7 per cent, and tallow for 10.6 per cent.[79] The English 'market share' is unlikely to have significantly exceeded 10 per cent after the early years of the century.

77 Bazilevich, 'Kollektivnye chelobit'ia', p. 107.
78 Arel, *The Muscovy Company*, pp. 111–17; Lyubimenko, *Les relations*, p. 86.
79 *PRO* E 315/467, 190/24/4, 190/37/8, 190/38/1, 190/38/5. Valuations by Millard.

Peripheries of the Thirty Years' War

During the last years of his reign, in spite of his avowed pursuit of peace, James VI and I did not shrink from indirect and direct involvement in war. For example, he encouraged the levy of an expeditionary force in support of the cause of his wife's home country, Denmark. With the outbreak of the Thirty Years' War in 1618, as well as wanting to support the Protestant cause in general, James was also anxious to lend a helping hand to his daughter Elizabeth, the 'Winter Queen' of Bohemia. After much dalliance with Spain, he embarked on war with it just before he died in 1625, leaving a difficult inheritance for his son Charles.

Meanwhile, during the first years of his reign, Tsar Mikhail Fedorovich under the tutelage of his father the Patriarch Filaret concentrated on recovery from the Time of Troubles, on consolidation of internal stability and peace with former interventionists. However, there is no doubt that the outbreak of the Thirty Years' War aroused the interest of observers in Moscow as well as in London.

In London, this was reflected in the expansion of newspaper activity. Between 1621 and 1625, the *Weekly Newes* reported on developments not only in 'Bohemia, Austria, the Palatinate, the Grisons, the Lowe Countries' and 'in Europe' or 'Christendome' generally but also in 'East India' and 'the whole world'.[80] Meanwhile, in Moscow, 'manuscript bulletins'[81] known as *vesti-kuranty* were collected by the Diplomatic Chancellery from a wide range of sources. Like their printed counterparts in London, the *vesti-kuranty* were stimulated by the events of the Thirty Years' War. For example, in 1620, a translation was completed of a German 'notebook' with news from Poland, France, Bohemia, Silesia, England, Holland, Italy, Hungary and other countries. Among other developments recorded was the levy of 2,000 Scots for service on the continent. The *vesti-kuranty* were read aloud to the tsar and his boyars, as indicated in their margins by the notes of the translators themselves. Meanwhile, in Britain, circulation was far less restricted, but by no means completely free. Before the 1640s, the Privy Council kept a firm control on the printing of domestic news, while corantos or news-sheets dealt widely with foreign affairs even if avoiding controversial subjects for the most part.[82]

Charles I was more adventurous than his father from the first, continuing the war with Spain and commencing hostilities with France in 1626. He persevered with involvement in Germany through a subsidy to Denmark to carry on the war against the Empire. In the 1630s, however, he was sending bullion to help

---

80 Scott, *England's Troubles*, p. 15. The Grisons were a Swiss canton.
81 Cracraft, *The Revolution*, p.102.
82 Kotkov, *Vesti-kuranty*, 1600–1639gg., pp. 3–8, 38; Cust, 'News and Politics', p. 62.

Spain maintain its army in Flanders. Parliamentary leaders suspected 'a design to alter the kingdom both in religion and government'.[83] Such apprehension about the king's purposes in his foreign policy were to combine with disaffection from many aspects of his domestic policy to lead towards the crisis of the 1640s.

From 1623 to the end of the Thirty Years' War, as noted above, no British embassy was sent to Russia. Nevertheless, the significance of that war in the history of the Stuarts and Romanovs may be illustrated through an examination of the contribution of two individuals, both bearing the same name although not closely related. Sir Alexander Leslie of Auchintoul, probably stemming from the Balquhain, Aberdeenshire, branch of the family, is not to be confused with the more renowned bearer of the name, from the Balgonie branch, Fife, whose career we shall examine first.

This Alexander Leslie became Earl of Leven, and we shall call him Leven to avoid confusion with the other. By 1638, Leven had been in Swedish service for 30 years, excelling as Governor of the fortress of Stralsund among other outstanding contributions. In that year, Stuart relations with Sweden were exacerbated by Charles I's resumption of negotiations with Spain. In 1638, too, as Steve Murdoch notes, 'Charles I faced a rebellion in Scotland not too dissimilar in motive to the Bohemian Revolt of 1618' with the proclamation of the National Covenant, characterised by another authority, Allan Macinnes, as 'a revolutionary alliance of the landed and commercial classes intent on redressing constitutional and nationalist grievances in the State as well as upholding the Presbyterian version of the Reformed tradition in the Kirk'.[84] With Swedish support, Leven returned to his homeland, where he led the Scottish army in the Bishops' Wars, 1638–40, inaugurating the showdown between Charles I and many of his subjects on both sides of the border. Moreover, along with Field Marshal Leven, 3 major generals, 18 lieutenant colonels and colonels, 6 majors, more than 40 captains and about 120 lesser officers left Swedish service to form the bulk of the leadership of the Scottish army.[85]

Some of the lesser-known Alexander Leslie's earlier years were spent in both Swedish and Polish service. Probably during the Time of Troubles, certainly in 1618, he had close contact with Russians when he was taken prisoner along with other Polish soldiers at a siege of Smolensk, a frontier city changing hands on several occasions with which he was to be closely connected. He was taken to Moscow where he was lucky enough to find some foreign residents, probably

83 Kenyon, *Stuart England*, p. 117.
84 Murdoch, *Scotland and the Thirty Years' War*, pp. 7–8, including the quotation from Macinnes.
85 Grosjean, *An Unofficial Alliance*, pp. 166–73; Kenyon and Ohlmeyer, *The Civil Wars*, pp. 16–23.

associated with the Muscovy Company, who stood surety for his parole until his inclusion in an exchange of prisoners. In 1626, he became a colonel in the Swedish army and was soon sent off to England and Scotland to engage more soldiers for the service of Gustavus Adolphus. Soon after his return to Sweden in 1629, he was given another foreign assignment, to Moscow. After his release from Swedish service, Alexander Leslie arrived again in Moscow in January 1630 with a retinue of six servants and a military staff of two captains, three lieutenants, an ensign and a clerk as well as a Dutch military expert. Tsar Michael personally received Leslie and presented him with gifts in recognition of his semi-official military mission. As soon as he had gained some knowledge of the state of the Russian army, Leslie suggested that regiments be formed along Swedish lines, and members of his staff were assigned to organise two such regiments during the summer of 1630, while Leslie himself went back to Sweden to report to Gustavus Adolphus.

By this time, the Swedish king was confident enough of an imminent Russian attack on the Poles to break off negotiations with Poland for an extended truce. Leslie himself came back to Moscow in the late summer of 1630 to confirm the unofficial agreement between Sweden and Muscovite Russia on mutual assistance, accompanied by more than 60 people, including his own family. Leslie and other Swedish emissaries urged the Russian government to make war against Poland at the earliest possible moment, reiterating proposals for the modernisation of the Russian army and the employment of several regiments of foreign mercenaries.[86]

Leslie's suggestions met with the Russian government's positive response, and he was soon sent off on another recruitment mission in the Protestant countries of the north, Roman Catholic recruits being specifically banned. Early in 1632, Charles I Stuart received from Tsar Mikhail Romanov a letter in which the tsar explained why he had been forced to prepare for war against the Poles because of their flagrant misbehaviour, before going on to make a request for the hire of soldiers and purchase of weapons. Charles replied in a friendly manner, since, although his policy was neither clearly conceived nor consistently executed, and his difficulties with Parliament were already reducing his ability to conduct it, he appears to have shared the general British sympathy with the Protestant cause especially as represented by his sister's husband, Frederick, the Elector Palatine and titular King of Bohemia. Early in 1632, support for Mikhail meant encouragement to Gustavus Adolphus and the Protestant cause in general. On 25 May 1632 the Privy Council issued a general warrant in the name of the king, authorising 'Sir Alexander Lesley, Collonell, as Thomas Sanderson, Lieutenant Collonell, or

86 Porshnev, *Muscovy and Sweden*, pp. 72–87; Stashevskii, *Smolenskaia voina*, pp. 63–4, 70.

anie that shall be employed by either of them, to take up and transport the afore-
said number of two thousand voluntiers . . . provided that the said Leavies be in
no kinde employed against anie of his Majesties friends and Allyes.'[87]

From the Russian State Archive of Ancient Acts in Moscow, we have, among
other documents, muster-rolls of the mercenary soldiers inspected in 1632
by the boyars Prince Dmitry Manstriakovich Cherkasskii and Prince Boris
Mikhailovich Lykov, indicating a predominance of Scots.[88] These documents
also make clear the import into Muscovy of modern military ranks such as
'kapitan', 'maior' and 'kvarter-meister'.

As winter 1632 approached, difficulties of supply and discipline already
augured poorly for the multinational army being mobilised for the implementation of its major task, the recapture of Smolensk.[89] During the following
year or so, the multinational army failed in this task, and for a variety of
reasons, among them dissension between Scots and English. Leslie himself
shot the Englishman Lieutenant Colonel Thomas Sanderson, allegedly for
treason. The hopes of the Russians and of the Swedes for victory over the Poles
and the imperial forces, already dashed by the death of Gustavus Adolphus in
November 1632, were now more thoroughly obliterated. Pamphlets were
produced on the other side to celebrate the victory. Their short titles are variants of *Wahre und gründliche Relation, Glaubwürdige Zeitung* and *Gründlicher
Bericht* and their contents can be summarised under two headings: description
of the war itself; and the Polish triumph. As part of the surrender ceremony,
Colonel Charles Hubert placed 15 French flags before the king, while Colonel
'Alexander Lessel' led three regiments to lay down 8 flags in like manner.
Colonel 'Mattesson' and old Colonel 'Kitte' were other Scots in the surrender
parade. Another detachment brought 8 flags of the English nation, along with
the corpse of Colonel Sanderson after his murder by Colonel 'Lesle'. An account
continues: 'Very awful to look at during this procedure was the fact that the
defeated noblemen took with them their wives and children, the ill ones as well
on sledges behind the regiments. Because of lack of horses, the army had to
take the sledges, which was very shameful.' At the end of the ceremony, the
whole Polish army sang '*Te Deum laudamus*' and the Polish Chancellor
proclaimed that the Lord was the Prince of Victory, giving 'the worthy ones the
power to win and the unworthy ones the defeat'. While the Muscovite army was
superior in number, 'because of fate and hunger they had to lay down their

87 Porshnev, *Muscovy and Sweden*, pp. 101–2, 129; Phipps, *Britons*, pp. 260–1.
88 *RGADA*, fond 210, no. 78, listy 1–2, 14 March 1632.
89 Popov et al. (eds.), *Akty moskovskogo gosudarstva*, St Petersburg, 1890, vol. I, pp. 420–1,
   497, 501.

weapons and swear on the articles. Thank God for this victory. At least all the traitors and deserters are known and they will be punished.'[90]

A leaflet, translated from German into Spanish and published in Madrid and Seville in 1634, is *Relacion verdadera de la Insigne Vitoria que Alcanzo el Rey de Polonia, contra el gran Duque de Moscovia, y otros confederados suyos, todos enemigos de nuestra Santa Fe, y de las Coronas de la casa de Austria . . .* As part of its title, it lists the commissaries signing the peace agreement including 'El coronel Leslie Escoces'. Another leaflet in Spanish, also published in 1634, with a title beginning *Las Continuas Vitorias . . .*, observes how it was to the advantage of the King of Spain that the Polish king had defeated 'los Cismaticos Moscobitas' along with their allies including 30,000 Turks and 30,000 Tatars. And so the Christian religion had overcome that of the 'maldito Mahoma'.[91]

The War for Smolensk, then, was deemed by contemporaries to be of importance for the whole of the continent, and must be considered the centrepiece of Muscovite involvement in the Thirty Years' War, supported by English, Scottish and other foreign mercenaries. For his part, Alexander Leslie must have been aware of the significance of the activities of Scots on both sides[92]. Without doubt, they played a significant part in the modernisation of the Russian army in particular.

Leslie's later career was not insignificant. First, he survived charges against him in both Moscow and London for the murder of Sanderson. In April 1634, Leslie was due to be tried by the 'high Courte' in Moscow, but proceedings were delayed by a fire raging through much of the city. In May, a majority of the merchants trading in Moscow agreed that Leslie could not be accepted as a member of the Muscovy Company until the trial had taken place. But Thomas Wyche and some supporters held a further meeting at which they made Leslie a member. The others complained about this to the Company in London and probably to the government, too. But then, on 23 September 1634, a writ was issued in the name of the king in London granting Leslie a pardon.[93]

From 1634 to 1637, Alexander Leslie was probably for most of the time in Russia. Certainly in December 1637 he left it, although possibly after just returning from abroad. Tsar Mikhail appears to have received a letter of intercession from Charles I on behalf of Leslie, and gave him, as a parting present, sables to the value of 150 roubles, also providing him with five sleighs, an appropriate

90 These pamphlets are located in the City Archive, Gdan'sk, catalogued by title.
91 These pamphlets are located in the British Library, catalogued by title.
92 For Scots on the Polish side, see Bieganska, 'Scots'. And see Frost, 'Scottish Soldiers', pp. 209–12.
93 Dukes, 'The Leslie Family', pp. 410–12, 419–21.

entourage and victuals. Among the items of food and drink listed in another document from the archive in Moscow are a quantity of beef, two sheep, two geese, two hares, ten chickens, along with several buckets of wine and beer.[94]

Soon after this, he composed a 'Missive of the Swedish Colonel Alexander Leslie to Tsar Mikhail Fedorovich from Narva about the knightly Polish Order instituted in 1638'. The editor of the published document suggests that it was a translation into Russian of an original in Latin dated 5 June 1637. As well as sending the letter, Leslie volunteered to raise a force in opposition to the Polish Order, which had been blessed by Pope Urban VIII for its persecution of Orthodox breaking away from the Uniate adherence to Rome. Among other exclusions, the letter noted: 'Russians should not be admitted to this newly instituted order, because they have their own faith and ranks, and their own sovereign, and are not devoted to our faith and ranks, nor accustomed to our crown.'[95]

Certainly, Leslie was well placed at Narva to catch the crosswinds of religious conflict blowing through the Baltic in the late 1630s as the Thirty Years' War continued. As well as Polish Roman Catholic knights, there were various Protestant enthusiasts doing all they could to spread their own messages throughout Central and Eastern Europe. To take the promoter of universal peace John Durie alone, we know that he was in Stockholm from May 1636 to July 1638 as part of the great endeavour to unite the spirits of the brethren in the Reformed Churches. It is well within the bounds of possibility that news of this activity reached Leslie in Narva, rather less likely but by no means impossible that he had heard of the National Covenant drawn up in Scotland a few months before the dispatch of his 'Missive' to the tsar. Even more intriguing is an episode occurring some years later. In January 1645, the proselytising polymath Samuel Hartlib wrote a letter to the Committee of Both Kingdoms [Scotland and England] seeking permission to promote 'the publicke Religion, Iustice and Liberty of the three kingdoms amongs forraners . . . and to propagat the sacred effect of the most Solemne and National Covenant'. In a letter of 9 April 1648, Cyprian Kinner informed Samuel Hartlib that during a recent visit to Warsaw he had heard that Leslie, the brave commander of the Scottish army, was not very well educated but already knew German well and would pay at least £1,000 to be taught Latin by an easy method. G. H. Turnbull suggests that this Leslie is Alexander, Earl of Leven. But Leven was in Scotland in 1648. Could this in fact be Sir Alexander Leslie of Auchintoul, seeking to spread the Word further?[96]

---

94 *RGADA*, fond 35, opis 1, no. 132, list 8, 27 October 1637.
95 Budde, 'Poslanie', pp. iii–vi, 20.
96 Turnbull, *Hartlib*, pp. 175–88, 439; Terry, *The Life*, p. 446; Murdoch, *Scotland and the Thirty Years' War*, p. 8. See generally Dukes, 'New Perspectives'.

While merchants and others departed at the time of the mid-century crisis, Leslie stayed on to help Tsar Aleksei weather that crisis, then to capture Smolensk in 1654. He then became Governor of that city, where he met mercenaries of later generations such as Thomas Dalyell and William Drummond before his death in 1661 or 1663. Before that, after accusations that Leslie had shot at a cross surmounting the local church and that his wife had forced her servants to eat meat on Orthodox fast days and kept them too busy to attend to their religious duties, as well as throwing an icon into a fire, they escaped a trial by opting for naturalisation.[97] On 18 September 1652, Alexander was re-christened Avram as he became an Orthodox Russian. Immediately after the ceremony, Leslie, his wife and children received presents from Tsar Aleksei Mikhailovich himself. Among those given to Leslie were: a crucifix of gold set with precious stones; a sheepskin coat lamellated with marten, with a beaver collar; damask gloves; a shirt with a buttoned collar and breeches made of taffeta; an upper belt made of silk with a gold tassel; a lower belt made of silk; silk braid with silver binding; a hat made of velvet; and boots and shoes made of Turkish leather. Leslie and his son had an audience with the tsar and were given more presents as well as 200 roubles. Leslie was also granted an estate of 1,200 *cheti* (approximately 1620 acres), along with 200 roubles per month pay and 45 roubles per month expenses. In addition, he was given six horses along with winter and summer fodder and three deliveries of firewood per week. He was to receive daily a generous ration of drink, with the thirsts of six servants being taken care of, too. Although Leslie had now become a subject of the tsar, he never forgot his origins, which have been remembered by his descendants up to the present day.[98]

Incidentally, Leslie was by no means either the first Scotsman to receive landed property in Russia or the first to become naturalised. For example, in 1600, Robert Dunbar received an estate of 400 *cheti*. In 1623, James Lunn, alias Yakov Lunev, was summoned to the Patriarch's office for his conversion. He declared that 'his father arrived from the Scottish land under Ivan Vasilyevich of All Russia, of blessed memory, and he was born here in Moscow'. Brought up a Lutheran, he was now ready to become Orthodox.[99]

About four years after the naturalisation of Alexander Leslie and his family, in August 1656, a kinsman noted that 1,000 Scottish soldiers recently arrived in Königsberg were not happy with their allowance of black bread, and were better pleased by the oatmeal that they had at home. Here were fellow-countrymen at the

---

97 *The Travels of Olearius*, pp. 244–6; Pascal, *Avvakum*, p. 176.
98 Dukes, 'New Perspectives', pp. 186–9.
99 Fedosov and Nozdrin, 'Lion Rampant'. More generally, see Reger, 'Baptizing Mars', pp. 401–7

other end of the process to the russifying Leslies.[100] But some of them might have moved on to Russia to become members of a later generation devoting much of their lives to the service of the Romanovs while not completely forgetting their earlier allegiance to the Stuarts. As we shall see, relations between the two dynasties were no more than fitfully maintained throughout the Interregnum but were resumed on a regular basis after the Restoration of 1660.

The Peace of Westphalia

To conclude our investigation of the period from 1625 to 1649, we should note that the Thirty Years' War involved nearly the whole of society as well as almost all the states of Europe. This was widely asserted to be the case at the time, for example in a pamphlet published in London in 1648 with the title *We have brought our Hogges to a Faire Market*:

> In these late, bad and worst of times, wherein all the Christian World hath been imbroyl'd with Warre, and all the miseries of Sword, Fire, and Famine; when Nation did rise against Nation, and Realme against Realme; the Swede against the German Emperour, the Pole against the Russian, the Spaniard against the French, the Hollander against the Spaniard, and France in most bloody and cruell Civil War with itselfe. When all those Kingdomes and Territories were... drencht and neer drownd with blood and slaughter, these Kingdomes of England, Scotland and Ireland were... the onely... spectators and lookers on... [yet] Warre we would have at any rate or price whatsoever... killing and cutting throats, robbing, rifling, plundering... spoyling, and ruinating one another (under the fair pretences of Religion and Reformation) with more barbarous inhumanity and cruelty, then could have been committed here by... millions of Turkes, Tartars, or Cannibals.[101]

In 1647, the first publication in Russian of a secular work, via Dutch from German, J. J. Wallhausen's *Kriegskunst zu Fusz . . . (The Art of War on Foot)*, had already indicated that there were both internecine and public (foreign) wars, and that internecine wars were 'considered the most pernicious by all the pagan scribes'. Internecine wars were no stranger to seventeenth-century Muscovy.

---

100 *RGADA*, fond 210, opis 1, no. 270 listy 944–5, 3 August 1656. We thank Dr Boris Morozov for giving us a copy of this document.

101 Quoted by Scott, *England's Troubles*, pp. 48–9. Ironically, Scott makes no substantial reference to Russia in his description of the European context. His work, therefore, can be taken as a recent example of the persistence of the view that Europe in the seventeenth century consisted mainly of the West.

There was a particular relevance to the observation that public wars included 'those wars which are waged against those who flout and banish God's honour and word and who are the enemy of every Christian, such as the Turks, Tatars, pagans, and barbaric peoples'. In Muscovy, the distinction between internecine and public wars had been blurred, making its own predicament rather more serious than that of most if not all of its Christian fellows.[102]

In 1648, the Peace of Westphalia marked the end of the Thirty Years' War. As Derek McKay and Hamish Scott point out, 'the peace was one of the most important in European history and it has often been seen as opening the modern era of international relations'.[103] However, such a view has sometimes been disputed. Benno Teschke, following Robert Brenner, has argued that this modern era begins with significant developments in commercial and social rather than diplomatic and political relationships. Therefore, in Teschke's view, the origins of the era should be sought in the rise of British economic activity from the later seventeenth century onwards, with 1688 marking the final removal of the Stuart kings a more significant date than 1648.[104]

As far as Europe as a whole is concerned, we should not be misled by the fact that the documents comprising the Peace of Westphalia made little reference to Muscovite Russia, giving the tsar the title of 'Magnus dux Moscoviae' and introducing him solely as the ally of Sweden.[105] As Heinhard Steiger makes clear, the 'christlicher Friede' and 'pax christiana' were ecumenical rather than denominational. Steiger asserts: 'Catholics, Lutherans and Calvinists were partners in the treaties; the Orthodox were also included with the grand prince of Moscow in the IPO [*Instrumentum Pacis Osnabrugense*] and thereby joined the community of international law'. Even the Ottoman sultan 'formed a part, if only in a modified manner, of the community of law'. However, there was no mention of the British Isles, cut off from the continent and increasingly beset with their own problems.

After years of talk that threatened to be as prolonged as the action, a series of agreements, the most important of which comprised the Peace of Westphalia, brought the war in general to an end in October 1648, although Spain and France in particular were to keep it going until November 1659. By the principal terms of

102 Grabar, *The History*, pp. 15–17. The 'pagan scribes' are almost certainly classical, especially Roman, not from the same origin as the more recent enemies of Christendom.

103 McKay and Scott, *The Rise*, p. 3.

104 Teschke, *The Myth*. Christov, 'Liberal Institutionalism Revisited', is a brilliant plea for a reading of Westphalia as history.

105 Vainshtein, *Rossiia*, p. 3. This belittling version of the tsar's title provoked an angry response from the Russian government. See also Kobzareva, 'Vestfal'skaia mirnaia sistema'. A comparison may be made with the situation obtaining at the end of the First World War, when 'the Maximalist Government of Russia' received scant mention in the Treaty of Versailles. See Thompson, *Russia*, pp. 400–2.

the peace, France gained Alsace, the Dutch Republic consolidated its rise and Sweden retained a foothold in Northern Germany. Switzerland achieved formal separation from the Empire while Brandenburg expanded within it. The Austrian and Spanish Habsburgs lost some of their pretensions, although Ferdinand III, Holy Roman Emperor since 1637, gained some consolation from his confirmation as King of Bohemia, where upstart Protestantism had been suppressed, as well as in Hungary and Austria. Outside these hereditary dominions, however, both Lutheran and Calvinist heresies continued to thrive as the local rulers saw fit. According to Heinhard Steiger, the Roman Catholic Counter-Reformation could not now achieve complete success; indeed, the pope was involved in the peace 'not as the religious leader of Europe or the world, but as the secular ruler of a territory'. In the view of John Elliott:

> This Europe, as shaped by the Peace of Westphalia, was to be a continent in which the secular interests of states were to be of more importance in the conduct of international affairs than their religious differences. In this more secularised continent, the papacy, which had been relegated to the sidelines in the Westphalia negotiations, ceased to be even the nominal arbitrator of Christendom. Indeed, it was a symptom of the changing times that the very term 'Christendom' was more and more to yield pride of place to 'Europe'.[106]

The Thirty Years' War was an important stage in military development, Gustavus Adolphus showing the way with a well-drilled and disciplined army which possessed a national core even though it contained many mercenaries. In this chapter, through an examination of aspects of the careers of the two Alexander Leslies, we have seen how, via Sweden, and supported by their comrades, they came to play an important part in the destinies of the Stuart and Romanov dynasties. Leven, whose distinguished career we have briefly summarised, fought for Gustavus Adolphus before leading the Scottish army in the Bishops' Wars of 1639 and 1640. As we have indicated at greater length, Sir Alexander Leslie of Auchintoul helped the Russian army on the first stages of its modernisation as well as exercising a not insignificant cultural role in his anti-Catholicism and conversion to Orthodoxy. Both Alexander Leslies were far from alone.

Conclusion

More generally throughout Europe, the Thirty Years' War marked a significant step forward towards the formation of the absolutist state, of which the national

---

106 Steiger, 'Concrete Peace', p. 443; Elliott, 'War and Peace', p. 39. According to Aston, *The Fifteenth Century*, p. 87, the adjective 'European' was coined by Pope Pius II (1458–64).

army would be an essential part. To pay for it and other vital needs, improvements in the economy had to be encouraged and more efficient means of taxation had to be devised. These in turn made necessary a more smoothly working administration and improved system of law. The monarch, previously exercising a personal rule through divine right, now had to look for additional support in secular ideas as his commands merged with the edicts of the state. Agreement had to be reached with the clergy, the nobility and leading townsmen, since absolutism needed a firm social basis. But national assemblies were often restricted in the interests of centralisation. More coercive methods often had to be found for keeping the peasantry in subjection, especially in the Centre and the East of Europe, including Russia, where serfdom became entrenched during the reign of Aleksei. Peter Brown has observed: 'With Aleksei we see a confluence, in their Muscovite context, of autocracy and bureaucracy.'[107] While the nobility was dominant, leading merchants and churchmen also figured in this confluence. The kingdom of England, Scotland and Ireland played a distinctive, even exceptional, part in the process, with the execution of Charles I halting any movement in the direction of absolutism. While the personality and policies of the king no doubt contributed to his own downfall, the nature of the three kingdoms and of the relationship between them was also significant. So was the weighty influence at the centre of London, where the merchants of the Muscovy Company and other organisations gave full voice to their ambitions.

Soon after the end of the Thirty Years' War, then, crisis was widespread throughout Europe and the British Isles, affecting the destinies of both Stuarts and Romanovs, and the relations between them. Before that crisis, the writing was on the wall for Stuart absolutism, while Romanov absolutism was in process of consolidation. Aleksei was confident enough to abolish the Muscovy Company's privileges, while the English Parliament vied with King Charles to preserve them. As we shall see, the pursuit of the restoration of those privileges was to prove fruitless in the second half of the seventeenth century.

Through most of the first half, while the Atlantic loomed on the horizon for the Stuarts, the Romanovs looked for a route to the Pacific via the north-east passage as they sent expeditions to the remotest edges of Siberia. Nearer home, in Europe, they aspired to a stratagem almost forgotten in the old world. Having been on the receiving end of the Northern Crusade, the Russian dynasty now sought to revive crusade to the south, against the Moslem infidels. Preoccupied with events nearer home, the Stuarts considered this a challenge too far.

---

107 Brown, 'Tsar Aleksei Mikhailovich', p. 145.

FOUR

Crisis, Interregnum and Restoration, 1649–1663

Crisis

Political crisis was widespread throughout Europe in 1648–9, with Russia at the eastern extremity far from untouched, and offshore Great Britain shaken by the overthrow of the predominant form of government throughout the continent, monarchy.[1] To varying extents, all three of our prime foci of attention, commerce, diplomacy and war, were involved in change associated with the crisis. From around the middle of the seventeenth century, a quickening of the pace of capitalist development is detectable, reflected in both overseas activity and commercial rivalry nearer home, for example in the Anglo-Dutch contest that the Dutch appeared to be winning for the next 20 years or so.[2] Following Westphalia, and the growth of international law, a new diplomacy was apparent, not least in Muscovite Russia. L. A. Iuzefovich writes: 'Ritual became etiquette, ideology was replaced by aesthetics, both becoming more noticeable in the years of the reign of Aleksei Mikhailovich.'[3] By 'ritual' and 'ideology', Iuzefovich appears to mean religious rather than secular, by 'etiquette' and 'aesthetics' secular rather than religious. Certainly, among the significant steps taken was the introduction in 1657 of armed protection for an ambassador from the Ukrainian *hetman* Khmelnitskii, a measure to be extended to other European ambassadors, including those from 'the Polish, English and Dutch kings'.[4] Protocol and ceremonial changed also in the British Interregnum, then with the Restoration. Obviously, Cromwell's government could not look upon monarchy in the same way as its Stuart predecessors and successors. Equally, noting that the Dutch republic was not given the treatment accorded to monarchy, M. S. Anderson points out that 'England suffered to some extent from a similar gulf between her real status during the Interregnum of 1649–60.' Then, the emissaries of Charles II could not restore the *status quo*. Generally speaking, M. S. Anderson asserts, 'The second half of the seventeenth century saw a distinctive movement away from the erratic lavishness which had marked much of this

---

1 Some of the first original arguments were collected in Aston, *Crisis in Europe*. For a later collection, see Parker and Smith, *The General Crisis*.
2 Israel, *Dutch Primacy*, pp. 197ff.
3 Iuzefovich, *'Kak v posol'skikh obychaiakh'*, p. 205.
4 Murov, *Istoriia gosudarstvennoi okhrany Rossii*, p. 43.

aspect of international relations in earlier decades.'[5] Meanwhile, the torch of military revolution was passed by the Swedish army of Gustavus Adolphus on to Cromwell's New Model Army, to name but one. Among those playing leading roles in the formation of Russian elite regiments from 1648 onwards were exiled adherents to the Stuart cause, Generals William Drummond, Thomas Dalyell and Daniel Crawford.[6]

Returning to the political crisis in particular, everybody knows how Charles I met his end, but few are aware that Alexis faced mortal danger in the years 1648–9, even fewer realising that the two experiences were part of a crisis affecting most of Europe and providing a new paradigm for inter-state relations. So let us begin with the less familiar of the two experiences, leaving overall evaluation for later.

The tsar and his entourage were well aware, via the *vesti-kuranty* newspapers and other sources, of key political and constitutional events in the British Isles as well as on the continent, possibly suggesting parallels to their own fate. Let us look at what was happening to the tsar in the period leading up to the execution of his brother monarch, Charles I.

On 1 June 1648, Aleksei Mikhailovich was returning to Moscow from a visit to a monastery when, as on similar occasions before, a crowd complained about injustices and violence being inflicted upon the people, not by the tsar himself, but by his leading advisers. Attempts by the tsar's entourage to quell the crowd led to further insurgence. Some unpopular officials were killed, and the tsar's favourite saved only on condition that he was dismissed and sent into exile. In June, there were both attempts to appease the people and yet more disturbances. Some nobles and merchants petitioned successfully for the summons of the *zemskii sobor*, the Assembly of the Land. Unrest flared up again in Moscow and in other towns, but the worst was past. Among the officers involved in the suppression of the unrest were the Scottish colonels Mungo Carmichael, Alexander Crawford and Alexander Hamilton. Alexander Leslie, by now a general, was also summoned to Moscow for this purpose.[7]

As an important contribution to the restoration of order, S. F. Platonov pointed out that 'Tsar Alexis took a very active part in the discussions with the crowd', to many of whose wishes he had to accede.[8] Moreover, according to S. V. Bakhrushin, he had to bribe the *strel'tsy* musketeers to make a 'popular request' for the return of the tsar's favourite, since the tsar's oath concerning the

---

5 Anderson, *The Rise of Modern Diplomacy*, pp. 51, 60.
6 Malov, *Moskovskie vybornye polki*, pp. 15–16, 47, 65–6.
7 See Murdoch and Grosjean, 'Scotland', *SSNE Database* entries on these Scottish officers.
8 Quoted by Bakhrushin, 'Moskovskoe vosstanie', p. 53.

man's exile could officially be broken in such a manner. As Bakhrushin suggested: 'In state conditions alien to all constitutional juridical forms, there was created a unique reciprocal relationship of the supreme power and the people, in which was possible a formal agreement between the tsar and his subjects reinforced by an oath. Thus peculiarly was composed the political life of Moscow.'⁹

Bakhrushin and other Soviet historians downplayed the significance of the support given to the tsar by the patriarch and the Church. Moreover, they may have exaggerated the part played in this life by 'the people', but it most certainly showed itself in moments of crisis such as 1613 and 1648. Nevertheless, the last word in 1649 was with the nobles and merchants who welcomed the resolution of the crisis sanctioned by the Assembly of the Land, the *Ulozhenie* or Code of Laws of 1649. For, although the Code's preface declared that it aimed at justice for all, the institution of serfdom was firmly entrenched and other concessions made to the wishes of the nobles and merchants. Thus, in an informal alliance with the upper strata of Muscovite society, the Romanovs consolidated their absolutism at the same time as any pretensions the Stuarts might have had in the same direction were crushed.¹⁰

As a response to the regicide of 1649, as we have already pointed out, a decree was issued attacking the trading practices of the Muscovy Company. Muscovy Company merchants were expelled from interior cities to Arkhangel'sk; henceforth no English merchants were permitted to trade with any city within the Russian dominions: '1649 At which time the said Emperor taking further distaste at the horrid and detestable murder of your Maj. Royal Brother of Blessed memory', responded by banishing out of his territories 'all such merchants and Traders . . . belonging to the city of London looking on that city as the Head of Rebellion'.¹¹ The Muscovy Company's Charter was cancelled, so 'reducing it to the same status as the Dutch and other foreigners'.¹² The repercussions were profound. Politically, Dokhturov's embassy (described in Chapter 3) was to be the last to England for 16 years, until after the Stuart Restoration. However, as the relationship had normally been economically based for the English, it was the economic sanctions, not the political disruption, which were to have the greatest effect. Nevertheless, a contemporary argued that 'These new confusions in

---

9 Ibid., p. 59.
10 For a fuller treatment, see Dukes, *October*, Chapter 1, 'The General Crisis of the Seventeenth Century'.
11 'The Humble Remonstrance of John Hebdon, Resident of his imperial Majesty', 16 March 1660' – *PRO*, SP 91/3, fols 77r–79v. The *ukaz* was presented to John Osborne, indicating that he was considered the royal Representative and Muscovy Company Representative in Russia.
12 Phipps, 'The Russian Embassy', p. 258.

Brittaine, Ireland, France, Poland, Russia, elsewhere are to me the prolouge to that great Act',[13] so placing Russia firmly within the fold of those countries which some historians consider to have been afflicted by a 'crisis' suffered during the middle of the seventeenth century.[14]

Thus, although regicide was the stated reason for the revocation of trade privileges, other factors had a role to play: as in 1646, political and economic reasons could be combined with the opportunity of appeasing social discontent. In 1649, for example, 164 deputies from Russian towns petitioned Aleksei, complaining that foreign mercantile competition was causing poverty and hunger amongst Russian mercantile families. In the context of the domestic disturbances, Aleksei decided to act: the Revolution in England, Scotland and Ireland was a convenient political pretext for revoking the Muscovy Company privileges. Of course, were Aleksei not to react in any way against the overthrow of monarchical rule and the imposition of republicanism, he would be displaying a dangerous political weakness.

If the privileges were to be revoked, customs duties previously unpaid would form an additional and valuable source of income for the Russian Treasury. Thus perhaps, as Phipps suggests, 'the same action might have been taken even if the King had triumphed over Parliament in the Civil War'.[15] However, Loewenson argues that, although political and economic motives were apparent, 'it would be wrong to presume that the shocking news from England was looked upon merely as a welcome pretext. The extent to which Moscow was impressed by the fact that the English "killed to death their King Carolus" is shown by the striking differences between the receptions accorded to the representatives of Charles II and of Cromwell.'[16]

In a brief historical survey of the Muscovy Company's existence, Patrick Gordon examines the differing reasons surrounding the revocation of the privileges. The evidence he cites agrees with the thesis that it was for economic, rather than political, reasons that the privileges were revoked:

> but the Hollanders and Hamburgers haveing found the way hither also, began to trade without any Corporation, yet encreased so, that the Hollanders especially in tyme gott great advantages of the English and outwitted (to give it no worse terme) the English and even trapan'd them into many things and then delated

13 'Letter, John Saddler to Samuel Hartlib', undated. The Hartlib Papers, 46/9/23A.
14 R. O. Crummey, 'Muscovy', accepts the application of the term to Russia.
15 Phipps, 'The Russian Embassy', p. 257. Note, however, Phipps states on p. 272 that 'Trade and politics had combined to make Aleksei's abrogation of the Muscovy Company's Charter of Privileges inevitable.'
16 Loewenson, 'Did Russia Intervene', p. 15.

them. For they had gott some of the English to bring up their goods under the notion of their owne so to avoid the paying of custome, whereby the Tzaar was cheated of his revenues. So that it was in agitation, by the instigation of the Hollanders & Russia Merch.ts, whom they had drawne to their party, to disan-null these priviledges but their not being sufficient proofes, and the English forwarned, keeping themselves closser and by their splendid way of liveing haveing gained the goodwill of the Nobility, and those of the poorest merch.ts & tradesmen by trusting, the business was delayed, untill the unhappy tragedy of the murder of King Charles the First, whereat occasion was taken, upon a more generous account to banish the English, and take away ther Privileges, yet afterwards they were permitted to trade paying custome as others.[17]

However, for all the supposed hidden reasons for the revoking of the privileges, the Russians, as Gordon notes, were always to insist that the regicide was the one and only reason.

There is a strong case for maintaining that the modern era began in 1649 with the execution of Charles I after a formal trial, not just a straightforward murder, as had always been a threat to heads of state. And this is no superim-position of a theory of 'crisis', for upsets affected monarchs and their subjects alike. In a survey of the years up to 1650, for example, James Howell wrote '. . . to take all nations in a lump, I think God almighty hath a quarrel with all mankind, and given the reins to the ill spirit to compass the whole earth.' Howell described events in Africa, China and Turkey before turning to those in Europe including the following:

> The Emperor of Muscovia going on in a simple procession upon the Sabbath day, the rabble broke in, knocked down and cut in pieces divers of his chieffest counsellors, favourites, and officers before his face; and dragging their bodies to the mercat place, their heads were chopped off, into vessels of hot water, and so set upon poles to burn more brightly before the court-gate.[18]

In Moscow, then, the heads of some of the entourage; in London, the head of the monarch himself.

Just before his execution, Charles I allegedly said that it was his duty to God first, and to his country to clear himself as 'an honest man, a good King and a good Christian'. Charles denied responsibility for the war with Parliament. He forgave those responsible for the sentence of death, and called for a national

17 Gordon, Diary, 23 June 1666, vol. 2, pp. 221–2.
18 Howell, *Familiar Letters*, pp. 411–12.

council to settle the affairs of the Church. He insisted that he desired the liberty and freedom of the people but he also insisted that a subject and a sovereign were 'clear different things' and duty to the king was clearly laid down in the laws of the land, laws which he had not sought to change in an arbitrary manner. He proclaimed himself 'the Martyr of the people'. He also denied popery, attesting that 'I die a Christian according to the profession of the Church of England, as I found it left me by my father ... I have a good Cause and I have a gracious God; I will say no more.'[19]

Soon after the king was executed, his alleged last words were reported in English pamphlets and newspapers.[20] Not long later, although it is impossible to be precise, these words came out in translation in a Russian 'newspaper'. The *vesti-kuranty*, to which we have already referred, are by no means an obscure source. But they have been little used by historians.[21] This is rather surprising as it surely is noteworthy that Tsar Alexis and surviving members of his entourage received a detailed account of the execution of Charles and his immediately preceding speech. They probably listened to it rather than read it, for the *vesti-kuranty* were 'manuscript bulletins' rather than printed newspapers, and not circulated around the court, even less beyond it. Papers bearing news, nevertheless.

The translation of the king's alleged final words and their circumstances came into Russian via German – *tsesarskii iazyk* – and Swedish. The original is still recognisable, but inevitably the triple translation leads to some distortions. For example, in the original, Charles asks for a glass of claret. In the Russian version, this becomes a glass of Rhenish. A patriotic German translator perhaps. A more significant mistranslation perhaps crept in at the Swedish stage in the reference to the king dying a Christian 'according to the profession of the Church of England', which is rendered '*po svoei kal'vinskoi kirg'skoi vere v Aglinskoi zemle*' – according to his Calvinistic church belief in the English land. Was this a conscious attempt to set the Lutheran Church clearly apart from the Church of England?[22]

19 Wedgwood, *The Trial of Charles I*, pp. 213–19.
20 For example, *King Charles his Speech made upon the Scaffold*. The much published and most influential royal meditation *Eikon Basilike* (*The Royal Image*), probably composed by the king's chaplain John Gauden, also made its first appearance soon after the execution.
21 The most detailed study is by a philologist: Schibli, *Die ältesten russischen Zeitungsübersetzungen (Vesti-Kuranty)*. For an early notice, see Waugh, 'The Publication of Muscovite kuranty'.
22 Kotkov, *Vesti-kuranty, 1648–1650*, pp. 82–5. Maier and Pilger, 'Second-hand Translation', pp. 232, 234 point out that the translation from Spanish via Dutch of the Peace Treaty between Spain and the Netherlands, Münster, 1648 was done 'extremely carefully'. The tsar received 'a Russian translation that was just about as clear, as understandable and as correct' as the Dutch version. Alekseev, *Angliia i Anglichane*, pp. 92–3, refers to another work on the execution of Charles I translated from Latin by Epifanii Slavinetskii, *O ubienii kralia Aggel'skogo*.

We do not know for sure what effect the Russian version had on Tsar Aleksei, or even if he heard it, but we may be permitted to speculate that he still had it in mind at Kolomenskoe in February 1663 when he was taken ill and forced to make a sudden exit from a banquet after proposing a toast to the 'glorious martyr Charles I'. Quite possibly, he thought of his own relationship to his people and the Orthodox Church. No doubt, the Moscow 'Copper' Revolt of the previous year, 1662, was also on his mind.[23]

We are on more certain ground in the observation that at the time of the mid-century crisis, the *vesti-kuranty* continued to give a detailed picture of developments in Europe's offshore archipelago. Thus, in the six-month period from May to October 1649, 12 out of 28 numbers of the *vesti-kuranty* made reference to information on the further progress of the Revolution in England, Scotland and Ireland as Cromwell sought to consolidate his hold on the three kingdoms.[24] These references present a reasonably accurate account of the Revolution's progress, if very little of an analytical nature.[25] There are some interesting renditions, for example, *bol'shoi dumnoi boiarin* for high official. There are some surprising neologisms, notably *rebelri*, which, according to the editors of the *vesti-kuranty* from the Russian Academy's Institute of the Russian Language, might signify the Levellers.[26]

Swedish involvement in the relay of news from London to Moscow takes on a further dimension in a communication of 9 June 1649 from Stockholm to Moscow. This was actually sent by the Scottish Colonel Alexander Crawford to his brother Colonel 'Ivan' Crawford and Lieutenant Colonel 'Ivan' Leslie. Alexander Crawford wrote that he had arrived safely in Stockholm on 6 June and brought news with him from Scotland while he was also expecting further news from Riga. As well as showing concern for the pay and conditions of officers and men, he also reported that the Marquises of Hamilton and Huntly had been executed for leading opposition to the new regime, but that the Scots still hoped to carry war to the English.[27]

When we look at English newspapers in the period from May to October 1649, along with news of events from other parts of Europe including, for example, the struggle of the Venetians to hold Crete against the Turks, the few reports from the

---

23 Longworth, *Alexis*, p. 154. Among those called upon to suppress the 'Copper' Revolt, so called because of the replacement of silver coinage by copper, was Patrick Gordon and several brother Scottish officers, who had enrolled in Russian service in 1661.

24 Maier, 'Newspaper Translations'.

25 We are grateful to Dr Micheál Ó Siochrú, formerly of the University of Aberdeen, for his confirmation of the accuracy of this observation.

26 Kotkov, *Vesti-kuranty, 1648–1650*, pp. 96–7.

27 Ibid., pp. 108–9, 146–7.

eastern end of the continent mostly concern the Revolt of the Cossacks against the Poles. For example:

> The Cossacks commit many insolencies still, and being expostulated with, put it upon the Russian Pesant-Rebells . . . Meanwhile there arrived Ambassadours at Muscove, from the King, and from the said Generall [Khmelnitsky], in one day, though neither admitted, wanting some Epithites in the Title. Who can tell, saith a Letter, but the old Prophecie may come to be verified yet, foretelling, that in the yeare 1650 the Kingdome of Poland would be covered over with Horse-shoes.[28]

The imbroglio of Poland, Russia and the Cossacks is too complicated to explain in detail, although it should be pointed out that it constituted an important preliminary to the Thirteen Years' War, 1654–67, between Muscovy and Poland. To quote a recent authority: 'To a greater or lesser extent, the Cossack uprisings of early modern Ukraine, the most important of which were raised under the banner of Orthodoxy, were part of a whole series of social and political conflicts that rolled across Europe in connection with the upheavals precipitated by the Reformation and Counter-Reformation.'[29]

In the English newspapers, there is some mention, too, of the Russian embassy to Sweden throughout the summer of 1649, ending successfully on 17 November 1649:

> The three ambassadors of Muscovia after they had happily determined their Negociation, had their dispatch, accompanyed with three great Chaines of Gold, each of which, was pendant to the Portraiture of the Queene, enriched with Diamonds. The Gentlemen and principall Officers of their followers had also given them each one a great Goblet of silver guilded, and to all the meaner followers other lesse Presents. The same day they had their audience of taking leave of her Majesty, she invited him to a dancing, which was to be danced before her. These ambassadors have been defrayed, during all the time they have been here, and the Ships that are appointed for their transportation are also furnished with all necessary provisions.

Enough of contacts, on to comparisons of the distribution of information via newspapers in the two societies. This need not be a matter of great concern, since there are very few meaningful comparisons to make. Consider quantity.

---

28 *A brief relation*, 18–25 December 1649, p. 179, Thomason 90:E.587[2], *EEBO*.
29 Plokhy, *The Cossacks*, pp. 343–4.

From 1641 to 1659, there were more than 350 publications in England that could be called newspapers. (Perhaps Daniel Defoe's memory was deceiving him some years later when he wrote in his memoirs of the Great Plague of 1665: 'We had no such thing as printed Newspapers in those days . . .') In Russia, there was one, and that unpublished, scarcely deserving the name 'newspaper'. In England, to quote authorities on the subject, 'twenty years of interregnum threw censorship into such utter disarray that certain periods seemed to be entirely free of it. Political information and commentary could therefore circulate almost without limitation.' In Russia, a political culture in which the Orthodox Church is usually said to have played a central role militated against open discourse: after the *vesti-kuranty* had been read to the tsar and the boyars, they were kept secret in the Chancellery archives. It is worthy of note, too, however, that in Russia's immediate Roman Catholic neighbour, the *Merkuriusz Polski*, begun in Krakow and Warsaw in 1661, was, to quote the authorities on the subject again, 'an isolated venture of its kind and failed to find an audience'. The principal reason that they advance is the failure of 'urban development comparable to what had been essential to a political information business elsewhere'.[30] In Protestant Sweden, the *Ordinari Post Tijdender* was first printed in 1645 for Johan von Beijer, the Postmaster in Stockholm, in his official capacity.[31] The nature of the capital city, encouraging literacy, appears to have played its part here. Such observations could open the door to speculation about the situation in Muscovite Russia.

For the moment, we must agree with Gary Marker that seventeenth-century Russian printing 'seems not to have acted as a leading agent of secularization'. At the same time, however, we are reminded by the same authority of the 'thousands of individual works that were produced by hand in the seventeenth century. Whole genres that had been part of written culture for some time remained outside of printed culture throughout the seventeenth century.' These would include fables, fairy tales and epics, but also works of history and travel accounts, not to mention the *vesti-kuranty* that we have concentrated on here, deemed by other leading authorities to be 'a highly attractive linguistic source for the study of seventeenth-century Russian vernacular language'.[32]

We will return to the question of publication as a fomenter of progress and crisis in our conclusion.

30　Dooley and Baron, *The Politics of Information*, pp. 11–12. Quotation from Defoe, *A Journal of the Plague Year*, p. 7.
31　*The Birth*, pp. 34–5.
32　Marker, 'Russia and the "Printing Revolution" ', pp. 271–2; Maier and Pilger 'Second-hand Translation', p. 209.

Interregnum

Contact between Aleksei and Prince Charles, first initiated in 1648, continued after the regicide. In, 1649, the royalist Sir Peter Wyche received a familiar-sounding reply to his enquiry about the restoration of Muscovy Company privileges. A decision was expected once 'His Imperiall Majesty shall have concluded the war with the King of Poland and with the Crimean Khan.'[33] In 1649, too, Prince Charles decided to send 'Lord Baron John of Culpepper' as his 'Extraordinary Embassador' to Moscow. Culpepper was a royalist and had fought for Charles I during the Civil War, appearing in a 'List of those who were in the garrison of Worcester at its surrender.'[34] Before his departure to Moscow, Parliament declared: 'That Charles Stuart, eldest son of the late King, James his second son, . . . Sir John Culpepper . . . and all those who have been plotting or assisting the rebellion in Ireland, be proscribed and banished as enemies and traitors, and die without mercy, wherever they shall be found within the limits of this nation, and their estates be confiscated.'[35]

Culpepper's mission was to announce officially 'the unnaturall rebellion raysed by Our Subjects of England, against the King Our late Royall Father . . . by those monsters of mankind.'[36] He passed through Hamburg early in February 1650. A hostile English newspaper noted:

> The Lord Culpepper is come to Hamburgh with five or six attendants, he is going to Muscovia Ambassador from the Prince, his followers report a chiefe part of his Embassie is, to demand a debt which that State, was owing to Queene Elizabeth, but I believe begging, and to doe mischiefe to the English Merchants, that will not supply him with Money, are the principall occasions of his journey.[37]

In Danzig, Culpepper talked with 'the English frequenting his lodgings and giveing information' against merchants who had trade with the Commonwealth.[38]

---

33 *PRO*, SP 91/3, fols 184–5; Paeffgen, *Englisch-russische Wirtschaftsbeziehungen*, p. 161.

34 *CSPD*, 1645–1647, p. 456, 29 July 1646.

35 'March 14, 1649. Order in Parliament'. *CSPD*, 1649-1650, no. 27, p. 39.

36 'Charles to Aleksei, 16 April 1649'. *RGADA*, fond 35, opis 2, list 83. See also 'William Sandys Journeying and Labour in Charles the Second's Service', *HMC* 39th Report, Xv.2, Hodgkin Mss, 1897, p. 119.

37 *A brief relation*, Bremen 17 January 1649[1650?], Thomason 91: E.592[7], *EEBO*. As may be seen from the following footnote, this date is erroneous.

38 A letter from 'Capt. Meade to Sec. Nicholas' dated February 3/13 1650 states 'Lord Culpepper came to Hamburg three days after me, and went forward on his voyage the next morning.' *CSPD*, 1649–1650, no. 14, p. 505. On Culpepper in Danzig, see *PRO*, SP 88/16, Part II, fol. 210.

Arriving in Moscow in May 1650, he asked for a one hundred thousand rouble loan, but was to receive only twenty thousand roubles, and this was paid in kind – grain and furs.[39] Five thousand quarters of grain were sent from Russia to the exiled Prince Charles (now Charles II in Scotland); both Osborne and Hebdon signed the receipts as the Royal Representatives in Russia.[40] According to a later report made by Hebdon, Lord Culpepper also attempted to have the Muscovy Company privileges restored, but was rebuffed by an indignant tsar, apparently inclined to punish supporters of regicide. Aleksei allegedly declared: 'When your Majesties Ambassador, the Lord Culpepper, did in your Majesties name solicit his Imperial Majesties for the restoration of the said merchants, His Imperial Majestie gave him for answer, that he did not expect your Majesties Amb. of all men should interceed for such that had aided with the Rebels, but rather have fought for severer punishment to have been inflicted on such people.'[41]

However, the letter Culpepper was to deliver did not explicitly or implicitly request the resumption of privileges. Indeed, Charles II revealed an awareness of the reasons for their revocation: 'not doubting, but that your Imperiall Ma.ty in Your great Wisedome, will clearly discerne, how much it concerns all Soveraigne Princes, to provide for the safety of their owne persons.' If we are to believe the London-based Muscovy Company merchants, Culpepper was responsible for Aleksei's order that they 'depart his dominions': 'This, we think, was caused by Culpepper, Ambassador of the pretended King of Scots, then residing there, the Emperor having sent or lent a large sum to the said King.'[42] *En route* back to the exiled Charles II in France, Culpepper was possibly involved in the publication in the Netherlands of a pamphlet entitled *A Declaration of His Imperiall Majestie, The Most High and Mighty Potentate Alexea, Emperor of Russia and Great-Duke of Moscovia*, protesting against the murder of Charles I.[43]

It would appear that Culpepper wanted privileges restored only to the royalist elements within the Muscovy Company. Among these royalist elements, 'John Vicars, alderman of London, and Jon. Osborne, Russia merchants' had received a

---

39　This was gratefully acknowledged: 'Charles II to Aleksei, 30 July 1655'. *RGADA*, fond 35, opis 2, no. 85 (copy). Another copy in *PRO*, SP22/60 fol. 76. See also 'Thomas Coke to the Council of State, April 1651, 5th Paper, *HMC*, Portland I, p. 583: 'The Lord Culpepper came from Russia to the Hagh where he now is, and brought eyther in money or credit a great summe with him for the Kings service.'

40　Phipps, *Britons in Russia*, p. 150.

41　'The Humble Remonstrance of John Hebdon, Resident for his Imperial Majestie ... 16 Mar 1660' – *PRO*, SP 91/3, fols77r–79v.

42　'Charles II to Aleksei, 16 April 1649', *RGADA*, fond 35, opis 2, no. 83; *CSPD*, 1653–1654, no. 149, p. 340. Muscovy Company 'list of our houses and debts' valued at 30,000 pounds.

43　*A Declaration*; Loewenson, 'Did Russia Intervene', pp. 13–20; Roginskii, 'Missiia', pp. 96–102.

pass from the Council of State to pick up a detained ship of theirs in Holland and from thence sail to Russia.[44] It appears that John Osborne again acted against the interests of the London-based Muscovy Company merchants in 1651, when a petition was brought against him.[45] It is possible that, because of Osborne's royalist convictions, his daughter ('a religious discreet good natured, & well bred maid; of sober well composed & well featured carriage & countenance, of about eight & twenty years of age, able to guid a house & governe children') was said to 'intend if the troubles continue heer, to go this Summer to her Father'.[46]

At the Restoration in 1660, royalists were to believe that 'of all Christian Princes, the Tzaar alone had never acknowledged, nor kept any Correspondence with the usurper Cromwell, as also the King dureing his exile had received other good offices from the Tzaar'.[47] If we examine the diplomatic links of Charles II and Cromwell and the second Romanov tsar, Tsar Aleksei Mikhailovich, from 1650 to 1660, we can see that this was only partly true. The diplomatic links between the Republic and Aleksei did end in failure; for success, privileges would necessarily have been restored to the Muscovy Company. The 'other good offices' imply that, whatever the true political allegiances and affiliations of Muscovy Company members in London, some, at least, of the Muscovy Company merchants in Moscow were royalists.

During the period of the Republic, as in the Time of Troubles, the Muscovy Company based in London increased its interest in trade to Greenland as its ability to trade to Russia decreased.[48] However, Russian goods were still being imported into England by hired Dutch ships. Indeed, one Muscovy Company official states that this 'was done for 2 reasons, viz., that we have them for half the freight of English ships and the Dutch give content . . .'[49]

Moreover, attempts were made to: recover trade links with Russia; discover the causes for the breakdown in diplomacy between Russia and the Commonwealth; and examine the Muscovy Company's role in the disruption and so reveal how the diplomatic initiative had passed to the royalists in exile.[50] The Council of State, for example, asked 'what remedies the company thinks fit to be applied for their recovery, and deliver it to Mr. Thurloe'. However, all these

---

44 *CSPD*, 1650, p. 542, 15 May 1650.

45 *CSPD*, 1652–1653, no. 90, p. 71.

46 'Nicholas Stoughton to Samuel Hartlib, 19 March 164/52'. *The Hartlib Papers*, 46/12/12A.

47 Gordon, Diary, 23 June 1666, vol. 2, p. 222.

48 See, for example *CSPD*, 1653–1654, no. 33, p. 362; no. 66, p. 379; no. 74, p. 380; no. 18, p. 392; no. 19, pp. 392–3; no. 69, p. 421.

49 *CSPD*, 1656–1657, no. 4, I, pp. 227–8.

50 'February 20, 1650. Council of State. Day's Proceedings. 3. To send to the Governor of the Russia Company, for an account of what they did unto the letter from Parliament to the Emperor of Russia.' *CSPD*, 1650, p. 5.

deliberations were, according to 'Fras. Ashe, Governor, and the Company of Merchants trading to Russia' in a letter to the Committee of Foreign affairs, to produce no 'resolutions or encouragement as to proceeding in that trade, on account of the committee's other weighty affairs'.[51]

It is perhaps a measure of the domination of diplomatic links with Russia by trade interests that the only diplomatic missions to Russia during the Commonwealth period were sent at the instigation of the Muscovy Company. The purpose of their mission was to regain the privileges that they had lost. Therefore, it is hardly surprising that the diplomatic initiative had passed to the royalists abroad, since Cromwell was committed primarily to the conquest of Scotland and Ireland, and to the First Anglo-Dutch War (1652–4).

In 1654, with the Treaty of Westminster and the ending of the First Anglo-Dutch War, the 'Governor and Company of Merchants trading to Russia', having petitioned Cromwell successfully 'that some fit person recommended by the merchants be sent at their charge to the Emperor of Russia as the Protector's agent, to restore and settle the trade between England and Russia according to the ancient privilege',[52] promised to pay the expenses of such an embassy.[53] The man chosen as 'his Highness' [Cromwell's] agent', William Prideaux, had an audience with Tsar Aleksei in Moscow in February and March 1656.[54] He also talked with the Governor of Archangel, Boris Ivanovich Porkin, about the duties that English merchants would have to pay and other matters. Porkin merely reiterated the government's position and gave a negative answer to Prideaux's question about the possibility of trading past the White Sea port.[55] Prideaux also tried to settle some of the outstanding claims left in the wake of the 1649 fiasco. For example, he claimed that the loss of John White's potash monopoly in 1649 had resulted in losses of R4,000. However, the Russians vehemently contested the claim, arguing that such a figure was incompatible with the modest scale of production.[56] Similarly, Prideaux's enquiries about restoring the Muscovy Company's privileges received a reply that was to become familiar to English merchants and diplomats in the second half of the

51 *CSPD*, 1651–1652, no. 19, p. 266; no. 53, p. 301.
52 *CSPD*, 1654, no. 13, pp. 202–3. There is reference to draft letters at *CSPD*, 1649–1650, no. 11, p. 469 and a plan inspired by the Council of State, for '. . . the Revenue Committee, to furnish the merchants trading to Russia with money necessary for sending the letter from the Parliament of England to the Emperor of Russia not to exceed [£]500 . . .' in January 1650 at *CSPD*, no. 20, p. 488. For this purpose, 'Col. Wm. Hawley to be employed', *CSPD*, 1649–1650, no. 15, p. 491. The letter does not appear to have been sent.
53 'Council of State Day's Proceedings, 8 June 1654'. *PRO*, SP25/75, fol. 354.
54 Lyubimenko, 'Anglo-Russian Relations', pp. 52–3; *CSPD*, 1654, no. 4, p. 219.
55 Arkhangel'skii, 'Diplomaticheskie agenty Kromvelia', p. 122.
56 *Thurloe Papers*, vol. 3, pp. 575–7.

century: the ongoing war prevented immediate action on the issue but a satisfactory solution would be worked out thereafter.[57] Evidently, the embassy was not a success, but it is interesting to note that Prideaux blamed the harassments and delays he endured at the hands of Russian authorities on the deliberate mistranslation of his interpreter, the royalist John Hebdon.[58] (This ability of royalists in Moscow in effect to sabotage diplomatic missions provides, as we shall see, the precursor and model for anti-Williamite and pro-Jacobite activities in the 1690s.) By August 1656 Prideaux had returned from Moscow to England, his mission fruitless.[59]

While Prideaux was engaged in his embassy to Moscow, Swedish diplomats in London and Stockholm were simultaneously attempting to form an alliance with the Commonwealth. The evident collapse of Anglo-Russian trade had not gone unnoticed by the Swedes with their ambitious schemes for diverting Russian trade to the Baltic. Indeed, Philip Crusius von Krusenstiern had already proposed that the English move their operations to Reval. This project had then attracted growing attention in Sweden due to the deterioration of Russo-Swedish relations under Queen Christina.[60] The Swedish residents in Russia, Karl Pommerening and Johan de Rodes, both took pains to push the Crown's agenda with English merchants. Pommerening conducted negotiations with them in 1650 and found considerable willingness to move, provided that Sweden could offer them privileges comparable to those lost a year earlier. The atmosphere in Stockholm became even more favourable to rapprochement with the Commonwealth after 1651 when the Swedish government – at first unofficially – came to accept Cromwell's government as legitimate. De Rodes met with Prideaux during the latter's embassy to Russia.[61] Meanwhile, Krister Bonde conducted talks with the Commonwealth in London in 1655–6. He offered military and naval aid and reciprocal trading privileges – concessions for Swedish herring fishing off the British coasts and freedom to trade to America – in return for lighter duties for English ships in Swedish harbours, and, most importantly, a joint Anglo-Swedish effort to divert Archangel trade to Narva, Nyen and Reval. Bonde made concrete promises for the right of

57 Arkhangel'skii, 'Diplomaticheskie agenty Kromvelia', p. 129.
58 Ibid.; *Thurloe Papers*, vol. 3, pp. 387, 602, 698.
59 In 1659 Prideaux, 'an ancient gentleman, who has been employed in Russia and travelled in the Levant', was nominated by the Levant company to replace the deceased Spencer Bretton as Consul to Smyrna. *CSPD*, 1658–9, p. 309. See also *CSPD*, 1659–1660, pp. 266, 267; Phipps, *Britons in Russia*, p. 28.
60 Troebst, *Handelskontrolle-'Derivation'-Eindämmung*, pp. 331–2, 334 ff.
61 Ibid., pp. 341–2; Arkhangel'skii, 'Diplomaticheskie agenty Kromvelia', pp. 123–4.

emporium for both the Muscovy and Eastland Company in Narva, Nyen and Riga respectively. However, he was forced to concede the reluctance of the Muscovy merchants to move to Narva, although the Eastland Company did petition for a move to the city. While any diversion of White Sea trade to the Baltic would allow Sweden directly to monitor and regulate trade to Russia, English ships would potentially be hostage to Dutch-inspired economic dislocation within the Baltic. The proposed alliance was not implemented, owing to the outbreak of the Russo-Swedish war in 1656.[62] The state of Cromwellian diplomatic negotiations simultaneously occurring in Stockholm were discussed in a report written 'For my Lord Bradshaw', who was thus fully aware of the complexity of the situation.[63]

The next embassy, sent under the rule of 'Olivarius Protector Reipublicae Anglia, Scotia et Hibernia' to 'Alexis Mychaylowich', was presided over by Cromwell's Resident in Hamburg, Special ambassador 'Ricardus Bradshaw'.[64] This news was noted by the court in exile.[65] Richard Bradshaw's embassy was sent to Moscow on 12 April 1657, intercepted briefly *en route* by Patrick Gordon and other Stuart sympathisers mistaking Richard for Lord Bradshaw, one of the regicides.[66] It returned that autumn. Its primary mission was, of course to restore Muscovy Company privileges. But its timing, following the Peace of Paris of 1657 bringing the first Anglo-Dutch War formally to an end, allowed Bradshaw 'to propose himself as mediator for the conclusion of peace between Russia and Sweden', at war since 1656. In effect, as Russia was poised to capture Riga and thus become a Baltic power, it could have become a possible ally for the Protectorate, as well as affording English merchants free transit trade in the Baltic and a shorter route to the Moscow market. However, in recognition of the growing *realpolitik* of the British government, Bradshaw's instructions allowed for the possibility of a 'second-best' outcome of free trade and unlimited access to the Russian interior,

---

62 Roberts, *Swedish Diplomats*, pp. 146–50; Troebst, *Handelskontrolle-'Derivation' – Eindämmung*, pp. 341–2. Kobzareva, *Diplomaticheskaia bor'ba*, pp. 289–90, takes a negative view of the Russo-Swedish War, 1656–61, concluding that it delayed the end of the Russo-Polish Thirteen Years' War, 1654–7, without achieving a lasting foothold on the Baltic Sea.

63 'Copy Letter, John Dury to Lord Commissioner Lisle' undated. *The Hartlib Papers*, 24/2/33A.

64 'Letter from Cromwell to Aleksei, 10 April 1657'. *RGADA*, fond 35, opis 2, no. 87. *CSPV*, 1657–1659, no. 29, p. 34; no. 33, pp. 38–9; no. 67, pp. 87–91. *CSPD*, 1656–1657, p. 310: 'To advise his Highness to send Rich. Bradshaw, his resident at Hamburg, as envoy to the Great Dukes of Muscovy', p. 300, no. 15, p. 304.

65 'April 18/28 1657, Lieutenant-General Middleton to Secretary Nicholas'. *CSPD*, 1656–1657, p. 345.

66 See, for example, Robertson, *Passages*, p. 28.

including the capital. Nevertheless, Bradshaw's permission to enter was delayed, and then he returned to London empty-handed.[67]

Hebdon argued later that: 'Lastly when the rebells did send their Ambassador [Bradshaw] to his Imperial Majesties, his Imperial Majestie suffered not the said rebell to tread into his Territory. And no notice being taken of him nor his message, forced him to returne from Riga.'[68] However, since documentation does reveal that Bradshaw presented his proposals to the 'Illustrissime Domine Cancellarie', signing the memorandum himself, on the 19/29 September 1657, it is likely that Hebdon is overstating his case.[69] On this occasion, perhaps as Bradshaw was not a Muscovy Company member, the Commonwealth assumed responsibility for the cost of his mission, estimated at £500.[70] Moreover, it is highly likely that merchants whose sympathies lay with the new Republic would have provided the Commonwealth with information on Russia during this period. One contemporary noted that: 'To discover the affairs of others they [the English during the Republic] do not employ ambassadors, but use spies as less conspicuous, making use of men of spirit but without rank and unlikely to be noticed.'[71] Whatever Bradshaw's real motivations were, they were treated with utmost suspicion in Moscow which was awash with rumours of a Swedish descent on Kola in order to drive the Russians out of the Eastern Baltic, some of which they had conquered in 1656–7. Thus, Bradshaw was viewed as a Swedish spy.[72]

Commerce

The steep deterioration of relations between Britain and Russia quite evidently found its counterpart in Anglo-Russian trade. While next to no quantitative information survives on commercial relations in the early 1650s, gloomy reports by Prideaux suggest that both shipping and operations in Archangel were minimal. Writing on 10 September 1654, the envoy lamented the limited time to conduct trade, a problem amplified by the narrow geographic area now open to the English merchants. Both these factors, as well as Dutch competition, had enabled the Russians to shift the terms of trade in their favour. The lack of specie

67 *Thurloe Papers*, vol. 6, p. 278; Arkhangel'skii, 'Diplomaticheskie agenty Kromvelia', pp. 134, 136.
68 'The Humble Remonstrance of John Hebdon, resident for his Imperial Majestie, 16 Mar 1660'. *PRO*, SP 91/3, fols 77r–79v.
69 *RGADA*, fond 35, opis 2, no. 88.
70 Birch, *A Collection*, vol. 6, p. 278; *CSPD*, 1657–1658, no. 10, pp. 301, 558; *PRO*, SP 25/106–68; Aylmer, *The King's Servants*, pp. 127–9.
71 *CSPV*, 1655–1656, no. 194, p. 143.
72 Rukhmanova, 'Bor'ba Rossii', pp. 187–90; *RGADA*, fond 210, Moskovskii stol, No. 279, 1657–60gg., listy 143, 149.

on both sides further limited mutually advantageous exchange. Lastly, the ongoing war and a plague epidemic in central Russia prevented some merchants from coming to the Arctic coast.[73] A near total collapse of Anglo-Russian trade was the consequence.

A highly disagreeable task awaited the fellows of the Muscovy Company as the seventeenth century passed its midpoint. After years of tension with the Russian authorities and relative decline, the Company was now forced to speedily wrap up its elaborate operations in the Russian interior. Perhaps the greatest loss involved the forced sale of 16 houses along the Moscow–Archangel axis. The Company jointly owned a total of seven houses: two in both Archangel and Moscow, and one each in Kholmogory, Vologda and Iaroslavl'. The floor space of the Kholmogory, Vologda and Moscow properties totalled 486,191 sq. ft, of which the massive facility in Vologda accounted for nearly three-quarters, and the two Moscow houses – led by the 92,868 sq. ft 'New House' – for just over a quarter. The Kholmogory house was a relatively modest affair with 6,468 sq. ft. The total value of these properties, as assessed by the Company in 1649, was R9,407.[74] Individual members of the Company owned a total of ten houses in 1649. John Osborne had a house in Archangel and two in Vologda. Thomas Wyche, John White, Richard Duncombe, John Dee, Robert Cocks and Thomas Steistet owned one house each in Vologda. Anthony Tivery had a house in Iaroslavl'. The combined floor space of six of these houses was 463,870 sq. ft, led by Osborne's 290,472 and 72,618 sq. ft properties in Vologda. The total value of the Kholmogory, Vologda and Iaroslavl' houses was estimated by the Company to be R3,110 in 1649. Apparently also merchants other than owners stayed at some of the privately owned houses.[75]

To make matters worse, the Russians did not hesitate to exploit the weakness of the English merchants. Among other things, Ivan Andreevich Miloslavskii, keen to acquire the Company's new Moscow house, claimed that no compensation was warranted for the building valued at R6,202, since it had been a gift from Ivan IV. A new appraisal by a group of the leading merchants known as *gosti* almost a year later put the value of the New House at only R2,700. The House was eventually bought by the Treasury which, however, withheld the payment because of R3,000 arrears by Osborne on his caviar monopoly.[76] The process of financial redress was slow elsewhere, as well. In the first year after expulsion, while none of the general (Company) houses was sold, only

73 *Thurloe Papers*, vol. 2, pp. 597, 605; Arkhangel'skii, 'Diplomaticheskie agenty Kromvelia', p. 123.
74 Arel, *The Muscovy Company*, pp. 280–1, 283.
75 Ibid., pp. 293, 295–6.
76 Ibid., pp. 515, 517–18.

two of the eight houses owned by individuals were sold in Vologda as well as the one of this type in Iaroslavl'. In the spring of 1650, the Company responded to pressure to sell the remaining properties with the statement that 'it did not expect any buyers' because the houses were 'too foreign in construction', that is to say they were too expensive.[77]

New appraisals conducted by the Russians sharply reduced the value of the buildings, in some cases to as little as one-tenth of the original estimate. For instance, the Iaroslavl' house in January 1653 was finally sold to the city's trading quarter (*posad*). The company house in Vologda went to David Ruts as partial repayment for a R426 loan. Thomas Wyche's Vologda house was acquired by a local church, again in repayment for a loan to the priest.[78]

Also the task of recovering outstanding debts proved daunting. By August 1651, the Company had managed to get back only R13,667 of the total R26,857 owed to it. The Investigations Chancellery reported that R4,816 of the remainder was, in fact, irretrievable owing to death, old age of debtors, clerical errors, etc. By the end of 1653, owing to considerable resistance by Russian elite merchants, the total outstanding loans still amounted to R7,959.[79]

This state of affairs may have contributed to formulation of plans to attack Archangel. While concrete data are scarce, there were rumours in 1654 – possibly concocted by the Swedes – that the English had sent a fleet of 25 men-of-war to Archangel. The information was conveyed by Reval burgher Cordt Meuseler to his Novgorod counterpart Petr Mikliaiev in July, and de Rodes reported similar rumours within weeks.[80]

In a slight turn for the better, John and Thomas Hebdon were admitted into the Russian interior already in the 1650s. In 1658, Samuel Meverall and John Dombel were given a five-year permission to visit Moscow in return for services rendered to the Crown. The grant was renewed after the Restoration in 1663 and 1668.[81]

The incipient recovery in Anglo-Russian trade becomes more impressive when simultaneous developments in the Baltic are taken into consideration. While the interest of the English merchants in Narva had a great deal to do with their setbacks in Archangel, their position also benefited from legislative reforms. The Navigation Acts especially allowed them to gain a market share from the Dutch much more dramatically than on the White Sea route. In essence:

---

77 Ibid., p. 520.
78 Ibid., pp. 522–5.
79 Ibid., pp. 526, 539–30.
80 Roginskii, *Poezdka*, p. 75; *Sostoianie Rossii*, p. 238.
81 Gurliand, *Ivan Gebdon*, pp. 6–8; *RGADA*, fond 35, 1678 g., delo 241.

The Acts of 1660 (Act of Navigation) and of 1662 (Act of Frauds) excluded Dutch tonnage from the importation into England of essential Baltic products: flax, hemp, timber, tar, pitch, and potash. Imports were legal only in British-owned vessels or in vessels belonging to the country of which the imported goods were the 'growth, production or manufacture.' Goods imported in ships not built in England paid a higher import duty.[82]

In fact, the exclusion of foreign merchants from the English Baltic trade was not absolute, as we shall see later.

Restoration

After the Restoration of Charles II in 1660, London was flooded by foreign ambassadors. Ostensibly recognising the return of the pre-Civil War polity, however, they did not suppose that the old order had indeed been restored; the problems which had caused the Civil War were not to be solved by Charles II.[83] For its part, the Muscovy Company pushed for what it could have reasonably expected – the restitution of its privileged trading position in Russia – recalling that: 'The Emperor granted ample priviledges onto the said society, to trade freely in his dominions without paying any customs tolls or any other duties for themselves, or any of their goods and merchandises . . . with many other immunities . . . which in consideration of wholly good services done by their nation to the Russe.'[84]

However, although the political position in Britain had ostensibly returned full circle, the economic advantage accrued by the Russians in the intervening years, in addition to the stronger position of the tsarist regime after the crisis of 1648–9, was too great to allow them to agree to a return to the old economic order. As Lyubimenko was to comment, 'the Company did not realise for a long time that its exceptional position in Russia had come to a definite end', adding that during the next fifty years every letter and every messenger from England to Moscow insisted without success on the restoration of the old privileges.[85]

The first contact between Aleksei Mikhailovich and Charles II was made, semi-officially, by John Hebdon, the tsar's commercial agent in the Netherlands. Hebdon arrived in London in 1661, his mission to recruit 3,000 soldiers for Russian military service. Without diplomatic credentials but with only a letter of

82 Åström, 'The English navigation laws', p. 3.
83 See Seaward, *The Restoration*, for a discussion of this issue.
84 'In the Humble Narrative of the Government and Company Merchants Trading to the Dominions of the Emperor of Russia, read 28 Mar 1661 by P.C.'. *PRO*, SP 91/3, fol. 81r–v.
85 Lyubimenko, 'Ango-Russian Relations', p. 49.

safe-conduct, he managed to persuade the English Privy Council that he was, in fact, the tsar's representative in London. A note in the margin of this letter 'Received and read by Committee appointed to treat with the Muscovite Amb. 28 Mar 1661', suggests that Hebdon had indeed succeeded in raising his status from that of 'Resident' to that of 'Ambassador'.[86]

Hebdon then offered congratulations to Charles II in the tsar's name.[87] While he was in London, Muscovy Company merchants persuaded him to intercede with Aleksei on his return to Moscow for the re-establishment of trading privileges.[88] The king too was called upon to make his contribution. One letter read: 'The petitioners, knowing that the person employed in this negotiation is not only thoroughly acquainted with the afffaires and suffering of this company in Russia but also in the highest favour . . . do most humbly supplicate' that Charles II 'will be graciously pleased to attest all opportunities to once again restore ancient amity between the two kingdomes'.[89]

Hebdon attempted to portray himself as a selfless servant: 'having no self interest in what I have said more than what tends to the honour of my sovereign and benefit of my nation.' In a further proclamation of devotion to duty and the royal will, Hebdon explains that he 'shall be glad to spend the rest of my life and small fortune . . . in the joint service of my sovereign the King's Majesty and his Imperial Majestie my master in this or any other service'. He advised Charles II to send an ambassador to Russia in order to restore the 'ancient amity' between the two countries – the implication being that 'ancient amity' existed in a period when English merchants enjoyed trading privileges; 'amity' had been underpinned by trade concessions, and not political alliance, according to the English. The Russians, however, wanted to reform a relationship based on a different set of assumptions, which, however, 'may and will tend to the benefit of the King's Maties subjects the Muscovy Co and increase of trade to this nation'.[90]

86 'Charles II to Aleksei, 10 May 1661'. *PRO*, SP 91/3, fols 85r–86v; 'Privy Council Committee Meeting, 22 March 1661'. *PRO*, PC2/55, fol. 178; Privy Council Minutes, 29 March 1661, *PRO*, PC 2/55, fol. 57. Although the 3,000 soldiers were not forthcoming, 1661 was the year in which Patrick Gordon and his fellow Scottish officers entered Russian service.

87 'John Hebdon's Remonstrance to the King, March 1661'. *PRO*, SP 91/3, fols 82r–83v; 'Charles II to Aleksei, 10 May 1661' – *PRO*, SP 22/60, fol. 78.

88 'The Humble Narrative and Petition of the Government and Company Merchants Trading to the Dominions of the Emperor of Russia, read by the Privy Council Mar 28 1661'. *PRO*, SP 91/3, fols 81r–v.

89 'The Humble Petition of the Government and Company of Merchants to Muscovie Russia, from John Joliffe Gov. 28 Mar 1661'. *PRO*, SP 91/3, fol. 84.

90 'Additional Remonstrances of John Hebdon, Resident of His Imperial Majesty 28 Mar 1661'. *PRO*, SP 91/3, fol. 82r–v.

Hebdon returned to Russia bearing a letter from Charles II that announced the 'happy and wonderful restoration' of the Stuart monarchy, thanked Aleksei for his aid during the years of exile and requested that Muscovy Company privileges be restored.[91] In a reply, which acknowledged Charles II as rightful ruler, Aleksei apparently signified a return to the friendly relations both countries had enjoyed before the regicide of 1649. This letter acknowledged the problem of Muscovy Company privileges, and proposed the exchange of ambassadors to discuss the matter.[92]

Charles II may have also been petitioned 'By his Majesties Council for Virginia' who recommended this 'naturally riche, spacious, and exceedingly well watered, very temperate' province. The petitioners added that 'those rich Furrs, Cordage, and other Comodities, which, with difficulty and danger wee now drawe from Russia, wilbe had in Virginia, and those parts adioyning, with ease and safety'. As trade with Muscovy was relatively easy before the revocation of the Muscovy Company privileges in 1646 and 1649, and as this document was drawn up 'By his Majesties Counsell', the evidence points to the document's origins in the first years of the Restoration. It appeared then that the Muscovy Company privileges would be restored, while the position of Virginia and the American colonies as a new source of raw materials would be relegated.[93]

Prince Petr Semeonovich Prozorovsky's embassy to Charles II, 1662–3, entered London, with its retinue of 150 men, on 27 November 1662. As Patrick Gordon put it: 'At which tyme the English conceived hopes of being restored to their Privileges for in the yeare 1662 the Tzaar not to be behind with the other Christian Princes sent a splendid Ambassy (and a person of greater birth and quality, as had been sent any where befor) to congratulate great Brittaines King his happy restauration . . .'.[94] Prozorovsky was the principal ambassador, and his deputies were Ivan

91 'Charles II to Tsar Aleksei, 10 May 1661'. *RGADA*, fond 35, opis 2, no. 89. (Copy: *PRO*, SP 91/3, fols 85–8.)

92 'Tsar Aleksei to King Charles II, 28 July 1661'. *PRO*, SP 102/49, fol. 39. Konovalov, 'England and Russia' p. 60, makes the distinction between a *de facto* recognition of Cromwellian rule during the Interregnum and a *de iure* recognition of the Restoration Government.

93 'By his Majesties Council for Virginia' [undated]. *The Hartlib Papers*, 61/3/2A–3B. This petition would have been written between 1628 and 1662, the period in which Samuel Hartlib compiled his information.

94 Gordon, Diary, 23 June 1666, vol. 2, p. 222. Gordon had already attempted to engage in diplomatic activity earlier that year by bribing Russian officials in an attempt to join the Russian ambassador's proposed embassy to Persia; the money had been accepted, but the post was not forthcoming. Gordon, Diary, 13 January 1662, vol. 2, pp. 148v–149. Gordon's interest in diplomatic activity can also be attested by his observation: 'The Hollands Ambassadour Mr. Boreel received in Mosko'. Gordon, Diary, 25 October 1662, vol. 2, p. 155. See also 16 September, 1662: 'Pass for Jo Hebdon, jun., to go into the Baltic sea to receive the three Russian ambassadors'. *CSPD*, 1661–1662, vol. LIX, p. 489.

Afanasevich Zhelyabuzhsky and Ivan Stepanovich Davydov. His Scottish interpreter was 'Sir Andrew Forrett Colonell'.[95] The ambassadors were banqueted and
feasted at a royal reception at Whitehall on 29 September 1662. Contemporary
witnesses describe the event as both costly and unusually splendid.[96]

On this occasion the cost of the embassy would not be borne by a Muscovy
Company that had been suffering greatly reduced profits. Fr. Giavarina, the
Venetian Resident in London, explained the motives of the Muscovy Company
in a report to the Doge, 28 July 1662:

> On their pleading that they could not bear the expense for lack of money, they
> were summoned before the Council of State and told that it had always been
> done in like cases and were urged to do it now. But they absolutely refused to
> spend a farthing, not so much from lack of money as because in past years the
> Grand Duke of Muscovy has deprived the English of all the privileges they
> used to enjoy in his dominions, so that the trade there is rather a loss than a
> gain, and they will not agree to such an expense. Accordingly the king will be
> obliged to meet it himself, an innovation that will be very costly.[97]

As the Venetian resident attested, the Prozorovsky embassy was paid for out of
government funds.[98] The Muscovy Company would not pay for diplomatic
embassies to Russia until its privileges had been restored. Thus, if cost-effective
relations were to occur, diplomacy had to concentrate on restoring the 'ancient'
privileges and so make good the serious financial losses suffered by the Company
during the Interregnum. The restoration of privileges would enrich the Muscovy
Company, while the king could pass the burden of the cost of such missions to

95 'Charles II to Aleksei, 2 June 1663'. *RGADA*, fond 35, opis 2, no. 92. Gordon mentions
    Forrett or Forrat in 1662: 'Colonell Cornelius von Bockhoven haveing been taken pris-
    oner the year before by Polotsko came to Mosko, and shortly after him, Co.ll Forrat who
    had been taken prisoner at the same time.' Gordon, Diary, 25 October 1662, vol. 2, p. 155.
96 *The Diary of Samuel Pepys*, III, p. 428, and *The Diary of John Evelyn*, III, p. 349. See also:
    PRO, PC 2/55, fol. 56; *CSPD*, 1661–1662, no. 94, p. 574: petition 'for the keeping of
    such outlandish beasts as shall be presented to His Majesty by the Russian ambassador',
    28 November 1662. For the text of Prozorovsky's ambassadorial speech at the royal
    audience, see: Martynov, 'Prince Prozorovsky's Ambassadorial Speech', pp. 50–7.
97 *CSPV*, 1661–1664, p. 167. In the 'Additional Remonstrances of John Hebdon, Resident for
    His Imperial Majesty of all Russia 28 Mar 1661', Hebdon writes of the Muscovy Company
    that it '... were then able, and did at all times defray all charges, both for the fitting out,
    and also for the maintenance then of the King's Maties Amb.'s and allowed maintenance
    here to al such Amb.'s which at any time came from the Emp.'s to the King. Yet now such
    is ther condition at present that they are not able to do the like.'
98 *CSPD*, 1661–1662: (no. 56), p. 462; *CSPD*, 1663–1664: (no. 71), p. 126, (no. 72), p. 127,
    (no. 117), p. 181, p. 186, (no. 100), p. 322.

a prosperous Muscovy Company. Thus, the actual diplomatic negotiations consisted of attempts to regain the revoked Charter of Privileges.[99]

Prozorovsky succeeded in obtaining the repayment of the 1650 loan to Charles II of R20,000, paid in kind, but he could gain no further loan (to be repaid in Russian hemp and potash) from either Charles II or the Muscovy Company. The Russian ambassador was not empowered to discuss the restoration of privileges, but left Muscovy Company officials with 'sufficient assurances' that a favourable answer would be forthcoming were Charles II to send his own ambassador to Moscow.[100] To this end John Hebdon was knighted 'in the presence of your Imperiall Maties great Ambassador Knez Peter Semenovich Prosorofscoe'. Because of his diplomatic experience in both courts, Sir John was recommended by the king as the means 'of promoting Our mutual interests'. Prozorovsky left England carrying letters from Charles II for Tsar Aleksei, in which Charles II wrote: 'We shall endeavour on our part to advance, improve, and increase all those meanes and opportunities which may cause our present confederation to transcend all that has been before us.'[101]

Konovalov argues that Aleksei, in analysing the conventional diplomatic style of the royal letters, was to think mistakenly in terms of an Anglo-Russian political alliance. He then asks how Aleksei, with any understanding of the nature of the English position, could not realise that the English protestations of loyalty towards Russia were evoked solely by trade considerations and by the prospect of regaining their exclusive rights in the Russian market? Were the Russians not aware that the England of Charles II did not regard the Russia of Tsar Aleksei Mikhailovich as a power eligible or needed as a political ally?[102] However, we should rather question the assumption – in light of the undeniable mercantile rivalry that existed with the Dutch – that the Russians could be fooled by the diplomatic style of royal letters. Not only did the Russians perfect the style themselves, but Dutch diplomats in Moscow would have forcefully and repeatedly

---

99 Council Notes between Charles and Lord Chancellor Clarendon, November 1662. Chancellor Clarendon to Charles II: 'I pray remember the entertaining these ambassadors will be chargeable to you . . .' See Bryant, *The Letters*, p. 111.

100 'Privy Council note to the Muscovy Company, 25th March 1662'. *PRO*, PC 2/58, p, 358. See also, Gordon, *Diary*, 23 June 1666, vol. 2, p. 222: 'These ambassadours, in their conferences and discourses, giveing great hopes of the priviledges . . .'

101 'Charles II to Aleksei, 7 July 1663'. *RGADA*, fond 35, opis 2, no. 94. (Copy: 'Charles II to Aleksei, 7 July 1663'. *PRO*, SP 91/3, fol. 102.) See: Lyubimenko, 'Anglo-Russian Relations', p. 56, n.1. Hebdon advised the Navy Commissioners: 'The ship wanted for Archangel, to bring over 280 tons of hemp, a present from the Emperor of Russia, might convey over the Russian Ambassador and his company, 115 strong to the said port. Recommends the bearer, Capt. Green, for the voyage.' *CSPD*, 1663–1664, (no. 10), p. 115.

102 Konovalov, 'England and Russia', p. 64.

pressed arguments which undermined, diverted and neutralised any tendency to take proposals at face value. The Dutch even managed to brief Prozorovsky during his journey to London. He received 'instructions from some private persons in Holland, a nation the declared enemies of the English in point of trade'.[103]

In the early 1660s, nevertheless, Dutch opposition to English mercantile ambitions was not as pronounced as before. Moreover, in the Treaty of Kardis, signed between Russia and Sweden in 1661, Aleksei acquiesced in Sweden's acquisition of large areas of the eastern Baltic, and John Dury in Stockholm noted that 'There is a great Inclination here in those who Rule to keep a firme Peace & good Correspondence with England, although there are some that would rather have a breach.'[104]

Conclusion

Unfortunately, however, the Restoration of the Stuarts was not to realise widespread hopes as 1663–4, the 'year of promise', ended in failure. The aims of British diplomacy towards Russia were to be at last clearly and irrevocably revealed. The previously prominent, even dominant, position of the role of the Muscovy Company in securing these aims was to be exposed, but its power to maintain that position was being undermined by the lack of success. For their part, the Romanovs gave increasingly transparent excuses for the delay in revival of the Muscovy Company's privileges, while the Stuarts would not give a clear answer to appeals to join in a crusade against the Moslem Turks.

As the gap between the rhetoric and reality of commerce, war and diplomacy grew, the role of the Muscovy Company as a link between the two dynasties was collapsing under the strain of the contradictions: Restoration Stuart economic self-interest withered in the face of Romanov imperial ambition. Under Tsar Mikhail foreign policy was aimed at strengthening a tenuous domestic order; now under Tsar Aleksei it sought to consolidate and expand the Muscovite state as well as its international standing.

Moreover, we are speaking of the continuing clash of two world views. The Stuarts, in the wake of Cromwell's ambitious 'Western Design', were looking increasingly to the wider world, while the Romanovs, still on the receiving end of the imperial ambitions of others as well as beginning to exercise them again themselves, drove harder bargains as they also widened the focus of their interests, to the east into Siberia as well as to the west into the Baltic.

---

103 *CSPD*, 1663–1664, no. 88, p. 20.
104 'Letter, John Drury to Samuel Hartlib, Amsterdam: 5/15 July 1661'. *The Hartlib Papers*, 4/4/26A–B.

FIVE

The Struggle for Revival, 1663–1676

If, in the first half of the seventeenth century, the Romanov regime faced a precarious existence, by the early 1660s absolutism in Russia was firmly rooted. With the restoration of the House of Stuart, Charles II's primary political objective was to strengthen royal authority and legitimacy throughout his three kingdoms. An active alliance system abroad could increase trade and so protect state economic interests. This necessitated a greater diplomatic effort, and a more active navy.

Accordingly, the maintenance of Russia as a provider of naval supplies continued to be important for Stuart ambition. However, it was not in Romanov interest to restore Muscovy Company trading privileges, at least until a military alliance with the Stuart regime was brokered. Even then, it is difficult to conceive how such an alliance could significantly reduce Ottoman and Tatar vassal encroachments through the Black Sea coast to the Ukrainian steppe and periodic marches on Moscow itself.

The New Diplomacy

With neither a military alliance nor the restoration of Muscovy Company privileges apparent, diplomacy was left to fill this uneasy vacuum. Unfortunately, as yet there were no fixed norms for protocol and ceremonial. Moreover, basic priorities differed: while Paris and the Hague were the most important posts as far as the Stuarts were concerned, the Romanovs conducted their first discussions about diplomatic procedures with Poland in 1672, Sweden in 1674, and the Holy Roman Empire in 1675.[1] Rather than identifying or addressing the fundamental divergence in Stuart and Romanov state interests, however, diplomats on both sides offered cultural explanations to account for the failure to achieve a breakthrough. What was to become the leitmotif of Stuart–Romanov relations in this period was especially pronounced in the first Embassies of the Restoration period, beginning with Carlisle and Dashkov, when hopes and expectations were highest.

---

1 Jones, *Britain and the World*, p. 39; Iuzefovich, '*Kak v posol'skikh obychaiakh*', p. 204.

In July 1663, an embassy from Charles II left for Russia,[2] led by Charles Howard, the first Earl of Carlisle, carrying letters to the tsar.[3] With Carlisle travelled his wife (Countess Anna of Carlisle, daughter of Edward, first Lord Howard of Eserick), his son (Edward, Viscount Howard of Morpeth), Andrew Marvell (as Secretary to the embassy),[4] Colonel Walter Whitford,[5] and a chaplain.[6] Guy Miege accompanied them and wrote an account of the embassy.[7]

Konovalov argued that the personality of Carlisle made him entirely unsuitable for the post of ambassador at such a critical time in the history of Anglo-Russian relations.[8] It seems that in choosing Carlisle, Charles II considered that his noble status would impress upon the Russians the seriousness with which the forthcoming negotiations were to be treated by the British. However, in reality, Carlisle was poorly equipped to conclude successfully negotiations of any sort that required patience, tact and understanding – in short, diplomacy. Sir George Downing, a family relation, reported: 'He hath no language and so must wholly trust his secretary', while Carlisle's brother-in-law commented that he was of more use for parade than for 'business'.[9]

2 *CSPD*, 1663–1664, no. 144, p. 184 – 'June 27, 1663. Capt. Thos. Tedderman to [Sam. Pepys]. Has arrived in the Hope and awaits orders from the Duke of York. If he is to transport the Earl of Carlisle for Russia, begs an additional allowance of stores.' Captain Tedderman transported Carlisle in the *Hope*, whilst it seems that Captain Sayers transported the presents in the *Kent*. Sir John Hebdon to Sir. Wm. Batten, 29 June 1663. 'Recommends Capt. Robt. Sayers, who is well versed in the navigation for Russia [as pilot in the *Kent*, which is to carry Lord Carlisle an ambassador.]' *CSPD*, 1663–1664, no. 150, p. 186. Capt. Tedderman leaves a report of '. . . his voyage to Archangel to transport the Earle of Carlisle and his lady, and of his return to England. Bad weather has much worn the sails and the rigging.' *CSPD*, 1663–64, no. 119, p. 304. See also: 'Sir Wiliam Morice to the Earl of Winchilsea, 1663, July 2' – *HMC* 71, Finch Mss, vol. I, 1913, p. 264.
3 'Charles II to Aleksei, 23 January, 1663' – *RGADA*, fond 35, opis 2, no. 91; 'Charles II to Aleksei, 25 May, 1663' – *RGADA*, fond 35, opis 2, no. 90; 'Charles II to Aleksei, 30 June, 1663' – *RGADA*, fond 35, opis 2, no. 93.
4 Robbins, 'Carlisle and Marvell', pp. 8–17.
5 *CSPD*, 1663–1664, no. 73, p. 156 – 'Petition of Colonel Walter Whitford to the King, for money towards equipping him to return to Russia with the Earl of Carlisle, who goes ambassador.'
6 *CSPD*, 1663–1664, no. 49, p. 198 – 'The King to [the Master and Fellows of St. John's College, Cambridge.] Requests them to dispense with the absence of Brian Turner, fellow of their college, who is in attendance on the Earl of Carlisle, ambassador extraordinary to Russia, still allowing him the profits of his fellowship, and admitting him college preacher, although his catechizing is only partly performed.'
7 *A Relation of Three Embassies*. Konovalov, 'England and Russia', p. 67, states: 'Miege's book is an apologia for the Ambassador's actions: the author is at pains to attribute the failure of the Embassy in Russia to the disloyalty, unreasonableness, and ill will of the Russians, and to present the Ambassador's actions in the best possible light.'
8 Konovalov, 'England and Russia', pp. 65–6; Phipps, *Britons in Russia*, p. 162.
9 'Sir George Downing in a Letter to Lord Clarendon, from the Hague, 1st of April 1664' – Konovalov, 'England and Russia', p. 65.

It is fair to point out that Carlisle, with no previous diplomatic experience, displayed a confidence and assurance that bore no relation to his abilities. But the context of Anglo-Russian relations must be remembered. The Russians had realised in the 1640s that there were no advantages or benefits to be gained for Russia if English merchants were to have exclusive custom-free rights to both Russian markets and Russian products. The New Customs Tariff of 1653 implicitly recognised this. Thus, it could be reasonably argued that whoever the ambassador, and whatever his character, the outcome of the embassy would have been the same. It is also fair to note that there is evidence (lacking for other ambassadors to Russia) to suggest that Carlisle had researched papers on previous Embassies relating to Anglo-Russian diplomacy.[10] Carlisle's misfortune was not that he sabotaged negotiations through his stubbornness and obduracy, but that he gave the Russians an excuse for doing what they had wanted to do from the outset. Ultimately, Anglo-Russian diplomatic relations were characterised not by a misunderstanding or failure to understand each other's views but by a collision of interests. Compounding this problem were the niceties of diplomacy both new and old.

On entering Archangel harbour on 23 August 1663, Carlisle at once informed the foreign community of his arrival: Patrick Gordon noted 'We had notice of the English Ambassadour the Earle of Carlile his arrivall at Archangell with his Lady and a great traine.'[11] After a slight delay caused by the late arrival of a second ship[12], Carlisle left Archangel on 12 September and reached Vologda on 17 October. Letters were sent ahead by the embassy to Moscow. Gordon wrote:

> I received a Letter from the English ambassador and another from M. Bryan, showing that some things were wanting from the ambassadors suit desireing me to provide them so quietly that no body should know, the things were two silver trumpets with banners wherein my lords armes (wch were sent me)

---

10 *CSPD*, 1663–1664, no. 59, p. 170. 'June 15, 1663. Jo. Cooke to Williamson. Sec. Morice wishes him, for dispatch of the Earl of Carlisle, to search for all instructions to ambassadors or agents in Russia, or similar papers, and send them to him; he will safely return them.'; see also, no. 84, p. 175.

11 Gordon, Diary, 6 September 1663, vol. 2, p. 175.

12 *CSPD*, 1663–1664, no. 6, p. 225 'August 1, 1663, York. Sir Thomas Glower to Sec. Bennet. The ship that carries the King's goods to Russia is driven by storms to Burlington.' On September 15, Gower writes a fuller account of what had transpired to Secretary Williamson (ibid., no. 64, p. 272): 'The ship driven back was that which contained the King's present of horses, &c., to the Czar of Muscovy, and the goods of the ambassadors; it was driven from the coast of Norway to Burlington. They had many wants, little money, and no directions in case of accident; sped them away, and helped them with necessaries.' See also *CSPD*, 1663–1664, no. 50, p. 168.

12 halberts or partisans with fringees of his livery etc. I returned ansr 2 dayes thereafter that all should be ready to content & in due tyme.[13]

Hebdon commented on the dignity of Carlisle's initial reception and the civility of the Russians towards his embassy. Carlisle, he wrote, 'hath binn treated by the Emperors officers with the greatest civility and as honourable as possible as these parts afford.'[14] But the roads were to prove impassable, Carlisle complaining of the 'slowness of the winter and the greater slowness of those sonnes of winter the Muscovites'.[15] And so, wrote Gordon in Moscow, 'wee had notice that the English Ambassador was keeping his Christmas at Vologda'.[16]

Despite evidence, including Carlisle's own testimony, which argues for Russian goodwill towards the embassy, Carlisle was later to claim that his entry into Russian territory was marred by 'the pride and rusticity of the Muscovites'.[17] Gordon wrote of Carlisle, 'takeing himself to be affronted at his first reception at the Sea Port, and then much more at his comeing into Mosko, which, albeit done by a mistake and not of purpose, he urged the reparation thereoff with too much heat, whereupon followed some irritations on both sides'.[18]

Konovalov comments that the 'high handedness and sharp protests represent the carping and imaginings of a haughty nobleman rather than the grievances justified by fact'. However, he adds, the Russians were also 'very troublesome and incorrigible in matters of ceremony', for they were to insist that Aleksei was to be referred to in all royal correspondence, as 'Tsar' instead of 'Emperor', 'Serene' in place of 'Illustrious'.[19] Moreover, it was admittedly an ambassador's duty, as the embodiment of the sovereign power he represented, to insist upon details of procedure, through the observance of which his nation's honour was upheld.[20]

---

13 Gordon, Diary, 15 October 1663, vol. 2, p. 176. Thomas Bryan was a Muscovy Company merchant: *CSPD*, 1661–1662, no. 17 and no. 32, p. 97; Phipps, 'The Study of Britons', p. 35. Lachs, *The Diplomatic Corps*, p. 55, confuses the position: 'During the intervals when England had no organized mission to Russia, communications between the King and the Czar were entrusted to English merchants settled in Moscow who received, translated, and passed on all necessary messages. One of their merchants, Thomas Brejn, received the semi-official title of vice-agent after the departure of Charles Howard, earl of Carlisle, but he received no recommendation from the Crown.'

14 'Sir John Hebdon to Sir George Carteret, 18th of November 1663, from Vologda' – PRO, SP 29/88, fol. 16v, and also *CSPD*, 1663–1664, no. 10, p. 344.

15 'Lord Carlisle to Charles II, 12 March 1663' – PRO, SP 91/3, ff 103–4.

16 Gordon, Diary, 1 January 1664, vol. 2, p. 179.

17 Konovalov, 'England and Russia', pp. 67–8 for examples.

18 Gordon, Diary, June 23, 1666, vol. 2, p. 222r-v. See also Gordon, Diary, 6 February 1664, vol. 2, p. 181v.

19 See 'Lord Carlisle to Charles II, 12 March 1663' – PRO, SP 91/3, fol. 103.

20 Lachs, *The Diplomatic Corps*, p. 97.

Nevertheless, on this occasion, Carlisle's petty, point-scoring tactics were to provoke complaints from the Russians as well as harden their attitude.[21] He was not alone. At least, at a lower level, among his entourage, apparently, was a loyalist stout enough to challenge to a duel a Scottish lieutenant in the tsar's army who extolled his master to the diminution of the king. The duel was won by the champion of 'His Majesty of Great Brittaine'.[22]

Carlisle entered Moscow on 6 February 1664. On 11 February, Gordon noted: 'The English Ambassadour had his first audience being convoyed up in the usuall manner all the presents being drawne and carryed befor him. The infantry being ranged on both sides of the way, and the Crimlina or Castle full.'[23] Carlisle, ever mistaken in his assumptions, still considered there to be a chance that British diplomatic objectives could be realised. After his first audience with Aleksei on 11 February 1664, he wrote to Charles II that he had been 'informed from several good hands that it is agreed in Councill that the former priviledge shall be granted'.[24]

Gordon lists the dates of the various conferences and audiences with Aleksei in which Carlisle was to participate, commenting on the outcome that 'The Earle of Carlisle had his 3d conference, and all with little satisfaction.'[25] The Russian non-negotiable position was made clear to Carlisle on 10 March 1664, when two councillors visited and informed him that Aleksei 'would promise Priviledges as soon as the warr with the Pole and the Crim. were ended'. Yet Carlisle still thought it pertinent to write to Charles II that 'I stick to it to have the Priviledges first granted' before the king would agree to a Russian loan.[26]

Carlisle argued that Russia had a moral obligation to repay English merchants for the sacrifices made in lives and money whilst opening up the White Sea trade route. But this argument failed to persuade, as did offers to mediate at the peace talks between Russia and Poland as the price of restored privileges. In the final agreement, the 1628 Charter was to be partially restored, with the option left open to restore it fully once the wars were finished. In short, 10 English merchants as opposed to the 24 of 1628, were to be able to travel from England

---

21 'Russian Complaints against Carlisle, July 1664', in Konovalov, 'England and Russia', Appendix III, pp. 95–104. A summarised and partially translated version appears on pp. 79–82.

22 *A Relation*, p. 302.

23 Gordon, Diary, 11 February 1664, vol. 2, p. 182.

24 'Carlisle to Charles II, 12th of March 1664' – *PRO*, SP 91/3, fols 103–4.

25 Gordon, Diary, 29 February 1664, vol. 2, p. 182v.

26 'Carlisle to Clarendon, 12th of March 1664' – Konovalov, 'England and Russia', pp. 87–91; see p. 89. Information concerning the progress of this Embassy was rapidly disseminated across Europe to other British diplomats on active service. See Bennet, *The Earl of Arlington's Letters*, Vol. II, pp. 18–20.

to Moscow, via the port of Archangel, but, like any other merchants, they would have to pay duty. This, then, was the conclusion to the embassy. Could this be considered a partial success?

At a final audience with Aleksei, Carlisle refused to accept the tsar's gifts. Gordon reported:

> I had notice by my sert & letters that on the 17th the English Ambassadour had refused the Emperours present of sables, saying it was not fitt that he should make any advantage for himself seing in his masters business for which he came he had received no satisfaction, and that 2 dayes thereafter the present which at his first audience he had presented from himself was returned.[27]

Carlisle placed responsibility for the failure of the embassy to restore the Muscovy Company privileges fully on the nature of the Russians themselves. He observed:

> For they are a people who neither know to manage affairs nor practice courtesy, and (as far) as truth and honour, they would think it a disreputation to be guilty of them. Hence it is that to give the Ly is here accounted no affront and to profess themselves slaves is their only ingenuity.[28]

This observation was repeated in a letter to Secretary Bennet:

> What else was to be expected in a country where as other beasts change their colors twice a yeare, the rational beasts change their soules thrice a day? . . . Or what Priviledges could Merchants hope for where Embassadors must all depart from theirs?[29]

This, of course, is disingenuous in the extreme, and a shallow excuse for Carlisle's own failings.

Fear that the impact of Carlisle's report would have a detrimental effect on Anglo-Russian relations prompted the Russians to send an embassy to London, led by the *stolnik* Vasilii Yakovlevich Dashkov along with the *diak* Dmitrii Shepulin. The embassy's aim was to refute Carlisle's interpretation of events and to complain about his undiplomatic conduct. Gordon argued that it was Carlisle's refusal of the tsar's presents 'which offended his Tzarasky Matie so

---

27 Gordon, Diary, 28 June 1664, vol. 2, p. 189.
28 'Carlisle to Charles II, 14 June 1664' – *PRO*, SP 91/3, fols 105–6.
29 'Carlisle to Secretary Bennet, 14 June 1664' – *PRO*, SP 91/3, fol. 107.

highly, that he dispatched a stolnick Vasily Yakufleuf sin Diaskow, in the quality of Envoy to the King to complaine of the Ambassadourr'.[30] Had the Russians known in the autumn of 1664 that Carlisle had attempted to form an alliance between Britain and Sweden that would have been against Russian interests, Dashkov would have been ordered to undermine this very serious threat to Russian security. Such an alliance would have had disastrous consequences for Russian economic and political relations with West European states.

Gordon reported that Carlisle's embassy 'went on from Mosko towards Sweden' on 24 June 1664.[31] From Stockholm, where he was found to be 'in a very high esteme universally for many very good qualityes',[32] Carlisle wrote a series of letters to Lord Clarendon, detailing the advantages that an alliance with Sweden would bestow upon English trading interests. This alliance could have opened up 'without paying Custome'[33] direct English trade with the Baltic city-ports of 'Narva, Nijen, Revell, Riga and Pernow'.[34] An Anglo-Swedish blockade of Archangel would have severely disrupted Dutch shipping, and Russia would have been forced to become reliant upon her only gateway west – the Baltic ports. Secretary of State Sir Henry Coventry noted that Carlisle 'seeme very willing to a warre with Musco ... the thing they seeme earnestly to desire is that wee would impede the Trade at Arche Angel and so oblige the Muscovites to bring all theyre commoditys to Narva – and so be transmitted by the Baltique'.[35]

Carlisle's *A Memorandum on Trade with Russia* argued that such a blockade would have been in British interests. We learn from it that the Baltic ports are open more months of the year, are closer to Britain and pose fewer navigational and natural hazards than Archangel. The Baltic ports are also closer to the hinterland areas in which the exported products were produced. Moreover, the Swedes would uphold religious freedom, thus increasing the 'quality of life' of the proposed English merchants. Perhaps they would also assure English merchants of privileges.

The threat of war was very real. On 4 November 1665, Clarendon instructed Coventry to 'do all you can to engage and dispose them [the Swedes] to warr

---

30 Gordon, Diary, 23 June 1666, vol. 2, p. 222v. See also Gordon, Diary, 26 July 1664, vol. 2, p. 190: 'Vasily Yakufleovitz Deskov ordered & sent to England to complaine of the Earle of Carliles comportment here.'
31 Gordon, Diary, 28 June 1664, vol. 2, p. 189.
32 'Henry Coventry to Arlington, Stockholm, 10 March 1666' – PRO, SP 95/6, fol. 39.
33 'Carlisle to Clarendon, 12 March 1664' – Konovalov, 'England and Russia', Appendix I, pp. 87–9.
34 'A Memorandum on Trade with Russia, C 1664–65' – Konovalov, 'England and Russia', Appendix II, pp. 93–4.
35 'Coventry to Clarendon, from Stockholm, lst of October 1664' – Konovalov, 'England and Russia', p. 77.

upon Mosco, in which they will receive all the assistance and support from hence they can reasonably expect'.[36] Sir Thomas Clifford reported from Stockholm that, in effect, the main issue of diplomatic conflict between Russia and Britain since 1649 could be settled if the government were to 'send two or three frigates to block up Arch Angel, which is said will be force enough to divert trade from the place and bring it to Riga and the Baltic'.[37] Two years later, perhaps with these suggestions in mind, Carlisle was instructed that 'so has been the hereditary maxime of all our Kings Ancestors to keepe the balance evin in the Baltic'.[38]

This sequel to Carlisle's mission to Moscow forms part of the context of Dashkov's embassy to London. Dashkov left Archangel on 25 September 1664 and reached London on 22 December. Here he presented Charles II with a document listing the complaints from the tsar's councillors against Carlisle's conduct. The complaints centred on Carlisle's obstinacy and stubbornness in Russia. For example, Dashkov cited Carlisle's allegation that Ambassador Prozorovsky had purposefully asked for an impossibly large loan two years earlier, so that its refusal could justify the Russian decision not to re-grant privileges. This, Charles II was informed, was a 'slur on the personal honour of the Tsar himself'.[39] However, after the loan was refused, Prozorovsky still accepted Charles II's gifts, diplomatic conduct that Carlisle did not emulate. Gordon reports that Dashkov:

> who comeing into England had but a cold reception, and getting but 3 dayes defrayment, was permitted to live upon his owne, yet, the Earle of Carlisle returning to England upon the relation of his negotiation was justifyed and his comportment approved, thereafter, giveing the Envoy a visitt (whereat he was much surprized), promised his assistance for his friendlyer usage, and so, out of an excess of generosity, interceded with the King so farr that he gott full restitution of what he had disbursed, and was dismissed honourably.[40]

On this occasion, apparently, Carlisle demonstrated an unusual concern for Prozorovsky's plight.

Dashkov had a last audience with Charles II on 17 April 1665, where both sides assured each other of their friendship and amity and exchanged letters to that effect. Charles insisted to Aleksei that:

---

36 'Clarendon to Coventry, 4 November 1664' – Konovalov, 'England and Russia', p. 78.
37 'Sir Thomas Clifford to Charles II, November 1665' – Konovalov, 'England and Russia', p. 83.
38 'Instructions for one sent to Sweden, 1666' – *PRO*, SP 95/6, fols 102, 108; see fol. 104.
39 'Russian Complaints against Carlisle', c. July 1664 – Konovalov, 'England and Russia', p. 101.
40 Gordon, Diary, 23 June 1666, vol. 2, 222v.

James VI and I, after John de Critz the Elder, *c.* 1606, National Portrait Gallery, London

Tsar Mikhail, 'Great State Book', 1671–1672, *Portrety, gerby i pechati Bol'shoi Gosudarstvennoi Knigi 1672g.* (St Petersburg: Arkheograficheskii institut, 1903)

Charles I, After Sir Anthony Van Dyck, *c.*1635–1636, National Portrait Gallery, London

Tsar Aleksei, 'Great State Book', 1671–1672, *Portrety, gerby i pechati Bol'shoi Gosudarstvennoi Knigi 1672g*. (St Petersburg: Arkheograficheskii institut, 1903)

Charles II, John Michael Wright or studio, *c.* 1660–1665, National Portrait Gallery, London

Tsar Fedor, I. Saltanov(?) Daniel Waugh Collection

James VII and II, Unknown Artist, *c.* 1690, National Portrait Gallery, London

The Regent Sophia, *c.* 1689, Abraham Bloteling of Amsterdam, Lindsey Hughes

Fabian Smith, Guildhall Library, London

Grigorii Mikulin, Unknown Artist,
Daniel Waugh Collection

Earl of Carlisle, William Faithorne, 1669,
National Portrait Gallery, London

Petr Prozorovskii, Unknown Artist,
Daniel Waugh Collection

Patrick Gordon, Frontispiece, *Passages from the Diary of Patrick Gordon of Auchleuchries, 1635–1699*, Aberdeen: Spalding Club 1859.

Petr Potemkin, After painting by Godfrey Kneller, Daniel Waugh Collection

Sir John Hebdon, Ferdinand Bol, 1659, Sarah Campbell Blaffer Foundation, Houston

Vasilii Golitsyn, Unknown Artist, Daniel Waugh Collection

London before the fire, Ashmolean, Oxford

Moscow Blaeu, *Theatrum orbis terrarum*, 1643, Aberdeen University

Arkhangel'sk, Blaeu, *Theatrum orbis terrarum*, 1643, Aberdeen University

Vologda, Cornelius de Bruins, *Reizen over Moskovie*, 1711, Rijksuniversiteit, Groningen

Narva, Merian, Ashmolean, Oxford

We find noe evidence or argument to perswade Us that hee the said Earle of Carlisle hath been wanting in his respect of your Imperiall Matie nor in his duty to Us according to the character wherewith Wee honoured him, though hee could have been born with some failings of his in the latter, rather than with the last miscarriage in the former, haveing so unchangeable an inclination and resolution to maintain a perpetuall Brotherly Love.[41]

All this despite the letters plotting war and economic conquest that were now flowing regularly between London and Stockholm. Charles also offered his assistance in the mediation of a Russo-Polish peace.[42]

Because of Russian fear of the English plague, which was to reach its peak in September 1665, Dashkov was quarantined in Pskov on his return from London. The Russian Chancellor refused to see the letter he carried from Charles II. William Parker, one of the Muscovy Company merchants, opened it and after translation brought a copy to the Chancellor.[43] Another ironical and paradoxical consequence of the London plague can be seen in the circumstance that it caused the closing of Archangel without an English blockade and yet stopped the news reaching Moscow that both the British and Swedes had, at the very least, conspired to harm Russian economic interests. The Dashkov embassy, like the English plague, was also to harm Anglo-Russian relations, according to Gordon, who reported in June that 'Vasily Yak. Deskov returned without satisfaction as to his complaint against the earle of Carlile, haveing had but a cold reception, yet by the bounty of the King at his dismission recompenced.'[44]

Gordon and Charles II

The Second Anglo-Dutch war (1665–7), that had broken out unofficially in June 1664 in the colonies and at sea, was officially declared on 4 May 1665. The war created a demand for naval supplies in both Britain and Holland. It delayed all thought of blockading Archangel as it became imperative to secure the existing trade routes, rather than attempt a blockade which would both split British naval forces and divert their attentions towards forcing a new trade route through the Baltic. As this was a sea in which Dutch frigates could operate with greater freedom than the English, their home bases being closer and their knowledge of the shipping conditions greater, the Baltic option would indeed have been very

41 'Charles II to Aleksei, 20 March 1665' – *RGADA*, fond 35, opis 2, no. 95.
42 Paeffgen, *Englisch-russische Wirtschaftsbeziehungen*, p. 170.
43 'William Parker to his Brother' – *PRO*, SP 91/3, fols 114r–116v.
44 Gordon, Diary, 10 June 1665, vol. 2, pp. 210v–211; *CSPD*, 1664–1665, Feb. 1665, no. 141, p. 230, 'Grant to the Earl of Carlisle of 1000 l. on his return from his embassy to Russia.'

risky. The Dutch traded primarily with the Baltic ports for wheat, rye, hemp, tar, pitch and timber. Moreover, they dominated trading activity: for example, from 19 June to 16 November 1650, no less than 986 of 1,035 ships passing into the Baltic from the North Sea were from the Netherlands.[45]

Moreover, it seems that leading members of the Muscovy Company were not willing to risk the disruption of trade caused by the proposed move from Archangel, with all its consequent risks. Clarendon, in a letter to Coventry in Stockholm, dated 7 December 1665, stated the strong Muscovy Company objections and listed the imponderables and risks involved if the White Sea trade route were to be exchanged for that of the Sound, Archangel for the Baltic city-ports of Narva, Reval and Riga. The Muscovy Company merchants, Clarendon wrote:

> who having allwayes driven their Trade by Archangell, will never be willing to change that course, wee do not yet know what number of ships will be required for the stopping that Trade, nor what Preivileges and benefitt wee shall receive by putting it into the other chanell.[46]

Why, however, did these objections become apparent only in late 1665? Could it be that the threat of, and then actual naval warfare with Holland, was to impress upon the minds of the British chief ministers their dependency on Russia for hemp, timber and potash?[47]

With or without restoration of their privileges, the British could not afford to alienate Russia. John Bryan, the Muscovy Company resident in Moscow, received a letter of December 1665 from Charles II to Aleksei, and passed it on to the Russian court.[48] The letter requested that Russian naval supplies – such as masts and tar – be sold only to the British, with their purchase at Archangel by the Dutch forbidden. As Gordon put it in his Diary:

> But now the warr which the king had with France & Holland being like to continue, by the advice of the Moskovia Merchants, the King did writt to the Tzaar by post, showing of the warr he had with France & Holland, & how that

45 Davies, *A Primer*, p. 9. Barbour, 'Dutch and English Merchant Shipping', pp. 261–90.
46 'Charles II to Aleksei, 29 December 1665' – *RGADA*, fond 35, opis 2, no. 97. (Copy: *PRO*, SP 22/60, fol. 86.) See also comments by Aström, *From Stockholm to St. Petersburg*, pp. 13–23.
47 'Charles II to Aleksei, 12 April 1665' – *RGADA*, fond 35, opis 2, no. 96. This letter concerns an Anglo-Dutch dispute between 'a certaine Holand Merchant called David Rutts, together with Thomas Hebdon an English Merchant now residing in Russia' and 'John Osborn an English Merchant now residing in Russia'.
48 'Charles II to Aleksei, 29 December 1665' – *RGADA*, fond 35, opis 2, no. 97. (Copy: *PRO*, SP 22/60, fol. 86.)

he was informed that the Hollanders brought much materialls for their shipping from Russia, which he desired might not be permitted them, and that it
might be free for his Ma: subjects to buy such Materialls.[49]

In January 1666, the Navy Commissioners were fully aware that Holland was
'obliged to venture as far as Russia for her next years supply'.[50]

The Muscovy Company was far from alone in being prepared to risk war
with Holland. The Levant Company, the East India Company and the Royal
Adventurers Trading to Africa had all brought anti-Dutch petitions before
government ministers prior to the outbreak of war, even though, according to
Steven Pincus, all realised that an Anglo-Dutch war 'would be a short-term
economic disaster'.[51]

On 23 June 1666, Gordon was summoned to the Russian Diplomatic
Chancellery to carry Aleksei's reply to Charles' letter. Gordon reports 'the
reasons of sending this message' and tells why it was the Russians were 'sending
a stranger, and why me and not another'.[52] The reasons reflect the combination
of circumstance, chance and deliberate decision. In August 1665, Gordon,
because of the death of his brother, had submitted a petition 'desireing to be let
for England for a tyme'.[53] Moreover:

> no Russe was found willing to go with it [Aleksei's reply], fearing such cold
> entertainment as Diaskow had gott; for notwithstanding it was knowne how
> that he had been sufficiently rewarded and honourably dismissed, yet he
> atributed all this to his owne dexterity, and the fear the King had of offending
> his Tzaarsky Majestie, averring that none thereafter would be defrayed but for
> three dayes, as the ministers of other princes; that all things wer ten tymes so
> dear as in Mosko; and many difficulties more; which, with the Russians unwill-
> ingnes to allow any minister so much money as to maintaine him at any court,
> and also loth to offend the Hollanders, (who had now engrossed all the trade
> almost here), by a publick message, it was resolved to send some stranger, and
> me especialy, because I had petitioned to go thither the year befor, and being
> one of his Majesties subjects, might haply have friends at court.[54]

This then was why Gordon was first considered then chosen for this delicate,
yet unpopular diplomatic mission.

49 Gordon, Diary, 23 June 1666, vol. 2, pp. 222v–223.
50 *CSPD*, 1665–1666, no. 18, p. 188.
51 Pincus, 'Popery, Trade and Universal Monarchy', p. 29.
52 Gordon, Diary, 23 June 1666, vol. 2, p. 223.
53 Gordon, Diary, 1 August 1665, vol. 2, p. 213.
54 Gordon, Diary, 23 June, 1666, vol. 2, pp. 223r–223v.

Liubimenko argued that the Russians were willing to employ foreign nationals in minor diplomatic roles: Andrew Forrett, an army officer with language skills, was translator and special assistant to the Russian embassy of 1663.[55] However, in this case, Gordon was not accompanying a Russian ambassador as an aide, but was leading a diplomatic mission with the role of envoy. In the context of Anglo-Dutch commercial rivalry and open warfare, and its consequent effect on Russian exports, Gordon's mission was not insubstantial.

Konovalov suggested that Gordon was chosen for the diplomatic mission because the Russians recognised that he had excellent connections at the Stuart court, and these connections could be used to Russian advantage.[56] However, Gordon had never previously visited London and had no connections with the English political establishment. His contacts were with the Scottish military high command, and these because of the part that he had played in securing the release of Generals Thomas Dalyell and William Drummond from Russian mercenary service.[57] Gordon had received letters from General Dalyell and Lt. General Drummond, carried by Colonel Whitefuird 'as also a large & particular relation of the passages & estate of effaires in Cristendome'.[58] Indeed, it was both Drummond and Dalyell who were to recommend the unknown Russian envoy to the Scottish Secretary of State, the Earl of Lauderdale. Drummond noted:

> that Gentleman Coll Patrick Gordon Envoye from my old Master the Zaar is a sole discreet young man becaus he is a Scott and imployed about the matter of trad[e] which concerns England, bestow upon him some thing beyond the ordinaire to honor him in his reception and audiences and I doubt not but you will be pleased with him.[59]

Dalyell reinforced this impression:

> My Loird thar is a Gentleman cam from Musko calit Colonel Gordon he is veray ambisheus of your patroneg all I ken say of him is he is a pretay sober and a

55 'Charles II to Aleksei, 2 June 1663' – *RGADA*, fond 35, opis 2, no. 92. (Copy: 'Charles II to Aleksei, 27 May 1663' – PRO, SP 22/60, fol. 80); Liubimenko, *Les Relations*, p. 238; Gordon, Diary, 25 June 1666, vol. 2, p. 224: 'his M. graced me with a 100 Rubles for my jorney and a 100 Rubles for my pay in advance.'

56 Konovalov, 'England and Russia', p. 49.

57 Dukes, 'Problems', in Smout, *Scotland and Europe*, pp. 143–66.

58 Gordon, Diary, 1 October 1665, vol. 2, p. 214v. Gordon only began writing to these Generals in April 1665. Before then his British contacts consisted of his 'Father, unkle & brother John in Scotland'. Gordon, Diary, 11 January 1665, vol. 2, p. 224.

59 'Drummond to Lauderdale, 9 October 1666' – BL, Add. Ms 23125, fols 122–3.

veray Siuel[civil] man what he is cam for I kno not bot it wil import to yor Lordship himselfe. Begen pardon for this boldness.[60]

Gordon himself had also written to Lauderdale, describing himself as '(being not only a stranger to yo'r L. but to my owne native Countrey in a manner)'.[61] These recommendations would then have been passed on to the Court of St James, where background information on a Russian envoy was needed.

Gordon, while not a fully professional diplomat, had some knowledge of the contemporary political scene. Evidence within his Diary attests to some interest in diplomatic occurrences in this period. For example, in September 1664, 'Lt. Coll. Vasily Mich: Tepkin sent to Polland with business previous to the Ambassy to be sent to the Parliament or Seym.'[62] In December of the same year, Gordon writes: 'This yeare in the month of August a treaty betwixt the Roman Emperour & the Turkish sultan concluded for 20 years.'[63] He also appears to have taken an interest in Russo-Georgian diplomatic relations: 'The Prince of Georgia called Nicolay Davidovits received with state in Mosko.'[64] In another entry, crossed out, Gordon indicates that he was at least partially aware of the troubled relations between the two trading rivals: 'In the beginning of March was the great sea fight betwixt the English & Holl.'[65]

From 1667, when A. L. Ordyn-Nashchokin became director of the Diplomatic Chancellery, according to Norman E. Evans, he 'seems to have been responsible for a noticeable increase in the number of foreigners employed as diplomats by Tsar Alexei Mikhailovich (1645–76) in preference to the incompetent and fantastically uncouth Russian nobles who had long excited the contempt of the western European courts to which they were accredited.'[66] This perhaps overstates the case, as it is difficult to discern any considered Russian policy towards employing foreign nationals, while the bad manners of the Russian nobles were not generally noted. It appears that the staffing of Embassies and diplomatic missions to London was made on an *ad hoc* basis, in response to the prevailing availability of qualified people. However, the only agreements reached between Russian and British diplomats after the revocation of the Muscovy Company

---

60 'Dalyell to Lauderdale, Leithe 2 October, 1666' – *BL*, Add. Ms 23125, fol. 108.
61 'Bruges 16/26 Sept 1666. Gordon to Lauderdale' – *BL*, Add. Ms 23125, fol. 96. Copy held in *AUA*, Ms 3051/2/9.
62 Gordon, Diary, September 1664, vol. 2, p. 194v.
63 Gordon, Diary, December 1664, vol. 2, pp. 201–201v The conditions of the Treaty are listed.
64 Gordon, Diary, 19 April 1666, vol. 2, p. 218.
65 Gordon, Diary, June 1666, vol. 2, p. 220.
66 Evans, 'A Russian Royal Letter', p. 76. See also O'Brien, 'Early Correspondence', pp. 606–19.

privileges concerned troops and military provisions. Therefore, the fact that
Gordon was a soldier and in a position to evaluate the possibilities of acquiring
men and *matériel* in England and Scotland could have been of considerable
advantage.

Irrespective of a formal blockade of Archangel, which could have been ruinous
for Anglo-Russian relations, the Anglo-Dutch war had reduced the volume of
Muscovy Company trade.[67] As it was, relations between Britain and Russia were
at extremely low ebb – no privileges had been granted to Carlisle's embassy,
Dashkov had spoken only of insults and dishonour, Muscovy Company ships
were even prevented from entering Archangel for fear of the plague. In an atmosphere of distrust and suspicion, then, Gordon was to deliver a letter from Aleksei
to Charles II, replying to that of 29 December 1665, and to present Aleksei's
compliments to the king.[68]

On 28 June 1666, Gordon paid his respects to 'the Boyar Elia Danielovitz & his
Lady who with others there were very kind to me'[69] and then set off in company
with his brother-in-law Charles von Bockhoven, Captaine Rae, Peter Pile an
apothecary, Caspar Staden, and two servants with six 'yempshiks', 13 persons
altogether.[70]

Having written in advance to Hebdon and Lauderdale from Bruges about the
nature of his mission, he arrived in Dover on 1 October, and the next day reached
London, where he 'was heartily welcomed by Sir John Hebdon & Family'.[71] As
well as offering hospitality, Hebdon shared with Gordon his knowledge and
understanding of Restoration diplomatic protocol and practice.

Hebdon was able to offer advice in two capacities: as a Muscovy Company
official and as an ex-Russian envoy to London. Earlier that year he had
proposed to supply the Navy with 'hemp, tar, and masts from Russia, in the
event of a rupture with Denmark, which would obstruct the trade in the east'.[72]
That is to say, if Britain went to war with Holland, the latter would control the
sea passage into the Baltic and thus cut naval supplies from Danzig and Riga.

---

67 *CSPD*, 1666–1667: no. 158, p. 44; no. 138, p. 129.
68 Gordon's diplomatic instructions from the Diplomatic Chancellery are stated in a letter
    to Lauderdale, 26 September 1666 – *BL*, Add. Ms 23,125, fol. 196. 'The money was brought
    to me, with his M. letters & instructions' on 27 June 1666. See also, Gordon, Diary, 28 June
    1666, vol. 2, p. 225.
69 Gordon, Diary, 28 June 1666, vol. 2, p. 225.
70 Gordon, Diary, 30 June 1666, vol. 2, p. 226. A 'yempshik' or 'iamshchik' was a post
    horseman funded by the state who enjoyed special quarters in Moscow.
71 Gordon, Diary, 2 October 1666, vol. 2, p. 247.
72 *CSPD*, 1665–1666, no. 108, pp. 392–3: 'Sir John Hebdon to the Navy Comrs.' Hebdon
    provides us with a good example of a man unashamedly bearing the burden of dual
    responsibilities.

Thus, British naval integrity was hostage to an unblockaded Archangel. This advice was to enable Gordon to implement his official Russian diplomatic instructions, and also adapt his mission to the fact that, due to the Great Fire of London, which had raged between 2 and 6 September, destroying much of the city, the court was officially in mourning. So he kitted out himself and his brother-in-law in an appropriate manner.[73]

Hebdon was thus able to greatly help Gordon on his first diplomatic mission; he had the expertise, experience and contacts that Gordon at this stage in his career had yet to cultivate. Via Lauderdale, Sir John arranged the first informal audience with Charles II for the evening of 9 October. Gordon duly handed over the tsar's letter, which stated that the Dutch were to be forbidden to buy any naval supplies from Russia and that the English would be permitted to purchase Russian shipping material once the plague was over. Gordon wrote in his Diary:

> I found his Majesty standing under a Canopy bareheaded with many nobles about him. Being entred the Roome and performed the usuall reverences, I tooke the Emperours Letters from my brother in law, after I had the short complement, his Ma. was pleased to receive the letters with his owne hand and gave them of imediately to one standing by, and asked me for the good health of his ma: which I answered after the ordinary way, then his M: was pleased to say that this message so much the more acceptable, that the Tzaar had been pleased to entrust one of his owne Subjects with it. and caused tell me, that I might use the freedome of the Court.[74]

In October and November, Gordon sent memorials to 'the Secretary office & concerning my business and held meetings with the Lord Chancellour in which the Privileges were discussed'.[75] On 13 November, 'wee debated the business I came for, as also that of priviledges very sharply'.[76]

In late 1666, according to James Sutherland, 'the only paper the King's subjects were allowed to read was the official *The London Gazette*, and from that they could learn little more than what was happening in foreign countries.'[77] This paper was instituted by Charles II himself in 1666 as a bi-weekly

---

73 Gordon, Diary, 9 October 1666, vol. 2, p. 247v.
74 Gordon, Diary, 9 October 1666, vol. 2, 248r–v.
75 Gordon, Diary, 5 November 1666, vol. 2, p. 251.
76 Gordon, Diary, 13 November 1666, vol. 2, p. 251.
77 Sutherland, *The Restoration Newspaper*, p. vii. For a general history of *The London Gazette* from 1665–99, see Handover, *A History*, chapters I–III. The original newsletters can be read in the British Library on microfilm – *BL*, OGE 70. (Hereafter, *London Gazette*, date and no. of issue.)

(Mondays and Thursdays) newsletter. It printed an 'official' summary of polit-ical, diplomatic and military events[78] that had been reported by its foreign correspondents, as well as domestic news of interest to its readership – the activities of the king and royal household.[79] These correspondents were usually diplomats, merchants, soldiers, travellers and spies.[80] All information passed from the European informants back to the office of Henry Bennet, the Earl of Arlington and Secretary of State for the Southern Department, Middleton, then on to the editor, Joseph Williamson.[81]

Some of the government officials Gordon was to meet were connected with *The London Gazette*. In late December 1666, he dined with the Earl of Middleton,[82] and then in early January 1667, again: 'I dined with my Lord Middleton, and was very kindly entertained.'[83] During the previous six months, Gordon had been in constant contact with Moscow, receiving 14 batches of letters, some of them containing diplomatically important information. For example, 'Received Lts from Doctor Colins dated Mosko 25 7.bris from Mr Bryan . . . whereby I had notice of the birth of a Prince called John.'[84] Almost certainly, using such information and making use of his London contacts, Gordon became a Moscow correspondent for *The London Gazette*.[85]

He also consolidated his friendly relations with Dalyell and Drummond, having written to the former on seven occasions and received eight replies. In

---

78 Williams, *A History*, p. 23: 'no other journal could have the authority of the *Gazette*, deriving information from the source: the court. It might not say all but what was said was correct.' Macaulay, *History*, p. 406: 'whatever was communicated respecting matters of the highest moment was communicated in the most meagre and formal style.' *The London Gazette*'s first number was the twenty-fourth of *The Oxford Gazette*, and its publication in early February 1666 marked the court's return to London from Oxford after the plague.

79 Muddiman, *The King's Journalist*, p. 195: *The London Gazette* 'contained little domestic news other than the Royal Proclamations and a number of advertisements. Schwoerer, 'Liberty of the Press', p. 207.

80 All correspondents are listed in Fraser, *The Intelligence*, Appendix IV, pp. 153–5. Foreign correspondents sent dispatches from Moscow, as well as other Eastern European cities, for example Königsberg, Danzig, and Warsaw. News which concerned Eastern Europe usually ran under the byline 'Warsaw'. For example, *The London Gazette*, no. 27, 'Warsaw, January 25th'. News discussed included Russo-Polish relations. *The London Gazette*, no. 48, 26–30 April 1666, ran a news item under the byline: 'Riga, April 5'. *The London Gazette*, no. 99, 25–29 October 1666, contained the byline: 'Narva, September 21'. These were exceptional reports.

81 *The Diary of John Evelyn*, vol. IV, p. 38: Arlington, who had succeeded Secretary of State Nicholas, October 1662 'remitted all to his man Williamson'.

82 Gordon, Diary, 28 December 1666, vol. 2, p. 253v.

83 Gordon, Diary, 8 January 1667, vol. 2, p. 255v.

84 Gordon, Diary, November 1666, vol 2, p. 251.

85 See Pernal, 'The London Gazette', pp. 1–17.

November 1666, both generals had played a leading role in suppressing the Covenanter Rebellion in Scotland. Gordon would have been well aware of the details of this action, which he would have relayed to Russian officials upon his return.[86]

Leaving London, Gordon made the point of saying farewell on 22 January to both Secretaries of State and his Diary noted that this courtesy was especially directed towards the Earl of Middleton 'to whose kindness I was very much obliged'.[87] Earlier that day Gordon had been commanded by Charles II: 'Colonell Gordon, I have a servant there in Russia called Gaspar Calhoffe, for whom I have written diverse by me to your Emperour I wonder that at our desire he doth nor dismiss him pray speake to the Emperour that he dismiss him'.[88]

In London, Gordon had made an excellent impression, having been given freedom of the court by Charles II as a special mark of favour.[89] Furthermore, as he left, the king 'commanded to give me 2 hundred pounds sterling upon the account of my expences and a gift'.[90] Konovalov commented that through 'tact and commonsense' Gordon succeeded in restoring Anglo-Russian relations and 'in some measure' was responsible for the revival of British trade interests in Russia.[91] On a personal level, Gordon had made contacts within the Stuart court and at the heart of government.

Gordon was to return to Moscow with a letter from Charles II to Aleksei: 'Your Imperial Maties letter bearing date the 29th June pass came to Our hand by Yo.r Imp.ll Maties Colonel Patrick Gordon being in answer to Ours dated by Our Courte at Oxford the 29th day of December last'.[92] The letter informed Aleksei that the plague in England was over,[93] and thus, implicitly, the Russian rationale for closing Archangel to the English was now rendered redundant and trade must be re-established. The letter went on to ask Aleksei to forbid the Dutch but allow the Royal Navy to buy and transport masts and tar 'out of your

---

86 This information is taken from: Gordon, Diary, late July/August 1666–January 1667, vol. 2, pp. 244v–256.

87 Gordon, Diary, 22 January 1667, vol. 2, p. 258.

88 Gordon, Diary, 22 January 1667, vol. 2, pp. 257v–258.

89 On 9 October 1666, 'The Kings Lock Smith by order brought [a key] wch opened the doores to the Parke, Galleries and pr passages in the Court, to whom I gave 20 shillings & to his attendants. my name being graved on it', Gordon, Diary, 9 October 1666, vol. 2, p. 249.

90 Gordon, Diary, 10 December 1666, vol. 2, p. 252v.

91 Konovalov, 'England and Russia: Two Missions', p. 49.

92 'Charles II to Aleksei, 25 January 1667' – *RGADA*, fond 35, opis 2, no. 98. The letter itself is badly damaged – the middle portion is either unreadable or missing. However, the text of the letter is reproduced in: Gordon, Diary, January 1667, vol. 2, pp. 258v–260v: 'The Copy of [Royal?] letter to the Emperour of Russia, 28 December 1666'.

93 Gordon, Diary, 27 May 1667, vol. 2, p. 273r–v.

Imp.n Ma.ties Dominions by such persons as ye officers of our Navy shall employ and in such quantity as they shall desire.'[94]

Luckily, Gordon realised in time a mistake in the superscription of this royal letter, 'Illustrissimo written for Serenissimo'. And so, he had 'desired Sr John Hebdon to represent the matter to the Secretary of State, telling that I durst not for my head carry such a letter with me and that it was well knowne what a great deale of stirr there had been in Mosko with the Earle of Carlisle in Mosko about that word, the Secretary very readily promised to amend it.'[95]

When Gordon reached Moscow, the Diary records that in June 1667 'being at last permitted to come into the Prikase I presented his M. letters to the Boyar, and thereby gave my statine knigy or a relation of my Negotiation. The Boyar told me that I must have a litle patience before I could be admitted to his Ma.ties hand.'[96] This action marked the formal end of his diplomatic mission on behalf of Aleksei.

By 20 August 1667, Gordon was able to write his third letter to Williamson apologising: 'I had not omitted writting to you by these two last posts had not his Majesties business hindered me.'[97] In July, he had written: 'wee have no passages heer wherof befor this you cannot but have had information by your other Correspondents.'[98] Gordon informed Williamson of the postal service, its efficiency and the routes: via Riga and Mr Benjamin Ayloffe from Moscow to London; and from London via Danzig and Riga to Moscow. As with other correspondents, Williamson, Secretary of State and editor of *The London Gazette*, used Gordon as an extra-diplomatic unofficial source of information. The first of Gordon's letters, written in Lübeck, a stopover on the way to Moscow, sets the tone, content and style of all other letters: 'ther shall be nothing worthy of observation in the Eastern parts *that shall* [italicised words deleted] escape you.'[99] As Gordon returned to Moscow, the New Trade Statutes were being drawn up in Moscow. They provided greater protection for Russian domestic trade by 'imposing heavier burdens upon, and restricting the field and scope of activities of foreign merchants in Russia.'[100] Before this letter was sent, Gordon through his correspondence, had begun to build upon the friendships he had made in London: he received Prince Rupert's letter in favour of his father-in-law from 'Sir John Hebdon and to his son the esquire.'[101] These petitions were successful

94 'Charles II to Aleksei, 25 January 1667' – *RGADA*, fond 35, opis 2, no. 98.
95 Gordon, Diary, January 1667, vol. 2, pp. 257r-v.
96 Gordon, Diary, June 1667, vol. 2, p. 274.
97 'Gordon to Williamson, 20 August 1667' – *PRO*, SP 91/3, fol. 131.
98 'Gordon to Williamson, 9 July, 1667' – *PRO*, SP 91/3, fol. 130.
99 'Gordon to Joseph Williamson, Lubeck, 22 March 1667' – *PRO*, SP 82/11, fol. 101.
100 Konovalov, 'Patrick Gordon's Dispatches from Russia, 1667', p. 54.
101 Gordon, Diary, 9 March 1667, vol. 2, p. 268.

and by early July Gordon informed Williamson: 'P.S. Coll Bockhoven for whom the King did writt to the K. of Pol [King of Poland] was at liberty befor the letter came, yet doth he most humbly acknowlege his Maties favor in tending it, and all those who assisted it.'[102] Gordon had also written 'to Doctor Davison in Varso [Warsaw]', another correspondent of *The London Gazette*.[103] Thus, it is possible to argue that although Gordon's embassy and his diplomatic role officially ended with the delivery of Charles II's letter to Russian bureaucrats in Moscow, 'his Majesties business' was now, since he was *The London Gazette*'s Moscow correspondent, to continue to fall within Gordon's competence.

More New Diplomacy

In response to the royal letter of 1667, which Gordon had carried to Moscow, Aleksei sent two Russian envoys, Mikhail Nikitich Golovin and Fedka Akishev, with the news that the Truce of Andrusovo had been arranged between Russia and Poland. The Treaty, which brought to an end the Thirteen Years Russo-Polish War (1654–67) and confirmed Russian retention of Smolensk and part of Ukraine, was signed on 20 January 1667. Gordon would have passed this information on to Williamson and Hebdon, after he himself 'had notice of the 13 yeares truce betwixt the Emperour of Russia & the King of Polland'.[104]

Carlisle had been promised that, when the war was over with Poland, the question of privilege restoration would be addressed. Moreover, the Russian envoys were to carry back to Russia the message that the British had made peace with Holland at the Treaty of Breda, 21 July 1667, so ending the Second Anglo-Dutch War (1665–7).[105]

Throughout the period of Gordon's stay in London, Muscovy Company members and, in particular, Sir John Hebdon, (a member of the Court of Governors of the Muscovy Company) petitioned Charles II to allow another diplomatic mission to be sent to Moscow. The aim was to recover the Muscovy Company privileges and so restore a trade advantage. For example, on 11 December 1666, Hebdon sent proposals to the Navy Commissioners 'for the providing hemp, tar, masts, tallow and other naval stores from Russia . . . Desires his proposal be kept a secret from the merchants, that another may not

---

102 'Gordon to Williamson, 9 July 1667' – *PRO*, SP 91/3, fol. 130.
103 Gordon, Diary, 15 March 1667, vol. 2, p. 269.
104 Gordon, Diary, 12 March 1667, vol. 2, p. 268v.
105 'Charles II to Aleksei, 20 September 1667' – *RGADA*, fond 35, opis 2, no. 101. (Copy: *PRO*, SP 104/175, fols 47–49.) Charles acknowledged Aleksei's last letter dated 'the fourth of June last presented Unto Us in Our Royall Court by your Imp.all Maiesties Envoye Mixhala Nikiticha Golovinka.'

plough with his heifer.'[106] Persistent rumours of a Russo-Polish peace treaty meant that within hours of its unofficial confirmation, the British embassy was to begin its journey. 'Sir John Hebdon, Knt one of the Gentleman of Our Royall Privy Chamber' was to be sent to Russia as 'Envoy Extraordinary'[107] armed with detailed instructions.[108]

The embassy left for Moscow in the spring of 1667 and returned in the autumn of the following year. Patrick Gordon would certainly have briefed Hebdon in London concerning the prevailing Russian predisposition to restore the privileges and he certainly knew of the intended embassy. Moreover, as a correspondent of Williamson, editor of *The London Gazette*, he reported on political, diplomatic and military events in general and proved to be a valuable source for detailing evidence of the progress of the embassy in particular. On 29 October, Gordon gave details to Williamson about the depressed state of Muscovy Company trade to Russia:

> wee have had at Archangell this year about 32 or 35 ships, 9 whereof Hamburgers and Bremners, the rest Hollanders, and a very slight trade by reason of our new projects and imposts. Litle action in thes parts at present, this not being the season for it.[109]

This reiterated a comment Gordon had made earlier in the month: 'Our trade by reason of the impost and these Marine Warres is greatly decayed.'[110] He also related details of Hebdon's diplomatic progress, which was no doubt partly impeded by his abrupt resignation from Russian government service.[111]

The tsar received Hebdon on 20 September 1667.[112] This reception followed a meeting on 15 September 'in the Ambass Office – what good will be done wee cannot know as yet'.[113] Throughout the embassy, Gordon acted as a second

---

106 'Sir John Hebdon to the Navy Comrs.' 11 December 1666. *CSPD*, 1666–1667, no. 64, pp. 337–8.

107 'Charles II to Aleksei, 28 April, 1667' – *RGADA*, fond 35, opis 2, no. 100.

108 'Hebdon's First Set of Instructions' – PRO, SP 104/175, fols 3–7. 'Hebdon's Second Set of Instructions' – PRO, SP 91/3, fols 12Or–123v. Hebdon was to complain at the amount of money his Embassy was afforded; he asked for £500, but was to receive less. 'Treasury Warrants, April 1667' – PRO, SP 29/88, fol. 129. *CSPD*, 1667, p. 65: Hebdon to receive £360 for his equipage.

109 'Gordon to Williamson, 29 October 1667' – PRO, SP 91/3, fol. 135.

110 'Gordon to Williamson, 1 October 1667' – PRO, SP 91/3, fol. 133.

111 'Orders are gone . . . hence to let Sir John Hebdon com[e] forward to Mosco.' 'Gordon to Williamson, 20 August 1667' – PRO, SP 91/3, fol. 131. Konovalov, 'England and Russia: Two Missions', p. 58.

112 'Gordon to Williamson, 1 October 1667' – PRO, SP 91/3, fol. 133: 'On the 20th passat Sir John Hebdon his Majesties Envoy had audience.'

113 'Gordon to Williamson, 15 October 1667' – PRO, SP 91/3, fol. 134.

opinion for Williamson in his attempts to gauge and assess the likelihood of the ban on privileges being revoked. To this end, Williamson contacted Gordon, who replied: 'Nothing could be mor acceptable to me as yours of the 23 Aug: I shall not faile in requitall to acquaint you of what passeth heer, which at present is very little.' This letter again ends with an ever-polite reminder of their symbiotic relationship: 'I hope you will inform me at all times the state of our owne countreyes which is the one thing I most value, as likewise to be esteemed.'[114]

Hebdon carried back to Charles II a letter from Aleksei dated 15 June 1667.[115] As well as being Charles II's Envoy Extraordinary to Russia, Hebdon was also to become, simultaneously, the new principal agent for the Muscovy Company; earlier in the century, Smith and Digby had both acted in the same dual capacity.

In April 1668, Sweden entered the Triple Alliance, signed on 13 January 1668, with Britain and Holland, against the power of France. The Swedish resident in London asked Charles II if British diplomats could mediate between Russia and Sweden. Sir Peter Wyche (1628–99) was chosen as Charles II's Envoy Extraordinary to Russia in 1669. Sir Peter Wyche was a scholar of Geography, a professional diplomat and a Charter Member of the Royal Society, for whom he was to write a treatise on his visit to Russia. His embassy lasted from 4 February until 24 November 1669.[116] As well as attempting to mediate between Russia and Sweden, Wyche was instructed to enquire about the restoration of Muscovy Company privileges.[117] In January of 1668/9, the British resident in Warsaw had reported on how political realignment now presented opportunities for trade:

From Moscow we have news that the Czar has concluded a peace with the Persian Sofi, vice, that in Future none at all of the Merchandizes shall be transported anymore into Turkey nor into Italy but to the countreys wch makes a great joy here and there, for it has bine all wayes the merchantes complaints, and if it be soe, some doe not doubt of recouvering their losses sustain'd.[118]

---

114 'Gordon to Williamson, 15 October 1667' – *PRO*, SP 91/3, fol. 134.
115 This action is acknowledged in: 'Charles II to Aleksei, 15 January 1668' – *RGADA*, fond 35, opis 2, no. 102.
116 *Calendar of Treasury Books*, vol. III, 1669–72, p. 1; p. 10; p. 183; p. 186. Wyche was to receive £400, half for equipage and half 'for three months' ordinary as envoy to Muscovy'. Konovalov, 'Patrick Gordon's Dispatches from Russia', p. 58, has stated that Wyche's embassy 'is a subject deserving of separate study'. Such a study has yet to be undertaken. Wyche's treatise for the Royal Society gave details of how grain was kept, about birds, frost and the effects of cold on substances such as oil, blood, iron and steel. Royal Society Library, RBO/4/30.
117 'Instructions to Sir Peter Wyche, 18/19 January, 1668/69' – *PRO*, SP 104/175, fols 178–9.
118 *PRO*, SP 101/39 (unsorted.)

Wyche was in constant contact with London on his journey to Moscow. It was reported on 9 March that 'Tomorow or the next day Sr Peter Wyche intends for Dantzick, though the Earle of Carlisle persuaded him to remain there til he heard from England, for that there was not so great necessity for his going to Russia.'[119] *The London Gazette* reported: 'Riga, May 3. The first instant arrived here Sir Peter Wiche, his Magesty of Great Britains Envoy to the Court of Muscovy, having been on his way civilly Treated and Complimented by the Magistrates of Dantzick, and afterwards entertained at Coningsberg and Prussia.'[120] On reaching Moscow,[121] Wyche presented his credential letters to the tsar and a memorial to the Diplomatic Chancellery, seeking permission to intercede in the Russo-Swedish dispute.[122] Charles called for the restoration of privileges and protection 'on behalfe or for Our Subjects and Merchantes residing and trading in your Imp.ll Ma:ties Dominions.'[123]

However, Wyche was told that he could also mediate between Russia and Sweden – but only when the war in the Crimea had ended. Similarly, the Muscovy Company privilege 'to trade without paying customs' would be restored once 'His Imperiall Majesty shall have concluded the war with the King of Poland and with the Crimean Khan.'[124] After a final audience with the tsar, Robert Yard, secretary to Wyche's embassy, was to summarise its achievements in a letter to Williamson: 'in some things he had had a very unsatisfactory answer, in others he had obtained none at all.'[125] However, *The London Gazette* of 12–16 August[126] was less emotive and more understated in describing these meetings: 'Several debates have been lately held in this Court about the establishment of Trade with foreign Princes to which the Czars Factors have been called in for their advice, but nothing is concluded.'

Polish opinion, according to a correspondent writing from Danzig, considered this diplomatic mission to have been such a failure that it was predicted: 'If the Pole and the Muscovites should have Warr they hope England will assist ag.st the

---

119 'Robert Yard to My Master' [Williamson], 9 March 1669' – *PRO*, SP 82/11, fol. 18.
120 *The London Gazette*, 23–29 May 1669, no. 365: 'Sir Peter Whyche came to Riga the 17th of Aprile though no letters from him as I heare of.' 'Swanne to Sec. of State, Hamburg 4 May, 1669' – *PRO*, SP 101/39 (unsorted).
121 *The London Gazette*, 2 July–2 August 1669, no. 387, 'Moscow, June 23'.
122 'Wyche's Memorial to the Diplomatic Chancellery, Summer 1669' – *PRO*, SP 91/3, fols 180v–181r.
123 'Charles II to Aleksei, 15 January 1668/69' – *RGADA*, fond 35, opis 2, no. 102. (Copy: *PRO*, SP 104/175, fols 175–7.) *CSPD*, October 1668–December 1669, p. 163 – 'January 20, 1669: Warrant to Sir Edw. Griffin to pay 10l. to Gideon Royer, for embellishing with arms, badges, &c. a letter sent to the Emperor of Russia, by Sir William Wyche, Envoy Extraordinary.'
124 'Wyche's Reply, 1669' – *PRO*, SP 91/3, fols 184–5.
125 'Yard to Williamson, 9 August 1669' – *PRO*, SP 91/3, fols 174r–v.
126 *The London Gazette*, 12–16 August 1669, no. 391.

Muscovites.'[127] Before leaving Moscow, Wyche was informed that Dashkov had left for England – his diplomatic mission was to discuss the restoration of Muscovy Company privileges.[128] Another report noted: 'Sir Peter Wyche is leaving Moscow; and that Emperor has some thoughts of sending an Envoy to England, to make a compliment of the privileges, &c., enjoyed in those territories by the English, and to desire his Majesty to be umpire in the diferences between him and the Swede.'[129] But Wyche was to report that Dashkov, on reaching Riga, was conveniently detained by the Poles. Wyche himself left directly for Poland and was issued with a new Privy Seal for this purpose on 24 November 1669.[130]

During this period, mercenary officers recruited from England or Scotland into the Russian army carried letters between the Stuart and Romanov monarchs. However, individual couriers aside, the next diplomatic exchange in 1673 involved the son of the immigrant Dutch merchant Andrei Denisovich Vinius, who had founded and owned the famous ironworks at Tula. Andrei Andreevich Vinius was described in the state papers as 'a person with seven or eight attendants' and 'a person of good parts, an admirer of arts or anything that is ingenious . . . being postmaster general of Russia and Muscovya.'[131] His mission was to rally Britain, France and Spain into a political and military alliance with Venice, Poland and Russia against the Ottoman Empire. Paul Menzies, another Scot in Russian military service, had the task of recruiting the papacy to the cause – all Christian European monarchs were to fight against the Turkish infidel.[132] *The London Gazette* reported: 'Dantzick, April 17 . . . the Czar of Muscovy hath at several times sent to acquaint the King with the great inclination he has, to employ with him all the Force of his Empire against the common Enemy of Christendom, which how far that Monarch will manifest, when there may be occasion, time must show.'[133] Regarding Vinius in partic-ular, the Venetian secretary recorded that 'the Muscovite minister pretends that he has no further commission, though he is ready to listen, for the sake of remaining on his travels at the cost of this country.'[134]

127 'Dantzick, 12/22 March, 1669/70' – *PRO*, SP 101/39 (unsorted).
128 'Wyche to Lord Arlington, 17 August 1669' – *PRO*, SP 91/3, fols 176v–177v.
129 *CSPD*, October 1668–December 1669, p. 495.
130 'Yard to Williamson, 15 September 1669' – *PRO*, SP 91/3, fols 178r–v.
131 *CSPD*, 1672–1673, pp. 613, 618; *CSPD*, 1673, pp. 1–2: See also, p. 10 and p. 194. These refer-ences reveal personal, rather than inter-state diplomatic, detail concerning the Envoy's stay in London.
132 Dukes, 'Menzies and his Mission', pp. 88–94. For an examination of Russo–Venetian relations of this period, see Longworth, 'Russian–Venetian Relations', pp. 88–94.
133 *The London Gazette*, 5–8 May 8 1673, no. 779. See also: *The London Gazette* issues no. 785, 809, 821.
134 *CSPV*, 1673–1675, no. 50, pp. 32–3.

In fact, Vinius was specifically instructed to find out about the international situation. He duly reported on the Anglo-French alliance against Spain, as well as the international relations of the Pope and the Empire. Among other observations made on his return, he pointed out that Great Britain had a mixed system of government, monarchical, aristocratic and democratic, going on to explain that this was government by one person, by leading individuals, and by the people respectively. Where important matters such as war, peace and finance were concerned, Vinius noted that the king summoned parliament, whose workings he went on to describe in some detail. He contrasted the limited monarchy of Great Britain with the absolute monarchy of France.

In London, Vinius had two audiences before King Charles II, with his brother the Duke of York and other lords in attendance. But the Russian envoy was not to gain Stuart support for the Romanov cause. In a letter carried by Vinius, Charles explained that Britain was geographically in no position to aid Russia in an Ottoman war: 'The great distance between Our Kingdomes and that of Poland cuts off all possibility of sending any Land forces thither; And for those of the Sea, (wherein our Strength and Power chiefly consists) as thay would have but little influence upon the Turkish Sultan in his Warres against Poland.'[135] Although the Third Anglo-Dutch War (1672–4) was underway, this explanation was not completely credible. After all, British (largely Scottish) mercenary regiments had fought for Sweden, Poland and Denmark throughout the century, while substantial numbers of British soldiers were in the tsar's service at the time of the Vinius mission.

Commerce

In spite of the, at times, fervent diplomatic activity, the second half of the seventeenth century became an era of relative decline for the English in Russia. In the late 1650s and 1660s, typically only four ships a year made the journey to the White Sea. However, there were years when only one English vessel was dispatched to Archangel and at least a couple of years with no shipping whatsoever. Moreover, British commercial presence in the Muscovite interior continued to be minimal. In 1659, two English merchants were allowed to journey with their wares to Moscow. By 1664, the number of such individuals had reached four to five each year. In 1669, there were only two English

---

135 'Charles II to Aleksei, 9 April 1673' – *RGADA*, fond 35, opis 2, no. 104. (Copy: *PRO*, SP 104/183, fols 128–33); Vinogradoff, 'Russian Missions to London', pp. 50–4; Kazakova, 'A. A. Vinius', pp. 351–5, 359–60.

merchants present in Moscow. Clearly, the English were having trouble in fully exploiting the privileges secured by Carlisle's mission.[136]

There was little sign of the Muscovy merchants being able to do much with more generous privileges, unless the real goal was merely to restore the intermediary role they had enjoyed between the Russians and the Dutch up to 1646. The English community had limited influence on the Muscovite market. A rather typical example is the failure of Richard Gasrunt in 1666 to acquire a monopoly in masts and tar in the name of John Hebdon.[137] In 1670, the share of English merchants of the duties collected in Archangel was only 9.7 per cent (R3,498 out of R35,968). This proportion rose only very marginally to 10.4 per cent in the following year. In 1673, Thomas Hebdon was the only English merchant at the Archangel fair. His duty payments – R326.78 – constituted less than 1 per cent of the total collected.[138]

The number of English ships visiting Archangel annually never exceeded four and in some years, it was only two. For example, in 1668, the Company commissioned only two ships, with a total capacity of 540 tons, for the London route, and one 100-ton vessel for Leghorn. In 1669, the Company had insufficient subscriptions of tonnage for one 'considerable shipp' and only 10 tons for Leghorn by the original deadline. In 1676, however, subscriptions for London temporarily reached 1,500 tons, with another 105 tons 'for the Straits', i.e. Italy.[139] By the mid-1670s, English merchants served only the Leghorn–Archangel route in addition to direct trade with London. The known

---

136 *PRO* E 190. The numbers of interlopers from ports other than London seldom exceeded two in any given year; Martens, *Rossiia i Angliia*', p. 35; Demkin, *Zapadnoevropeiskoe kupechestvo*, I, p. 47.

137 Kellenbenz, 'La signification économique', pp. 44, 58.

138 For instance, in 1667, the Muscovy Company resolved to exempt its ships from duty payments 'in regard of the danger of the tymes by reason of the Warrs'. Additional expenses were incurred due to the need to commission convoy protection. At the same time, the Company incurred considerable expenses in the late '60s for special Envoys to the tsar for the purpose of regaining lost privileges, yet with no success. *GHL*, Ms 11,741/1, pp. 13, 15, 38; *RGADA*, fond 137, Arkhangel'sk, 1670 g., no. 5, fols 22–3, 25v; no. 6, 1671 g., fol. 21; 1673 g., no. 7, fol. 38v.

139 In 1670, the subscriptions were already higher: 491 tons for London and 506 tons for Leghorn, enough for four ships. This was followed by 569 and 56 tons respectively in 1671. In 1674, subscriptions for London totalled 517 tons. In 1678, 720 tons was subscribed for London and 21 tons for Leghorn. The corresponding numbers in 1679 were 641 and 57 tons respectively. In 1680, 1,000 tons was underwritten for London and 134 tons for Italy. *GHL*, Ms 11,741/1, pp. 25, 27, 40, 61–2, 96, 122, 156, 191. Sometimes, the small volumes of shipping turned out to be insufficient and, for example, in 1676, there was a request for a 270-ton early ship. Similar pleas were made in 1678 and 1681. In 1679, the Company actually agreed to reduce subscriptions by 51 tons to fit everything on the available vessels. *GHL*, Ms 11,741/1, pp. 121, 171–2.

total value of English exports to Russia was £17,765 in 1663, compared to Russian exports to England of £24,000. The corresponding figures in 1669 were £40,000 in English goods and a surprisingly small total of £9,239 in Russian exports.[140] Even the more generous of these figures would have given the English a very modest 'market share' of perhaps 6–8 per cent, with the total value of Archangel's exports typically varying between R600,000 and R800,000 in the 1670s and 1680s.[141]

By 1667, the Company had 'desisted from setting forth shipps for the Whale fishing in Greenland' and agreed to permit London soap makers to effectively take over the business. However, in 1670, one 140-ton ship was sent to Greenland and the Company agreed to 'incourage to inlarge this ffishing'. There is little evidence of sustained success, even though another ship followed in 1671.[142] At the same time, at least some Russian goods came to England from Hamburg and Narva. Indeed, the status of Narva's trade was a source of great controversy for the Muscovy Company, which, *de iure*, still had the right to levy duties on it. However, many of the ships returned to Hull, Newcastle, York and elsewhere, which made control more difficult and forced the Company to send special supervisors to the leading outports. Moreover, many of the ships claimed to have departed from Reval, which belonged to the Eastland Company's sphere.[143] Given its limited scale of operations, the Company remained highly vulnerable to accidents. In 1673, only two English vessels returned home, having spent the winter in Archangel. In 1674, the total number was three. In September 1675, an English vessel was wrecked off the Irish coast on its way home. In 1676, two English vessels returning from Russia were thrown on to an island off Cape North, although a Dutch vessel rescued some of their equipment.[144] By 1675, English trade with Russia was described as being in a state of total decay, although a plan was developed to secure a contract for the Company to export 400 barrels of caviar per annum, which was deemed sufficient for equipping two vessels.[145]

Conclusion

The struggle for the revival of the special relationship was failing as the diplomatic impasse represented fundamentally divergent state interests, as well

---

140 Demkin, *Zapadnoevropeiskoe kupechestvo*, I, p. 75.
141 Repin, *Vneshniaia torgovlia*, p. 89; *RGADA*, fond 137, opis Arkhangel'sk, nos 5–9, 11, 13–15, 17, 20, 22, 23, 25–6, 29, 31a, 32.
142 *GHL*, Ms 11,741/1, pp. 16–17, 34, 43, 48, 57.
143 *GHL*, Ms 11,741/1, p. 9 and ff., 57–8.
144 Lyubimenko, *Les relations*, p. 272.
145 Ibid., p. 271; *CSPD*, 1675–6, p. 241.

as a different interplay of foreign policy and domestic order for the Stuart and Romanov regimes. The Romanovs were adhering to their belief that there were no advantages or benefits to be gained from restoring the exclusive rights and privileges of the Muscovy Company. The Stuarts would not be drawn into a pan-Christian war against the Ottoman 'infidel'. In 1672–3, 'widely seen as a watershed in England and Europe',[146] Vinius was among Russian representatives sent throughout the continent to bring the powers into the crusade as Turkish incursions grew. The Third Anglo-Dutch War began to the accompaniment of a French invasion of Holland. The interests of the two dynasties were again divergent.

146 Miller, *The Stuarts*, p. 167.

SIX

Towards Termination, 1676–1688

The period 1676–88 in Stuart–Romanov relations witnessed regime change in both Russia and Britain. Tsar Aleksei died in 1676, and was succeeded by Fedor III. At Fedor's death in 1682, Sophia was declared Regent for young joint tsars Ivan V and Peter I. Three years later, in 1685, Charles II was succeeded by his brother James VII of Scotland and II of England. At the beginning of the period, renewed diplomatic initiatives designed to increase commerce and tie Britain to a Europe-wide military political and military alliance against the Ottoman Turks were mounted, but rhetoric of commitment continued to fall short of reality then and later. There was no lack of effort, but differences in levels of political will and strategic orientation, resources and capabilities could not be bridged.

Late Diplomacy

With the death of Aleksei in 1676, and the accession of Tsar Fedor III, formal diplomatic exchanges were resumed between Britain and Russia. Information had continued to reach London from letters sent from Moscow, via Riga to Danzig. One such letter could easily have been sent by Patrick Gordon: 'I have this day from Mosco dated 5/15 Januar as followeth . . . Wee are talkeing here of sending an Ambassador to England to restore, to that Nation, their former Previledges of a free Staple wch I may wish may prove true.'[1]

Fedor's first imperial letter to Charles II announced his accession, the death of Aleksei and expressed a desire that the two countries should remain in peace and friendship. A translation of this letter mentioned 'opening a trade for Persian silks at Archangel'. The letter was to be 'communicated to the Company, to make a fit use of it so far as the interests of that trade may be concerned in it'.[2] Charles's reply, carried back to Russia by the Russian diplomat Trefan

---

1 'Sanderson to Williamson, 9 January 1675', PRO, SP 88/14, fols 13–14. For a unique description of the funeral procession see: Appendix: *The London Gazette*, 13–16 March 1675/1676, no. 1077. Mosco, February 11.

2 'Fedor to Charles II, 8 February 1676', PRO, SP 91/3, fol. 205; *CSPD*, 1676–1677, p. 209.

Nemchinov, expressed his 'condolences and congratulations', and reaffirmed the brotherly relations between the two countries.[3]

The Muscovy Company,[4] led by John Hebdon, son of the deceased Sir John Hebdon[5], who wished to be considered as envoy, attempted to make use of this opportunity by petitioning Charles II to renew attempts at re-securing the lost privileges. Moreover, the Muscovy Company merchants John Gold and John Joliffe had informed Charles II in July of 1675 'of the great decay of English trade in the dominions of the Emperor of Russia, occasioned principally by his taking away the English privileges and banishing all the English from Moscow, and confining them to that non-inhabitable port of Archangel'. They had petitioned Charles II that with Fedor 'having made profession of great friendship to his Majesty, there is now the opportunity in some measure to renew trade and settlement in those dominions' by 'his letter to the Emperor'.[6]

Hebdon's petition was successful and it was commanded that he receive money from the Lord Treasurer.[7] His embassy, including a chaplain, Christopher Bateson, left England on 16 September 1676 and returned on 15 July 1678.[8] His instructions gave the reasons for employing him 'as well as for the good opinion we have of your fidelity to Us and Our service, as more especially for the knowledge your education in those parts must have given you in the language, customes & particular forms of that Countrey'.[9] He received two diplomatic letters, as well as his diplomatic credentials as envoy, which he was to present at the first meeting with Fedor. The tsar was reminded of the 'benefit and advantage of Our Subjects who have been found so many ages so usefull to

---

3 'Charles II to Fedor, 11 September, 1676', *RGADA*, fond 35, opis 2, no. 105 (Copy: *PRO*, SP 91/3, fols 213–14). 'Charles II to Fedor, 12 September 1676', *PRO*, SP 104/118, fols 25–6: 'in your letter of ye 8 of February last, by the Bearer Trefann Memithenore, your Envoye, of the death of the most illustrious Princes, our most dear Brother Alexie Michaelowich'. 'Russian Envoys Pass in Latin', *PRO*, SP 104/118, fols 26–7.

4 'The Humble Representative of the Moscovia Company' 1676', *PRO*, SP 91/3, fols 302–4.

5 'The Humble Proposalls of John Hebdon, 1676, *PRO*, SP 91/3, fols 206–7, 243–4. John Hebdon Esq. was the son of Sir John Hebdon, who had died in 1670.

6 *CSPD*, 1675–1676, p. 241. See also: ibid, no. 106; ibid, no. 107. But it was the death of Aleksei, rather than Fedor's profession of friendship, that provided the impetus to this diplomatic contact.

7 *CSPD*, 1676–1677, pp. 299, 301; *CSPD*, 1676–1677, p. 344.

8 *CSPD*, 1676–1677, p. 332.

9 'Hebdon's Instructions, 30 September, 1676', *PRO*, SP 104/118, fol. 34.

one another in their Trade and Commerce'. [10] Charles then made a fresh request for 'the re-establishing of the English Company in their Ancient Priviledges and Settlement in Russia' now that the war with the Crimean Tartars and the Poles was over. [11] If general privileges could not be restored, Hebdon was instructed by the Muscovy Company to attempt to acquire specific concessions for their merchants. [12] These included the 'right for the merchants to live in various cities and the exemption from the payment of custom duties and fees'. [13]

Hebdon's first audience of 2 April 1677 was reported to London:

> I have just now advice from Riga That they had letters dated Prim May from Mosco wch tell them Monsr Hebdon had audience from the Czar: 2 d April wth all tokens of Esteem and friendshipp, that the Czar was very weake two Lords being forced to raise him up from his chair, at his askeing of our Kings good health and that hee expected in a few dayes to be admitted to a conference. [14]

It was followed by a second audience on 8 May. Here Hebdon presented the second letter that argued for the resumption of privileges. However, the Russian position was unchanged: the resumption of war was expected in the Crimea and only a temporary truce, as opposed to a permanent peace, had been signed with the Poles. Furthermore, Fedor was aware of the revenues that would be lost were privileges to be restored. Again, supposed military necessity was to mask commercial expediency as a reason for not renewing the privileges.

10 'Charles II to Fedor Alexeowich, 16 September, 1676', *RGADA*, fond 35, opis 2, no. 106. (Copy: 'To the Emperor of Russia by Mr. Hebdon, Charles II to Fedor, 16 September 1676', *PRO*, SP 104/118, fols 31–2.) See also: 'September 27, 1676. Warrant to Sir Edward Griffin for payment of 30l. to Gideon Royer, the king's writer, flourisher and embellisher, for writing, flourishing and embellishing three skins in vellum . . . being for three letters to the Emperor of Russia one whereof was sent by his envoy, Trefann Memthenore, the other two by the King's own envoy, John Hebdon.' *CSPD*, 1676–1677, p. 340.
11 'In Russia Mr Hebdon's Cred.lls', *PRO*, SP 104/118, fols 29–31, and 'Mr. Hebdon's Instructions, 30 September 1676', fols 33–7. See also: 'Charles II to Fedor, 16 September, 1676', *RGADA*, fond 35, opis 2, no. 107.
12 'Instructions from the Right Worshipfull the Governor and the Fellowship of English Merchants for the Discovery of New Trades, Usually called the Muscovia Company unto John Hebdon, Esq., 16 September, 1676', *PRO*, SP 91/3, fols 210–213.
13 Phipps, *Britons in Seventeenth-Century Russia*, p. 181. See also: *CSPD*, 1673–1675, p. 599, 20 February 1675, for a proclamation prohibiting the importation into England of cordage or cable yarn, except 'such as is made in Russia from the hemp of that country.' The proclamation was aimed at the relief of the plight of English rope makers.
14 'Sanderson to Williamson, 5 June 1677', *PRO*, SP 88/15, fol. 16. See also fols 14 and 18 for references to Hebdon and confirmation that 'an Rich. Daniel at Riga' who acted as a link in the information flow between London and Moscow. 'Sanderson to Williamson, 16 February 1675', *PRO*, SP 88/14, fol. 15: 'Mr. Richard Daniel a merchant of our Company at Riga.'

In Moscow, other foreign diplomatic representatives were attempting to influence the direction of Russia's foreign policy. The Danish resident, Fredrick Gabel, supported by the Dutch representative, Van Keller, pushed for a Russo-Danish offensive treaty against Sweden.[15] Perhaps stimulated by this political agitation, and in disappointment with the failure of the Russians to restore the lost Muscovy Company privileges, Hebdon proposed, in a letter to Williamson, the initiation of an Anglo-Polish war against Russia together with a withdrawal of merchants and, probably, a blockade of Archangel, too.[16] Making use of Van Keller's 'observations', Eekman has argued that Hebdon, rather than pressing for an Anglo-Polish attack upon Russia, promoted an Anglo-Swedish alliance. However, as Hebdon's own letters contradict this, Van Keller must have been mistaken.[17]

Certainly, the proposition had echoes from the previous decade when Carlisle had proposed an Anglo-Swedish alliance against Russia and a blockade of Archangel in 1664. However, in 1677, the idea did not receive as considered a response. Charles II thought it a 'wild notion'. Moreover, since the blockade would have been coupled to 'immediately warning off all his [Charles II's] subjects out of Russia', the ideas of the embargo of personnel into Russia and the demand that those present leave 'immediately' were equally untenable.[18]

Hebdon delayed his departure, arguing that he had to collect debts owed both to English merchants[19] and to his late father for expenses incurred on an earlier diplomatic mission to Russia.[20] He insisted that he would depart only when an order to that effect was received from Britain.[21] In particular, he requested privileges for a group of 26 merchants, although his instructions required him to omit the less prominent merchants from his list in the event of Russian intransigence.[22] The Russians in reply merely repeated their old arguments about the impossibility of taking action until the arrival of a lasting peace. In response, Hebdon even offered to send 52 warships to the Baltic in

---

15 Eekman, 'Muscovy's International Relations', p. 54.
16 'Hebdon to Williamson, February 27, 1677', PRO, SP 91/3, fols 235–6.
17 Eekman, 'Muscovy's International Relations', p. 55.
18 'Williamson to Hebdon, May 11, 1677', PRO, SP 104/118, fol. 45.
19 'Hebdon to Williamson, October 23, 1677', PRO, SP 91/3, fols 269–70.
20 Hebdon stated that the Russians owed his father 337 rubles, but the Russian government was to claim that, on the contrary, Sir John's estates owed the Russian government 3,000 rubles. See, 'Fedor to Charles, November 14, 1677', PRO, SP 102/49, fol. 42.
21 'Hebdon to Williamson, 12 June 1678', PRO, SP 91/3, fols 257–8. Lachs, *The Diplomatic Corps*, p. 16, does not interpret Hebdon's insistence upon a king's letter to initiate his departure as a delaying tactic: '. . . but he was not permitted to do so without expressed permission of the King; this he finally received, at the advice of the Company, late in 1677.'
22 PRO, SP 91/3, fols 235 ff., 261 ff.

order to eliminate any Swedish threat. More revealingly, however, Fedor professed awareness of the loss of revenues that restoring the privileges would cause to the Muscovite Treasury.[23] Hebdon, disappointed and incensed by the negative Russian attitude, was now ready to resort to extreme measures. He suggested that English merchants should leave Russia within six months and proposed that those remaining should be declared rebels and have their goods confiscated. The Russians grew increasingly frustrated over the envoy's behaviour. He was eventually forced to leave in March 1678 after one of his servants murdered a Russian, something that, in turn, caused a diplomatic incident.[24] Fedor, in letters to Charles II, complained of public brawling, the fatal wounding of a Russian soldier by Charles Jordan, and general unseemly, unruly and not to say undiplomatic behaviour, initiated and encouraged by the envoy of Charles II.[25]

Hebdon was told by Williamson that an 'Enclosed Memoriall from the Dutch Amb.r happened to come to his Maties hands charging you with a very great miscarriage in point of conduct in your employment there.'[26] Hebdon was reminded and cautioned that 'upon the whole his Matie requires you to conduct yr self, as to the Bounds of yr Businesse & Negotiation with the instructions you carried with you, & not to meddle in anything further'. Van Keller most probably sent a relation of this incident to the Dutch ambassador in London in an attempt to disrupt Anglo-Russian relations by having Hebdon recalled. In a letter dated 17 June 1677, he wrote: 'I am counteracting Hebdon's plans as much as I can.'[27] Van Keller was formally appointed diplomatic representative to Moscow by the States General in 1677, and so this attempt to disgrace Hebdon would have indirectly promoted his own position within the diplomatic community.

Charles II promised to investigate the allegations, reinforced by a Muscovy Company petition stating that they did not know 'what effect it may have to the damage of that trade'[28] and that 'the said John Hebdon may bee punished according to the crimes and misdemeanours he has committed shall appeare to be

23 Paeffgen, *Englisch-russische Wirtschaftsbeziehungen*, pp. 178–9; Herd, *General Patrick Gordon*, p. 73.
24 Paeffgen, *Englisch-russische Wirtschaftsbeziehungen*, pp. 179–80.
25 'Fedor to Charles II, February 27, 1678', *PRO*, SP 102/49, fol. 43; 'Fedor to Charles II, September 1, 1678', *PRO*, SP 102/149, fol. 44; *CSPD*, 1678, Addenda, 1674–1679, p. 582. Gordon, Diary, 18 March, relates a pertinent incident.
26 'Williamson to Hebdon, 11 May 1677', *PRO*, SP 104/118, fol. 45.
27 Eekman, 'Muscovy's International Relations' p. 55.
28 *CSPD*, 1678, Addenda, 1674–1679, p. 601. Hebdon had been specifically warned before leaving England that 'wee foresee there may be some difficulty in the thing, and therefore it will require your best care and adresse in the management of it.' 'Mr Hebdon's Instructions, September 30, 1676', *PRO*, SP 104/118, fol. 35.

deserve[d]'.[29] Despite the fact that Gordon was aware of Hebdon's quarrelling, he reported that Hebdon 'certainly hath used all dilgence and possible endeavours, and too his great expenses and trouble hath maintained his Royal Majesties honour to the utmost'.[30] Hebdon had the chance to set out his own account before Charles II, being informed that 'It will be expected for you at yr returne, that you give unto my hand in writing not only a narrative [but also] an account of the present state of the last Court & Country, in all particulars, according to the standing Rule, set down for all to see that serve his Maty abroad in any character'.[31] Hebdon left for home in March 1678.

In 1680, Prince Peter Potemkin was sent by Fedor as ambassador to both Britain and France. *The London Gazette* reported: 'Moscow, July 27. We are told that the Czar has resolved to send ambassadors to England, France and Spain, and other Courts to notifie his marriage, and to exhort those Princes to enter into some common engagement against the Turks'.[32] This mission was apparently more concerned with generating goodwill rather than raising substantive issues. Potemkin had an audience with Charles II in November 1681:

On Thursaday his Majesty gave audience to the Russian Ambassador, who brought a present from the Duke of Muscovy of fine silk hangings, carpets and some sables. His Majesty received him very kindly and has him placed in Lady Williams' house at Charing Cross and allows him 25 l. a day as long as he stays here.[33]

It had appeared to one seasoned Russianist in Stuart diplomatic service that Muscovy Company privileges would be restored. Sir Peter Wyche wrote on 24 January/4 February 1680/1: 'I visited on Saturday the Muscovite Envoy, who was here in his way to France, Spaine, and then (as he told mee) to England; Hee seemed to insinuate, he was to offer the Trade as wee enjoy'd it formerely, and as

29 'Charles II to Fedor, 13 June, 1678', *RGADA*, fond 35, opis 2, no. 108. (Copy: *PRO*, SP 104/118, fols 53–5.) See also Tsar's reply: 'Fedor to Charles II, January 23, 1679', *PRO*, SP 102/49, fol. 45.

30 'Gordon to Williamson, 28 January 1678', *PRO*, SP 91/3, fol. 276.

31 'Williamson to Hebdon, 20 July, 1677', *PRO*, SP 104/118, fol. 46. See also: 'Extract from a letter relative to John Hebdon. Envoy of the King of England to Moscow, 1677/1678, February 20', *HMC*, 36 Ormonde Mss, New Series IV, (1906), p. 115.

32 *The London Gazette*, 13–16 September 1680, no. 1547. See also: Lossky, 'Dutch Diplomacy'; 'Wyche to Sec. of State, 8/18 February 1680/1681', *PRO*, SP 82/16, fols 251–3 (see especially fol. 252).

33 *CSPD*, 1680–1681, p. 591. Ambassador Prince Peter Potemkin saw, 'by the ambassadors particular command', 'a play called the Tempest and later 'the second part of the siege of Jerusalem.' *CSPD*, 1682, p. 24.

I was promised, it should be restored.'[34] However, Fedor's letter to Charles II expressed a willingness only to remain in friendship and amity.[35] In reply Charles II acknowledged he had received 'notification of the favourable Peace, your Imp.ll Maty has lately concluded with the Poles, which has been imported to Us by your Imperiall Maties Ambassador Peter Ivanowich Potemkin Stolnik and Gentleman of Uglitz'.[36] But no mention was made of the possible restoration of the Muscovy Company privileges. Private conferences and discussions held between the ambassador and Muscovy Company officials were also to prove fruitless.[37] This was the first and last embassy from Fedor to the Court of St James. Charles wrote one more letter to Fedor before the tsar's death, in which he closely catalogued the continual failure of each bid for restoration of Muscovy Company privileges, ending the letter: 'We have thought fitt at present to mention to your Imperiall Majesty the many disappointments Our Subjects have made with the Cause of their Trade within your Imperial Majesties Dominions.'[38]

Gordon And James II

In 1682, Tsar Fedor Alekseevich died. He was succeeded by two more of Aleksei Mikhailovich's sons, one from each of his marriages, Ivan and Peter (the future Peter the Great), with their sister Sophia as Regent. As was customary on such occasions, a letter was sent by messenger (Dmitrii Simonovskii) to inform Charles II of this news.[39] Charles replied with the usual protocol of condolences

---

34 'Sir Peter Wyche to [Sir Leoline Jenkins], January 24/February 4, 1680/81', *PRO*, SP 82/16, fols 241–133, see fol. 241r. According to 'Proposals submitted to the Committee for Trade by the Provost of Linlithgow to the Secretary of State, 1681': '. . . the improving of the Muscovia traid will be worth the consideration . . ', *SRO*, PC 12/17.

35 'Fedor to Charles II, September 14, 1680', *PRO*, SP 102/49, fol. 46.

36 'Charles II to Fedor Alekseevich, 9 January 1681/2', *RGADA*, fond 35, opis 2, no. 110.

37 'W. Blaithwaite to the Governor of the Muscovy Company, November 29, 1681', *PRO*, SP 104/119, fol. 22. Vinogradoff, 'Russian Missions', p. 61: 'Then my Lord Conway, Secretary of State, asked him if he had any Power to treat about Trade, or the restoring of our Priviledges, which werre very great in K. Charles the first time, but after his Death were taken away; to which he answered no.' See also: *HMC*, 24 Rutland Mss Report XII.5, (1889), p. 60 and p. 63 for descriptions of the Russian ambassador's reception and conduct in London.

38 'Charles II to Fedor Alekseevich, 12 April, 1682', *RGADA*, fond 35, opis 2, no. 111. (Copy: *PRO*, SP 104/118, fols 62–8.) See also: 'Mr Warwick [to Secretary of State], Stockholm, June 19, 1682', *PRO*, SP 95/12, fol. 19.

39 'Ivan and Peter to Charles 11, June 9, 1682', *PRO*, SP 102/49, fol. 47. Vinogradoff, 'Russian Missions', pp. 63–4; Evans, 'A Russian Royal Letter', pp. 75–82. Another version of this letter interestingly refers to both tsars: 'Our Czarskie Highness', but only one by name 'Duke Ivan Alexeowich': 'Ivan and Peter to Charles II, 9 May 7190', *PRO*, SP 104/119, fols 39–41. See also: 'Credential of the Russian Envoy, 9 May 7190', *PRO*, SP 104/119, fols 69–70; 'Recredential to the Envoy of R. 1682', *PRO*, SP 104/119, fols 71–2.

and congratulations, expressing a hope that the troika of mutual interest – 'Friendship, good Correspondence and Entercourse of Trade' – which bound the two countries together, would now be strengthened.[40]

In 1684, Hebdon tried to become an envoy to the tsars, but his petition that 'in regard of great sums expended by him and his father in his Majesty's service, an order for his allowance to be made up equal to that of other envoys to Muscovy and that in lieu of his great debt he may be put into some suitable employment' met with no positive response.[41]

For his part, in the course of 1685, as during the proceeding 20 years as a commanding officer, Patrick Gordon would have had a keen interest in Russo-Turkish, and Russo-Polish relations.[42] Not only did peace with neighbouring countries mean that Muscovy Company privileges would be restored, but in principle it signalled Gordon's release from Russian military service. Because Gordon was stationed in Kiev during this period, he was fully conversant with the main thrust of European political efforts to create a common military alliance against the Ottoman Empire. In March, he wrote: 'Ambassadors from the Pope, Rom. Emp. State of Venice, Schach of Persia, & other Princes were to be in Varsavo all perswading & offering assistance for continuance of the warr against the Hereditary enemy of Christendome.'[43] Gordon was in regular correspondence with diplomatic sources in Moscow and received 'particular letters from the Hol: Resident with Complements and Forreign Newes'.[44] Moreover, Gordon also realised that a greater toleration of Catholics and Catholicism within Russia hinged upon a successful outcome of the contemporary diplomatic negotiations taking place in Moscow.[45]

He was soon to learn of an event of great significance for Roman Catholicism back in Britain. Whilst in Kiev, he 'received notice by gazets & letters from Mosko of the death of our King & that the Duke of York was succeeded to all his

---

40 'Charles II to Ivan and Peter, November 24, 1682', *RGADA*, fond 35, opis 2, no. 112. (Copy: *PRO*, SP 104/118, fols 41–3).

41 *CSPD*, May 1684–February 1685, p. 244.

42 In January of 1685 Gordon notes the return of 'Michael Suslow whom wee had sent to Poland & Hungary', describing his 'relation in writeing, wherein he magnified the great victoryes as well as the Losses of the Christians in Hungary'. Gordon, Diary, 14 January 1685, vol. 4, p. 53.

43 Gordon, Diary, 21 March 1685, vol. 4, p. 66.

44 Gordon, Diary, 8 February 1685, vol. 4, p. 59. He had written regularly to Van Keller amongst others, petitioning to be released from Russian mercenary service. For example, in 1685, he was to write on 4, 10 and 24 March.

45 Gordon, Diary, 8 February 1685, vol. 4, p. 59: 'from P. Schmidts informing, that, the Rom: Emp: former Ambassadours Stallmaster Kurts was shortly to be in Mosko with letters from the Emperour to the Tzars'. See Hughes, *Sophia*, pp. 125–6, for details of these negotiations.

Kingdomes & Dominions whom God long preserve'.[46] Having referred to one island 'Carolina',[47] he now named another 'Jacobina'.[48] Gordon's professional interest, his religious persuasion and political loyalties combined to maintain a high level of understanding and a varied, almost unique, perception of political, social, economic and military events across a broad geopolitical plane.

The occasion for a new embassy had arisen, and Gordon, again petitioning to be allowed to return to Scotland, was to have his wish fulfilled the following year. In fact, he was to become the next official but informal envoy between Regent Sophia and James II and VII, between Russia and Britain. Gordon was to toast, for the first time, the health of King James, with fellow Scottish countrymen: 'being our King's birthday, wee kept it with all the usuall Solemnity. drinking his Ma-ties & other usuall healths in wyne out of my owne wineyard'.[49] And now, he was to go to London to meet James on behalf of the Russian government.[50]

Events in 1686 began well for Gordon. On 18 January, he 'sollicited the Boyar [V. V. Golitsyn] about my going out of the Countrey and was bidd bring a petition'.[51] The following day, he 'had orders to be lett of my wyfe & children staying in Mosko in pledge'.[52] In late January, over a four-day period, he was dismissed but ordered to return, by the very centre of power in Russia. He was 'at their Ma-ties hands, receiveing a Charke of brandy out of the yongest his hand, with a command from him to returne speedily'.[53] Then, he 'was at the Princesse [Sophia] her hand who required me to returne speedily, and bring at least one of my sonnes with me';[54] He 'tooke my leave of the Boyar who desired me to returne speedily & not to drowne him my Cationer, and to writt to him by every Post'.[55] Then, on 29 January, Gordon paid his respects to the foreign diplomatic community in Moscow and received further instructions from the Russian government:

46 Gordon, Diary, 23 April 1685, vol. 4, p. 70.
47 Gordon, Diary, 14 April 1685, vol. 4, p. 69v.
48 Gordon, Diary, 12 May 1685, vol. 4, p. 73.
49 Gordon, Diary, 14 October 1685, vol. 4, p. 91v.
50 Phipps, *Britons in Seventeenth-Century Russia*, p. 328: 'Gordon was again in England in 1669 and 1686 but on each occasion he carried no letter from the Tsar and apparently had no diplomatic function to conduct: however, both times he undoubtedly met with government officials and with members of the Muscovy Company.' This quotation represents the standard understanding of Gordon's diplomatic achievements in the 1680s. See Hughes, 'V. T. Postnikov's 1687 Mission', pp. 447–60.
51 Gordon, Diary, 18 January 1686, vol. 4, p. 100v.
52 Gordon, Diary, 19 January 1686, vol. 4, p. 100v.
53 Gordon, Diary, 26 January 1686, vol. 4, p. 101.
54 Gordon, Diary, 27 January 1686, vol. 4, p. 101.
55 Gordon, Diary, 28 January 1686, vol. 4, p. 101.

I dined with Mr Boetenant and diverse others and afterwards in the towne, tooke my leave of the Secretary of Estate, and Mr. Vinius, from whom I received a verball comission, by order of the Chieffe Minister of Estate [V. V. Golitsyn], concerning their Ma-ties effaires. In the Slabod I tooke my leave of the Hollands Resident, and others my nearest ffriends.[56]

This mission, then, did have a diplomatic bias; the absence of formal royal correspondence is explained by the fact that Gordon received, as he writes, a 'verball commission'. We would thus expect Gordon, when in London, to attempt to make strenuous efforts to meet with and talk to King James, in order to comply with V. V. Golitsyn's order. He would also use this opportunity to launch a concerted effort to secure his release from mercenary service in Russia. Indeed, the visit ended with King James promising to petition the tsars for Gordon's release. When his release was not granted, Gordon attempted through the influence of his position to gain the post of British envoy to the tsars. This would allow for another attempt at release from Russian service, also ensuring that some of his grievances were redressed.[57]

As Gordon shows himself to be well aware of the social and political under-currents of this period, we likewise should place this Roman Catholic profes-sional soldier and Russian envoy at the Court of St James in his contemporary context. The reign of King James VII and II (henceforth James II) has been interpreted in various ways, but the main argument concerns whether or not James intended to impose an absolutist regime in the three kingdoms. To support the view that both Charles II and James II consciously sought to strengthen the powers of the Crown during the 1680s in order to impose abso-lutism, historians have highlighted the idea that royal prerogative was employed to appoint judges, purge the militias and pack Parliaments.[58] A fear of 'Popery and arbitrary government' had became a dominant theme of British politics after 1673; James's conversion to Catholicism, a childless queen and an alliance with France raised the spectre of Catholicism being imposed forcibly upon the three kingdoms by a Catholic monarch aided by a Catholic French army. In response, Parliament passed a Bill that required all office holders to subscribe to a 'Test', which denounced the Catholic doctrine of transubstantia-tion, and, in James's view, so denied the Crown the services of loyal and

---

56 Gordon, Diary, 29 January 1686, vol. 4, p. 101v.
57 Gordon was accompanied by his son James, and two servants, 'Shenka' and Daniel. It is possible that 'Shenka' was the only Russian to visit Scotland in the seventeenth century. We owe this information to D. G. Fedosov.
58 For example, Jones, *The Revolutions*, pp. 128–75.

deserving subjects. James was forced to resign his offices. His marriage to Mary Beatrice, a 15-year-old Catholic and youngest daughter of the Duchess of Modena encouraged Parliament to exclude James from office: three exclusion bills were passed before Parliament between 1679 and 1681. The bills argued that James had: 'been perverted from the Protestant to the popish religion, whereby . . . great encouragement hath been given to the popish party to enter into and carry on most devilish and horrid plots and conspiracies for the destruction of his Majesty's sacred person and government, and for the extirpation of the Protestant religion.' If James were to succeed to the throne, then it was argued that 'nothing is more manifest than that a total change of religion within these kingdoms would ensue'.[59] In the face of Whig opposition, James had to leave England, ruling in Scotland as Duke of York.[60]

Upon his accession to the throne, internal opposition in England against his supposed desire to 'establish' or 're-establish' Catholicism upon the country continued. It has been argued that James II only wanted to place Catholics on an equal footing with Protestants, for them to be able to worship freely and hold public office. He did not believe in a forcible imposition of Catholicism but wanted willing converts: he was to condemn the religious persecution in France following the Edict of Fontainebleau (8 October 1685) as both impolitic and unchristian.

Indeed, forcible conversion was recognised as unfeasible as Catholics represented no more than 2 per cent of the population and the great majority of the army was Protestant. To be sure, Catholics were not evenly distributed throughout society. They were concentrated amongst the households of the gentry and the nobility, and had a greater profile among the elite – conversions in those surrounding the king were especially noticeable.[61] However, James had no Catholic heir, since his heir presumptive was his daughter Mary, a Protestant married to a Protestant husband, William of Orange. James's belief in the hereditary principle did not allow for a change in the order of succession. He believed that the monarchy was a sacred institution, and that the principle of

---

59 Kenyon, *The Stuart Constitution*, pp. 387–9. James, Duke of Albany, was well aware that the Exclusion Crisis was heavily publicised on mainland Europe. For example, Wyche reported from Hamburg of 'the most dismale account of our affaires which Holland sends hither with every Post'. 'Wyche to [Secretary of State], Hamburg, 26 October/5 November, 1680', PRO, SP 82/16, fol. 191. Apart from *vesti-kuranty*, the Russian government received a wide-ranging report, 'Stateinyi spisok d'iaka Vasilia Mikhailova', *RGADA* fond 35, opis 1, kn. 20, l. 228ob.–235, as published by Kobzareva, 'Zelo narod . . .', pp. 27–9.
60 Whilst in Edinburgh, he encouraged cultural institutions by founding the Royal College of Physicians, the Advocates Library and the Order of the Thistle. See: Ouston, 'York in Edinburgh', in Dwyer, Mason and Murdoch, *New Perspectives*, pp. 133–55.
61 *HMC* Dartmouth, I, p. 36; Miller, *Popery and Politics*, p. 12.

hereditary succession was divinely ordained. In the last analysis he was answerable to God alone.[62] However, James lacked the financial resources which would be needed were he to, as the Protestants feared, emulate the French model of absolutism. On the eve of the Revolution of 1688, even after zealous attempts to promote Catholic officers within the army, the Earl of Perth complained that 'the hundredth man in it is not a Catholic and we have scarce any officers of that persuasion.'[63]

The debate concerning James's real intentions misses the point: the willingness of his subjects to defend his person actively and engage an enemy to secure his throne, depended upon their perceptions, false or not, of his supposed intentions. And James was unable to rectify or reverse the hellish fantasies of Catholic rule which were so strongly imprinted in the popular imagination, fantasies not assuaged by his overt and implicit support of Catholics in the army and his pressure on both the English and Scottish Parliaments to abolish what Protestants called the 'great guard and security to our church', the Test Act.[64] As one historian has noted, 'Under the terms of the Test Act of 1673, the King could commission Roman Catholic officers into the army for a maximum period of three months, after which time they were to swear the oaths of supremacy and allegiance.'[65]

This policy was initiated in 1685 in response to the Monmouth Rebellion, which highlighted James II's military weakness. During the preceding Argyll's rebellion, part of the militia, although not the Scottish nobility, had defected to the rebels. The Scottish nobility supported King James because he was 'the keystone in the conservative Royalist political and cultural structure, which they hoped to build as the basis for a great renaissance of Scottish achievement'.[66] James was able to argue before the English Parliament that the militia had proved unreliable and therefore should be replaced by a large standing, professional army. It was not his peaceful Roman Catholic subjects who had revolted, and thus to grant commissions in his standing army to Roman Catholics would only improve its standards and discipline, increase its professionalism, and serve to secure his safety. An unreconstructed army might prove unreliable in a future crisis.[67]

Therefore James intended to double the army to 19,000 officers and men and discipline and train these troops through summer and autumn military manoeuvres. Recruitment was to be open to the most able and loyal of his

62 Daly, 'The Idea', pp. 227–50.
63 *HMC* Stuart, I, p. 31.
64 *The Diary of John Evelyn*, IV, pp. 484–7.
65 Childs, *The Army*, p. 20.
66 Lenman, 'Scottish Nobility', pp. 143–4.
67 For an argument along these lines, see Grey, *Debates*, p. 353.

subjects, and 100 Catholic officers were commissioned. But a standing army was traditionally associated in the English mentality with a tyrannical regime, such as Cromwell's. The equation of 'popery' and 'arbitrary government' allowed it to be considered axiomatic that if Catholicism was to be established then so also must absolutism. Moreover, 'That the French king was a militant Roman Catholic and an absolute monarch reinforced the association between the two in the minds of most Englishmen.'[68]

Patrick Gordon, a military officer, loyal to the Restoration monarchs and a Catholic, received many letters outlining the occurrence of these rebellions and the debate in the country concerning the consequences. For example, 'I had a perfect acco-t of the defeat of the Earle of Argile in Scotland & Duke of Monmouth in England.'[69] It is into this political and social environment (the king pressing for toleration of Roman Catholics and the repeal of the 1673 Test Act, the majority of his subjects resisting change), that Gordon's diplomatic mission of 1686 must be placed. In March, just before Gordon's arrival, James II informed the Secret Committee which dealt with Scottish affairs that he wished the Scottish Parliament to remove the Penal Laws and so thereby admit Catholic officers into the army. The Test was to be replaced by a simple oath of allegiance.

On Gordon's long journey from Moscow to London, there had been time to discuss Muscovy Company business with merchants in the towns he passed through. On his arrival in England, however, Gordon found his very movements circumscribed by the proposal to allow Catholic officers to serve in the army. On 5 April, accompanied by his sponsor Lord Melfort and his old friend in Moscow General Drummond, Gordon was introduced 'to His Ma-tie, in the comeing out of his bedchamber, who was pleased to receive me very graciously. And having kissed His Ma-ties hand with the usuall ceremonies, and a short complement, w-ch I made, His Ma-tie asked many questions concerning the Tzars, the countrey, the state of effaires, the militia and the government . . .'[70] Later that same day Gordon was again 'attending His Majestie' and on this occasion was introduced to Prince George of Denmark, the husband of Princess Anne. On 16 April, Gordon went 'to Court, and waited upon the King, in the Park, at his walke, as also in the evening.'[71]

Gordon's behaviour during this period is very much that of a courtier cum diplomat. He 'hears devotion' at 'St James's chapel on numerous occasions during

68 Speck, *Reluctant Revolutionaries*, p.11; Miller, *James II and VII*, p. 92.
69 Gordon, Diary, 30 September 1685, vol. 4, p. 89v. See also: Gordon, Diary, 21 September 1685, vol. 4, p. 88.
70 Gordon, Diary, 16 April 1686, vol. 4, p. 122v.
71 Gordon, Diary, 17 April 1686, vol. 4, p. 123.

his stay,[72] and this was clearly the privilege of foreign diplomats. Gordon mixed freely with the diplomatic community in London, especially those whose countries were connected with Russia, whether through trade or because they were member states of the forthcoming Triple Alliance of Sweden, Holland and Britain. For example, on 11 May, 'I heard devotion at the Venetian Ambassadours & dined with many friends at the Dutch house by St. James, & were soberly merry.'[73]

On 21 April, Gordon had another personal discussion with King James II: 'Attending His Ma-tie at his walke in Arlington Gardens, he was pleased, walking up and downe the alley, to speake with me about halfe an houre, enquiring particularly of our manner of government, our garrisons, souldiers, armes, & manner of warring, the business of Czegrin, and many other things.'[74] James owned a considerable amount of colonial property and a substantial number of shares in trading companies. Moreover, a large amount of his revenue came from overseas trade, and so he had a real interest in commercial expansion.[75] Thus there was every reason for him to discuss the perennial bone of contention between Britain and Russia – Muscovy Company trading privileges – although there is no specific record of him doing so.

The next day, Gordon wrote that 'According to *my ordinary custome* [authors' italics], I went and waited on the King, at his walking in the Parke.'[76] Gordon related many details of court life and of his frequent meetings with the king and of their discussions, including during a royal visit to Chatham.[77] He even moved his location to within easy walking distance to the Court of St James to reduce coach fees.[78] However, while much of the contact between the king and Gordon had personal and non-diplomatic implications for him, it must nonetheless be clear that Gordon was in London as a Russian diplomat, and gained frequent access to King James largely because of this status. But we must also realise that this was a low-key mission, the commission only 'verball'. *The London Gazette*[79]

---

72 For example: 18 April; 23 April; 25 April; 9 May; 13 May. See: Gordon, Diary, April–May 1686, vol. 4, pp. 118v–126v.

73 Gordon, Diary, 16 May 1686, vol. 4, pp. 126–7v.

74 Gordon, Diary, 21 April 1686, vol. 4, p. 123. Gordon had played a distinguished part in the siege of 'Czegrin' or Chigirin in 1678. For a judicious appraisal, see Brian Davies, 'The Second Chigirin Campaign', pp. 97–118.

75 Miller, *James II and VII*, p. 168.

76 Gordon, Diary, 22 April 1686, vol. 4, p. 124.

77 Gordon, Diary, 26 and 27 April 1686, vol. 4, p. 123.

78 Gordon, Diary, 19 April 1686, vol. 4, p. 123.

79 *The London Gazette* 22–26 April 1686, no. 2123. Other audiences were recorded. For example, Whitehall, April 25: 'Count Salazar, Envoy from the Marquis de Gastomaga Governor General of the Spanish Netherlands, had Audience of the Majesties, being conducted by Sir Charles Cottrell Master of the Ceremonies.'

and contemporary commentators[80] describing the programme of the king
during this period make no mention of Gordon.

The nature of the king's conversations with Gordon on fortifications and
other military matters suggests that he was actively attempting to recruit the
Russian general into the army, which he was at that time attempting to reform.
The need for the maintenance of the security of the three kingdoms, not to
mention the possibility of foreign war, was all too evident. As Gordon desired
to leave Russia, this embassy must have seemed an ideal forum through which
he could display his potential usefulness to the king. This was no idle conjecture. As he left London, Gordon paid one last visit to the king at Windsor,
where James questioned him closely, 'enquireing where & how long I had
served abroad, and many other things relateing to military effaires, to all which
I answered as well as I could, his M. was graciously pleased to tell me that I
should make hast to returne, and that he would have a care of me & do for me
what he could'. Half an hour later, on kissing the queen's hand and on being
introduced to her by the king, Gordon was again comforted by the king who
told him 'you must not stay long there [Moscow], and wee shall write to the
Tzaars about you.'[81]

Gordon must have left with the impression that the king would petition the
tsars for his release from Russia, so that he could exchange Romanov mercenary service for Stuart diplomatic or military service. As Lachs has noted,
'under the later Stuarts the accepted method of rewarding a diplomat for
service overseas was political preferment at home'.[82] In Gordon's case, it is more
likely that he would have followed the career paths of Dalyell and Drummond
and found a niche within the military establishment. Furthermore, in view of
the fact that prior to his departure from Russia Gordon had received letters
from British governmental sources suggesting 'something extraordinary might
be expected as far as military activity is concerned', it is inconceivable that
Gordon was unaware that those within the Stuart political establishment were
actively considering his recruitment into the Stuart army.[83]

Gordon left London for Scotland. Arriving in Edinburgh on 28 May, he was
welcomed by his clan chief who was also commander-in-chief of Edinburgh
Castle: 'the Duke of Gordon came to me, & welcomed me very kindly, afterwards

80 Luttrell, *A Brief Historical Relation*, I, p. 375 onwards.
81 Gordon, Diary, 14 May 1686, vol. 4, pp. 127r–v. 'James was more of a stickler for ceremony
    than Charles; but he was still more accessible than most monarchs and still met foreign
    ambassadors in the Queens' apartments after dinner.' Miller, *James II and VII*, pp. 121–2.
82 Lachs, *The Diplomatic Corps*, p. 161.
83 Eekman, 'Muscovy's International Relations', p. 49.

diverse other particular ffriends gave me the honour of a visitt.'[84] Over the next few days he was introduced to leading members of the Scottish political and cultural elite, for example, the Lord Chancellour, the Lord Commissioner, the Earls of Errol, Airly, Dumfermline, and Aberdeen, the Dukes of Hamilton and Queensberry and the Marquess of Atholl.[85] Gordon's arrival in Edinburgh coincided precisely with the debates within the Scottish Parliament over the issue as to whether or not to allow the recruitment of Roman Catholics into a proposed standing army. Gordon had previously monitored the state of play. On 5 May, for example, he had recorded: 'this night the letters came from Scotland of the Parliaments actions, and how it was scarsely carryed, that, in their answer to the Kings Letter they should call the Kings ffriends Rom. Catholicks.'[86]. Gordon followed the debates; on 1 and 3 June he 'went to the Parliament house.'[87] However, by 14 June, when Parliament was adjourned, nothing was decided. According to a contemporary report:

> Our great expectation was what the Parliament of Scotland would do towards taking away the penal laws against the Roman Catholics, but tho' they would be willing to ease all and tolerate some particular families and persons, yet they will not absolutely annull the laws, which being news unacceptable its thought the session will be shortened.[88]

After Edinburgh, Gordon made his way north to Aberdeen where he had the opportunity to settle his concerns over the estate of Auchleuchries and meet old friends and family. There, he received from London a 'copy of the Kings letter which was to be sent in my favours', as well as copies of those from the Duke of Melfort to 'Kniaz Vasily Vasiliovits Golitzin chieffe Minister of State in Russia'

---

84 Gordon, Diary, 28 May 1686, vol. 4, p. 130.

85 Gordon, Diary, 31 May 1686, vol. 4, p. 130v.

86 Gordon, Diary, 5 May 1686, vol. 4, p. 126. On 29 April, 'the Earl of Morray, his Majesties high Commissioner, made a speech to them, in the close of which he recommended them the giveing ease aand security to the Roman Catholiks.' Luttrell, *Brief Historical Relation*, I, p. 376.

87 Gordon, Diary, 1 and 3 June 1686, vol. 4, p. 131.

88 *HMC* 75 Downshire Mss, vol. I (1924), Parts I and II, p. 184: Newsletter 1686, June 14 Whitehall. See also: 'The Parliament in Scotland have gott passed several acts on behalf of themselves, but done nothing in behalf of the Roman Catholiks; which 'tis said his Majestic is displeased at, and hath prorogued them.' Luttrell, *Brief Historical Relation*, I, p. 381; Gordon, Diary, 15 June 1686.

and a letter from the Duke of Gordon to the tsars.[89] Gordon set sail for Moscow from Aberdeen on 15 July.[90]

On 31 August 1686, he 'came to the stranger sloboda [settlement] about 5 aclock afternoone'.[91] He was soon greeted by Golitsyn and Tsar Ivan on 1 September: 'being the Russes new yeares day, I went to the towne, was very kindly welcomed by the Boyar Kniaz Vasily Vasiliovitz Golitzin, and afterwards see the Eldest Czaar & the procession'.[92] Then, on 3 and 10 September, he dined with Golitsyn; on the second occasion 'after dinner had much discourse, yet nothing of carrying on the warr only of my jorney & my effaires'.[93] Unfortunately, however, letters from King James, received on 13 September and 29 November, only served to place Gordon under suspicion.

The first letter submitted that Gordon 'by the deceass of his Father is to inherit Lands for which he is to performe personall Service unto Us. And Wee having use for the service of such of Our subjects, as have been bred up in the military Employments, Wee do therefor desire of your Imperiall Ma-tie that you would dismiss the said Patrick Gordon, with his wyfe, Children, Family, & effects out of your Dominions'.[94] On 17 September, Gordon was able to report to London that Golitsyn appeared 'very earnest to know, whither his Sacred Majesty would send any Ambassadour or Envoy hither in haste'. Gordon added that he had 'given them a hint of some things which are looked upon there as uneasy ... and I doubt not but some things may be gott redressed and rectified, and some good besides done for the honour and advantage of the English Nation: if dexterously managed'. Gordon is most likely referring to the Muscovy Company privileges.[95]

89 Gordon, Diary, 14 July 1686, vol. 4, pp. 137v–138v.
90 *The London Gazette*, no. 2167, 'Hamburg, August 9th 1686' makes clear that Gordon could not have been the newspaper's only Moscow correspondent: 'The letters from Moscow, of the 3rd of last month [Gordon was in Aberdeen] inform us, that an Envoy was arrived there from the Cham of Tartary.'
91 Gordon, Diary, 31 August 1686, vol. 4, p. 143v.
92 Gordon, Diary, 1 September 1686, vol. 4, p. 144: 'Gordon to the Earl of Middleton, 26 July 1687', *BL*, Add. Ms 41842, fol. 157: 'I hope in September to be in Mosko where I shall be ready to contribute all I can for his Sacred Majesties honour & interest.' Gordon had also written to the Earl of Middleton on 12 August whilst at Riga: Gordon, Diary, 12 August 1686, vol. 4, p. 141.
93 Gordon, Diary, 3 and 10 September 1686, vol. 4, pp. 144r–144v.
94 'James the Seventh' to 'Our Most dear Brothers the Lord great Czaars, 29 May 1686', *RGADA*, fond 35, opis 2, no. 113. 'James the Seventh' as he wrote petitioning for one of his Scottish subjects. Gordon makes a copy of 'the King's letter which was to be sent in my favours'. Gordon, Diary, 14 July 1686, vol. 4, pp. 137v–138.
95 'Gordon to the Earl of Middleton, 17 September 1686', *BL*, Add. Ms 41842, fol. 148. Printed: Konovalov, 'Sixteen further Letters', p. 83.

Although Gordon hoped for 'a good answer and to be gone from hence once in November or sooner'[96], the Russian response to the royal request for Gordon's release, indeed made two months later in November, was extremely unfavourable. On 16 November, the Diary records threats of internal exile 'in some remote place of their empire' having been intimated to Gordon 'by some Russes who pretended to be my friends'.[97] The matter came to a head on 22 November, when Golitsyn 'did fall out in great passion, against me, and bcause I vindicated my Self the best way I could, and had the great advantage of reason upon my syde, he was the more incensed so that in great heat he ordered me to be writt in for an Ensigne & sent away the next day . . .' The Boyar, 'with very high words & threats and reasoning without all reason or the least show of uprightnes, nor valuing or considering anything I said insisted that I should acknowledge my error & crave pardon and promise to serve in future . . .' Gordon, fearing exile 'to the remotest places of their Empire', was forced to 'acknowledge my error and crave pardon', and was further humiliated when this petition was rejected 'not being penned in humble enough tearmes'.[98]

Gordon was surprised when a second letter, signed by Middleton, arrived in Moscow on 29 November, again requesting Gordon's release from Russian military service. However, this letter did not propose Gordon's return to Britain, where anti-Catholic opposition might have made it difficult to appoint him to high military rank, but promotion in Russia, the tsars willing, to the post of 'Envoy Extraordinary to their Czaarish Majesties'.[99] On 3 December, the Dutch ambassador was already bleakly assessing its impact:

> This move appears very suspicious to me, because, if he were admitted to such a position, the most negative actions could be expected of him, regarding commerce as well as other respects. We now have the malignant and damaging Jesuits on our necks. I'll do everything I can to see which steps can be taken in this case.[100]

96 'Gordon to the Earl of Middleton, Mid-September 1686', *BL*, Add. Ms 41842, fol. 156. Printed: Konovalov, 'Sixteen further Letters', pp. 84–5.

97 Gordon, Diary, 16 November 1686, vol. 4, p. 146. From this time onwards, Gordon describes himself as being 'under a great cloud'. 'Gordon to Williamson, 3 December 1686', *BL*, Add. Ms 41842, fol. 150.

98 Gordon, Diary, 22 November 1686, vol. 4, pp. 147r–147v.

99 'Earle of Middleton to Gordon, 25 October 1686', *BL*, Add. Ms 42823, fol. 89. On the inside of the front cover of *BL*, Add. Ms 42823, we read the inscription 'Copies of Letters from Ld Midleton Sec. of State to diff. foreign Envoyes 1684.' The text is also reproduced in Gordon, Diary, 29 November 1686, vol. 4, pp. 148r–148v.

100 Eekman, 'Muscovy's International Relations', p. 50.

This second letter, read with Gordon's own remonstrance, was heard in the Privy Chamber on the 9 December, and the Russian response was forthright: 'L. G. P. Gordon cannot be Extraordinary Envoy from the King to the Tzaars. because he is to be in the great army in this expedition against the Turks & the Tartars, and . . . that if the King to maintain the brotherly love & amity with the Czaars will send any Ambas. or Envoy he shall be received graciously & with favour.'[101] Gordon was not to be punished further. As early as 11 December, his Diary noted that 'the Czaars had graced me, and had remitted my fault, and ordered me to be my former charge & so ended this stage play'.[102] In January 1687 Gordon, by orders of the tsars, was given command of select regiments of the Second Division during the ensuing campaign against the Crimean Tatars.[103]

Nevertheless, he appears to have continued to act for English merchants in Moscow on behalf of the Stuart cause. On 15 January, he wrote to Middleton: 'I hope to have opportunityes of preparing bussiness, and (albeit to my great expenses) must conforme and comply with his [Golitsyn's] humours to attaine to which may produce good effects, and be for his sacred Majesties interests.'[104] This was a convenient arrangement; King James had retained a loyal Moscow resident, but without the consequent financial burden.[105]

More Late Diplomacy

Throughout the course of 1687, Gordon reported on the last Russian diplomatic mission to London before the fall of James II: 'a diak of the ambassy Office is ordered to come to his S[acred] Majesty and to Holland, and will be with you with the first shipping, he carryeth nothing but compliments.'[106] Gordon named the *diak* in his Diary: 'had notice of Vasil. Simof. Poshwinikuf being ordered

101 Gordon, Diary, 9 December 1686, vol. 4, pp. 149v–150.
102 'Gordon to Williamson, 11 December 1686', BL, Add. Ms 41842, fol. 150.
103 Gordon, Diary, 3 January 1687, vol. 4, p. 155.
104 'Gordon to the Earl of Middleton, 15 January 1687' BL, Add. Ms 41842, fol. 154. This letter was carried 'by Mr Joseph Wulfe. ane English Mercht.' Gordon, Diary, 29 January 1687, vol. 4, p. 156v.
105 CSPD, January 1686–May 1687, pp. 360–1: 'February 7, 1687. Warrant. Extraordinary allowances to British Envoys, Residents, and Envoy Extraordinarys in France, Spain, Holland, Denmark, Sweden, Portugal, Flanders, Hamburg and Ratisbonne.' There is evidence to suggest that Gordon also continued to write for *The London Gazette*. For example, 'London Gazette, November 29–December 2, 1686, no. 2195' in its content and by the approximation of dates, was most likely: 'Newsletter from Moscow, Mid September, 1686' – BL, Add. Ms 41842, fol. 156.
106 'Gordon to the Earl of Middleton, 7 January 1687' – BL, Add. Ms 41842, fol. 152. Printed in Konovalov, 'Sixteen further Letters' pp. 86–7.

Envoy Extraord:. to his Ma. of Great Brittaine & to Holland.'[107] Gordon also offered a realistic assessment of the status of Anglo-Russian trade, but advocated keeping the issue of the privileges alive as a diplomatic bargaining chip:

> albeit I am told that the Privileges consideratis considerandis are scarce worth the asking, yet I am not of the opinion, that so just and honourable a pretence should let fall, befor any equivalent be granted. It will be fitt to represent to the Envoy the averseness they show here to pleasure his Majesty even in the most just and smallest matters . . . It will be needful to insist very much upon the privileges as the basis and cement of the friendship betwixt his Sacred Majesty and the Czaars . . .[108]

Ambassador Vasilii Timofeevich Postnikov, a secretary and professional diplomat in the Diplomatic Chancellery, visited London from September to December 1687. His mission can be interpreted as a sign of surgent Russian imperial power, rightly described by Lindsey Hughes as an attempt by Muscovy 'to carve out a more substantial niche in European affairs'.[109] Certainly, its costs were to be strictly regulated: 'The Emperor to accord expenses will not allow above seventy persons in the train of the Muscovite Ambassadors: the surplus of the train must be maintained by themselves.'[110]

Just as with Andrei Vinius's mission of 1672, so too was Postnikov's embassy one of many, including those of Ia. F. Dolgorukii and Ia. E. Myshetskii to France and Spain, B. P. Sheremetev to Venice, and V. Mikhailov to Denmark and Sweden. Vasilii Mikhailov also came to England, where he noted widespread public alarm about the king's pro-French and pro-Catholic policies as well as doing what he could to interest the king in an anti-Turkish coalition.[111] Postnikov himself went to Prussia, Holland and Florence as well as England, as part of a diplomatic offensive in the west 'undertaken in technical fulfillment of the clause in the treaty of "permanent peace" between Russia and Poland (26 April/6 May 1686), in which the signatories pledged to seek aid, both

---

107 Gordon, Diary, 4 January 1687, vol. 4, p. 155. Gordon used the ambassador to carry letters bound for Scotland. Gordon, Diary, 22 February 1687, vol. 4, p. 160v. See also Vinogradoff, 'Russian Missions', pp. 64–72; Konovalov, 'Sixteen further letters', pp. 87–8.
108 Gordon to the Earl of Middlefield, 25 January 1687, *BL.* Add. Ms 41842, fol. 184; Konovalov, 'Sixteen further letters', pp. 87–8.
109 See Hughes, 'V. T. Postnikov's 1687 Mission', p. 448.
110 *CSPD*, January 1686–May 1687, p. 347.
111 Kobzareva, ' "Zelo narod grub" ', pp. 24–9.

military and financial, of "other Christian monarchs" for the Holy League's war against Turkey.[112]

Postnikov's letter of credentials was wrongly addressed to 'James VII' – it omitted the 'and II'. Possibly, this was a reflection of the king's intercession on behalf of his Scottish subjects.[113] Certainly, we know how sensitive an issue titles could be in the seventeenth century.[114] However, in this case, the omission of 'and II' does not appear to have caused any embarrassment.

Nevertheless, in the letter carried back to the tsars by Postnikov, the king refused to lend money to aid a military offensive against the Turks. The letter stated that 'his Majesty was sorry his own Affairs would not give him leave to assist his Masters with Money to carry out the Warr against the Turks; and that, could he do it, as an inducement, the Czars ought to show some favour to the English Merchants by restoring them their priviledges which they formerly had.'[115] It also stated that 'such Ministers as We shall send Unto your Imperiall Majesties Court, shall live upon thier own expence, acording to Our appoint-ment and allowance, without receiving or expecting any money or provision from your Imperiall Ma.ties or your successors.'[116] While Postnikov resided in London, he received a £50 allowance and was accommodated rent-free. He appealed for a greater allowance.[117] Point 4 of a reply refused this request, but point 3 appears to have hinted why: '3. That his Matie thinks ye renewing ye ancient priviledges wch ye English enjoyed in their trade to Russia, will much conduce to continue, and even to increase the friendship between their Matiees & good Correspondence between their Subjects.'[118]

Possibly, this response was influenced by the activities of Patrick Gordon in Moscow. Certainly, on 7 February 1687, Gordon could finally observe: 'I received letters from England adviseing me in what forwardnes my business of being his

112 A 'Copy of the Legue betwixt the Muscovites and the Poles agt the Tartars Ricd from the Envoye of Russia at a Conference with their Lords', *BL*, Add. Ms 48125, fols 177–88. It lists 33 articles. See also: *The London Gazette*, 7–10 November 1687, no. 2293, Whitehall, 8 Nov.: 'This day the Envoy from the Czars of Muscovy had Audience of Their Majesties, in the usual manner, being conducted by Sir Charles Cottrell Master of Ceremonies.' *HMC* 75 Downshire Mss, vol. I (1924), Parts I and II, p. 266 and p. 268.

113 'Translation of the Envoye of Muscovy his Credentialls', *BL*, Add. Ms 48125, fol. 175. 'Ivan and Peter to James the Seventh 10 Feb. 7195', *PRO*, SP 104/119, fols 81–4. In the margin over 'the Seventh': 'This error in ye stile happened by their following ye last letter w.ch ye Lord Melfort sent in answ.r to one yt. Came by Gen.ll Gordon in 1686.'

114 See, for example, Longworth, 'Russian–Venetian Relations', p. 386.

115 Vinogradoff, 'Russian Missions', p. 70.

116 James II and VII 'to Our most Deare Brothers, the Great Lords, Czars Ivan and Peter' 4 December 1687, *RGADA*, fond 35, opis 2, no. 114. (Copy: *BL*, Add. Ms 48125, fol. 191.)

117 'The Muscovite Envoyes Mem.ll, 26 September 1687', *PRO*, SP 104/119, fol. 88.

118 'Answer to the Muscovite Envoy', *PRO*, SP 104/119, fol. 90.

Sacred Ma-ties Envoy was, and that my Credentialls, instructions, & equipage were all ready.'[119] However, March heralded the beginning of the Crimea campaign and so all diplomatic efforts on behalf of the Stuart king were to be put on hold until he returned to Moscow in September. But then: 'On the 9th [I] was at their Majesties hands, when with many gracious words I was prefered to be Generall [i.e. Maj. Gen.] and told that I should entertain no hopes of going out of the Countrey so long as the war lasteth, which troubleth me exceedingly.'[120]

In a letter to Meverell of 16 September, Gordon appeared to have expected an envoy from London concerning the question of the import of tobacco into Russia. At the same time he again made reference to the costs he had incurred as royal representative: 'I hope seing it was his Majesties affaires his Sacred Majestie will not suffer me to be a losser.'[121] As royal representative, he wrote to Middleton: 'I know not what to advise concerning your business with this Court, the busines of the import of tobacco will not go forward as I have learned, in other things only generall answers . . . wherein I can be serviceable to his Sacred Majestie and affaires, heveing notice, I shall according to my bound duty, I shall use my utmost endeavours.'[122]

In order 'to conduce to his Majestie takeing notice of my expenses here', Gordon asked Meverell to advertise the fact 'in the gazet there'[123] that on 14 October, as he put it in his Diary, 'Our most gracious soveraigne his birthday with the Usuall Joviality haveing all his S. M. borne subjects & many descended of them at the feast.'[124] In *The London Gazette* issue of early December, a paragraph under the byline 'Moscow, October 22' duly describes how 'Lieutenant-General Patrick Gordon . . . being his Majesty of Great Britain's Birthday, the said General solemnized it here, making a great Entertainment for all his Majesties subjects.'[125]

---

119 Gordon, Diary, 7 February 1687, vol. 4, p. 158v.
120 Gordon, Diary, 9 September 1687, vol. 4, p. 182.
121 'Gordon to Samuel Meverell, 16 September 1687', BL, Add. Ms 41842, fol. 159.
122 'Gordon to Middleton, 26 September 1687', BL, Add. Ms 41842, fol. 160. The American colonies of Virginia and Maryland produced tobacco and in 1681 Lord Culpepper, the Governor of America, had attempted to gain permission to export into Russia. Gordon procured this monopoly in 1695. Gordon, Diary, 8 February 1695, vol. 5, p. 447. On 13 February 1695, Gordon writes 'Mr. Woolfe sent me his acot which amounteth in all to 185 Rubles, 8 Grivnes 14 deniskeens.' Gordon, Diary, 13 February 1695, vol. 5, p. 447.
123 'Gordon to Meverell, 22 October 1687', BL, Add. Ms 41842, fol. 164.
124 Gordon, Diary, 14 October 1687, vol. 4, p. 182v.
125 The London Gazette, 8–12 December 1687, no. 2302.

Commerce

As we have seen, the Muscovy Company's ever more desperate efforts to regain their lost glory received a new lease of life from a change of guard in Moscow following Aleksei Mikhailovich's death in 1676, but resulted in failure.

In general, however, a new era of détente gradually set in the second half of the 1670s, in spite of the general xenophobia of Fedor's regime and the tense relations with foreign merchants in the wake of the 1667 New Commercial Code. In 1676, the tsar informed the Muscovy Company of 200 bales of silk brought by Armenians to Moscow.[126] In 1681, Joseph (Osip) Woolfe requested a passport for Moscow where he wished to collect outstanding debts. By 1684, Woolfe, along with his brother John, journeyed to Moscow for an entire year. Eventually, in January 1687, he received the most generous of the permits granted for the Russian interior. This was in recognition of the profits he had generated for the Treasury by selling caviar and potash and of the nearly R12,000 he had paid in customs duties in 1682–7. The charter allowed him to trade freely in the Russian interior, although duties were to be paid in accordance with the New Commercial Code. He was also given the right to keep houses in Moscow, Archangel, and 'on the Dvina'. Woolfe may also have traded in rhubarb. A letter discussed at the Muscovy Company meeting of 12 December 1684 alleged that he and Dutch merchant Adolf Houtman were jointly exporting 100 *pud* of rhubarb each year. Woolfe became a large-scale operator, repeatedly sending early ships, for example two vessels in 1684 and even more in 1686. He also sent at least one early ship in 1687 and two (some 400 tons) in 1688. By 1689, Woolfe was also supplying ships for the general shipping.[127]

In 1690, a group of English merchants including Andrew and Jeremy Styles, 'Nicholas Cohn' (perhaps George Caren), and William Light, who all traded in Archangel on a permanent basis, were similarly granted permission to return to the interior. Even they, however, had been visiting Moscow for several years: Andrew Styles and James Pindecke since 1683, 'Cohn' and Light since 1688.[128] In total, some ten English merchants a year visited the Russian interior in the late

126 *GHL*, Ms 11,741/1, p. 125. See also Fedor's April 1676 letter to Charles II, informing of future Armenian silk trade at the Archangel fair: *PRO*, SP 91/3, fols 208–9.

127 *RGADA*, fond 35, 1681 g., d. 2, fols 1, 35, 42–3; fond 159, opis 2, d. 3825, fols 1–2; Demkin, *Zapadnoevropeiskoe kupechestvo*, I, p. 47; *GHL*, Ms 11,741/2, pp. 51, 57, 68, 83, 92, 114.

128 Apparently, the pre-1690 passports were identical to those issued to Dutch and Hamburg merchants and never explicitly identified the merchants in question as English, something that had allowed them to also circumvent the travel restrictions of 1677. Repin, *Vneshniaia torgovlia*, pp. 333–5; *RGADA*, fond 35, 1690–1 gg., d. 258, fols 1, 13–14, 24.

1680s and early 1690s.[129] In the 1680s, the Company even made some attempts to revive its trade in Persia. In 1683, Thomas Sandes was allowed to organise a mission there with a 440-ton ship and another mission followed in 1691.[130] Nonetheless, as late as 1689, the Dutch resident, Johan Willem van Keller, described the sorry state of Anglo-Russian trade: 'At this court there is not a single English minister. And the number of English traffickers here is not very considerable either; there are no more than six, four of whom live ordinarily here in town, and two others in Archangel.'[131]

In 1681, the Muscovy Company dispatched six ships to Archangel, a total of 1,550 tons. Even then, two early ships had to be dispatched the following spring to collect the overflow. In most subsequent years, the number of ships varied between four and six, but there were years with ten or eleven as well. In 1682, an average year, the subscriptions were 690 tons for London and 417 tons for Leghorn, yet a 350-ton early ship had to be sent the following spring. Total subscriptions again rose to 1,050 tons for London and 163 tons for the Mediterranean. By 1689, the total subscriptions were 2,392 tons for London and 335 tons for Leghorn. The average size of the ships increased markedly from 200–250 tons in the 1670s to 300–350 tons in the 1680s. In years with more ships, it was customary to let one or two depart one to two weeks after the regular departure date of late June or the first days of July. Similarly, early shipping in April or May became common. In 1689, early shipping alone attained 547 tons.[132] Perhaps because of capacity constraints, Company members were in some years allowed to ship goods on any vessel beyond the confines of centralised subscriptions.[133]

In spite of the Acts of Trade and Navigation, the exclusion of foreign merchants from the English Baltic trade was not absolute. Indeed, the implementation of the measures was fraught with confusion and controversy and thus, starting in the 1680s, it was apparently 'legal to import hemp from Netherlands,

---

129 The right was explicitly granted to Jeremy and Andrew Styles, James and Philip Woolfe, John and James Pindecke, John Edwards, Gabriel Ward, George Caren (?), and William Lock. *RGADA*, fond 35, 1681 g., d. 2; 1688 g., d. 257; 1690 g., d. 258.

130 *GHL*, Ms 11,741/2, pp. 14–15, 152.

131 Eekman, 'Muscovy's International Relations', p. 51.

132 In 1684, the subscriptions for London attained 1,392 tons, as compared to 30 tons for Leghorn. The corresponding figures in 1685 were 2,000 tons and 79 tons respectively. In 1690, 2,462 tons was subscribed for London and 135 tons for Leghorn, and this, as well as early shipping, was permitted in spite of an embargo. *GHL*, Ms 11,741/1, pp. 216–21, 231; *GHL*, Ms 11,741/2, pp. 24–5, 100, 130, 136–7.

133 Archangel continued to divert trade from other areas of the Company's operations. Thomas Sandes in 1686 requested permission to send his Greenland-bound ship to the White Sea, should they 'be disappointed of their Lading of Oyle'. *GHL*, Ms 11,741/2, p. 69.

provided the hemp was of European origin and was carried in British-owned bottoms'.[134] Subsequently, the spirit of the law was respected until wars once again complicated the supply situation in the 1690s.

However, S. E. Åström's analysis of the Hull Port Books for 1683 and 1685 shows clearly that the Netherlands and Hamburg entirely lost their position as intermediaries of the Baltic naval stores. In London, the situation was not essentially different, with very small quantities of flax continuing to be imported from Hamburg. Consequently, increasing numbers of British ships did indeed begin to make trips to the Baltic.[135]

The Navigation Acts also gave a major advantage to Swedish ships towards the end of the century. While a total of 515 non-English vessels came to Britain from Sweden and Swedish possessions in Michaelmas 1691–Michaelmas 1697, there were just 240 English vessels sailing in the same direction.[136] Thus, an increasing share of the total now consisted of Swedish vessels. In the words of John Robinson, an English diplomat who was an expert in Swedish affairs:

> When Sueden has been engaged in a War, the English Ships have had the whole Employ: but in Times of Peace, the Advantage if so great on the Suedish side, and Merchants so much encouraged by Freedom in Customs to employ their Ships, that English Bottoms cannot be used in that Trade, but only while Sueden is unprovided with a Number of Ships sufficient for the Transportation of their own Commodities.[137]

English shipping in Narva benefited from a political rapprochement between Sweden and Britain. A treaty of friendship and commerce had been signed in 1661 and further supplemented by the friendship, defence, commerce, and navigation treaty of March 1665. Paragraph 23 of the latter treaty allowed English merchants to buy wholesale goods in Sweden. Its paragraph 24 ensured the right of Swedish and English merchants to establish commercial partnerships and guesthouses in the other country. Stade, Landskrona, and Narva were singled out as possible sites in Sweden. These rights had been reaffirmed when the treaty was renewed in 1672. Moreover, the government issued a plea for the

---

134　Moreover, in 1672–4, 'great quantities of potash were freely shipped from Hamburg.' This
　　is likely to have came originally from Archangel, however, given the limited involvement
　　of Hamburg merchants in the Baltic. Åström, 'The English navigation laws', p. 5.
135　*PRO*, E 190/317/6, E 190/328/1; Åström, 'The English navigation laws', pp. 7–10.
136　Ibid., p. 15.
137　Quoted in: Åström, 'The English navigation laws', p. 14.

English to come to the Baltic and Narva.[138] The numbers of English ships passing the Danish Sound increased dramatically. The annual average in 1661–74 was below 10, but then it rose to 20–30 by the late 1670s. In 1683 and 1700, 51 and 71 ships, respectively passed the Sound.[139]

A sizeable and influential English colony soon emerged in Narva and lent an important stimulus to Russian trade in the area. Narva almost certainly constituted the most attractive base of operations in the Baltic. It was very well connected, via waterways and roads alike, with the commercial centres of north-western Russia, Novgorod and Pskov. There was no powerful bourgeoisie or ancient regulations to limit their room for manoeuvre. Similarly, direct Russian trade of the type seen on the Neva route and in Nyen was impossible in Narva due to the local geography and regulations. In Narva, the English could also have much more direct access to the Russian merchants than in Riga, where all trade was intermediated through the city's own burghers and violations of the relevant rules were invariably punished. In addition, customs duties were lower than in Riga, the English were allowed to maintain their own warehouses and, last but not least, they were since 1684 free to practise their own religion and bring in a preacher, Charles Thirlby.[140] After 1688, the English were allowed to have their representative in the City Council. They also enjoyed the warm support of the Ingrian Governor General Göran Sperling. As of 1688, too, they were allowed to stay in Narva beyond the previous limit of two months a year.[141] Naturally, the decision of the Swedish government to focus its derivation policy primarily on Narva increased the attractiveness of investing in the city.

The relatively long-standing efforts of the local and central authorities since the beginning of the century to attract English merchants to Narva, largely in a bid to reduce the domination of the Hanseatic German merchants, began to bear fruit in the 1670s. By 1679, at least seven people of British descent were active as merchants in Narva: William Johnson Kettlewell, Richard Bacon, George Pierson, Willian Linch (Lint) of the Eastland Company, Thomas Leffers (Loftus), William Ramsay, and Alexander Gilbert.[142] The two leading members of the community, Kettlewell and Loftus, had come to Narva much earlier: Loftus initially in 1666 and Kettlewell in 1670. Both of them became full burghers, and Kettlewell, whose wife since 1683 was a daughter of the city's

---

138 Erpenbeck, 'Die Engländer, p. 484; Fahlborg, *Sveriges yttre politik*, I, pp. 87–91; Küng, 'Inglise kaubandus Narvas', p. 12; Åström, *From Stockholm to St. Petersburg*, p. 24; Piirimäe, *Kaubanduse küsimused*, p. 91.

139 Tabeller over Skibsfart, I.

140 Åström, *From Stockholm to St. Petersburg*, p. 75; Åström, *From Cloth to Iron*, pp. 125, 131.

141 Erpenbeck, 'Die Engländer in Narva', p. 488; Küng, 'Inglise kaubandus Narvas', p. 14.

142 *RA*, 1583–1707, Östersjöprovinsernas tull- och licenträkenskaper, vol. 34.

burgomaster Johann Christoph Schwartz, was even granted a monopoly of a tobacco mill. Loftus, having returned permanently to Estonia in 1678, moved to Narva in 1686–7 and, starting in May 1688, served as the British representative on the City Council for a ten-year period. He was eventually succeeded by Henry Browne, brother to Johan Browne who served as a British agent in Reval. Pierson, Gilbert, and Bacon, at least, also got married in Narva, as did William Walker who came to Narva in the 1680s.[143]

Not all British residents of Narva became citizens, and the process was not always voluntary. The Crown tended to ignore pleas by non-citizens in order to increase the ranks of the tax-paying population of Narva. Loftus complained to the king in 1678 that Narva wanted to force him to become a citizen. Gilbert was fined in 1689 for refusing to become a burgher.[144] E. Küng has found records of nine Englishmen taking the citizenship oath in Narva. They were rope master John Langerwood of Nottingham (1681), William Kettlewell (1682), Captain John Küssell (1682), Thomas Loftus (1687), Alexander Gilbert (1689), Captain Johan Noting of Newcastle (1692), Captain Philip Wuddus (Woodhouse ?) of Hull (1692), Captain Georg Buorges of Hull (1692), and William Walcker (Walker?), originally from Yorkshire (1693).[145] Apparently there were also some 'fake naturalisations'. Merchants could minimise their costs by passing the Danish Sound as Swedish citizens, thus free of duty, yet arriving in England as Englishmen. This type of behaviour of questionable legality represented an attempt to circumvent Reval in Narva's export trade. Export trade via Reval, real or alleged, was used as a way of eluding the Muscovy Company's still extant *de iure* control over Narva's trade. Thus, in 1672, Henry Slater claimed that his flax and hemp had been imported from Reval and not Narva, as the Company was claiming. The Russia Company set up special controls at the ports of London, Hull, and Newcastle for the purpose of collecting 1 per cent licence payments on wares imported from Narva. In 1696, the Eastland merchant Nathaniel Gould was alone in paying the Russia Company £50–60 on his Narva trade valued at £5,000.[146]

143　Åström, *From Cloth to Iron*, p. 130; Erpenbeck, 'Die Engländer in Narva', pp. 487–8, 491; Erpenbeck, 'Die Bürgermeister Narvas', p. 39 ff.

144　Åström, *From Cloth to Iron*, p. 130; *RA* Livonica II: 210; *KARA* Narva, Rådsturättens dombok 1689, fols 164, 182, 193, 206; Erpenbeck, 'Die Engländer in Narva', p. 488.

145　Küng, 'Inglise kaubandus Narvas', p. 15.

146　An English shipbuilder John Russell became a Narva citizen in 1693 so as to be able to serve as the captain of the Narva ship the *Fortuna*. In 1696, however, he was found to be in violation of the Navigation Acts and the ship was detained in England in 1696–9. Gilbert appears to have been involved in a similar situation in 1691. Erpenbeck, 'Die Engländer in Narva', pp. 494–5.

The English imported a typical array of naval stores via Narva: flax, hemp, potash, tar, pitch, bar-iron, and timber. The naval stores were virtually entirely of Russian origin, the iron Swedish.[147]

The English also came to play a key role in the tobacco trade, which in turn became an essential component of Narva's Russian trade long before such commerce was legally established on the White Sea route. However, operations were complicated by the repeated efforts by the Swedish state and the local merchants to impose limitations on this trade. For instance, in 1662, all tobacco merchants were asked to surrender their holding to the new monopoly.[148] Following rampant smuggling, a royal resolution issued on 14 May 1666 allowed Narva merchants to import large quantities of tobacco past the tobacco monopoly for the purpose of re-exporting it to Russia.[149] However, the tobacco inspector limited his supplies to Narva until the Swedish Commerce College in 1669 found that Narva and Nyen sold all their tobacco to Russia and the government's derivation policy would thus benefit from liberalising tobacco trade in the two cities. A resolution to the effect was duly issued on 26 May 1669.[150]

By the mid-1670s, the English became the main suppliers of colonial tobacco to Narva.[151] Tobacco occupied the first place among their imports into Narva. In fact, the English exported little else to the Gulf of Finland, lagging far behind other nationalities as salt, cloth, wine, and paper importers and completely insignificant in the herring trade. The English tobacco trade created a source of conflict with the local burghers. Although Karl XI had liberalised Narva's tobacco trade in 1669, in October 1675, after intensive lobbying, he had granted Narva burghers a monopoly in tobacco. All foreigners now had to sell their tobacco to Narva merchants before proceeding to Russia.[152] In 1677, Narva burghers tried to force foreigners to sell their tobacco within two weeks. However, as of 1678, foreigners could sell their tobacco to Narva merchants at the prevailing market price for two months. After this, the local prosecutor was

---

147 Åström, *From Cloth to Iron*, pp. 128, 131; Erpenbeck, 'Die Engländer in Narva', pp. 492–3.
148 Küng, 'Tubakakaubanduse riiklik', p. 6; *Samling*, III, pp. 110–14, nos. 3–8; *EAA* 1646–2–253, fol. 65; 1646–2–243, fols. 12–13; *EAA* 1646–2–132.
149 *EAA* 1646–1–1, fol. 101v.
150 *EAA* 1646–1–1, fol. 111; 1646–2–192, fol. 11; 1646–2–291, fols 70–1; Küng, 'Tubakakaubanduse riiklik', p. 9.
151 Indeed, many of the vessels coming from Danzig, France, and Amsterdam were English. For instance, in 1694, the English ships coming from Danzig carried 2,725 pounds of tobacco. Küng, 'Tubakakaubanduse riiklik', pp. 4–5.
152 Piirimäe, 'Torgovye otnosheniia Rossii so Shvetsiei', pp. 65–81; *EAA* 1646–1–1, fol. 127v; 1646–1–2, fols 551–2.

authorised to force a sale.[153] The extension was undoubtedly once again due to capital shortages in the city. Apparently, until that point, the English had typically conducted their own tobacco trade independently. A royal resolution in September 1673 countered Narva's complaints by pointing out that English merchants had significantly increased Narva's trade volumes.[154]

Under the circumstances, the English were unlikely to surrender an attractive business opportunity without some resistance. In October 1677, a group of English merchants complained that the Narva authorities were violating the commercial treaty between Britain and Sweden, which supposedly authorised the English to trade freely in any commodity.[155] A dispute between the representatives of the Crown and the local authorities ensued. The following spring, the Council repeated its position and called on the English to offer not only their tobacco, but also their wine and herring to local merchants for the standard two-week period.[156] Since September 1678, all foreigners had to take their tobacco to the City Hall basement where it was to be weighed and offered for sale to local burghers for a period of two weeks. The purpose of this measure was to alleviate the financial demands of tobacco trade on the city's own merchants. The English were also accused of selling wine illegally to Russia.[157]

Conclusion

Great changes in the tobacco trade among others were to ensue towards the end of the century. Indeed, as we shall see, it is possible to suggest that a commercial revolution took place. But before then, there was political revolution, involving the end of the Stuart kings and the consolidation of the Romanov tsars.

During the years up to 1688, the alleged Stuart attempt to establish absolutism on the French model resulted in failure. James II had neither the money nor the social support for such a departure from the English tradition. The situation in Scotland and Ireland was somewhat different, as we shall see. Further

---

153 In 1679, even the king declined a request by Reval merchants to export tobacco to Russia through Narva. *EAA* 1646–2–38, fols 52v, 68–9; *EAA* 1646–1–2, fols 578–80.

154 In May 1676, the Muscovy Company included tobacco on the list of permissible export goods on the Archangel and Narva routes. Küng, 'Inglise kaubandus Narvas', p. 13; Erpenbeck, 'Die Engländer in Narva', pp. 484–5; *EAA* 1646–1–1, fols. 101v, 127v.

155 *EAA* 1646–2–176, fol. 63.

156 Küng, 'Inglise kaubandus Narvas', p. 13; *EAA* 1646–2–176, fol. 64; 1646–1–91, fols 157v–8; 1646–1–92, fol. 515.

157 Ibid., p. 13; *EAA* 1646–2–38, fols 68–9; 1646–1–1, fol. 117v; 1646–1–92, fols 479, 487–8.

afield, if colonial trade flourished, foreign policy was not a success, in particular adherence to Louis XIV's France, the model of absolutism. Meanwhile, following the Russian tradition, even before the seizure of sole supreme power by the future Peter the Great, Romanov absolutism was already on a more secure foundation. Of course, there were still problems, unrest among the *streltsy* musketeers and others in the towns, among the peasants and Cossacks in the rural areas. The frontiers were still far from fixed, with incursions from the Turks and their henchmen the Crimean Tatars ever-threatening.

SEVEN

Endgame, 1688–1698

In the years 1688–9, the so-called 'Glorious and Bloodless Revolution' occurred in the British Isles. The Stuarts in the person of James VII and II were ejected from the throne. Although the 'revolutionaries' clearly recognised the importance of dynastic continuity, James and his supporters, as firm believers in primogeniture through the male line, could hardly accept Mary, William III's wife and daughter to James, as a valid continuer of the dynasty. Meanwhile, great changes were taking place in 1689 in Russia, where the Regent Sophia was overthrown by the younger tsar, her half-brother, the future Peter the Great. These two events, both of enormous significance for our major theme, will be examined in some detail here. Then, we will trace developments during the ensuing decade after the events from the point of view of their implications for the traditional Stuart–Romanov relationship.

Let us be clear. In many, indeed in most respects, our story is at an end by 1689. The special relationship between the Stuart and Romanov dynasties was over. However, as is well-known, so to speak, the Stuarts were dead, but would not lie down. Their hopes for a return to the throne lived on in the Jacobite movement. As far as Jacobite influence over the Romanovs was concerned, a key figure continues to be Patrick Gordon, whose significant meetings with the Stuart kings Charles II and James II have already been described above. Significant encounters with the most renowned Romanov tsar, the future Peter the Great, will be described in this chapter. However, the hopes of the Jacobites in Russia were finally dashed by the meeting between William III and Peter I, later the Great, in September 1697, followed in December 1699 by the death of Patrick Gordon.

A further word of clarification may be necessary before we embark upon our description and assessment of the final years of the special relationship of the Stuarts and Romanovs. Our focus on Scotland does not mean surrender to 'Scotophilia' (any more than our frequent references to Gordon mean surrender to 'Gordonophilia'). We must remember that the major movements for the restoration of the Stuarts, in 1715 and 1745, arose in the home of the dynasty, where the strongest support could still be found. Moreover, peripheral to the major centre of the government, Scotland presented strategic advantage to Jacobitism, too.

The Birth of Jacobitism In Russia

1688, a fallow campaign year in Russia, saw another upsurge in diplomatic activity on behalf of King James. Gordon continually promised the Earl of Middleton that he would 'not be wanting in any thing that I can to promote his Sacred Majesties interest in this place'.[1] To this end he continued to involve himself with the diplomatic affairs in Moscow, renewing old diplomatic contacts within the foreign community and strengthening new ones. In the first week of the *annus horribilis* for Stuart monarchical ambitions, for example, Gordon 'dined by the Holls. Resident with the Polis Envoy'.[2] It is clear that throughout the year Gordon interacted with other foreign diplomats resident in Moscow, partly discussing Muscovy Company affairs and partly representing the interests of the king. It is likely a celebration followed the news of the birth of James Francis Edward on 10 June 1688: 'Wee had the joyfull newes of the birth of the Prince of Wales, whom God preserve. who was borne Junii 10 betwixt 9 & 10 houres & 15 minutes in the morning at St. James.'[3] At the same time Gordon, the trusted military commander, who in the course of his professional duties was naturally to meet with high-ranking members of the Russian nobility, acted as an intermediary between them and foreign diplomats. For example, 'And. Art. [Matveev] came to me & moved me to go with him to the Holl. Resident.'[4] As royal representative in Moscow, Gordon even recommended his son James to Middleton for service in the Stuart diplomatic corps: 'He hath the Latin, French, Dutch, and Polonian Languages in some measure, and upon that account may be usefull for other employments as well as military.'[5]

Barely a month later, Gordon was to attempt to disrupt the diplomatic efforts of his daughter's godfather – 'the Hollands Resident Johann Wilhelm van Keller' – who was pressing the Dutch interpretation of events in Britain and the recognition of William of Orange as William III. Stuart supporters in Moscow were rallied to the cause, and the Jacobite movement in Russia was conceived.

Gordon took it upon himself, as the most senior royalist from Great Britain, to justify the actions of King James: for example, 'at a Feast by Elias Tabort, where much discourse about our King haveing set fast the Archb-p of Canterbury & 6 other b-ps in the Tower, w-ch I maintained to be reasonable &

---

1 'Gordon to the Earl of Middleton, 28 February 1688' – *BL*, Add. Ms 41842, fol. 165; Gordon, Diary, 28 February 1688, vol. 4, p. 197: this letter was written in a 'copy book of letters', as yet undiscovered.
2 Gordon, Diary, 16 January 1688, vol. 4, p. 194.
3 Gordon, Diary, 16 July 1688, vol. 4, p. 208.
4 Gordon, Diary, 19 January 1688, vol. 4, p. 194.
5 'Gordon to the Earl of Middleton, 10 May 1688' – *BL*, Add. Mss. 41842, fol. 167.

just.'[6] Explaining and justifying the royalist cause within the foreign community was one challenge. A more pressing and harder task was to win through the sea of misinformation, misunderstanding and rumour which swept through Moscow in the late summer and autumn of 1688 to strive for victory beyond the foreign community, within the Russian court and especially within the Diplomatic Chancellery.

On the face of it, the Dutch were outgunned. The main sources of non-Russian-based foreign information came from: two Catholic powers via the Polish and imperial envoys; the Catholic Gordon, in direct contact with Melfort, Middleton, and leading members of the Scottish political establishment as well as being connected to *The London Gazette*; and the Protestant Dutch envoy. Thus Gordon, in conjunction with the Polish and imperial envoys from two powers closely involved in the formation of Russian foreign policy at this time, and with their masters, the king and emperor, both pro-Jacobite, should have been able to offset Dutch efforts to justify the usurpation of a hereditary line with an interpretation of events which was consistent, continuously updated and thrice underpinned. What to Russian interests was a trading partnership compared to a military alliance?

And yet, on 30 August, Gordon was confronted while dining with Golitsyn with the following argument about King James and his subjects:

> 'Wee could agree well enough with your Kings father & brother, but wee cannot come to right with this, he is proved proud beyond all measure'. I makeing as if I understood only his not sending any hither answered that the King because of his great troubles in his owne dominions, had not leasure to think of business lying so farr of as I thought. He said moreover that the English could not subsist without their Commodities as leather, hempe, potash, tallow & masts to the which I gave a compliant answer.[7]

A month later Gordon 'dined by Elias Tabort where was the Boyar K. V. V. and most of that party'.[8] The implication was that 'that party' represented the pro-Orangist faction in the Russian court. If so, Golitsyn was in fact anti-Stuart in disposition. This can possibly be explained by the lack of Stuart interest in the Crimean campaigns, upon whose success Sophia's Regency had staked its political credibility. Golitsyn had already notified the Dutch resident that King

6 Gordon, Diary, 12 July 1688, vol. 4, p. 207v.
7 Gordon, Diary, 30 August 1688, vol. 4, p. 210v.
8 Gordon, Diary, 29 September 1688, vol. 4, p. 213v.

James was guilty of 'favouring the Turkes too much'.[9] For Gordon, the irony of the situation was to become apparent. Paradoxically, the Crimean campaigns that the Regency had mounted against the Turks should have been of major concern to the Stuart king. By attacking the Turks and their Tatar allies in the Crimea, Russia divided and thus weakened the Turkish assault upon Habsburg territory, allowing Leopold to withdraw his imperial troops from Hungary and post them to the French border, so relieving French pressure upon Holland over the summer of 1688. Thus, especially with the removal of the threat of the French capture of Phillipsburg on the Rhine, William was freed to launch his amphibious attack upon Britain.

In his effort to steal the Dutch thunder, Gordon had to be first with the news of any event, so that he could set the agenda and define the parameters of debate in the growing propaganda war. In this exercise, it was important to have one spokesman actively peddling a consistent line. Gordon had the authority to unite the pro-Stuart elements within the foreign community. Moreover, through his experience, contacts and high military rank, he also possessed the status necessary to be given a hearing in Russian governmental circles and so the potential ability to neutralise anti-Jacobite Dutch propaganda.

Thus, in October 1688, Gordon began to propagandise the Stuart cause. The ceremonial occasion of the king's birthday launched Jacobitism in Russia. Gordon used this focal point as a means of appealing to a sense of patriotism and fostering loyalty to the ruling legitimate monarch, recording in his Diary for 14 October:

Wee celebrated the Kings birthday with those of his Sacred Ma-ties subjects who were here and others of the best quality among whom was the Polls Resident, & were all merry. At parting the Resident said to me that the King was happy who had subjects to remember him so cordially at such a distance.[10]

Nicholas Rogers argues that this type of occasion represented 'a singularly appropriate script in a world where royal anniversaries were solemnly observed to sanctify and legitimise the political order and where ceremonialism with its attendant festivities and folklore were still of decisive importance in fostering political allegiances'.[11] In private as well as in public, Gordon clearly promoted

9   Gordon, Diary, 17 November 1686, vol. 4, 146v.
10 Gordon, Diary, 14 October 1688, vol. 4, p. 215v.
11 Nicholas Rogers, 'Riot', p. 72.

his cause. For example, on 3 November: 'my Grandchild [by his daughter Katherine] Christened, & called Theodorus because borne on the day of that Sainct. Godfa-rs the Polls Resident Georg [blank] Demunt'.[12]

Throughout October, William of Orange had made repeated attempts to land an army in England. On 23 October, Gordon 'had notice of the Holands fleet gone for England upon the acc-ot (as is said) of the forcing the King to hold a free Parliament, & the preservation of Religion'.[13] The axe fell when:

> I received a letter from Mr. Fraser informing that the Hollanders great designe as they call it was now avowed against England, that they were gone with a fleet of 500 saile, at least that there were aboord of the Fleete 10000 men of all sorts, that the Prince went aboord on the 17th st veter. In the Gazetts of the 20th wee had the same.[14]

A successful and unopposed landing was made at Torbay on 5 November 1688. The news reached Moscow on 22 November.[15] Gordon immediately responded: 'I was in towne and had much discourse with the 2d favourite [Fedor Shaklovity] & some of the Councellours concerning the Holanders designe upon Our King, where I told them the truth'.[16] Gordon placed public duty alongside private concern. On 23 November, he wrote to Holland and London after his son's safety: 'I did writt to Mr. Meverell desireing to know the state of effaires there, & what is become of my sone. I writt also to Sir James Kenedy Lord Conservator of the Scottish Priviledges in Holand to the same effect'.[17]

Gordon was able to plan, collate information and co-ordinate his campaign with the help of the Polish resident. Newsletters offered encouraging reports of the fall of Philipsburgh to the French on 29 October. However, the danger to Holland had not been sufficient to halt the invasion of England a week later.[18] Gordon's youngest child's godfather, the Dutch resident, also provided 'a relation of all' concerning the *fait accompli*.[19] It seems that hard facts and first-hand eyewitness accounts were at a premium. Gordon received through Jacobite

---

12 Gordon, Diary, 4 November 1688, vol. 4, p. 218.
13 Gordon, Diary, 23 October 1688, vol. 4, p. 216.
14 Gordon, Diary, 12 November 1688, vol. 4, p. 219r–v.
15 Gordon, Diary, 19 November 1688, vol. 4, p. 219v: 'wee had currants or Gazettes of the 4th of N–r.'
16 Gordon, Diary, 22 November 1688, vol. 4, p. 220. The 'second favourite' was Fedor Shaklovity. See Hughes, *Sophia*, p. 216.
17 Gordon, Diary, 23 November 1688, vol. 4, p. 220v. That very day Meverell was sending Gordon news of James's safety: Gordon, Diary, 23 December 1688, vol. 4, p. 223v.
18 Gordon, Diary, 26 November 1688 and 2 December 1688, vol. 4, pp. 221–2v.
19 Gordon, Diary, 4 December 1688, vol. 4, p. 221v.

sympathisers in Riga 'an extract of a letter from London of the 6th of November, giveing notice of the Pr. of Orange his arrivall & landing at Torbay, Dartmouth, & Exmouth; he landed the fourth st. vet. & the next day had all his forces on land'.[20] Without delay, Gordon 'caused translate the extract of the letter from London which being read befor the Tzaars & counsell, gave great satisfaction'.[21] Following hard on the heels of this achievement: 'I rode to Pokrofska and dyned by the Boyar with the 2d favourite & diverse where much discourse about the effaires of England, where I told the truth & even passionately'.[22] Continuous briefings with informed and pro-Jacobite sources would have sharpened Gordon's argument and resolve.

On 13 January 1689, Gordon received 'the lamentable newes . . . of the King his haveing been forced by the infidility of his unnatural subjects to flee that he was <u>safely</u> [author's underlining] arrived at Dunkirk'.[23] William, with a large army that had to haul slow-moving wagons and artillery over impassable roads in order to engage the enemy, had successfully mounted a winter campaign. But James had provided weak military leadership. We can only suppose that after Russia the 'rigours' of an English winter, the distances involved, the relatively small size of the army, and the need for decisive leadership, would not have unduly taxed Gordon. He himself speculated:

had I been in a place where I could have been serviceable to his M: I should have vented my passion another way. I perceived even when I was there, that the Kings too great godness & credulity in intrusting disaffected & il principled persons in high charges could not but prove fatall. Notwithstanding all that hath fallen out I am sorry that his Matie did not, when I was in Scotland, lay his comands upon me to have stayed there albeit without employment, then might I have had occasion at this by me, to have given proofs of my loyalty and what I can do.[24]

20 Gordon, Diary, 9 December 1688, vol. 4, p. 222.
21 Gordon, Diary, 10 December 1688, vol. 4, p. 222v.
22 Gordon, Diary, 18 December 1688, vol. 4, p. 223. 'The Polls resident dyned by me where much discourse about State & other effaires.' Gordon, Diary, 16 December 1688, vol. 4, p. 223.
23 Gordon, Diary, 13 January 1689, vol. 4, p. 228. 'King was safely arrived at Ambleteuse, a new harbour betwixt Calais and Boloigne in France.' Gordon, Diary, 19 January 1689, vol. 4, p. 228.
24 Copy of Letter 'For his Grace the Duke of Gordon, at Paris, 15 November 1690': Gordon, Diary, vol. 4, pp. 58v–59. Childs has argued that James II and VII could have defeated William's forces after they had landed. Childs, *The Army of James II and VII*, pp. 177–81.

On 13 February 1689, the Crown of Great Britain was offered to William and Mary. In his acceptance statement, William stressed the misdeeds of James VII and II while casting doubts on the legitimacy of the Prince of Wales. William argued that he aimed to create a free and lawful Parliament and that he had been invited by the people to invade. Meanwhile, the Jacobite movement throughout Europe pressed for the restoration of the Stuart regime. In Russia, however, its chief proponent, along with many of its supporters, was to be neutralised by events for the next eight months. On 12 February, Patrick Gordon once again left Moscow at the start of the second Crimean campaign. He was not to return until 22 July and then to face the political crisis and its aftermath, which brought the future Peter the Great to the fore. Back in Scotland, on 11 April, the Convention had met in Edinburgh and declared William and Mary joint monarchs. The Scottish Crown was accepted by the House of Orange on 11 May.

The twin unifying articles of political faith amongst the Jacobite diaspora were a devotion to the deposed monarch and a desire to restore the House of Stuart to the British throne from its court in exile at the château St Germain-en-Laye near Paris. Fifty thousand, mainly Catholics, left Britain for the continent between 1689 and 1692 and the greatest rallying point for Jacobite exiles became the French army. A military atmosphere pervaded the court in exile itself, as there were 2,500 Irish soldiers in residence. A condition of the Treaty of Limerick between the Jacobite and Williamite forces on 3 October 1691 was that soldiers serving in the Irish army could volunteer to leave the country with all honours; Patrick Sarsfield led 11,000–12,000 Irish soldiers into exile in France.[25] Lord Melfort, a Catholic, was first Secretary of State and Lord Middleton, a Protestant, the other Secretary of State. However, feuds over religion and factionalism were to undermine the court at St Germain-en-Laye.[26]

In Russia, no such divisions amongst those who professed to be Jacobite appear to have existed. Some Jacobites within foreign communities have been characterised as 'numerous, well-organized, obstinate, competent in intrigue, and with a tradition of secret organization dating back to the Stuart exile during the Protectorate'.[27] Certainly in Russia those soldiers serving during the 1680s and 1690s had mainly arrived during the recruitment 'wave' of the 1660s, or, indeed,

---

25 'A regulation of the pay of the Irish Regiments come to France from Limerick.' Gordon, Diary, vol. 5, p. 111.
26 'The divisions between English, Scots and Irish among Jacobite exiles at the Stuart court, however, was a liability.' Cruickshanks and Black, *The Jacobite Challenge*, Introduction, pp. 3–4.
27 McLynn, *The Jacobites*, p. 172.

were first-generation descendants from soldiers who had arrived during the 1650s fleeing the Cromwellian regime. These men consequently had no first-hand experience of James's alleged misdeeds. Having been forced to flee, or escaping under the threat of expulsion, from a violently anti-monarchist Commonwealth, they were predisposed to support James. Indeed, William Speck has argued that 'to treat the events of 1688 in isolation from the upheaval of the civil wars would be absurd. Contemporaries were deeply conscious of the parallels which could be drawn between the experiences of their own times and those of their fathers.'[28]

Many, like Gordon in Moscow, were also Catholics. They thus had a vested interest in supporting a Catholic monarch. Moreover, owing to the relative isolation of Russian service from European contacts, and the extreme difficulty of leaving Russian service, mercenaries serving in Russia had only a partial knowledge of events in Great Britain. Such information tended to have been either filtered through to the foreign colony by official diplomatic or governmental sources and dispatches or through family contacts. Whilst the latter cannot be vouched for, it is not unreasonable to suggest that the former sources would have presented the ruling monarch, James II, in appropriately deferential and regal terms, in a manner designed to ensure and promote loyalty to the House of Stuart. Thus, John Miller's argument concerning the transient nature and the effect of time upon political allegiance in Britain cannot be made applicable to Moscow. Miller has written:

> As 1688 receded into the past, however, memories of James's misdeeds faded and a multiplicity of new resentments made Jacobitism seem to many – and not only to Tories – a serious alternative to an unpopular regime. Then, and only then, did it become easy for Tories to see James's expulsion and William's usurpation in isolation, and in simple, clear-cut terms, and so provide a rationale for adherence to the Jacobite cause.[29]

British mercenaries in Russia would have been more prone to be pro-Jacobite than Williamite from the outset.

Many Jacobites believed in the theory of kingship by divine, hereditary and indefeasible right. The king's authority came directly from God. The hereditary principle avoided disputes about succession. Indefeasible divine right meant that whoever had the divine right to be king could not lose it no matter what he did. In this respect the Glorious Revolution of 1688 was thus seen as a sacrilege;

28 Speck, *The Reluctant Revolutionaries*, p. 25.
29 See John Miller, 'Proto-Jacobitism', p. 19.

and there was no true *de iure* sovereign governing the United Kingdom after 1688.

Peter I's Assumption of Power

The whole of the foreign community in Moscow had seven months within which to dwell upon the implications of these seemingly abstract and theoretical concepts of divine, hereditary and indefeasible right, before Russia itself suffered its own 'revolution', a crisis in which the foreigners were visibly and potentially fatally required to express their political allegiance. The resolution of the crisis left Gordon as the undisputed military authority figure within that community and ideally placed to restart the push in earnest for Russian recognition of James VII and II as rightful ruler of Great Britain.

On 25 January 1688, Gordon noted in his Diary that there was 'a Councill day wherein did sitt both the Tzaars & the Princess, the Youngest Tzaar the first tyme'. The future Peter the Great, let us recall, was junior to his half-brother Ivan, while his half-sister Sophia had assumed power in 1682 as Regent during the minority of the joint tsars. By the end of May 1688, Peter was 16 years old, the same age as his grandfather Mikhail and father Aleksei at their accession. As Lindsey Hughes has written, 'there were indeed signs that Peter was now being groomed for power'.[30] Peter himself frequently attended court ceremonies, although he appears to have been happier sailing a newly discovered boat or commmanding his 'play' regiments.

In September 1688, Sophia appeared to be presenting, through promotion of herself as 'Self-Upholder, Autocrat and Regent', a legal and constitutional challenge to Peter's hereditary right to become tsar. On 7 September, Gordon wrote that there was 'great appearance and rumours of an insurrection among the streltsees' as well as tension between the younger tsar and Prince Golitsyn, Sophia's first favourite, regarding Peter's order for five 'fluitshiks', five drummers and others from Gordon's regiment to join him without informing Golitsyn. Trouble was brewing amid preparations for a second campaign in the Crimea in the following year. On 26 October, Gordon's own position as a foreign general was under attack from the patriarch, who, according to the Diary, said that 'a hertick hath the best people in our Empire under his command, but he was taken up smartly by all the Nobility, and even laught at'. The international complexity of the unfolding developments was illustrated by a Diary entry of 27 October:

30 Hughes, *Sophia*, p. 221.

another councill, how to proceed for money, what forces to send and whither, they beginning to apprehend some danger by the makeing of a peace, which in this juncture of tyme the Rom Emperour would be forced to, by the French invadeing the Empire and breaking the truce and doubting that their actions and expeditions would not be well interpreted, as not done sincerely and cordially, which they perceiving, and reason prompting them to beleeve that at the makeing of a generall peace the allyes would not include them, they began to cast about what was fittest for them to do.

As preparations continued for a campaign to be launched in the new year, on 13 November, Peter summoned the remaining drummers from Gordon's regiment to join him. On 5 December, Gordon learned that the Russian ambassador in Poland, was to go to Vienna to make certain that if peace were to be concluded with the Turks, the Russians would not be excluded from it.

Early in the new year, Tsar Peter's 'coming of age' was marked further with his marriage on 7 January 1689. There was a considerable amount of diplomatic activity, and the second Crimean campaign was launched by Golitsyn with Gordon in attendance but Peter at home conducting military and naval exercises. The campaign was a failure, although Sophia talked of 'incredible victories'. On the return of the army to Moscow in July, Gordon notes, 'with a great deale ade and entreaty the yongest Tzaar was brought to assent to the rewards which had been concluded to be given for our services'. On 27 July, Peter refused to receive the leaders of the army. Gordon observes that 'now there was plainly to be seen an open eruption or breach which was lyke to turne to animosityes'. On 31 July, according to his Diary, there were 'passions and humours increasing lyke to breake out into a Paroxismus'.

When Peter, fearing assassination, fled to the Troitsa [Trinity] Monastery, a choice had to be made. In his Diary entry for 4 September, Gordon clearly describes the event:

A Tzaars letter was brought into the Strangers Slabod [Foreign Quarter] being sent to the Generall persons & Colonells with all the other officers but no body mentioned by name. The order was in the name of the yongest Tzaar only . . . wee should imediately with all our armes and mounting repaire to his Ma-tie in the Monastery of Troitza.

Gordon took the letter to Golitsyn, who prevaricated, telling Gordon he would receive instructions as to how to respond to this order in the evening. The Diary records: 'I returned and made ready to be gone, and told the Colonells and other Officers whoe came to me for advice, that notwithstanding any order might be here given, I was resolved to go & would be gone in the evening, where upon all the great & small made ready.[31] Gordon gave his support to Peter as the tsar assumed supreme power for himself, ejecting his half-sister Sophia and her closest adviser Golitsyn.[32]

In this moment of political and constitutional crisis Gordon provided leadership. As the preeminent foreigner, royal representative and confirmed Jacobite, he probably swayed many to share his belief in hereditary succession in Great Britain as well as in Russia. This is conjecture, as is the interpretation of the events of September 1689 as a struggle of a modernising Peter versus a conservative Sophia. Nevertheless, throughout the 1690s, as Gordon strove for the Jacobite cause, he was also closely associated with Peter in preparations for the reforms that were to ensue at the end of the seventeenth century.

Having made a significant contribution to Peter's assumption of power, Gordon went on to assist the tsar along the road towards the acquisition of the title 'Great'. As General in the taking of Azov by the Black Sea, as Rear-Admiral in naval manoeuvres on the White Sea, and on many other occasions in Moscow, Gordon was Peter's companion and adviser.

Jacobitism and Peter I

The distinguishing feature of Jacobite ideological conviction was that William owed his position to conquest, not hereditary right. As John Miller has argued, 'much of the rationale of Jacobitism rested on a particular view of what had happened in 1688–9: a belief that James II and VII had been driven out by armed force and unjustly removed from his throne'.[33]

However, to win the campaign for the hearts and minds of the foreign community was useless unless real 'conversions' could be sustained within the newly emerging political elite. The faction that was to assume power after 1689 had to be influenced into propagating a pro-Jacobite foreign policy. In the 1650s, this had taken the form of refusing to countenance diplomatic ties with the new Republic. This was the benchmark against which Gordon's efforts would be measured. In the assessment of Eveline Cruickshanks, 'The main historical importance of Jacobitism . . . was its effect on British politics and

---

31 Gordon, Diary 4 September 1689, vol. 4, p. 253r–253v.
32 For description and analysis of this event, see Bushkovitch, *Peter*, pp. 160–9; Hughes, *Sophia*, pp. 221–41. Ivan V, joint tsar with Peter, died in 1696, 'having carried out his ceremonial duties to the last'. Hughes, *Sophia*, p. 247.
33 Miller, 'Proto-Jacobitism', p. 7.

British foreign policy, its influence on the politics of other European states and the contribution made by the Jacobite exiles to those states.'[34]

William III was able to call upon Moscow's resident Dutch diplomatic representatives, with their substantial expertise in Russian affairs, to secure the interests of his British subjects in Russia.[35] In other European countries and cities, those diplomats who had openly supported James II could be and were replaced. For example, the very day Wyche left Hamburg 'to make abod' in Spain, the new Williamite diplomatic representative moved into the vacated diplomatic residence.[36] However, Moscow proved an exception. Gordon's position as royal representative, although never fully formalised and regularised, was underpinned by his primary duty to his masters, that of military general. His actions during the 1689 'family troubles' left his position unassailable. Gordon appeared to be in a position to uphold Jeremy Black's assertion that it 'was not how many Jacobites there were, but what they could accomplish'.[37] Thus, the Dutch resident Van Keller, in a letter dated 1 November 1689, misjudged the situation, and wrote: 'At this Court here there is not a single English minister. And the number of English traffickers here is not very considerable either; there are no more than six, four of whom live ordinarily here in town, and two others in Archangel.' He then went on to ask if he should 'take care of the affairs of these few Englishmen'.[38] This impression that no 'English Minister' was in residence, and that British interests had been left unattended, was not to last. Gordon had returned from the Crimean campaigns and, in the following year, was to disrupt the first diplomatic contacts between William III and Peter.

What then is the evidence for Gordon co-ordinating the Jacobite campaign in Russia? Firstly, Gordon sought to re-establish contact with leading members of the old English and Scottish political elites who had fled abroad to form a government in exile. For example, he recorded in the Diary that 'haveing read in the Gazetts that the Earle of Melfort was to go from Paris to Rome I did writt to him, . . . recommending it to the care of the Marquis Angelus Gabrielli'.[39]

34 Cruickshanks, *Ideology and Conspiracy*, Introduction, p. 3.
35 'Sec. Sir Francis Windebank, 1689, May 31, Drury Lane' – HMC 23 Report, xii.3, Cowper Mss, II (1868), p. 230.
36 PRO, SP 82/17, fol. 54. Thomson, *The Secretaries of State*, p. 102, notes that William III 'was in a specially difficult position because he was forced to dismiss most of the diplomats who had served James.' For an appraisal of diplomacy under William III, see: Lane, 'The Diplomatic Service', pp. 87–109; Snyder, 'The British Diplomatic Service', pp. 47–68. D. B. Horn, 'Scottish Diplomatists', p. 8: it has been noted that 'The only Scotsman to hold a diplomatic appointment before the Act of Union was Admiral Sir David Mitchell.'
37 Black, *Jacobitism and British Foreign Policy*, p. 142.
38 Eekman, 'Muscovy's International Relations', p. 51.
39 Gordon, Diary, 4 December 1689, vol. 4, p. 262.

Over the previous 20 years Gordon had built up a reliable and efficient communications network stretching across northern Europe, consisting of merchants, Jacobite residents and correspondents of *The London Gazette*. For example, he wrote to his kinsman William Gordon, 'Let me hear from you as soone as possible, by the way of London, my Correspondent there is Mr Samuel Meverell, in Dantzick Patrick Forbes & James Adie, In Hamburgh Robert Jolly in Rotterdam James Gordon, In Riga Georg Frazer, In Narva Thomas Loftus & Thomas More.'[40]

Thus it was to these contacts that Gordon first turned and in a letter of 27 February 1690 to one of these well-briefed individuals, Samuel Meverell, Gordon fleshed out the embryo of his campaign to spread Jacobitism in Russia, noting:

> how steddable I have been and am and may be at this Court to the publick good of the Nation. Our Countrey men here will I hope advise the ffriends what I have done for them this present, and how I may be able to serve them here also, for there is not a day about wherein I cannot see & speake with his Matie who is now settled in the Government, is gracious to me beyond measure. pray let me know how much you have expended and to whom at Court I might make my address, I fear my old ffriends are out of date, and that my opinion may hinder the acquiring of new, albeit what hath hapened there doth not in the least diminish my care & endeavours for the welfare of the Nation. pray informe me who is Secretary for the Northern Province & for Scotland.[41]

Gordon had written a month earlier to the Earl of Aberdeen in a similar vein: 'I am very much grieved for the troubles, divisions & the distracted condition of that our poor Countrey. I pray God to grant peace & quietness, for there is nothing more as to my owne particular desire in this world as to come home & end my lyfe whence I received it in tranquility.'[42]

However, the method of his proposed return was to be that of conqueror, at the head of an army professionally officered by pro-Stuart mercenaries commissioned from the Russian army. On 8 May, he wrote to the Earl of Melfort:

40 'Memorandum for Captain William Gordon', in Dukes, 'Patrick Gordon and his Family Circle', pp. 24–9.
41 'Letter to Mr. Samuel Meverell, Mosco 27 Febry 1690', Gordon, Diary, vol. 5, pp. 48r–48v.
42 'Letter to the Earl of Aberdeen, Mosco 28 Jan 1690', Gordon, Diary, vol. 5, p. 47r. See also: 'Letter to the Earle of Erroll, Mosco Jan 1690', Ustrialov, *Istoriia*, vol. I, pp. 309–11, in which Gordon describes army campaigns and mentions the current state of the political situation in Russia after the change of government.

my designe and business was & is to offer my Service to his Sacred Majesty being ready & even passionately desirous to spend lyfe and all I have in the defence of his M: just right, [in the margin '& my service may be useful'] I only want his M. commands a comission without which I cannot safely adventure nor my service for in whatsoever quality or place my zeale & duty admits his Matie will employ me, I am ready & willing and with great celerity shall transport my Self to any place whence the King shall order me to receive his comands. It were fitt I had some blanke commission whereby I might engage such good officers as I may gett moved to a sense of there duty + my sonne James is in Scotland in his Maties service whom I have commanded to be constant & faithful.

Gordon ends the letter with the news: 'P.S. I have gott this Court to owne still his Sacred Matie & not to hear of any other.'[43]

Is it possible to imagine Gordon campaigning in the north-east of Scotland? Bruce Lenman describes the appropriateness of the region for such an activity, writing that 'the Gordon lands seemed to offer a reservoir of resources to any Jacobite army. After all, those lands included regions like the Enzie which were almost one hundred per cent Roman Catholic, and the Gordons were historically unique among the highland clans because of their ability to put significant cavalry forces in the field.'[44] Undoubtedly, Russia was a viable, if unrecognised, recruiting ground for Jacobite mercenaries, trained professional soldiers, who could have offered their services. Had such a professionally experienced officer as Gordon returned to the north-east of Scotland in 1686, it is possible he would have, with some 20 months in hand, put some 'bite' into the Scottish army and so bolstered the resolve of James II to stand and actively engage the enemy in battle. Cruickshanks and Black are agreed that any restoration was 'dependent on the availability of arms and troops supplied by or from other European states: France, Spain, Sweden or, in the 1750s, Prussia.'[45] However, the case has not previously been made for active recruitment from Russia of troops to form an invasion force to retake the Crown in the early 1690s.

43 'Letter to the Earl of Melfort, Mosco 8 May 1690', Gordon, Diary, vol. 5, p. 31r.
44 Lenman, 'Scottish Nobility', p. 154. Lenman goes on to postulate, p. 156, that the 'North-East was merely an extreme example of a common fact of Scottish life at the time of the Revolution: Jacobitism had more bark than bite.' The argument that one efficient and professional commanding officer in early modern Europe could make the difference to the outcome of a battle was stated by Carswell, *The Descent*, p. 19. That this officer could have been General Patrick Gordon has been postulated by Barnhill and Dukes, 'North-east Scots in Muscovy', p. 60, as well as Joseph Robertson, the editor of the Spalding Club, 1859 version of the 'Diaries'.
45 Cruickshanks and Black, *The Jacobite Challenge*, Introduction, p. 3.

As we have already seen, there were two elements of Gordon's campaign to spread Jacobitism within the foreign community: the proposal to actively recruit mercenaries from the Russian army to fight under the battle standard of the House of Stuart; and the hindrance of diplomatic recognition for the House of Orange. These twin pillars of the Jacobite strategy that Patrick Gordon had adopted, both defiantly active and openly supportive of the Stuart king, were perhaps influenced directly by the actions of his clan chief, the Duke of Gordon. As Daniel Szechi has observed, 'Jacobite society in Britain revolved around networks of kinship and sociability.'[46] In Scotland in particular, the nature of clan society itself promoted and fostered an affinity for the Stuarts. Thus, there was a profound intrinsic sympathy between the Stuart dynasty, with its patriarchal and authoritarian view of the role of kingship, and the clan structure. This sympathy was deemed by many in Scotland to have existed from time immemorial.[47] Statute law challenged the notion of authority resting upon hereditary jurisdiction, customary and traditional rights, and logically this legal and constitutionally based challenge was to threaten the clan chiefs' authority as much as James's. Also, there could reasonably have been a fear that if political power was not transferred according to the hereditary principle, then so too would the hereditary principle in economic power be discarded. Thus the role of the Duke of Gordon was pivotal in determining the response of his clan to the events of 1688.

The Duke of Gordon had been commander of Edinburgh Castle in 1689, and supported the position of James VII and II when Williamites 'sent another message to the Duke of Gordon to surrender the Castle of Edinburgh, which refusing he was proclaimed rebel to the state.'[48] In April 1690, the Duke of Gordon 'who had liberty upon his parol of honour, has, contrary to the same, withdrawn himself, and is gone to France.'[49] By November he was implicated in a plot: 'a body of men designed to goe for Scotland, to join the rebells there under the command of the duke of Gourdon, the lord Maitland, and the earl of Melfort.'[50] It was especially important for Patrick Gordon to establish the intentions of his clan chief[51] and he would have become aware of the breakdown of relations between two senior Catholic Jacobites in exile, the Duke of Gordon

---

46 Szechi, *The Jacobites*, p. 25.
47 Jackson, *Restoration Scotland*, pp. 45–59.
48 *CSPD*, 1689–1690, p. 38. Luttrell, *A Brief Historical Relation*, vol. II, p. 547, states that the Scottish Convention 'proclaimed him a rebell and traytor, forbidding all persons, on pain of treason, to correspond or treat with him.'
49 Luttrell, *A Brief Historical Relation*, vol. II, p. 34, April 23, 1690.
50 Ibid., vol. II, p. 100, September 2, 1690.
51 'For his Grace the Duke of Gordon, Mosco Nov. 15 1690', Gordon, Diary, vol. 5, p. 58r.

and the Earl of Melfort, supporting his kinsman. Thus, he complained that the Duke of Gordon, amongst others in the Scottish political establishment, had not received 'commissions in a general distribution he [Melfort] had made to the King's friends'. His opposition to Melfort's influence with the king 'was quickly communicated to their relatives and dependants'.[52]

However, Patrick Gordon continued his correspondence with both men in his successful bid to keep abreast of the news, especially Jacobite attempts being made to overthrow William of Orange. And, of course, he records such news in the Diary. For example: 'Wee had notice of the battell of Flewry which was fought on the 21 July St vet. the french victorizing. & that the Duke of Gordon was come to Paris';[53] 'In Preobravsinsky, wee had the newes of the sea fight betwixt the French & Hollanders & English';[54] 'Their maties came to Mosko in the evening the sadd newes of king James his overthrow in Ireland';[55] 'The Polls Resident gave me a visitt and told the many things concerning his private & publick effaires'.[56] It is probable that the possibility of Jesuit priests being allowed to return to Moscow was also discussed at this meeting. Then, 'I gave up another petition to his Matie about my Business. who gave it to Gabriel Golovkin to be written out shortly, & to be deferred to his M.'[57] As on previous occasions, the king's birthday became a rallying focal point for opposition to the House of Orange. It was a visible and public opportunity to declare ideological, political or constitutional loyalties, and must have had a powerful effect on those who took part. But such occasions also combined with the business of keeping good order in Moscow. For example: '18 regiments in the Fields at exercize where had like to be mischieffe came home late yet was merry with Countrey men drinking the Kings health.'[58]

From October 1690, the amount of references to 'my business' markedly increased. On 2 November: 'came home about 3 aclock in the morning my business spoke of & consulted above'.[59] Then, on 5 November: 'In Preobrasinsko &

52 Jones, *The Mainstream of Jacobitism*, p. 10. The contest for control of the Jacobite movement is discussed in Szechi, 'The Jacobite Revolution Settlement', pp. 610–28.
53 Gordon, Diary, 21 July 1690, vol. 5, p. 19: 'received a letter from the Earl of Melfort his sacred Maties Ambassadour at Rome 5th of August 1690, by post.' Gordon, Diary, 11 October 1690, vol. 5, p. 29. The reply was made the following month: 'For his Exc: the Earle of Melfort at Rome, Nov. 15 1690', Diary, vol. 5, p. 59.
54 Gordon, Diary, 4 August 1690, vol. 5, p. 21.
55 Gordon, Diary, 11 August 1690, vol. 5, p. 22.
56 Gordon, Diary, 7 September 1690, vol. 5, p. 26.
57 Gordon, Diary, 27 September 1690, vol. 5, p. 28.
58 Gordon, Diary, 14 October 1690, vol. 5, p. 29.
59 Gordon, Diary, 2 November 1690, vol. 5, p. 31. See also: 'In Preobrasinsko see & spoke with his Matic & spoke to some Boyars about my business', Gordon, Diary, 3 November 1690, vol. 5, p. 31v.

Ismailov where I was admitted to kiss the Emperess Dowager her hand was afterwards . . . with his Matie, came to the fyre in Pokrofska & afterwards to my house supped, rested & breakfasted my business consulted but nothing concluded.'[60] As the Catholic Jesuit priests in Moscow were expelled in October 1689, it is possible that the references to 'my business' indicate that Gordon attempted to mediate with Peter in order to retain their services in Moscow.[61]

In their absence, Gordon was obliged for the marriage of his daughter to make use of the Dutch minister. Tsar Peter was present, and no doubt would have ensured that all drinks were downed, especially were Gordon to combine the names of Peter and James in one all-purpose toast of health and prosperity. To this extent Jacobitism in Russia does not appear to have the characteristics of other Jacobite communities in the diaspora as described by Edward Gregg: 'From the moment James II and VII fled England for France in December 1688, Jacobitism became an exile movement, of necessity conspiratorial in organization and obsessed with the meaning of treason.'[62]

Peter's disaffection from the Stuart cause would not have been promoted by the diplomatic overture made by William III. A letter sent by him in January 1690 but that did not reach Moscow until December bore a superscription reading to the 'Czar and Great Duke Ivan Alexeiowich'. William referred to 'good and friendly intercourse' as the basis 'whereby the Trade and Commerce of both Nations will be advanced to the mutual benefit and advantage of our respective Subjects and Dominions.'[63] However, the letter neither made reference to the ending of the Regency in Russia nor commented upon the overthrow of James II and the accession of William III to the throne of Great Britain. It is also possible that the letter blundered in not referring to Tsar Ivan by his full titles. Gordon duly recorded in his Diary for 24 December:

> The Copy of the letter from the pretended King of England, calling himself Wm the 3d & dated the 3d of June, interpreted and no further notice taken of it, upon pretension that the Hollands Resident his name was not in it, It being

60 Gordon, Diary, 5 November 1690, vol. 5, p. 31.
61 For example: Gordon, Diary, 22 December 1690, vol. 5, p. 35v.
62 Gregg, 'The Politics of Paranoia', p. 52, raises delusions of persecution and fears of subversion within local Jacobite groups to the status of leitmotif for the movement as a whole.
63 William III to the 'Czar and Great Duke Ivan Alexeiowich' 31 January 1690, *PRO*, SP 104/120, fols 1–2. (On fol. 4 the introduction to the letter was rewritten, and both the tsars correctly named.) 'Warrant to pay to Gideon Royer, 'writer, flourisher, and embellisher,' his account of 10 l. for writing, flourishing, and embellishing, one skin of vellum with the King's arms, armaments, and badges, and for gilding and painting the labels for the seal, being for a letter sent to the Czar of Russia', *CSPD*, 1689–1690, p. 462.

sent to hime to be delivered publickley & solemnly, Another had been sent befor dated in Aprill but not haveing the full Title was returned by the Resident & sent, so that it seems they must have a third, and then a question if it shall be received for diverse reasons. I went to the Potiesny Hosse and see his Matie who was very gracious to me.[64]

A necessary first step to reversing the declining fortunes of Anglo-Russian trade must have been an accurate assessment of Russian attitudes to the new Williamite regime. If, according to normal Muscovite diplomatic practice, treaties were considered 'to have been concluded by a sovereign on his own behalf and for his heirs, that is, in the name of the State', what was the legal validity of existing trade agreements between Russia and a state which had deposed its king and overturned the principle of hereditary succession?[65] Were the treaty commitments agreed upon by his predecessor, James VII and II, to be upheld by William III? This indeterminate situation certainly allowed Gordon scope for raising legalistic, diplomatic and constitutional objections to the recognition of the 'Pretender King William'.

The rejection of William III's letter to Peter marked the high point of Jacobite hopes. The rejection was partly aided by confusion throughout Europe as to whether or not the House of Orange would retain control in the three kingdoms, since no European state was willing to recognise the emerging regime precipitately. For example, the British resident in Stockholm wrote:

Wee are of expectation of what the next letters will tell us of the French into Ireland, until we are some way or other delivered, tis to no purpose to speake to our Ministers here, who will governe themselves only according to the success of either side, and therefore are very desirous to know how matters go and are like to goe.[66]

On 11 August 1690, Gordon received 'the sadd newes of K. James his over throw in Ireland'.[67] Three months later, on 15 November, he wrote to his high-placed kinsman and fellow Jacobite the Duke of Gordon:

The sad revolution in our countrey, and the Kings misfortunes, wherein your Grace hath a large share, hath occasioned inexpressible grieffe to me, which

---

64 Gordon, Diary, 24 December 1690, vol. 5, p. 37. See also: Szeftel, 'The Title', pp. 59–81.
65 Grabar, *The History of International Law*, p.10.
66 'Mr. Duncombe to Secretary of State, Stockholm April 9th 1690', *PRO*, SP 95/13, fol. 120. See also fols 163 and 174.
67 Gordon, Diary, 11 August 1690, vol. 5, p. 22.

brought me in a sicknesse and even almost to deaths doore. Had I been in a place where I could have been serviceable to his Majestie, I should have vented my passion another way.[68]

Gordon blamed the revolution on 'the Kings too great goodness and credulity in intrusting disaffected and ill principled persons in high charges'. On the same day, Gordon wrote to the exiled King James II's Secretary of State, the Earl of Melfort, viewing the revolution 'as another conquest by a medley of forreigne nations' and wondering how his fellow-countrymen could 'endure so long such slavery and oppressions by forreigne forces'.[69]

January 1691 found Gordon consolidating his position amongst the Jacobite community in Moscow, but unable to halt diplomatic recognition. On 18 January, the Diary records: 'the English & other ffriends at a Feast with musick by me'.[70] The entry for 19 January relates how 'The D.[iak] prevailed upon to receive the P.[retender] K.[ing] W.[illiam] his letter to their Tz: M.'[71] On 24 January, 'the Hollands Resident gave up the letter from the P. of Orange giveing notice of his being advanced to the crowne of great Brittaine'.[72] It is possible that Gordon had been fighting a rearguard action in attempting to have this letter dismissed by using his influence to block its passage through the various layers of Russian bureaucratic officialdom. This campaign would have demanded a clear, reasoned argument to support his Jacobite position. However, he had now lost the initiative, since the Prince of Orange was recognised as King of Great Britain.

Possibly, all was not yet lost. A debate was still taking place in Moscow, fuelled, no doubt, by pro-Williamite newsletters translated into Russian and taken from *The Dutch Gazette*, pamphlets procured by the Dutch resident in Moscow, and even tracts translated by Il'ya Fedorovich Kopievsky, the Russian resident in Amsterdam.[73] Gordon also requested tracts from his network of contacts in west Europe, for example in a letter to a kinsman of 16 February 1691: 'pray if you meet with any bookes or papers set out in favour of King James

---

68 Gordon, Diary, 15 November 1690, vol. 5, p. 58.
69 Gordon, Diary, 15 November 1690, vol. 5, p. 58.
70 Gordon, Diary, 18 January 1691, vol. 5, p. 65.
71 Gordon, Diary, 19 January 1691, vol. 5, p. 65. 'A letter from the K. of Poll. to the Tzaars giveing notice of the Princes Jacob his mar: to the Princess of Newburgh', Gordon, Diary, 23 January 1691, vol. 5, p. 65v.
72 Gordon, Diary, 24 January 1691, vol. 5, p. 65.
73 Yu. K. Begunov suggests that it was Kopievsky who translated an anti-Jacobite interpretation of the events before, during and after the landing of Torbay and the Battle of the Boyne. The political system which existed during the reign of James II and VII was also criticised: Begunov, 'Opisanie vrat chestie . . .', pp. 60–93.

or anything impartiall relating to the tymes send me them . . . . pray let me here from you and know what passeth in our Countrey by yor shipping to Archangel.[74] Such tracts would argue the Jacobite cause, and they would be highly political in nature, concerned with the abstract notions and theories of divine right, hereditary principle, the duty of Christian subjects, the rightful subjugation of statute and common law to the Ancient Constitution.

It is thus highly likely that Gordon debated or discussed these issues with Peter, to whom he had daily access. To this extent, Gordon can be considered a tutor in constitutional law, kingship, current affairs and international relations to Peter. The importance of any such education in the field of diplomacy was underlined by Grabar, who asserted: 'When one speaks of Petrine diplomats, one must not forget that the leading and most outstanding diplomat was Peter himself. The entire direction of foreign policy emanated from him. Diplomats were the executors of his will, the transmitters of his intentions.'[75] This may have been true if one applies it to the eighteenth century, or even after the Azov campaigns of the seventeenth. However, at this early stage in Peter's career, the young tsar appeared more interested in fireworks, drill, hand-held grenades, siege craft and especially boats and shipbuilding. Gordon himself testifies to Peter's complete disinterest in diplomacy during this period: 'Lew Kirilovits & Kniaz Boris Alex: went to Pereslav to perswade his M: to returne, to receive the Persian Ambassadour, who being come to Volodinia was ordered to wait there.'[76]

In general, some have argued more recently, the most important contribution made by the Jacobite diaspora was the dissemination of its secular, as well as religious, ideas. Jacobites acted as a transmission belt; they helped spread the ideas of others. For example, Frank McLynn has observed:

The most controversial intellectual role played by the Jacobites on the continent was in the area of Jansenism and freemasonry. These were particularly tricky waters to swim in because of the attitude towards them of the Catholic

---

74 Gordon, Diary, 16 February 1691, vol. 5, p. 65, to 'Loveing Cousin'[who?] and signed 'Yor affectinate Kinsman.'
75 Grabar, *The History of International Law*, p. 43.
76 Gordon, Diary, 16 February 1692, vol. 5, p. 165. See also entries 23 and 28 February 1692, vol. 5, p. 166. Alexander Gordon, *History*, vol. III, p. 93: 'In the month of March 1692, an Ambassador came from Persia to the Czar, who caused draw up an army of twenty thousand men, along the front of which the Ambassador passed when he made his entry.' During the eighteenth century, 'efforts made to interest Peter the Great in the Jacobite cause and to involve him in the problems of the English succession' witnessed greater success, although 'the Jacobites interested Peter only in so far as they provided a weapon for the achievement of his aims in western Europe.' See Bruce, 'Jacobite Relations', p. 343.

church, the official protector and champion of the Stuart dynasty . . . Men like
the Duke of Wharton in Spain, Patrick Gordon and James Keith in Russia,
George Hamilton in Switzerland and Lord Wint in Rome all set up Jacobite
lodges.[77]

For the moment, let us resume our narrative from the early 1690s onwards.
Early in the decade, foreign 'policy', such as it was, was decided by Peter's
favourites and immediate family. It was these people, then, whom Gordon as
the leading Jacobite in Russia would seek to persuade and convince that it was
in their own interests not to recognise William III and to continue to support
James II and VII. Meanwhile, the Dutch continued to represent their king. For
example, Gordon's Diary for 7 March 1691 records: 'The Hol: Resident obtained
an Answer to the P. K. [Protestant King?] Wm letter.'[78]

Throughout 1691, Gordon continued to correspond with the Earl of
Melfort,[79] the Duke of Gordon,[80] and the Earls of Errol and Aberdeen.[81] As it
became apparent that Peter would not allow Gordon's release from Russian
mercenary service,[82] Gordon could only ruminate on the nature of loyalty and
the wisdom of monarchs:

it seems they had forgott the maxime of King James in his Basilicon Dorun
that Loyalty runneth in a race or lyne, whom it should they have trusted or
who was able to have maintained the Kings Authority and their interest if not
your G[race]. I remember K. Charles the first by evill Counsell, upon the acot

77 McLynn, *The Jacobites*, pp. 139–40. This overstates Gordon's role as there is no actual
    evidence in the Diary for the influence of Jansenism or freemasonry. Certainly, James
    Keith was influential in the introduction of freemasonry to Russia. See Chapter 8.
78 Gordon, Diary, 7 March 1691, vol. 5, p. 69v.
79 'received a letter from the Earle of Melfort dated at Rome the 12th of May acknowledging
    the reseat of myne of the 15th of November', Gordon, Diary, 7 July 1691, vol. 5, p. 85v: 'writt
    to the Earle of Melfort in answer to his dated at Rome 12th May', Gordon, Diary, 17 July
    1691, vol. 5, p. 87.
80 'received letters from the Duke of Gordon dated at London An: 90 April 12 enclosed a letter
    from Harie Gordon dated at varso 30 Marty 1691', Gordon, Diary, 18 May 1691, vol. 5, p. 79:
    'I did writt to Mr Guascomy his conveyance to the Duke of Gordon in answer to his of the
    12th Aprilis an:dm 1690', Gordon, Diary, 22 May 1691, vol. 5, p. 80; 'Red. from Duke of
    Gordon dated 22 July S.N. 1691', Gordon, Diary 27 September 1691, vol. 5, p. 98.
81 'writt to the Earles of Arroll and Aberdeen', Gordon, Diary, 8 August 169, vol. 5, p. 90.
82 'It hath been alwayes my great desire to have come home & passe the last of my dayes in
    my owne Countrey to the which I had great encouragement when I was last there, but
    noe the want of liberty of conscience there, & his Maties great favour here, hath put me
    almost out of all hopes, and yet I still imagine that I shall end my dayes there', Gordon,
    Diary, Letter 'to much honoured & Loveing uncle Mr James Gordon of Westertowne',
    vol. 5, p. 128.

of lessening the greatne of your house tooke away the Hereditary Sherifdomes of Aberdeen & Inverness from your predecessor as his great grandson nor did the Earldomes of Marr & Murray which albeit it did not make them recede from their Loyalty, yet it mad them less capable of serving their Maties in their need.[83]

In the power struggles at court the Duke of Gordon had evidently lost out to Melfort and it would appear that Gordon supported the position of his clan chief as he dropped contact with Melfort. As McLynn has appropriately noted: 'The aristocratic nature of the Jacobite movement evoked oligarchic solidarity and therefore the exiles were treated as honoured guests. There were no Jacobite ghettos; their principal problems were not economic but divided loyalties and dual nationalities.'[84] It is clear that divisions within their own ranks could marginalise and weaken some loyalists in Russia as elsewhere. From this period onwards, the references to Jacobite activity fade into occasional references celebrating the king's birthday,[85] or another depressing reversal of Jacobite hopes for restoration.

If Jacobite hopes for the conquest of the three kingdoms by amphibious assault upon Britain were further away than ever, in Russia Jacobites were closely associated with the emergence of a new navy. During the 1690s, Patrick Gordon continued and indeed strengthened his contacts with members of the Muscovy Company. This process was facilitated by the fact that his son-in-law was to become military governor of Archangel, and he himself was promoted to the rank of Rear Admiral. Between May and September 1694, Gordon's Diary records numerous meetings between himself, Peter and Muscovy Company merchants both in the town of Archangel and aboard Russian and English ships in the White Sea. With no privileges to revoke and Peter hungry for imports, these meetings were concerned with technological innovation and seamanship, not Jacobitism.[86]

With no official British resident in Moscow, the Muscovy Company merchants were satisfied with the informal arrangements. The relationship between Peter and the Company could be considered entirely commercial. In summer 1695, with a redistribution of diplomatic posts, the idea of a Williamite resident in Moscow was mooted, but nothing progressed. The diplomat Matthew Prior noted on 3 August:

83 Gordon, Diary, 'To the Duke of Gordon, January 12 1692', vol. 5, pp. 224v–25v.
84 McLynn, *The Jacobites*, p. 137.
85 Gordon, Diary, 14 October 1696, vol. 6, p. 49v.
86 References to letters from Gordon to 'Mr. Tho. Loftus' and 'Mr. Woolfe' are especially numerous. See: Gordon, Diary, 24 October–19 December 1696, vol. 6, pp. 49v–90.

A resident or envoy may in some smal time be sent to Venice, another to
Florence: be it either of these two places, at Ratisbon, Berlin (where may be,
His Majesty may send rather a resident than an envoy) at Stockholm,
Copenhagen or even Muscow, it is well provided I may serve my King, my
hero and my Master.[87]

In 1695 and 1696, diplomacy took a back seat, as Peter, accompanied by Gordon,
concentrated on the capture of the fortress of Azov by the Black Sea, ultimately
taken from the Ottoman Turks in July 1696.[88]

Commerce: New Moves

Even as the diplomatic relationship between Britain and Russia remained uncer-
tain and often difficult, and thus promised little formal basis for improved
commercial relations, signs of hope were beginning to reappear. Indeed, the
British fixation on formal privileges – a legacy of the extraordinary status of the
Muscovy Company during the reign of Ivan IV – had borne little connection to
the evolution of commercial relations during most of the seventeenth century.
The loss of the Muscovy merchants' special privileges by the middle of the
century had rendered the strategy of insisting on the restoration of the lost rights
effectively meaningless in any event.

The recovery of the Anglo-Russian commercial relationship began to gather
pace most noticeably in the Eastern Baltic where the significance of diplomacy
between the two countries was effectively nil. The drivers of Russian export
trade in the Baltic region were largely structural, above all the demography and
economic development of northwestern Russia and Sweden's Baltic possessions. Diplomacy came into them largely through Swedish-Russian relations
which, while frequently charged and relatively tense even at the best of times,
did permit a high and growing degree of pragmatism as far as cross-border
trade was concerned.

In Narva – and to a lesser degree the Neva port Nyen – English merchants,
mainly those belonging to the Eastland Company, tapped into a renaissance of
regional trade for which they could claim relatively little direct credit, but which
allowed them to revive a long-stagnant flow of Russian exports to the British

---

87 'Mathew Prior to [Arnold Jost Van] Keppel. 1695 August 3. N. S. Hague.' – *HMC*, 58 Bath
   Longleat III (1908), p. 61. It is notable that books dealing with the subject of British trade
   after 1689 are silent on the subject of Anglo-Russian trade until Tsar Peter's Great Embassy
   of 1697–8 nudges the issue into focus. For example, Crowhurst, *The Defence*, p. 45.
88 Herd, 'Peter I and the Conquest of Azov', pp. 61–78; Herd and Nekrasov, 'Britanskii
   istorik', pp. 195–205.

Isles.[89] They further substantially boosted their share of regional commerce by capitalising on their role as suppliers of Virginia tobacco, a highly sought-after commodity. Indeed by the mid-1670s, they were bringing little else to Narva and Nyen, something that resulted in interminable disputes with the local burghers desperate to gain control of the lucrative trade.[90] Punitive duties of 34 per cent were levied on tobacco, a figure that compared to 2 per cent on other imports. This, to the irritation of the local merchant community, fostered illegal trade. However, the English were obviously able to overcome these restrictions in part quite legally, since many of its members were Narva citizens. Very often, non-naturalised Englishmen worked in partnership with the local Narva burghers of English descent, thereby circumventing most of the Swedish mercantilist policies.[91] Undoubtedly in response to growing illicit tobacco trade, the Narva City Council in September 1698 considered a proposal to take over the keys of the English warehouses. However, the king evidently had authorised English tobacco trade with Russia by this time and the Council eventually found that the English could continue to store their tobacco in their own warehouses, rather than the City Hall. The changing situation was undoubtedly propelled by Peter I's decision that year to authorise British merchants to import tobacco to Russia.[92]

Although the English interacted primarily with Narva burghers, they also had direct dealings with Russian merchants, both in Narva and in Moscow and Pskov. In addition, they concluded deals in Russia through the Swedish commercial agents Thomas Knieper in Moscow and Daniel Stewen in Pskov. Dealings with the Muscovites were, as usual, based on credit and often led to disputes and, consequently, a lasting legacy in the Narva court records.[93] The

---

89 By the end of the century, there were 12 British agents working in Narva, typically in partnerships of two. Most of these people were not citizens or even permanent residents of Narva. The most important of them were Knipe & Hoyle, Collins & Bland, Thomas Moore & Thomas Meux, Robert Maister & Gabriel Dowker, William Beaumont, and William Walker & Thomas Dunn. Other names included Thomas Dowker, John Tyreman, John Taylor of the Eastland Company, Thomas Remington, Samuel Meux, John Miller, Francis Collins, Randolph Knipe, Thomas and Abraham Hoyle, Richard Walker, Robert Mallabar, and William Beaumont. Tyreman, a member of the Eastland Company, was an agent of a Newcastle merchant William Ramsay who imported linen from Narva. Thomas Dowker represented the Carleton family, William Walker acted as an agent for the Hull merchant Thomas Carter, and Alexander Gilbert worked for the London merchant house of Cary. Åström, *From Cloth to Iron*, pp. 128, 131; Erpenbeck, 'Die Engländer in Narva', pp. 492–3.
90 Küng, 'Tubakakaubanduse riiklik reguleerimine Narvas', pp. 4–5; Kotilaine, *Russia's Foreign Trade*, p. 366.
91 Price, *The Tobacco Adventure to Russia*, p. 39.
92 EAA 1646–1–107, fols 231–2; Åström, *From Stockholm to St. Petersburg*, p. 79.
93 Åström, *From Cloth to Iron*, pp. 128–9.

trouble was by no means always on the Russian side, however, and the relationship gradually became increasingly equal as the Novgorod lands regained their prosperity, effectively in anticipation of their restoration to the hinterland of the new capital of the Russian Empire in the eighteenth century. For instance, William Kettlewell ran into trouble with his Russian partners following losses of some Rtl 22,000 [*Reichsthaler*] when two of his ships, the *Castell von Narva* and *Das Narvische Wappen*, sank in the English Channel. By 1696, he was struggling to keep up his payments to Pskov merchants.[94]

The expansion in English shipping with the Baltic was very impressive when compared to the relative stagnation in Arkhangel'sk. The number of English vessels passing through the Danish Sound grew steadily to 20–30 by the late 1670s and as many as 71 in 1700. This was intimately linked to the growth of the English community in Narva. At least nine Englishmen became burghers of Narva between 1681 and 1693, which in turn further boosted trade since they were exempted from duties at the Danish Sound.[95]

During the period under review, the English were the second most important foreign commercial presence in Narva, eclipsed only by the traditionally dominant Lübeck merchants. By 1696, a total of 34 ships cleared the Narva customs for English ports and carried, among other things, over 77 per cent of Narva's total flax exports and just over 73 per cent of hemp. Both commodities were to a significant degree imports from the Pskov region. The English also were key buyers of potash, tar, and timber, again typically imports from Russia. Overall, the English in 1696 accounted for 20.4 per cent of the total value of Narva's export trade, which appears to have been quite representative of their market share during the closing years of the century. Even this figure is really an underestimate because many of the English now operated as Narva burghers.[96]

The Navigation Acts gave a major advantage to Swedish ships towards the end of the century, although some of them now began to favour merchants of English descent. While a total of 515 non-English vessels came to Britain from Sweden and Swedish possessions in Michaelmas 1691–Michaelmas 1697, there were just 240 English vessels sailing in the same direction.[97] A lion's share of the total now consisted of Swedish vessels. In the words of John Robinson, an English diplomat who was an expert in Swedish affairs:

94 Erpenbeck, 'Die Engländer in Narva', p. 492.
95 Erpenbeck, 'Die Engländer in Narva', pp. 481–97; Küng, 'Inglise kaubandus Narvas', pp. 12–16; Kotilaine, *Russia's Foreign Trade*, pp. 120–1.
96 Piirimäe, 'Udel'nyi ves', pp. 10–13.
97 Ibid., p. 15.

When Sueden has been engaged in a War, the English Ships have had the whole Employ: but in Times of Peace, the Advantage if so great on the Suedish side, and Merchants so much encouraged by Freedom in Customs to employ their Ships, that English Bottoms cannot be used in that Trade, but only while Sueden is unprovided with a Number of Ships sufficient for the Transportation of their own Commodities.[98]

The Great Northern War put an end to the existence of the English community in Narva. Protected through their neutral status, the English sent ships to Narva as late as 1700. In 1701, John Cary of London requested permission to sail to the war zone. It is not known whether such permission was granted or not, although he may have been a 'Herr Korie' who arrived there to arrange to move his business records to Reval. However, there were numerous violations of English rights. Bland and Holden had £600 worth of their goods confiscated by the authorities in 1700. The remaining English-owned goods were stored in warehouses and recorded in the so-called *Comptoirbücher*.[99] At least Henry Bland and Samuel Holden fled the advancing Russians to Reval, and the remaining members had their warehouses plundered by Swedish soldiers after the Russian siege was lifted. After a peak of 160 ships visiting Narva in 1695, foreign shipping was completely paralysed between 1704 and 1717. When the Russians returned in 1704, they raided the warehouses of the English community. In 1708, the entire population of Narva was moved to Vologda. Those resettling there included Kettlewell, Gilbert, and the widows Bacon, Browne and Pierson. They were allowed to return only after 1722, by which time St Petersburg had established itself.[100]

Improvements at Arkhangel'sk had to wait for longer for clear signs of a détente but, as was noted above, even there the situation gradually began to improve. By the early 1690s, some ten English merchants a year were active on the Dvina route and the Muscovy Company was seeking to revive its interest in Persia where a mission was organised in 1691, following an earlier one in 1683.[101]

The poor performance of the Muscovy Company had indeed prompted a growing number of people to begin to look for the causes of the deplorable state of Anglo-Russian commerce in the Company itself. In particular, a number of

---

98 Quoted in: Åström, 'The English navigation laws', p. 14.
99 Erpenbeck, 'Die Engländer in Narva', p. 496.
100 Åström, *From Cloth to Iron*, p. 132; Erpenbeck, 'Die Engländer in Narva', pp. 496–7; Hansen, 'Narvas Handel 1690–1722', p. 207 ff.
101 Demkin, *Zapadnoevropeiskoe kupechestvo v Rossii*, I, p. 47; Repin, *Vneshniaia torgovlia*, pp. 333–5.

critics of the company once again began to clamour for less restrictive membership criteria, in particular lower admission fees, which would have boosted the
resources devoted to Anglo-Russian commerce. A debate on the restrictive
membership criteria erupted by the mid-1690s; one pamphlet blamed the
decline of Russian trade squarely on the myopic policies of the Company: 'The
Trade of Russia being at present Ingrossed by Foreigners, will require great
Industry and Charges, to recover it to this Nation; and there those Merchants
who are to come into the Company for that end, humbly hope the Terms of
Admission will be moderate.'[102]

The question of fees was particularly important in the face of the steady
decline in the Company's membership. The number of 'fellows' had declined
from an already modest 31 in 1681 to 20 in 1698 and Samuel Heathcote claimed
in 1697 that there were only 12–14 active merchants. Nonetheless, in 1691, the
Company had made its membership criteria even stricter: 'That there shall be
noe more admissions of Members for ffines . . . but . . . only to admit such as
Claime by Service and Patrimony.'[103] The Muscovy merchants aggressively
lobbied against a proposed law to enlarge its membership, as well as another
proposed measure in 1689 to liberalise the woollens trade, a measure that
allegedly contravened their privileges. In the end, special provisions had to be
agreed for the adventurers.[104]

Under the circumstances, a growing number of people came to see tobacco –
the road to English success in the Baltic – as the key to unlocking the relative
crisis in Arkhangel'sk as well. These in fact included the Muscovy Company
itself. The issue of customs rates on tobacco was raised by the Company as early
as 1676–7 in connection with John Hebdon's mission to Russia. In 1686, the
Company discussed the idea of sending an envoy to Russian to discuss the
legalisation of tobacco trade.[105] However, the potential of the tobacco issue was
far more fully recognised by those determined to challenge the established
Russian adventurers. Various groups of merchants now came together determined to break the stronghold of the old Muscovy merchants on the back of the
general trend towards liberalising the membership criteria of English trading

102 *HU BBL GKLEL* 3081.18: 'Reasons for an Easie Admission into the Russia Company, 1695.'
103 *GHL*, Ms 11,741/2, p. 147. In response, one pamphlet denounced the virtual impossibility
     of joining the Company: 'Heretofore the [Russia] Company did permit Persons to Buy
     their Freedom for 60 l. But several Years since they made a By-Law, to Admit none into
     their Company, on any terms whatever, unless by Service. Whereas the Admissions into
     other Companies, may be had for 40 s. as aforesaid.' *HU BBL GKLEL* 3081.15: 'Reasons
     for Enlarging and Regulating the Trade To Russia and the Narve, 1695.'
104 Kotilaine, *Russia's Foreign Trade*, p. 118.
105 *GHL*, Ms 11,741/1, p. 151; Ms 11,741/2, p. 77; *PRO*, CO 388/1, fols 156–7; CO 391/1, pp. 200–1.

companies.[106] The earliest pioneers of this liberalisation were North American tobacco merchants. A document entitled 'Reasons For the Bill To Inlarge the Trade to Russia, As it Respects The Plantations of Virginia and Maryland' outlines the central issue: 'If the [tobacco] Trade be restrained to so few hands as at present it is, 'tis not reasonable to expect that a Liberty will be granted by the Czar to Import Tobacco into his Dominions; because He will see that His People cannot be supplyed but at such Rates as those Merchants please to set upon it, the Monopoly being in so few hands.'[107]

The tobacco merchants expected liberalisation to result in a veritable transformation of Russian trade. They anticipated annual exports of 20,000 hogsheads to Russia, enough to fill 40 ships of 200 tons each, something that in one stroke would have made the English truly serious rivals to the Dutch.[108] Several other merchants, not least those of the Eastland Company, joined this movement, recognising Russia's extraordinary potential as a supplier of naval stores and the advantages thus offered to English shipping on a number of levels. As stated by another pamphlet:

> Masts, Timber and Firr-Plank, Hemp, Pitch and Tar may be imported from Russia, at cheaper Rates that they can be had from Prussia, Denmark, Sweden or Norway . . . The Russes having no Ships of their own, all such Masts, Timber and Plank, and all other Commodities brought thence for England, will be Imported in English Ships; and so the Freight of them (which oft times is double or treble to the first Costs of the Goods) will be gained to this Nation . . . As a farther Consequence of the Russes having no Shipping, they will thereby be rendered uncapable of Entring into a Sea-War; and so we shall have the greater likelyhood of always enjoying a free and open Trade with them.[109]

The importance of the debate grew further when Peter I, in 1697, permitted the open sale and consumption of tobacco in Russia, evidently in response to the fact that illegal tobacco trade was rampant throughout his dominions. The British were galvanised to make tobacco the central plank of their Russian diplomacy when the government granted an exclusive tobacco contract to a Dutchman Thomas Fadomrecht. In April 1698, Peter, who was touring Western

---

106 Price, *The Tobacco Adventure*, p. 38.
107 *HU BBL GKLEL* 3081.6: 'Further reasons for inlarging the trade to Russia.'
108 Ibid.
109 *HU BBL GKLEL* 3081.15: 'Reasons for Enlarging and Regulating the Trade To Russia and the Narve, 1695.'

Europe at the time, agreed to grant the tobacco monopoly to Peregrine Osborne, Marquess of Carmarthen. Carmarthen, in fact, acted as the front figure for a group of a dozen merchants, who, having obtained the contract, admitted some 60 colleagues to their ranks and formed a partnership called 'the Contractors with the Czar of Muscovy for the Sole Importation of Tobacco into his Dominions' or 'the Adventurers in the Russia Tobacco Trade'. The Tobacco Contract guaranteed everyone associated with the company '"full liberty and protection" to live in any part of the Czar's dominions . . . and to trade with anyone or to employ anyone Czar's subject or alien'.[110] In fact, the tobacco merchants managed to secure privileges which the Muscovy Company could only – and with amazing persistence, did – dream of. The last formal plea for the restoration of the company's privileges was made to the king in 1697, nearly half a century after they had been scrapped.

Ultimately, the critics of the Muscovy Company won the day. The 'Act to Enlarge the Trade to Russia' finally passed in 1699 and the Company immediately saw a dramatic increase in its membership. At the meeting on 14 April 1699 alone, 73 new members were admitted, followed by another 15 on April 26 and 7 in May–June. Admissions of three to four new members at a time remained a regular feature of meetings in 1699–1700.[111] In the simplest terms, this amounted to a takeover of the old Muscovy Company by Eastland and other merchants eager to gain access to the naval stores of Russia. As controversial as the measure was, it greatly expanded the Company's resources. In 1701, when war cast its shadow on Baltic trade, 30 English ships headed for Arkhangel'sk and the history of the Company had come a full circle.[112] Once again, the English were the dominant commercial force in Russia, something that foreshadowed the more general passing of the torch – perhaps symbolised in the arrival of William of Orange – from Amsterdam to London as the commercial capital of northern Europe. It is interesting to wonder whether an earlier change of policy would have allowed the English to eclipse the Dutch already in the seventeenth century. There is little in the historical evidence to challenge the interpretation that the Muscovy Company – the founders and pioneers of Anglo-Russian trade – had become a self-seeking, even destructive, force and bore the responsibility for the decline of Anglo-Russian trade during most of the seventeenth century. They had a concrete and powerful example of what liberalisation could accomplish in the impressive success of their Dutch rivals. Yet it arguably took tobacco and a regime change in London to allow the

---

110 Price, *The Tobacco Adventure*, pp. 20, 23, 26–7, 38; *PRO* CO 391/10, pp. 181–3.
111 *GHL*, Ms 11,741/3, pp. 2, 5, 6–7.
112 *GHL*, Ms 11,741/3, p. 37.

English, very belatedly, to catch up with the far superior business strategies of their rivals in the Low Countries.

It is patently obvious that the reforms of the turn of the century turned the Muscovy Company from a small coterie of merchants into a strong and dynamic operation determined to conquer new markets. It is impossible to say whether a reorganisation earlier would have made a recovery of Anglo-Russian trade possible. On the one hand, tobacco only became legal in Russia in 1697, and the surge of the early eighteenth century was also connected with the Great Northern War. On the other hand, the impressive results of the reforms make it difficult not to characterise the strategy of the old Company as a failure.

The composition of English imports from Russia changed considerably during the second half of the seventeenth century. By the 1660s, English imports came to be dominated by potash, a commodity of particular importance for the growing textile industry. The English, first Simon Digby and then the Muscovy Company as a whole, controlled the potash monopoly in 1642–55. The Company's purchases of potash were some 282,960–694, 224 lb in 1647, 290,952 lb in 1648, and 181,440 lb in 1649. The English accounted for 13.9 per cent, or 1,638 barrels, of Russian potash sales in 1653–56. Potash was the single most important English import from Archangel by 1663, with total imports amounting to 720,384 lb, worth £9,648, or some 54 per cent of the combined value of London's imports from Russia. However, in 1669, potash imports reached only 243,600 lb, worth £3,045. Potash remained the leading import throughout the 1680s and 1690s. The 1699 total was 1,736,480 lb, whereas 2,682,998 lb was imported in 1700. The steady upward trend in potash purchases suggests a growing English dominance of the trade since, overall, Russian potash exports began to decline towards the end of the century.[113]

Naval stores came to assume a place of growing prominence among English imports from Russia. Especially important were the fibres, flax and hemp, which had historically left Russia in a processed form. However, the strong demand at home meant that unprocessed hemp and flax became increasingly important towards the end of the century. Flax purchases rose dramatically during the final years of the century with total imports attaining 1,137,990 lb in 1699 and 3,553,557 lb in 1700, making flax for the first time the leading import good from Russia. In the closing years of the century, flax, hemp, and potash together accounted for some two-thirds of total British imports. In 1679, the Company actually required its members to devote at least one-third of their

---

113 Arel, *The Muscovy Company*, pp. 398, 401, 406–7, 410–13, 413, 419–21, 425; Repin, *Vneshniaia torgovlia*, p. 133; Demkin, *Zapadnoevropeiskoe kupechestvo*, I, p. 101; *PRO* E 190, Customs 3; *BL* Add. 36785, fols 44–5, 91–2; *GHL*, Ms 11,741/1, p. 175.

shipping capacity to tallow and/or potash and evidence from subsequent Port Books suggests that the domination of potash was even more complete.[114] To properly appreciate the importance of Russia, the imports from the eastern Baltic would have to be added to these totals, since a significant proportion of them came from Muscovy.

Caviar continued to be of crucial importance for the Company, not least because of the lasting significance of the Leghorn route.[115] John Osborne, with John Hebdon, even managed to regain the caviar monopoly for the disgraced Muscovy Company for 1649–54. The monopoly was guaranteed by the Dutchman David Ruts who lent Osborne Rtl 14,000. The loan was repaid in 1651 with 100 barrels of caviar which Ruts sent to Venice. Thanks to his association with Osborne, Ruts, together with the Hamburg merchants Zacharis Belkens and Philip Verpoorten, bought 11,419 *pud* of black caviar (worth Rtl 26,408) from the tsar in 1653. The two Hamburgers appear to have held the monopoly for a while, but Hebdon regained it in 1655 by promising to export at least 500 barrels a year. B. G. Kurts claims that the monopoly was, in fact, controlled by a Florentine merchant in the years 1655–9. Hebdon did, however, dispatch a ship loaded with caviar at least in 1658. In 1670–8, possibly even a couple of years earlier, Belkens and Verpoorten held the privilege, and in 1698–1706 it appears to have been in the hands of I. Farius. Surviving quantitative estimates suggest an average of 400 barrels (some 16,000 *pud*) per annum. left the White Sea port in 1670–8. In 1698, however, the total was significantly lower: 113 barrels or 4,520 *pud*. The annual average in 1699–1702 was 160 barrels, or some 6,400 *pud*.[116]

Conclusion

While Anglo-Russian commerce was moving in new directions, the Jacobites in Russia were trying to proceed as before, holding to their belief in the old Stuart cause. By the end of the century, however, hopes were fading fast as Tsar Peter set off for a meeting with the usurper William III.

Then, on 29 November 1699, Patrick Gordon died, having performed a last important service for Peter in his leading contribution to the suppression of the

---

114 *PRO*, E 190, Customs 3; BL Add. 36785, fols 44–5, 91–2.

115 In 1591, the Company set a target annual export quota of 100–150 barrels (c. 89,600 lb). Arel, *The Muscovy Company*, p. 369 ff.

116 Ibid., pp. 369–72. Veluwenkamp, *Archangel*, pp. 87, 101–2; Repin, *Vneshniaia torgovlia*, pp. 202–3; *Sochinenie Kil'burgera*, pp. 209, 260; *Sostoianie Rossii*, p. 94; Gurliand, *Ivan Gebdon*, pp. 6–7.

revolt of the *strel'tsy* or musketeers during the tsar's absence from Moscow on his Great Embassy.[117] Meanwhile, until almost his dying breath, he had retained his interest in his native land, both for family reasons and because of his attachment to the Stuart cause. In the early eighteenth century, leading Jacobites such as Dr. Robert Erskine, Admiral Thomas Gordon, Major General Alexander Gordon and General James Keith would all benefit from the example that he had set, with no more success, however, in restoring the 'rightful king' to the throne.

117 Herd, 'Reformation, Rebellion and Russian Military Modernization', pp. 263–90.

EIGHT

Conclusion: Seventeenth-Century Legacy

In this final chapter, we will describe a great blow to the hopes of Jacobites in Russia, the meeting in Utrecht of Tsar Peter with the man who had in their view usurped the throne of James VII and II, William III. We will then proceed to review seventeenth-century developments in war, diplomacy and commerce, before drawing some conclusions. We will append a brief description of the putative last meeting between the Stuarts and Romanovs.

'The Great Embassy', 1697–1698

In March 1697, Peter set out on his first visit to the West. He hoped to organise a grand Christian coalition against the Ottoman Empire and its allies. He also sought to acquire a deeper knowledge of Dutch and British expertise, especially in shipbuilding, and to hire specialists to help him build the Russian navy and for other practical purposes.

Peter first met William III in Utrecht on 1/11 September 1697. Although Peter's tall figure and wild-eyed aspect could hardly be mistaken, he was supposed to be travelling incognito as a minor official of the embassy, 'Peter Mikhailov', under the leadership of his favourite, Francis Lefort. After ambassadorial formalities had been exchanged, therefore, the king retired to a separate room and a private meeting with the tsar ensued. It is unlikely that the two sovereigns were able to converse directly, although Peter had some acquaintance with the *Soldatendeutsch* lingua franca of seventeenth-century mercenaries. Possibly Lefort, who numbered among his accomplishments a number of languages (if little else), acted as interpreter.

Nothing is known for certain about the contents of the talks as far as Anglo-Russian relations were concerned. However, just a few weeks later on 14/24 October, Luttrell made the following entry in his 'diary':

> an abstract of the czars speech to his majestie, that 'twas not the desire of seeing Germany and Holland that made him leave his throne and victorious armies, but to see the most brave and generous hero of the age, that he had his wish, and was sufficiently recompenced for his travell in being admitted into the presence of his majestie, whose kind embraces had pleased him more than the taking Asoph and triumphing over the Tartars; and that the peace being

so near concluded, he could not have the opportunity, as Maximilian [Maximilian II Emanuel, Elector of Bavaria and Governor of the Spanish Netherlands] had, of fighting under the banner of England against France; but if the war continued, he and his armies were at his majesties service, and his ports should be free to his majesties subjects, who should have greater immunities then they ever yet have had.[1]

At about the same time, possibly drawn on by Luttrell, a version of the tsar's speech was published in French in London. A medal was soon struck showing the king receiving the tsar at the gate of his palace, with the city of Utrecht in the background and the following inscription below: PETRI ALEXIEWICZ CZAR MAGNIQUE GULIELMI REGIS AMICITIA TRAJECTI AD RHENUM, XI SEPTEMBRIS, MDCXCVII. [The friendly meeting between Tsar Peter Alekseevich and King William the Great at Utrecht, 11 September 1697.]

On 2 December 1697, Gilbert Burnet, Bishop of Salisbury, gave a sermon before King William at Whitehall on the occasion of the Peace of Ryswick, taking as his text II Chronicles, Chapter 9, verse 8, and comparing Peter to the Queen of Sheba:

And to make the Parallel to my Text run exactly, a much greater King, lying to a vaster Distance, leaves his Throne and Dominions in the midst of War, struck with the Fame, and amaz'd at the Actions of this Prince. Instead of a little Southern Queen, a mighty Northern Emperor, covered with Laurels, and us'd to Victories, resolving to raise his Nation, and enlarge his Empire comes to learn the best methods of doing it, and goes away full of Wonder, possessed with Truer Notions of Government.[2]

Although the Great Embassy of 1697–8 necessitated the public recognition of William III by Peter, Jacobites could draw at least a little hope and succour from the tsar's visit to London. Its basic purpose was to acquire military and technological assistance and materials.[3] This is confirmed by contemporary London

---

1 Luttrell, *A Brief Historical Relation*, iv, p. 291 as quoted by Loewenson, 'Peter I and William III', pp. 309–10.

2 'A Sermon Preached before the King, At Whitehall, On the Second of December 1697, being The Day of Thanksgiving For the Peace. By the Right Reverend Father in God, Gilbert, Lord Bishop of Sarum', as described and quoted by Loewenson, 'Peter I and William III', pp. 311–12.

3 Barany, *The Anglo-Russian Entente Cordiale*, pp. 20–4. For an overall survey of the literature, see Cross, 'Peter & Britain', in Cross, *Russia in the Reign of Peter the Great*, pp. 25–39.

newspaper sources as well as private diaries. For example, Luttrell writes in his 'diary' that the 'czar . . . is taking into his service all the land officers, ship carpenters, etc., that he can gett, to carry with him to Muscovy; and that his Majestie will permit several officers, at his request, to be employed under him against the Turks and Tartars.'[4] It is interesting to recall that Peter explicitly made reference to the ultimate purpose of these troops, to fight the Turks and Tatars. The proximity in time to the Azov Campaign served Peter's cause well. While official Petrine policy was to stress a commitment to fight in the south-eastern corner of Europe in return for soldiers, and sailors, many of these were Jacobites. Arguably, therefore, the Jacobites as well as William III made use of this embassy to bolster their position on the international scene. Nevertheless, the embassy dashed the hopes of the Jacobites in Russia for recognition by Tsar Peter.

One consequence of the Great Embassy was to kick-start diplomatic missions between the two countries: 'Our trusty and welbeloved Charles Goodfellow' was appointed 'to be our Minister and Consul Generall at Moscow' in September 1699.[5] The Muscovy Company attempted to have its privileges restored. However, in April, Peter had already made it clear that 'free trade' only would be tolerated.[6]

Without doubt, the Great Embassy's full recognition of William III had driven a significant nail, if not necessarily the last, in the coffin of Russian Jacobitism. In 1704, Charles Whitworth was appointed Envoy Extraordinary to Russia. He was instructed: 'as dexterously and with as little noise as you can, endeavour to informe Your selfe of the designs and Intentions of that Court, what Treatys may be entertained by the Czar, what his condition is as for Treasure . . . What matters the Ministers of other Princes and States and Treating and Negotiating there.' In particular, he was to attempt to resolve difficulties concerning the export of colonial tobacco, to such an extent indeed that he complained to a friend: 'since I have nothing but Export & Importation in my mouth, they [the Russian ministers] are apt to mistake me purely for a tobacco agent.' He confessed with some justification that Britain had 'great occasion for their [Russian] Trade, but little value for their Prince or people.'[7] There was little immediate hope, then, for the making of a new special relationship.

4 Luttrell, *A Brief Historical Relation*, iv, p. 280 – Tuesday, 21 September 1697.
5 'William III to Peter, 12 September 1699', *PRO*, SP 104/120, fols 16–17; 'Commission for Ch. Goodfellow Esqr. to be Consull in Moscow', *PRO*, SP 104/120, fols 22–3.
6 'Translation of the Czar's Letter to the King, 10 April 1699', *PRO*, SP 104/120, fol. 17.
7 'Instructions of Envoy Extra to Russia, Charles Whitworth, 29 September 1704', *PRO*, SP 104/120, fol. 45; Hartley, 'A Clash of Cultures?', pp. 49, 54.

We must be careful not to give too much emphasis to the general significance of the 'Great Embassy'. One of the major purposes of this book has been to argue that the revolution brought about by Peter in diplomacy, as in much else, has been exaggerated, and that Muscovite Russia asserted its presence in seventeenth-century Europe with some success.[8] We will underline this point, among others, as we turn to a retrospective.

Seventeenth-century Retrospective

This book is not a parallel history. That is to say, we have not attempted the impossible task of writing an account of both British and Russian development throughout the seventeenth century. Rather, we have attempted to uncover the nature of the special relationship between two dynasties and their subjects. What was the Stuart–Romanov relationship all about? What were the two sides after, what did they hope to gain and what did they gain in the event – the advancement of competing or complementary military, economic, and diplomatic interests? In answer to these key questions we have not selected evidence to support some preconceived abstract explanation that consciously set out to reinterpret the nature of this relationship in the seventeenth century. Rather, making use of many European languages, we have returned to the primary sources, particularly archival and printed documents relating to Stuart–Romanov diplomacy, commerce and military matters, along with a wide range of the secondary literature. On this basis, we have set out in predominantly chronological fashion our interpretation of these sources. Then, we have sought to locate this interpretation within the context of appropriate secondary literature.

In this concluding chapter we now have the opportunity to identify more clearly structures and processes, impute latent driving forces that help explain events in their contexts. We begin with a retrospective look at war and diplomacy, before moving to commerce and then drawing some general conclusions about the Stuart–Romanov relationship and what made it special.

War and Diplomacy

At the beginning of the seventeenth century, the Austrian and Spanish Habsburgs predominated in Europe, at the end the Bourbon French. Social disturbances were endemic and frontiers fluctuating nearer 1600, stability in

---

8 We disagree, therefore, with the arguments of Piirimäe, 'Russia, The Turks and Europe', and Matveev, 'Summit Diplomacy', who give emphasis to the Petrine revolution in diplomacy.

both regards more evident towards 1700. And what was seen widely as Christendom throughout the century was being increasingly recognised as the secular entity of Europe by the century's end. To illustrate the process for the continent as a whole, let us first take again the example of the pan-European conflict known as the Thirty Years' War, 1618–48.

The term 'Thirty Years' War' is not a later invention, but one already used by its contemporaries.[9] And yet, few of us today would accept the view of some of them, that the conflict was no more than a precursor to the final showdown between good and evil, heralding the Day of Judgement. We do need our explanatory tools, therefore, at the same time as accepting their limitations as well as our own. Inevitably, interpretations differ, depending on methodological approach as well as partiality of knowledge. Thus, employing a method which he calls 'dialectical or historical structuralism', the Czech Josef Polišenský put forward in a range of publications the thesis that the war was 'a military-political conflict rooted in the past, in which two models of European civilization confronted one another: those represented by the lands in which development toward a modern capitalist society had been halted, and the lands in which this development had been allowed to proceed'[10]. For the German Ronald Asch, on the other hand:

> In fact, there was one central issue justifying the contemporary judgement that the Thirty Years' War was a contest with a definite beginning and a definite end and with a structure giving coherence to the various military campaigns, not just an amorphous and haphazard series of individual wars: the constitution of the Holy Roman Empire and – inseparable from this question – the balance of political and religious forces in central Europe.[11]

Asch goes on to observe that the war was also in fact 'very much a European civil war as well as a contest between dynasties, princes and republics' and 'an important phase in the process of European state formation'. 'States' vied with 'estates' for supremacy, with military finance as an important bone of contention. He also suggests that the war is 'the best example of a political "event" which profoundly changed political and social structures, and perhaps even collective mentalities (though this is a field as yet largely unexplored)'.[12]

---

9 Parker, *The Thirty Years' War*, pp. xiii–xiv.
10 Polišenský, *Tragic Triangle*, p. 8.
11 Asch, *The Thirty Years' War*, p. 3.
12 Ibid., pp. 4–5, 7.

Another overall interpretation still worthy of serious consideration is that of the Soviet historian Boris Porshnev who wrote as follows. The aggressors were the Habsburg powers, in particular the Holy Roman Empire, aiming to suppress the resistance of the Protestant princes. Moreover, internal circumstances were more important than any aggression from France or any other foreign source. There were four categories of contradiction. They were, in apparent order of importance: state, between the Empire and the princes; confessional, primarily between Catholics and Protestants; national, including mostly Germans, Slavs and Hungarians; and social, between the classes. Porshnev argued that the actual order of importance was opposite to the apparent.[13] Now that in post-Soviet times, the class struggle is out of fashion, to put it mildly, full agreement with him might be foolhardy. Nevertheless, the disturbances at the conclusion of the war, as well as some of them in it, were at least partly social and deserve a full measure of appraisal.

There has been much discussion of the impact of the Thirty Years' War, 1618–48, in Central Europe and other parts of the continent. However, while the policies of other dynasties have been subject to close scrutiny, those of the Stuarts and Romanovs have largely been omitted from description of the great conflict. Let us take them in reverse order, since crisis struck the Romanovs before it overthrew the Stuarts, and since the Stuart story will be more familiar to most readers of this book.

Any overview of Muscovy looks first at the civil disturbances and foreign intervention known as the Time of Troubles (1598–1613) which shook the Muscovite state to its very foundations as Poland and Sweden threatened to take over large chunks of Russia for themselves, and even the Stuarts contemplated snatching a piece of the inheritance of the Romanovs. The arrival of this new dynasty, the Romanovs, marked the end of the Troubles but not the insecurity. Then, there is a period of concentration on internal consolidation and international inactivity punctuated by the localised Smolensk War (1632–4) until the wider conflict with Poland known as the Thirteen Years' War (1654–67), taking Muscovy into much of Ukraine and further into Europe.

After 1634, there were new directions in the general European war and a rupture in relations between Western and Eastern Europe.[14] Why? One important reason was the Muscovite government's preoccupation with internal problems. A visitor to Moscow, Olearius, wrote of the Russians: 'Once they are aroused, they are difficult to pacify; not withstanding the danger that may threaten them, they

13 Porshnev, *Muscovy*, pp. xi–xii.
14 Porshnev, 'Les rapports politiques', pp. 136–63.

resort to every kind of violence, and rage like madmen.'[15] Another reason was the difficulty in maintaining a stable peace with the immediate neighbours Poland and Sweden. According to a Polish historian, King Władysław IV confidently wrote to Charles I on 13 December 1633: 'a free road is open for us into the interior of the Muscovite realm.'[16] However, at least a few hopes were expressed that both Christian powers could unite against the Moslem infidels. In the end, the Peace of Polianovka was signed on 15 June 1634 without too much previous argument because it was very necessary for both sides. Poland retained Smolensk and other towns gained during the Time of Troubles, but King Władysław formally renounced his claims to the Russian throne.

So much for Poland, the old enemy: what of the former ally, Sweden? The Peace of Stuhmsdorf was made between Sweden and Poland in September 1635, the year that marked the moment of maximum Swedish expansion into continental Europe. This was the consequence partly of aspects of the internal situations obtaining in the German states and Sweden, partly of elements in the international situation in Europe. French diplomacy, along with British and Dutch as well as Swedish, worked hard to change the course of Polish foreign policy. According to the terms of the Stuhmsdorf treaty, Poland guaranteed its neutrality to Sweden and France. The entry into the war of France in June 1635 made a powerful impact on the final phase of the war, which also marked a major breach in the confessional struggle with Cardinal Richelieu's support for Protestant Sweden.

The ongoing struggle for the unification of the other Christian churches against Roman Catholicism was affected by the part played in relations between Eastern and Western Europe by the Ottoman Empire.[17] However, preoccupied by war with Persia and internal dissension, the Ottoman Empire was not really in a position either to exert pressure on the frontiers of Muscovy, or more generally to play a vigorous part in European international relations, for most of the period of the Thirty Years' War, even if it would have wanted to. Nevertheless, the threat of incursion by the Ottoman Turks, or by their allies the Crimean Tatars, or by other hostile elements to the south and east, was constant. Therefore, from 1635 to 1642, the Russian government concentrated on the construction of the Belgorod Defensive Line, such hopes of expansion as it entertained being for the time being directed towards Siberia.

Generally speaking, Russia adhered closely to the policy, which it adopted in June 1634, of avoiding any further close involvement in the Thirty Years' War

---

15 Olearius, *Travels*, p. 153.
16 Godziszewski, *Polska a Moskwa*, p. 10.
17 See, for example, Runciman, *The Great Church*, pp. 259–88, 335–7.

and the other affairs of Europe. The use of foreign mercenaries was strictly curtailed at the end of the Smolensk War, an exception being made only for officer instructors such as Sir Alexander Leslie who would assist the build-up of an indigenous army along modern lines. William M. Reger IV writes that regiments formed by Leslie and others 'bridged the divide between the seemingly aborted experiment with western military organization in the 1630s and the further development of the new-formation regiments after 1654. Without them, it is unlikely Russia could have mobilised adequately during the early years of the Thirteen Years War [1654–67]'.[18]

By the early 1640s, the Thirty Years' War was moving into its last phase, the only outstanding question being not who would win, but how convincingly? For the Franco-Swedish alliance was in the ascendancy, and the Habsburg side was heading for defeat. Nevertheless, the degree of the victory was of prime interest to two Baltic powers, Denmark and Poland. Swedish hegemony over the Baltic would mean for the former subservience, for the latter acceptance of the loss of Livonia and the danger of losing Western Prussia. And so, these two powers discussed joint action against Sweden, with Poland hoping for the acquisition of Silesia as a token of the Habsburg emperor's gratitude. A further possibility, never realised, was the incorporation in an anti-Swedish alliance of Muscovite Russia.

Away from the Baltic, another matter of great concern to the Muscovite government was heavy attacks in 1644 and 1645 by the Crimean Tatars encouraged by the Ottoman Turkish Sultan. Thus, there was some further talk of joint action by Poland and Russia, never implemented, against their common enemies to the south.

After the accession of Aleksei Mikhailovich in July 1645, Russian emissaries went to Warsaw to discuss such joint action. But there was reluctance on both sides to engage the Ottoman Empire in full-scale war, and a purely defensive alliance was concluded between Russia and Poland in September 1647. Meanwhile, the Muscovite government strove to repair relations with Sweden, sending ambassadors to Stockholm in 1646 and receiving them in Moscow in 1647.[19]

Meanwhile, what was happening in Great Britain? At the beginning of the seventeenth century, James VI and I also had a big idea, to be a prince of peace. He began his reign in England by coming to terms with the old enemy, Spain,

---

18 Reger, 'European Mercenary Officers', p. 240.
19 The above survey from Porshnev, *Frantsiia*, pp. 237–61; Vainshtein, *Rossiia*, pp. 202–10; Novosel'skii, *Bor'ba*, pp. 222–7, 295, 368–70. See also Soloviev, *History of Russia*, vol. 17, especially Chapter Two, 'Turkish Affairs, 1622–1643' and Chapter Three, 'Prince Valdemar, 1640–1645'.

France's predecessor as an aspirant to European hegemony along with the fellow Habsburg Holy Roman Empire. In the assessment of S. R. Gardiner, 'there seemed to be a chance that religious wars might be brought to a close'. Recognising that this was so, James embarked on a policy 'marked out for him by the facts of the case as well as by his own temperament'.[20] Peace was temporarily established, even in the potential flashpoint of the Netherlands. The murder of Henry IV of France in 1610 brought to an end for the time being the danger of wider war.

As part of his attempt to replace religious war by peaceful politics, James hoped to marry his elder son to the Spanish Infanta. Henry died in 1612, but was replaced as suitor for the hand of the princess by his younger brother Charles. Meanwhile, in 1613, Elizabeth, the daughter of James, was married to Frederick V, Elector Palatine and leader of an aggressive Union of German Protestant Princes. With the outbreak of the Thirty Years' War in 1618, and reversals for Frederick and the Protestant cause in general, James made an ultimately unsuccessful attempt at an alliance with Christian IV of Denmark, his brother-in-law. Parliament was unhappy with the continued prospect of the Spanish marriage, as was Prince Charles after a brief infatuation, and the royal favourite Buckingham. The heir to the throne was now involved in negotiations for a marriage alliance with France, which at first held out promise for relief of the Palatinate. However, by 1625, according to Gardiner, 'Never had an English government been more thoroughly discredited. James had shown himself incapable of making war. On March 27 James died, and Charles and his favourite were left to bear the brunt of the struggle in which they had heedlessly engaged.'[21] A much more positive appraisal came from Bishop Williams preaching the funeral sermon for the king he called 'Great Britain's Salomon' and declaiming that: 'None can be honoured of all Europe, but that he that held the Balance of Europe, and for the space of twentie yeares at the least, preserued the peace of all Europe.'[22]

After the death of the peace-loving James, the favourite that he had shared with his son, the Duke of Buckingham, pressed for war with Spain. As the French Princess Henrietta Maria crossed the channel to become queen-consort to the new king, Buckingham pressed for war with Spain. In 1627, however, he led a force for the relief of hard-pressed Huguenots in La Rochelle as war broke out with France. A miserable failure, the expedition aroused more parliamentary opposition to the foreign policy of the king and provoked the murder of

20 Gardiner, 'Britain under James I', p. 558.
21 Ibid., p. 578.
22 Patterson, *King James VI and I*, p. 357.

his favourite. By the end of the 1620s, peace was made with France and Spain, and Charles considered an alliance with both of them. However, the levy of Ship Money for the first time in 1634 led to a disastrous impact of foreign policy on domestic developments. We will not attempt to repeat this familiar story.

Relations with Russia in the first half of the seventeenth century were concerned mostly with trade, especially after James gave up his hopes of widespread peace. The Muscovy Company, which was in fierce competition with its Dutch counterparts, strove mightily to concentrate the government's attentions on this central issue. Meanwhile, the Russian government strove for recognition and support, informed about developments in the British Isles by *vesti-kuranty* 'newspapers' consisting mostly of translations from foreign newspapers kept by the Diplomatic Chancellery.

A lapse in actual diplomatic exchanges was brought to an end with the embassy of 1645–6 led by G. S. Dokhturov, sent to report on the death of Mikhail Fedorovich and accession of Aleksei Mikhailovich and to investigate the struggle going on between King Charles and his Parliament. We described this embassy in Chapter 3 above, along with its sequel, the decree banishing the merchants of the Muscovy Company to Archangel in June 1649, officially as a consequence of the execution of Charles I. By this time, as we noted, Muscovite Russia was experiencing its own serious social disturbances, leading to the composition of the *Ulozhenie* (Law Code) of 1649 and the confirmation of serfdom.

The widespread crisis culminating in 1649 provided a clear demarcation between the two halves of the seventeenth century. Yet events in the second half of the century were to show even more clearly what those of the first half, in particular the Thirty Years' War, had already demonstrated, that no consideration of 'the Christian world' could be complete without the inclusion of East along with West. However, religion as an element in international relations was in decline after 1649. Moreover, if we look at the characterisations of the Thirty Years' War as made by Polišenský, Asch and Porshnev, we can clearly see how the situation in Europe changed soon after hostilities came to an end. Now, more emphasis would have to be given to commercial rivalry extending beyond the continent into the wider world. The constitution of the Holy Roman Empire was no longer of central importance for European politics while states were consolidating their supremacy over estates, and, for the most part, maintaining control over society.

Of course, each part of Europe retained its own concerns. For an authoritative overview, let us turn again to Robert Frost, who adopts Klaus Zernack's designation of northeastern Europe as a region including Scandinavia, Poland–Lithuania and Russia, and follows him in opting for the wider term

'Northern Wars' rather than 'Baltic Wars' to describe international conflicts involving the region. Frost's first major focus is on what has traditionally been called the Livonian War, 1558–83, promoting the ascendancy of Poland–Lithuania as Ivan the Terrible failed to establish a firm foothold on the Baltic. The second Northern War, 1650–60, overlaps the Thirteen Years' War, 1654–67, between Poland–Lithuania and its upstart rival, Muscovite Russia, including the transfer of much of Ukraine from the former to the latter. The third or Great Northern War, 1700–21, leads to the triumph of imperial Russia under Peter the Great and the partial eclipse of Poland–Lithuania and those other erstwhile great powers, Denmark and Sweden.

Policies pursued on Europe's mobile steppe frontier continued to possess different emphases from those adopted in more settled parts of the continent to the west. State, national and social considerations all carried special nuances in Muscovy. Orthodoxy still kept Russia apart from other Christian confessions. The problem of the Ottoman Turks and their Crimean Tatar henchmen was particularly pressing. However, by the eve of the third Great Northern War, 1700–21, the process of modernisation, of the army in particular, was taken to a new level.

We overestimate the abruptness of this change if we see Peter the Great bursting into Europe where his predecessors had not previously made any impact at all. If H. D. Schmidt is correct in his assertion that the triumph of William III and the Grand Alliance over Louis XIV's alleged attempt to set up a universal monarchy and a united Catholic Christendom 'brought about the first major stage in the long process of western secularisation, the exchange of *Europe* for *Christendom* as supreme political collectivity',[23] we must not neglect the part played by Russia as well as Britain in this transition.[24]

Earlier, during the Interregnum from the execution of Charles I to the Restoration of Charles II, Oliver Cromwell sought to avoid foreign war, but also to support the Protestant cause and foster trade in Europe and the wider world while thwarting all plans for the restoration of the Stuarts. Unfortunately, Parliament bequeathed to him the First Dutch War, which had broken out in 1652. He was then widely criticised for too lenient a peace in 1654. Despite this leniency, tension with the Dutch over commerce and empire continued. As we have seen, Cromwell managed to establish commercial relations with Muscovy with a degree of success even though impeded by the propaganda of royalist sympathisers. He welcomed the outbreak of Muscovy's Thirteen Years' War with Poland in 1654 as the intensification of the struggle against Roman

23 Schmidt, 'The Establishment', p. 178. Schmidt's italics.
24 See Dukes, 'How the Eighteenth Century Began'.

Catholicism. Allegedly, he encouraged the breakaway Ukrainian leader, Bogdan Khmelnitsky, himself appraised by a contemporary as 'not less daring, not less experienced in politics than the English Cromwell'.[25] At first, he was enthusiastic about the Swedish invasion of Poland in 1655, although he became apprehensive about the danger of too sweeping a Swedish victory before warning about the consequences of too crushing a Swedish defeat at the hands of a Habsburg coalition. In a speech to Parliament in January 1658, he declared: 'If they can shut us out of the Baltic Sea, and make themselves masters there, where is your trade? Where are your materials to preserve your shipping?'[26] But Cromwell was also interested in the wider world, in the West Indies for example.

In Europe, the decline in Habsburg fortunes marked by the end of the Thirty Years' War was taken further in 1659 by the Peace of the Pyrenees, making that mountain chain the southwestern frontier of France, which also expanded to the north-east with the acquisition of part of the Spanish Netherlands. The Bourbon Sun King was on the rise, and international relations in Europe for the next 50 years or so were centred on Louis XIV's pursuit of glorious expansion. This challenge needed to be taken into consideration by the restored Stuarts along with continuing clashes with Holland, further negotiations with the Romanovs and ongoing concern for the nascent British empire beyond Europe.

The main British aim of the three Dutch wars (1652–4, 1665–7, 1672–4) was 'to destroy Dutch shipping and trade', according to J. R. Jones. A contemporary pamphlet declared that the Dutch pursued 'an universal sovereignty in the Baltic Sea, and the trade about the Northern Cape to Russia', so that 'in a few years if uninterrupted they will gain all the wealth in the world into their hands'.[27] However, there were also political motives in the Dutch wars. Steven A. Pincus considers that the first two in the series constituted 'a crucial turning point in English foreign policy ... the wider political nation of the later seventeenth century went to war to defend the national interest.' The English Republic sought 'to defend Protestantism and republicanism against the international threat of absolute monarchy', the Restored Monarchy 'to protect England from the unbridled economic ambition of a republican and religiously pluralist state.' Indeed, for J. R. Jones, the defeat of the Dutch in the third war was to be nothing less than 'the essential preliminary to the establishment of absolutism throughout the British Isles'.[28] To be sure, this third in the series was

---

25 Pierre Chevalier, quoted by O'Brien, *Muscovy and the Ukraine*, pp. 26–7.
26 Firth, *Oliver Cromwell*, pp. 370–89.
27 Jones, *Britain and the World*, p. 89; Pincus, *Protestantism and Patriotism*, p. 84, quoting *Europae Modernae*, pp. 62, 67.
28 Pincus, *Protestantism and Patriotism*, p. 450; Jones, *Britain and the World*, p. 81.

preceded by the Triple Alliance of Sweden, Holland and Britain of 1668 against the French threat, and in the late 1670s, 'it looked as though England would throw whatever weight she possessed into the European balances against France.' However, to follow again the argument of J. R. Jones, 'from 1681 until 1688 first Charles and then James abandoned any attempt to play an active role in European affairs, preferring instead to promise inaction in return for not very considerable, and rather irregularly paid, subsidies from Louis XIV.'[29]

In the late 1680s, as the paternalistic Stuarts were ejected from the throne for a second time, a convergence of international relations facilitated the replacement of James II by William III and Mary. The same process facilitated the rise of Romanov Russia.

In 1683, a Christian coalition under Jan Sobieski relieved Vienna from a siege by the Turks. The Poles and the Austrians remained concerned about the threat posed by the 'Ottoman infidel', as were the Russians. Could the Christian coalition be maintained and even extended?

Distinctive Russian contributions to the general cause in the 1680s were two campaigns against the Crimean Tatars, clients of the Turks. Having made a Treaty of Eternal Peace confirming earlier rapprochement with Poland in 1686, the Regent Sophia sent an army under V. V. Golitsyn south in 1687, partly in fulfilment of that treaty's terms. Meanwhile, the Ottoman empire was at war with Poland, Austria and Venice. The Russian campaign of 1687 failed, and so did another in 1689. Patrick Gordon sought to justify the action against the Crimean Tatars as integral to the grand Christian coalition by arguing that they acted as the wings of the Turkish bird. However, the reverses contributed to the overthrow of Sophia by the younger tsar, later to be known as Peter the Great. Patrick Gordon gave Peter loyal support, although he wished that he 'could have been serviceable to his Majestie' King James over in Ireland.[30]

The overthrow of James II, like the assumption of power by Peter, was facilitated by European war. In 1687, William of Orange received a letter from one of his promoters, the Marquis of Halifax, suggesting that Polish, Austrian and Venetian successes against the Turks might provoke France into action. When Belgrade was lost by the Turks in 1688, the promoters drew encouragement from Louis XIV's dispatch of troops into the Rhineland, causing his enemies to divert a considerable amount of their own forces but also to give cover to William for his descent on England. James now found it necessary to seek asylum from Louis.

29 Ibid., p. 99.
30 Dukes, 'How the Eighteenth Century began', pp. 6–9.

Peter continued campaigns against the Crimean Tatars, failing in 1695, succeeding at last in 1696. In March 1697, he set off on the Great Embassy, ostensibly to work for a crusade against the patron of the Tatars, the Ottoman Empire. His way was facilitated by the Treaty of Ryswick in May 1697, in which Louis recognised William of Orange as King of Great Britain and withdrew from Philippsburg and other acquisitions on the right bank of the Rhine. Later wars with France were to show more convergence.[31]

To sum up, this study has demonstrated that the Romanov regime placed conditionality at the heart of their diplomacy with the Stuarts – commercial privileges would be restored if the Stuarts entered into a military alliance. This had two benefits. Firstly, the ostensible purpose of a military alliance was to fight the Ottoman Empire on behalf of Christendom – the constant call for such an alliance stressed the Christian and European identity of the Romanov regime, and so legitimised it externally and consolidated domestic order at home. Secondly, the Romanovs, at least until the 1680s, had no real intention of mounting large-scale military campaigns in the south. Therefore, they had the luxury of asking for a crusade while knowing that it would not take place.

Accompanying the convergence in war and diplomacy towards the end of the seventeenth century, there was a significant shift in the fortunes of the Muscovy Company, marked by an increase in tobacco sales and a number of other considerations. Given the central importance of commerce in the Stuart–Romanov relationship, these developments are important enough to deserve attention in their own right. Addressing the commercial nature of the relationship raises an important issue: what was it that the Stuarts were really after in Russia? The Russians made Muscovy Company privileges a *quid pro quo* for military assistance, but they never received military aid on a sufficient scale that would have justified the concessions. Indeed, it was highly unlikely that Stuart official state military support through a formal legally binding treaty (as opposed to unofficial mercenary contributions, however substantial) would be forthcoming, as land-based campaigns on the steppe against the Ottoman Empire were, to put it mildly, not in accordance with the primary foreign policy concerns of the Stuart establishment. Given these geopolitical realities, Stuart policy towards the Romanov regime can best be described as a failed foreign economic policy, rather than simply a foreign policy. After all, the Dutch were driving Russian trade quite successfully with minimal concessions on the part of Muscovite authorities.

---

31 Rothstein, *Peter the Great and Marlborough*, in general.

Commerce

In most essential ways, the Stuart–Romanov relationship began and ended with trade. The formalisation of Anglo-Russian relations was the direct consequence of Chancellor's mission to Ivan the Terrible's 'realm of darkness' and the subsequent foundation of the Muscovy Company. The Company, in turn, became the key driver of English interests in Russia – at least as understood by them – and, from the London perspective, the *de facto* representative of the Tudor and Stuart monarchs in the faraway land.

The first formal document governing Anglo-Russian relations contained the Privileges granted by Ivan IV to the Muscovy adventurers. This was an event of momentous significance to both sides. As seen from the Kremlin, it represented an exceptionally generous offer to a new potential ally and friend, an attempt to tie the northwestern European kingdom to a formal relationship by giving its merchants a reason to come back for more. The English merchants, in turn, offered the Muscovite sovereigns, among other things, the prospect of enrichment by serving as distributors of Russian goods on the world markets – an important source of specie to a country lacking precious metals – while also supplying Russian with important commodities that were not available at home. Of particular importance for the ambitious ruler of Muscovy were the weapons that the English could provide, since Russian domestic arms production was minimal and the outputs of relative bad quality. The English Muscovy merchants became a critically important bridge between Russia and the world markets at a time when European economic integration was emerging as an important economic force and source of growth.

For the English, however, the generous privileges granted by the Muscovite sovereign arguably soon became a poisoned chalice and ultimately a pyrrhic victory. The merchants of the 'Russia Company' enjoyed an extraordinary first-mover advantage, being able to trade freely across Ivan's dominions, as well as to engage in transit trade with Persia and the Central Asian khanates. They did not have to pay duties and they were free to build bases in all key cities of Russia to provide the necessary logistical infrastructure for their commercial operations. For a while, they had a *de iure* monopoly over the northern passage to the White Sea. By the standards of bilateral commercial treaties, effectively all was given to them and little expected in return – at least in formal terms.

By giving the English effectively a *carte blanche* for their commercial operations in Russia, the rulers in the Kremlin fundamentally underestimated their own bargaining power and removed any incentives for the English to provide their new commercial partners with anything more than the minimum deemed necessary to ensure the continuation of their operations in the country. The asymmetry of the relationship was striking, but only sustainable for as long as the English did indeed remain in sole control of the northern route. Not surprisingly then, even as the Russians were hoping for a significant strategic contribution in the form of firearms and other *matériel*, the English soon began to slip. With both specie and arms supplies on the decline, it was painfully obvious that if it was a special relationship they were after, the Russians were struggling to get the English to reciprocate to any meaningful degree. For the Russians, this must have been not only a disappointment but in fact a major blow, since the alternative outlet to the western European markets, the Baltic, was ravaged by successive wars and crises as was the northwestern Russian Novgorodian hinterland that fed it, repeatedly devastated. Little remained of Great Novgorod, the erstwhile centre of Russian foreign trade, after the Livonian War and the Time of Troubles.

The limitations of the Muscovy adventurers' complacent tendency to take things for granted were quickly revealed when towards the end of the sixteenth century the Dutch merchants began to focus their efforts on the Muscovite market and soon established themselves as the predominant western commercial power in Arkhangel'sk. In effect, the English were faced with a rival subscribing to a fundamentally different business model from that of the favoured Muscovy Company. The Dutch merchants were not structured under the auspices of one company but several companies and partnerships which were in intense competition against each other just as much as they were against the English. Their relationship with Russia did not have a diplomatic dimension to speak of until much later. Thus, their exports and practices were driven by purely commercial, rather than 'national' interests. Moreover, their operations were based in Amsterdam, the pre-eminent entrepôt of international trade at the time where a wider array of goods was available at more competitive prices than anywhere else. They sailed on some of the best and most efficient ships in the world. And lastly, the merchants benefited from a great deal of financial innovation through creative credit and insurance arrangements. The stubborn insistence of the English on their privileges compared very unfavourably to this.

The problems linked to the diplomatic intransigence of the English were further compounded by the financial mismanagement of the Muscovy Company. Initially at the vanguard of reform – England's first joint-stock company opening up a vast new market – the Company within a couple of decades became a bastion of reaction. Indeed, the free trade lobby already dismissed the centralised company as a 'strong and shamefull monopoly' in 1604. The Muscovy adventurers, by contrast, claimed that their expensive investments in developing the Russian market necessitated a protective regime.[32] In the end, restrictive practices and narrow self-interest led to a steadily deepening financial crisis which the company sought to address through a variety of *ad hoc* measures, such as whaling in the Arctic, seeking direct access to the Siberian fur markets, and an ultimately abortive merger with the East India Company in 1618. In the end, however, these initiatives brought minimal relief and English trade with Russia declined to a mere shadow of its former self. The Company was further effectively torn asunder by two competing factions fighting it out over the fellowship's legal structure and profoundly confusing and frustrating the Russians with their unorthodox business practices.

Due to their insistence on the original privileges, which the Russians no longer had any reasonable basis for renewing, the English became the loudest but certainly not the most successful group of merchants active in the White Sea. Their demands began to sound particularly hollow as Russian merchants regrouped to exploit the fact that many of the Muscovy merchants supported the Puritan revolutionaries in the Civil War, although the privileges they operated under had been granted to the king of the country. The aforementioned petition to the 1648 Assembly of the Land was particularly devastating, but one difficult for the English to argue against with much credibility, especially as it seemed clear that the English complacency had resulted in concrete and extensive violations of the treaty provisions. Inna Liubimenko's assessment of the situation facing the Muscovy adventurers remains the most poignant descriptions of their predicament: 'the greatest advantage of the English – their duty-exempt status – had turned into its opposite – the greatest ill afflicting their trade.'[33]

The Muscovy Company in its original incarnation was dealt a dual, and nearly fatal, blow around the middle of the century. In 1646, the English were finally put *de iure* on an equal footing with the other nations active in Russia. Soon thereafter, the decapitation of Charles I and the establishment of the Puritan Commonwealth genuinely appalled the traditionally minded Russians and removed any remaining basis for granting the Russia adventurers preferential treatment. In 1649, the Muscovy merchants were expelled from the Russian interior. What many analysts of Anglo-Russian trade have tended to underestimate, however, is that by the time the deadly blow came, there was little left to kill. The English were marginal players in Russian trade, managing a fraction of the Dutch trading volumes but also now eclipsed by the northern German

---

32 Kotilaine, *Russia's Foreign Trade*, p. 95.
33 Liubimenko, 'Torgovye snosheniia', pp. 747–8.

merchants of Hamburg and Bremen. Their greatest asset was their extensive logistical infrastructure of warehouses and river barges. This allowed many English merchants to make money by serving as agents to the more successful Dutch and German merchants in the Russian interior. However, the practice was illegal and ultimately proved unsustainable.

The poor state of the Company constitutes a great paradox when viewed in light of the subsequent attempts to restore relations and, in a time-honoured fashion, restore the lost privileges. The expectation that a return to the 'old order' would have fundamentally transformed the commercial fortunes of the English must have been recognised as unrealistic by most of the players involved, including the Muscovy merchants themselves. From the narrow perspective of the Company, such a move would naturally have been beneficial in as much as it would have reduced costs and boosted profits. Moreover, it would have allowed the English to further develop their ability to serve the Dutch and the Germans, since they would have been able to operate more cheaply in the interior. However, the agenda of the Muscovy Company was blatantly redistributive rather than growth-oriented and it is likely that a mere restoration of the old charter would have sufficed to fundamentally transform the ailing enterprise.

In the realm of Anglo-Russian diplomacy, the English insistence remained a constant irritation to Russia policy-makers who had long ago recognised its futility. On the other hand, however, even the Russians seemed somewhat reluctant to drop the subject completely because it provided them with a bargaining chip that could in principle be used to win concessions in other areas. English pleas were tolerated, even if they were sometimes delivered with exceptional arrogance, and usually countered by promises to reconsider the issue once the political, security, or economic situation in Muscovy had stabilised.

The pointlessness of the Anglo-Russian diplomatic dialogue in the sphere of commerce was further underscored by the history of bilateral trade in the closing decades of the century. Where the English ultimately did succeed, their performance was in no way linked to the Muscovy Company or the privileges. The approach adopted by the English merchants in the Eastern Baltic, most notably Narva, was fundamentally different from that pursued by their brethren in the White Sea. Even if disputes about regulations and rights were far from uncommon in Narva, too, the basic business model was that of the Dutch: every man, or company, for him/itself, in free competition. Some English merchants further boosted their position by becoming burghers of Narva which allowed them to operate on an equal footing with the locals.

The case of Narva also allowed the English to engage in a commercial experiment that would prove of considerable value for the eventual change of fortunes in Arkhangel'sk. The eastern Baltic was an area where the English could sell their colonial tobacco to Russian merchants – whether directly or through the local burghers – without having to worry about the Russian ban on the sale of tobacco. The venture proved an enormous success. The English became the second-leading foreign nation in Narva (after the traditionally dominant Hanseatic merchants of Lübeck) and were soon bringing little else to Ingria. The same phenomenon was observed, albeit on a more modest scale, in the Neva port of Nyen.

Although both English fortunes and their treatment by the Russians had begun to improve in the post-Restoration decades, it was tobacco that ultimately made fundamental change possible in the White Sea as well. For this to happen, however, the old Muscovy Company had to be shattered and created anew. The old model had permitted a gradual recovery in shipping volumes, including the re-establishment of the Italian caviar trade as a regular component of English operations. Nonetheless, the annual number of ships seldom exceeded five even at the best of times and thus remained a modest fraction of what the Dutch could muster.

In the end, three circumstances of fundamental importance coincided at the close of the last Muscovite century. First of all, the new Russia tsar – Peter, eventually to be known as the Great – in 1697 decided to give up the government's long-standing and failing struggle to prevent tobacco trade and chose instead to boost government revenues by legalising the tobacco business. Secondly, the Muscovy Company itself now finally fell victim to the winds of liberalisation blowing in the London commercial community. After a protracted debate, its old restrictive rules were abolished by the parliamentary Act to Enlarge the Trade to Russia in 1699 and it was effectively taken over by the Eastland Company (operating in the eastern Baltic) and the Virginia tobacco merchants. An operation that had been in the hands of a small number of trading dynasties now suddenly had to open its doors to an influx of new members that fundamentally transformed its financial, human, and logistical resources. Lastly, the ability to export tobacco to Russia and the availability of unprecedented resources for doing so meant that English trade with the northern shores of the Muscovite realm suddenly exploded, especially once Peregrine Osborne, Marquess of Carmarthen, won the tobacco monopoly in 1698. A century that had been one of decline and seemingly interminable stagnation for Anglo-Russian commerce ended with a bang. By 1701, the main fleet sailing for Archangel already consisted of 30 vessels The Company returned to its roots of innovation and finally delivered on the promise of the late sixteenth century and, in fairness, did so more convincingly and impressively than probably any of the old Muscovy merchants could have imagined.

The great paradox of the Anglo-Russian trade relations in the seventeenth century is the striking fact that they have generated far more conjecture and erroneous conventional wisdom than they ever did concrete revenue. Perhaps because of the relatively well-known early history of Anglo-Russian trade and the initial successes of the Company, many subsequent observers have come to view the Muscovy Company as a relative success and the English as impressive and – by implication – successful pioneers of cross-continental trade. The facts of the matter tell a fundamentally different tale. The drivers of Russian foreign trade in the seventeenth century were the Dutch, as they also were in many other parts of the world, during their illustrious Golden Age. The English failure to compete against the Dutch was both striking and persistent. Their eventual success, by contrast, was made possible by the adoption of regulations and a commercial culture that owed a great deal to the burghers of the Low Countries.

There may be a temptation to use the evidence reviewed here as a basis for an unequivocally negative conclusion: seventeenth-century Anglo-Russian trade was a failure. The entirety of the relationship between the two dynasties points to a different conclusion, however. Trade was, and remained, the foundation of the bilateral relationship. It provided – throughout the century – a key reason for the two sides to maintain a dialogue. It offered the basis for a relationship that over time expanded into other areas and some of these new departures proved successful, even as positive results in the commercial sphere continued to elude the English. Trade was thus not only a source of frustration, but also an enabler. By permitting relations between the two sides to continue and intensify, it also provided the basis for its own eventual recovery, since the new privileges and opportunities at the end of the century undoubtedly owed a great deal to the diplomatic and military legs of the Stuart–Romanov relationship.

Stuarts and Romanovs – Conclusion

The activities of individuals, from those of Richard Chancellor and his men in the mid-sixteenth century onwards, have been central to our description of the manner in which the hopes for a 'perpetuall league of friendship' first enunci-ated in 1553 fluctuated over the following century and a half. All these individ-uals were subjects of a monarch (except during the Interregnum), and much the same goes for the Russians making a minor or major appearance in this book. Moreover, from one end of Europe to the other, monarchy was the keystone of governmental practice and theory. The Stuarts and the Romanovs therefore provide the overarching structure for our main chronological focus, the seventeenth century.

While our basic aim has been to tell a story, we have accompanied it with some analysis. Let us recapitulate. We have considered the relationship between the Stuarts and Romanovs to be special because it was based on trade, following the pattern set by their predecessors in the mid-sixteenth century after their relationship's accidental beginnings. The relationship was also notable because it was based on complementary rather than competing interests. While the Stuarts were, for most of the time, interested in commercial relations, the Romanovs sought domestic consolidation through promotion of military alliance against the Turks, stressing their Christian and European credentials. Furthermore, the relationship was characterised by its continuity, the sustained efforts of several generations of diplomats to press the interests of the two dynasties. A distinctive feature was the central participation in the relationship of the Muscovy Company, determining the form and substance of the relationship between the two states throughout much of the seventeenth century and reflecting the evolution of a private–public interface in foreign relations. Another distinctive feature was the significant participation of mercenary soldiers loyal to the Stuart cause in the consolidation of Romanov absolutism. From James VI and I to James VII and II, the Stuart monarchs interceded on behalf of their subjects, offering their military expertise to the Romanov tsars. The career of the most distinguished of the mercenaries, Patrick Gordon, illustrates the nature of the special relationship as well as influencing it.

While the relationship between the two dynasties could be deemed special, it was not top priority on either side. The Muscovy Company was a comparatively small organisation, struggling for survival with Dutch rivals. British attention was concentrated mainly on the Low Countries and France, while the Russian focus of interest was on Sweden, Poland and the Ottoman Empire. Britain increasingly looked westwards to colonies overseas as Russia expanded its own activities overland to the south and east. However, a remarkable commercial conjuncture at the end of the relationship, as accidental as that at its beginning, was marked by the import into Russia of tobacco from Virginia, a reflection of converging interests in a new phase in Anglo-Russian contacts involving a new relationship with the Dutch. Converging interests were also to be found in war and diplomacy at the turn of the century, from the consolidation of the future Peter the Great's power and ejection from the throne of James VII and II in 1689 to the concomitant struggles by Great Britain against France and Russia against Sweden at the beginning of the eighteenth century.

To turn to some concluding remarks on war, diplomacy and commerce, let us begin with the helpful concept of 'military revolution'. Defining the subject 'most simply as the replacement of small cavalry forces by huge gunpowder infantry armies', Marshall Poe goes on to review the extensive historiography of the subject, which again tends to ignore developments in Eastern Europe. He concludes that from about the middle of the sixteenth century to the middle of the seventeenth, 'under the impact of the military reforms, Muscovite state and society ceased to be medieval and set on the road to modernity'.[34] Here, the suggestion might be carried forward further through the later seventeenth century. As an illustration of this process, we have considered in earlier chapters aspects of the careers of British, mainly Scottish, mercenaries, including the two Alexander Leslies, Patrick Gordon and their many comrades in arms. However, in his analysis of the military revolution and political change, Brian Downing puts a more traditional viewpoint in his observation that 'Russia's contact with the West was light until Peter the Great's modernization efforts in the early eighteenth century'.[35] Obviously, we do not agree.

Robert Frost considers the interstices between the major conflicts, the first of them incorporating the Muscovite Time of Troubles with invasions by both Poles and Swedes and the Thirty Years' War, including the unsuccessful attempt by Muscovy to retake Smolensk. For this period, Frost posits 'a crisis of the whole principle of service in the eastern Slavic world',[36] suggesting that both Muscovy and Poland–Lithuania were confronted by the necessity to reorganise their military forces to defend the indispensable economic foundation of state power to be found in an agrarian economy becoming more commercialised and thus bringing about an increased social tension. Hence, Eastern European variations of the 'military revolution'. By the middle of the seventeenth century, the Muscovite army had modernised sufficiently to play an active part in what Frost calls the second Northern War, 1650–60, especially in the further conflict with Poland known as the Thirteen Years' War, 1654–67. To the West, a development of even greater significance was the emergence of the British navy. By the end of the seventeenth century, Britannia was poised to rule the waves, still making full use of naval stores from the Baltic.[37] The British, predominantly English, merchant navy allowed the Muscovy Company to play a central role in diplomacy as well as in commerce.

For the dominant realist school in the study of international relations, military power remains the most effective means of ensuring national security and state survival; therefore, military distribution of power remains essential. In the seventeenth century, diplomacy was a means of protecting and advancing state interests ultimately dependent on armies and navies. In our case study, the

---

34 Poe, 'The Consequences', p. 618.
35 Downing, *The Military Revolution*, p. 38.
36 Frost, *The Northern Wars*, p. 69.
37 See, for example, Ehrman, *The Navy*, pp. 60–5.

Stuarts gave emphasis to the navy, a force that the Romanovs before Peter the Great did not possess, as he himself was acutely aware.

However, realists also argue that the state is a prime actor in foreign policy and that state interests can be divorced from domestic concerns. Thus, state interests are driven by the accumulation of power in the international system and a state's power can only increase when another's decreases. This study demonstrates that the relationship between domestic and foreign policies in Stuart and Romanov seventeenth-century regimes was much more intermixed and diffuse than twentieth-century realist theory suggests is the case. This finding reflects the historical period within which this study takes place, a period marked by the emergence of the state and the gradual growth of an international system. Such a system is said to be in place when a full range of military, political and economic interaction occurs. This study helps locate the emergence and depth of that interaction. And so, light is thrown on the way in which the international state system in early modern Europe evolved.

This study also illustrates that in this period internal order was the key focus for both regimes and foreign policies served that primary domestic purpose. Institutional and political incentives shaped Stuart and Romanov policies and drove their diplomatic effort and both were founded on the need for domestic consolidation. The study of emergent international relations in the seventeenth century is the study of international relations through a comparative politics perspective – international relations was the arena in which the Stuarts and Romanovs could gain or lose domestic political advantage. In this period foreign and domestic policies were not distinct – despite the ahistorical certainties placed upon the Settlement of Westphalia by some recent contemporary international relations specialists. It is more relevant to talk of a mixture of international and domestic and politics than adopt the modern conception of their separation.

Thus, although material power (both military and economic) was an important determinant of inter-state relations, the Stuart-Romanov relationship also underscores the centrality of the role of institutions – the Muscovy Company in particular – in shaping the inter-state relationship. The seventeenth century gave birth to the Westphalian state order and international system, but this study argues that institutions mattered, that a multiplicity of cultural identities and the interpenetration of diverse foreign and domestic political units and loyalties were at play. Different types of solidarity between various transnational networks and organisations all suggested the continued salience of the medieval international system, rather than a more modern system based on the primacy of states.

While at times the Company appeared to be acting almost independently, for the most part it was subject to governmental direction. We have followed above the variations in Stuart (and Cromwellian) commercial policy, most of which may be placed under the heading of mercantilism. Observing that 'mercantilism can be thought of as the economic equivalent of absolutist state-building', Jarmo Kotilaine goes on to point out that the state played an especially important part in economically backward Muscovy, even more with Peter the Great's attempt to catch up.[38] In Britain, the ejection of the would-be absolutists, the Stuarts from James VI and I to James II and VII, meant a loosening of the bonds of mercantilism.

Of course, there was much more to the complex relationship of the Stuarts and Romanovs than war, diplomacy and commerce. For example, we have touched on the question of culture via the particular question of the newspaper. Just as Russia had no navy of any great consequence before the reign of Peter the Great, so it had no published newspaper before then, too.[39] However, the *vesti-kuranty* or 'manuscript bulletins' were an important source of information for the tsars and their entourages, as well as a reminder for us today that the Romanovs ruled a country where literacy and freedom of expression were both at a much lower level than in the country ruled by the Stuarts. We have also illustrated through the example of *The London Gazette* how information about Russia percolated through to the much more numerous and varied British newspapers. More work remains to be done on this subject, on the manner in which both printed and manuscript news was produced and circulated.

Another cultural question of central significance in the seventeenth century was religion, the influence of which has often deemed to be all-pervasive. Certainly, the reform in the Russian Church and the consequent Schism had profound consequences. The question of the part to be played in Great Britain by established and non-established churches was crucial to the tumultuous events of the seventeenth century. In both societies under consideration, there were fundamentalist movements opposed to Church reform. Interesting comparisons have been made between the Old Believers in Muscovy and the Covenanters in Scotland, for example.[40] Antipathy on the part of both the Orthodox and Protestant Churches to Roman Catholicism has constituted a major theme throughout the book. However, as we have noted, there was also a process of convergence in operation throughout the seventeenth century, appropriately summarised by Paul Bushkovitch: 'Both Reformation and Counter-Reformation had resulted in an enormous increase in the role of

---

38 Kotilaine, 'Mercantilism in Russia', pp. 144–6, 172–3.
39 However, Pokrovskii, 'Iz istorii gazety', p. 13, asserts that newspapers were to be found in Novgorod and Pskov as well as Moscow before the middle of the seventeenth century.
40 Cant, 'The Archpriest Avvakum'.

preaching among Protestants and Catholics, so that the Orthodox church, at least in Moscow if not the provinces, grew much more similar to the Christian churches of the West, in practice if not in dogma.'[41]

Cultural convergence was noticeable, too, in the arrival of secular culture, for example in the concept of Europe, as we have also observed. Much more could be written on this subject, of course,[42] but we must recall again that we have not set out to write a parallel history of Britain and Russia.

Our basic conclusion in the three principal areas of human activity to which we have given emphasis – commerce, diplomacy and war – is that throughout the seventeenth century in Europe, a similar process of convergence was in operation by the century's end. However, at the same time, as far as the focus of our study, the rule of the Stuarts and Romanovs, is concerned, the contrary movement – divergence – was clearly discernible.

In 1603, as we have seen, James VI, Stuart King of Scotland became James I of England without bloodshed or any kind of violence; in 1613, Mikhail Romanov was elected tsar before the horrendous Time of Troubles was completely over. Nobody could have predicted that, before the century was over, Stuarts would be ejected from the throne twice, Charles I in 1648–49 and his son James VII and II in 1688–89, while Aleksei Romanov would survive a severe crisis in 1648–49 and his son Peter would entrench his power in 1688–89. Why was this?

Some of the explanation of this divergence lies in the wider convergence in commerce, diplomacy and war. That is to say, there were three interlinked developments in the seventeenth century: the expansion of capitalism in Europe and beyond; the establishment of modern diplomacy; and the integration of war consequent upon the French attempt at hegemony. These developments killed any attempt by the male Stuarts at absolutism, while helping to consolidate Romanov absolutism.

By the end of the seventeenth century, the attempt of the Stuarts at absolutist control in the person of James VII and II had failed, and the constitutional monarchy of William and Mary had been introduced. According to at least one authority, this was because of the king's other preoccupation. Angus McInnes writes:

William's real interest was in the war against France, not in the English constitution. In consequence, during the course of the 1690s, he cheerfully signed away the royal position in order to get the necessary war supplies. He was the

41 Bushkovitch, *Religion and Society*, p. 179.
42 We have omitted the medical aspect, for example, as set out by Dumschat, *Ausländische Mediziner*, and Unkovskaya, 'Learning Foreign Mysteries'.

arch-saboteur, the quintessential fifth-columnist. He was, more than the feeblest native-born monarch, the betrayer of English absolutism.[43]

By no means all historians would agree with this assertion, any more than they could agree on a definition of absolutism or on the significance of the Revolution of 1688. For example, Robert Beddard finds the argument that James II tried 'to establish Catholic absolutism in England' unconvincing, and asserts that William III 'did more actual harm to the Church of England than James ever contemplated doing.'[44]

Meanwhile, on the other hand, the Romanovs were consolidating their own brand of government. For Peter, like William III, war was first priority, at least at the beginning of his reign. But, if William was a 'betrayer', Peter was true to the spirit of his predecessors. After the educational defeat at Narva in 1700, he went on to ultimate victory in the Great Northern War, consolidating absolutism as he did so.

Theoretical underpinning for his power came in his later years, 'in response to the challenges which Western ideas were posing to the Muscovite autocracy.'[45] Making use of some of these ideas as well as Russian traditions, *The Justice of the Monarch's Right to appoint the Heir to his Throne*, commissioned by Peter and probably composed mostly by Bishop Feofan Prokopovich, was published in Moscow in 1722. The work contains the following passage:

> And therefore the people cannot judge its sovereign's actions, for otherwise it would still retain the right to decide the common weal which it altogether renounced and conferred on its sovereign. A most heinous deed, therefore, was that done in the year 1649 by some powerful traitors in the Parliament of Great Britain against their king, Charles I: a deed cursed by all men and abhorred by the English themselves by the establishment of an annual day of mourning, and as far as we are concerned, a deed unworthy even to be remembered.

In his scholarly introduction, the translator Antony Lentin compares *The Justice of the Monarch's Right* with *The True Lawe of Free Monarchies*, written by James VI in 1597 a few years before he began the Stuart dynasty in 1603.[46] A century and a quarter on, the Romanovs in the person of Peter the Great claimed for themselves the rights which the Stuarts had by now lost.

---

43 McInnes, 'When was the English Revolution?', p. 392.
44 See review essay on 1688 by Beddard in *History Today*, June 2006, p. 62.
45 Benson, 'The Role', p. 254.
46 Lentin, *Peter the Great*, pp. 2, 32, 45, 209–11. See also Bushkovitch, *Peter*, pp. 440–1; Hughes, *Russia*, pp. 95–7.

There is a widespread view that Russia was not lagging behind the Stuarts, but following a different path. As well expressed by Endre Sashalmi, Muscovite ideology can be labelled the 'legally unlimited divine right of the tsars expressed mostly in theological symbols'.[47] Arguably, Prokopovich was building on this foundation, rather than replacing it.

Valerie Kivelson makes the important additional point that 'spatial analysis gives us unusually productive means of comparing early modern monarchies and highlighting what it was that truly made a difference in guiding historical development.' In Russia, the growth of serfdom locked most of the population to the soil. 'A legal language of rights fully grounded in place', therefore, 'substituted at a functional level for a more abstract discourse of rights and freedoms.' In England, meanwhile, 'individual, outright ownership' combined with a belief in natural rights.[48] In this connection, we need to recall that Scotland and Ireland, both containing 'frontier' regions differing radically from most of those in England, played a significant part in our story.

However, we need to remind ourselves again that we have not been aiming at a parallel history, describing all the vicissitudes of British and Russian history in the seventeenth century, but concentrating on the special relationship between the Stuarts and the Romanovs.

Epilogue: Last Meeting

After the death of Patrick Gordon in December 1699, his own purist version of the Jacobite cause[49] was kept alive in Russia by his kinsmen General Alexander Gordon and Admiral Thomas Gordon, Peter the Great's doctor Dr Robert Erskine and others. Allegedly, in 1717, Peter proposed a marriage between his daughter, the Grand Duchess Anna, and James III, the 'Old Pretender'. Of this suggestion, James wrote from exile in France: 'For God's sake get me out of this desert and well engaged with the Czar marriage.' But this proposal, even if it were made, was never realised, and no meeting occurred between James and his supposed bride, or their representatives.[50]

---

47 Sashalmi, 'Sixteenth-Seventeenth Century Muscovite Ideology', p. 172. See also Sashalmi's 'Some Remarks on the Typology of Official Petrine Political Ideology'.

48 Kivelson, *Cartographies of Tsardom*, pp. 213–14.

49 Harris, *Politics under the Later Stuarts*, pp. 208–9, analyses the phenomenon of Jacobitism, concluding on p. 228 that 'Jacobitism was a complex phenomenon, and generalisations about its nature and significance are difficult'.

50 Murdoch, 'Soldiers', pp. 7–8, 11. Corp, *A Court in Exile*, gives a good account of the Stuarts in exile in France, but says little about their international connections.

So when was the last meeting between representatives of the two dynasties? Possibly, albeit in a most tenuous manner, it was on 25 January 1740, when the Russian General James Keith had an audience with the Hanoverian King George II in London. The fact that Keith had been a participant in the 1715 Jacobite Rising was ignored. For example, the *Scots Magazine* described him as a 'Russian general in chief' who 'went from Scotland in 1716'. His status was underlined by his uniform, of the Izmailovsky Guards regiment.

Keith was not an ambassador. He had come to the British capital to press his claim for restitution of his family lands in north-east Scotland. When the Empress Anna had interceded by letter on Keith's behalf in 1738, George II replied that the case would be considered if 'the said Sieur Keith be sincerely disposed to abstain from all farther Misconduct towards us & will give us proper Assurances thereof & of his future Allegiance, before the Opening of the ensuing Session'. After his arrival in London, Keith gave no ostensible sign of disloyalty, indeed a close friend asserted that he 'acknowledged George II for his lawful king'. If, as some observers asserted, he was on an unofficial diplomatic mission to counter a French threat to harmonious Anglo-Russian relations, he would have been working against Jacobite interests. As Rebecca Wills convincingly argues, what might have been seen as a 'temporary professional obligation . . . inevitably prevailed as a survival practicality', even at the expense of 'a lasting personal loyalty to Jacobitism'. In other words, 'Russia had become less a place of exile than an escape from hopeless political compromise'. Moreover, 'Keith's example was mirrored to a greater or lesser extent by all those Jacobites who were able to establish themselves successfully in Russia.'[51]

Thus, before the '45, Russian Jacobitism was effectively dead, and the possibility of further relations between Stuarts and Romanovs had shrunk to virtually nothing. There was, however, a posthumous apparition in the shape of a letter to the Empress Elizabeth dated 28 September/9 October 1745 'signed on behalf of the Scottish Nation armed for justice' by 'M. D. D. P.', 'M. C. D. M.' and 'M. C. D. M.' and including the following passage:

> We hope, Madam, that YOUR MAJESTY will be touched by the conformity which may be found between her destiny and that of the Prince Charles Edward Stuart. Like him YOUR MAJESTY has been removed from the Throne of her Fathers, has seen it occupied by a Usurper, he has even more than She also has the grief of seeing himself proscribed by the Usurper, and condemned to a shameful death. Your Peoples finally recognising the the injustice done to

---

51 Wills, *The Jacobites and Russia*, pp. 156–62. A byproduct of Keith's visit to London was his induction into freemasonry, which he transported to Russia. Ibid., pp. 220–7.

you, have given back the Diadem that had been snatched from you; like you we carry to the feet of our Sovereign the Sceptre and the Crown, and we beseech him to accept these symbols of his legitimate authority.

The signatories expressed the hope that the empress would deign to indicate that she was ready to 'to hold out her arms to them in their hour of need as soon as their terrified enemies either scattered or joined them in order to restore in their climes days of serenity born of the reciprocal tenderness of the Sovereign and the Subjects'.[52]

The adherents of Prince Charles Edward Stuart stopped short of explicitly offering their prince as a prospective husband for the Russian empress. But the relationship of the Stuarts and Romanovs ended in 1745 as it had begun in1601, with an air of mystery.

52 *Lettre des Écossois à L'Impératrice de Russie*, from the National Library of Scotland, pp. 6, 7–8. M. C. D. M. is repeated.

Bibliography

Unpublished Primary Sources

British Archives

Aberdeen University Library (AUL)
Ms. 3051/2/9.
Ree Collection, Ms. 805, Ms. 2493.

British Library, London(BL)
Add. Ms. 11,741/2
Add. Ms. 23125
Add. Ms. 31128
Add. Ms. 36785
Add. Ms. 37356
Add. Ms. 37982
Add. Ms. 41842
Add. Ms. 48125
BL, OGE 70 396: *The London Gazette* (microfilm).

Guildhall Library (GHL), London
Ms. 11,741: Muscovy Company Minute books & treasurer's accounts, 1667–1955.

National Archives of Scotland (NA)
Privy Council (PC) 11/5A.
Privy Council (PC) 12/17.
Gifts and Deposits (GD) Hamilton Correspondence 406/1.

National Library of Scotland (NLS)
Carmichael and Gordon Papers, Ms. 109.

Public Record Office, London (PRO)
London Port Books E 315/467.
London Port Books E 190/3/4/24.
London Port Books E 190/37/8.
London Port Books E 190/38/1; 5.
London Port Books E 190/317/6.
London Port Books E 190/328/1.

CO 388/1.
CO 391/1; 10.

Privy Council 2/42; 55.
State Papers 14/8; 124. (SP)

State Papers 22/60.
State Papers 25/75.
State Papers 29/88; 266.
State Papers 41/124.
State Papers 69/10.
State Papers 82/11; 16; 17.
State Papers 88/2; 3; 6; 12; 14; 15.
State Papers 91/1; 2; 3; 4.
State Papers 95/12; 13.
State Papers 101/39 (unsorted).
State Papers 102/49.
State Papers 103/61.
State Papers 104/118; 119; 120; 125; 183.

Royal Society Library
RBO/4/30.

Sheffield University Archives, GB 0200 Ms. 61.
The Hartlib Papers. 4/4. 9/1. 9/17. 24/2. 45/1. 46/9. 46/12. 61/3. Now available on CD

Dutch Archives

Algemeen Rijksarchief, The Hague (ARA)
Liassen Moscoviën 7361, 1618.
Gemeente-Archief Amsterdam (GAA)
Notariële Archieven (NA)

Estonian Archives

Eesti Ajalooarhiiv, Tartu (Estonian Historical Archive) (EAA)
f. 1646 Narva magistraat (Narva Magistrate), n. 1, 2.

Tallinna Linnaarhiv (Tallinn City Archive)
Fond 230, n. BB37: Letters of the Gordon Family.

Russian Archives

Rossiiskii Gosudarstvennyi Arkhiv Drevnikh Aktov (RGADA)
Fond 9, opis 5.
Fond 11, opis 18.
Fond 96, opis 1.
Fond 35, opis 1, 2.
Fond 136, opis. 1
Fond 137, Arkhangel'sk, 1670 g., d. 5; d. 6, 1671 g.; 1673 g., d. 7.
Fond 142, opis 2.
Fond 180, opis 1.
Fond 210, opis 78.

Rossiiskii Gosudarstvennyi Voenno-Istoricheskii Arkhiv (RGVIA)
The Diaries of General Patrick Gordon of Auchleuchries. In six handwritten volumes.
Fond 846, opis 15, vols 1–6. [Cited by date, volume and page number.]

Swedish Archives

Riksarkivet, Stockholm (RA)
Handel och sjöfart, vol. 15.
Östersjöprovinsernas tull-och licenträkenskaper. Tullen i Novgorod 1583–1707. m.m.
vol. 34 (Kopior av orig. i RA). (KARA)

US Archives

Harvard University, Baker Business Library, Boston (HU BBL)

Goldsmiths'-Kress Library of Economic Literature (GKEL)

Published Primary Sources

Abelin, Johann Philipp. *Theatrum Europæum, oder, Ausführliche und warhafftige Beschreibung aller und jeder denckwürdiger Geschichten so sich hin und wieder in der Welt fürnemblich aber in Europa, und Teutschlanden, so wol im Religions Prophan-Wesen, vom Jahr Christi 1617. biss auff das Jahr 1629. exclus. bey Regierung deren beyden ... Romischen Keysern Matthiæa und Ferdinandi dess Andern ... zugetragen haben.* 21 vols (Franckfurt am Mayn: Bey Daniel Fievet, 1662–1738).
A Relation of Three Embassies From his Sacred Majestie Charles II to the Great Duke of Muscovie, the King of Sweden, and the King of Denmark preformed by the Right Honb the Earle of Carlisle in the years 1663 and 1664. Written by G[uy] M[iege] (London: Printed for John Starkey, 1669).
Acts of the Privy Council, John Roche Dasent (ed.) (London: His Majesty's Stationery Office, 1890 *(APC).*
Akty Moskovskago gosudarstva. N. A. Popov et al. (eds), vol. 1 (Sanktpeterburg: Tip. Imperatorskoi akademii nauk, 1890–1901).
Augustin, Baron de Mayerburg. *Relation d'un Voyage en Moscovie.* vol. I (Paris: A. Franck, 1858).
Barrow, John, Sir. *A Memoir of the Life of Peter the Great* (London: John Murray, 1832).
Bell, G. M. *A Handlist of Diplomatic Representatives, 1509–1688* (London: Royal Historical Society, 1990).
Bennet, Henry (Earl of Arlington). *The Right Honourable the Earl of Arlington's Letters to Sir W. Temple, Bar., from July 1665 ... to September 1670, etc. : (vol. 2. Containing a compleat collection of his Lordship's letters to Sir Richard Fanshaw, the Earl of Sandwich, the Earl of Sunderland, and Sir William Godolphin, during their respective embassies in Spain, from 1664 to 1674. As also to Sir Robert Southwel in Portugal.) [With a portrait]* (London, 1701).
Berry, L. *Works of Giles Fletcher* (Madison: University of Wisconsin Press, 1964).
Berry, L. and Crummey, R.O. (eds). *Rude and Barbarous Kingdom: Russia in the Accounts of Sixteenth-Century English Voyagers* (Madison: University of Wisconsin Press, 1968).
Bestuzhev-Riumin, K. N. (ed.). 'Pamiatniki diplomaticheskikh snoshenii moskovskogo gosudarstva c Anglieiu: tom 2, s 1581 po 1604 godu', *Sbornik imperatorskogo russkogo istoricheskogo obshchestva*, vol. 38 (St Petersburg: Russkoe istoricheskoe obshchestvo, 1883), pp. 340–52.
Birch, Thomas A. *A collection of the state papers of John Thurloe ... Containing authentic memorials of the English affairs from the year 1638, to the restoration of King*

Charles II. Published from the originals, formerly in the library of John lord Somers . . . and since in that of Sir Joseph Jekyll . . . Including also a considerable number of original letters and papers, communicated by . . . the Archbishop of Canterbury from the library at Lambeth . . . the Earl of Shelburn, and other hands. The whole digested into an exact order of time. To which is prefixed, the life of Mr. Thurloe: with a complete index to each volume (London: Printed for the executor of F. Gyles, 1742).

Bogoslovskii, M. M. and Lebedev, V. I. (eds). *Petr I: materialy dlia biografi.* 5 vols ([Moskva]: Ogiz, Gos. sotsialno-ekon. izd-vo, 1940–48).

Bond, Edward A. (ed.). *Russia at the close of the sixteenth century : comprising, the treatise "Of the Russe common wealth," by Giles Fletcher: and the Travels of Sir Jerome Horsey, now for the first time printed entire from his own manuscript* (London: Printed for the Hakluyt Society, 1856).

Brereton, Henry. *Newes of the present miseries of Rushia: occasioned by the late warre in that countrey. Commenced betweene Sigimond now King of Poland. Charles late King of Swethland. Demetrius, the last of the name, Emperour of Rushia. Together with the memorable occurrences of our owne nationall forces, English, and Scottes, vnder the pay of the now King of Swethland* (London: Printed [by N. Okes] for Iohn Bache, 1614).

Briet, Philippe. *Parallela geographiae veteris et novae* (Parisiis, France: sumptibus Sebastiani Cramoisy et Gabrielis Cramoisy, 1648–1649).

Bryant, Arthur (ed.) *The Letters, Speeches and Declarations of King Charles II* (London: Cassell, 1968).

Buganov, V.I. (ed.). *Vosstanie moskovskikh strel'tsov: sbornik dokumentov* (Moscow: Nauka, 1980).

Burnet, Gilbert. *The History of his Own Times.* vol. II (London: Gibbings, 1903).

Calendar of State Papers, Domestic, Foreign, Colonial, Venetian (CSPD) (CSPF) (CSPCol) (CSPV)

Calendar of Treasury Books, vol. III, 1669 – 1672 (London: H.M.S.O., 1908).

Care, H. *The Weekly Pacquet of Advice from Rome, or the History of Popery.* 4 vols (London: L. Curtis, 1679–1682).

Chamberlain, John. *Letters of John Chamberlain*, ed. N. E. McClure (Philadelphia: American Philosophical Society, 1929).

Chteniia v Istoricheskom obshchestve Nestora-letopistsa by Istoricheskoe obshchestvo Nestora-lietopistsa. XXIII (Kiev: Univ. tip., 1912).

Collins, Samuel. *The Present State of Russia in a Letter to a Friend at London* (London: Printed by John Winter for Dorman Newman, 1671). Available online, ed. Poe, Marshall.

Cross, Samuel H. (ed. and trans.) *The Russian Primary Chronicle.* Harvard Studies and Notes in Philology and Literature, vol. 12 (Cambridge, MA: Harvard University Press, 2003).

Debates. see Grey.

A Declaration of His Imperiall Majestie, The most High and Mighty Potentate Alexea, Emperor of Russia, and great-Duke of Muscovia, &c, Wherein is contained his Detestation of the Murther of Charles the First, King of Great-Britain and Ireland; his propensitie to restore King Charles the Second; That hee hath forbidden all Trade with England; and Meanes propounded for the establishing of a generall-Peace throughout Christendome ([London: s.n.], Printed in the yeere 1650).

Defoe, Daniel. *A Journal of the Plague Year* (London: Oxford University Press, 1959).

Dukes, Paul (ed.). 'Gordon and his Family Circle. Some Unpublished Letters', *Scottish Slavonic Review*, no. 10 (1988), pp. 44–67.

Early English Books Online. (EEBO)

Europæ modernæ speculum, or, A view of the empires, kingdoms, principalities, seignieuries, and common-wealths of Europe in their present state, their government, policy, different interest, and mutual aspect one towards another, from the treaty at Munster, Anno 1648 to this present 1665. (London: Printed by T. Leach for Tho. Johnson, 1665).

Evans, Norman E. 'A Russian Royal Letter of 1682', *Journal of the Society of Archivists*, vol. 3 (1965), pp. 75–82.

Evelyn, John. *The Diary of John Evelyn*, ed. E. S. Beer (Oxford: Clarendon Press, 1955).

Fletcher, Giles. *Of the Russe Commonwealth, 1591*, ed. Richard Pipes and John V.A. Fine, Jr (Cambridge, MA: Harvard University Press, 1966).

Foedera, conventions, literae, et cujuscunque generis acta publica, inter reges Angliae et alios . . . ed. Thomas Rymer, 20 vols. (London: J. Tonson, 1726–1735).

Foster, Elizabeth Read. *Proceedings in Parliament, 1610, vol. 2: House of Commons* (New Haven: Yale University Press, 1966).

Gardiner, Samuel Rawson (ed). *The Constitutional Documents of the Puritan Revolution, 1625–1660* (Oxford: The Clarendon Press, 1947).

Gordon, Alexander. *The history of Peter the Great, Emperor of Russia. To which is prefixed, A short general history of the country, from the rise of that monarchy: and an account of the author's life. In two volumes* (Aberdeen: F. Douglass and W. Murray, 1755).

Graham, Hugh F. (ed. and trans.) *The Moscovia of Antonio Possevino* (Pittsburg: University of Pittsburg Press, 1977).

Grey, Anchitel. Debates of the House of Commons from the Year 1667 to the Year 1694. Collected by the Honble Anchitell Grey, Esq, Who Was Thirty Years Member for the Town of Derby. 10 vols (London: Printed for D. Henry and R. Cave, and J. Emonson, 1763).

Hakluyt, Richard. *The principall navigations, voiages, traffiques & discoveries of the English nation made by sea or over-land to the remote and farthest distant quarters of the earth at any time within the compasse of these 1500 yeeres*, ed. D. B. Quinn and R. A. Skelton (New York: Viking Press [1965]).

Halkluytus Posthumus. See Purchas.

Herberstein, Sigismund von. *Notes upon Russia. being a translation of the earliest account of that country, entitled Rerum Moscoviticarum commentarii.* R.H. Major (ed.), 2 vols (London: Printed for the Hakluyt Society, 1851).

Historical Manuscripts Commission. Various, as indicated in footnotes. (*HMC*)

Howell, J. *Epistolae Ho-Eliane; familiar letters domestic and forren* (London: Printed for Thomas Guy, 1688).

Howell, James. *Familiar Letters on Important Subjects, wrote from the year 1618 to 1650.* 10th edition (Aberdeen: F. Douglass and W. Murray, 1753).

Jansson, Maija and Rogozhin, Nikolai (eds). *England and the North: The Russian Embassy of 1613–1614.* Memoirs of the American Philosophical Society, vol. 210 (Philadelphia: American Philosophical Society, 1994).

Journals of the House of Commons. (JHC)

Kenyon, J. P. (ed.) *The Stuart Constitution*, 2nd edn (Cambridge: Cambridge University Press, 1986).

Khevenhüller, Franz Christoph. *Annales Ferdinandei, oder Wahrhaffte Beschreibung Käysers Ferdinandi des andern, mildesten Gedächtniss:geburth, Aufferziehung und bisshero in Krieg und Friedens-Zeiten Vollbrachten thaten, geführten Kriegen und Vollzogenen hochwightigen geschäfften.* 12 vols (Leipzig: M.G. Weidmann, 1721–6).

King Charles his Speech made upon the Scaffold at Whitehall Gate, Immediately before his Execution, on Tuesday the 30. of Jan. 1648, With a Relation of the manner of his going to Execution. Published by Special Authority (London: Printed by Peter Cole, at the Sign of the Printing Press in Cornhill, near the Royall Exchange, 1649).

Konovalov, S. 'Seven Russian Royal Letters 1613–23', *OSP*, VIII (1959), pp. 118–34.

Konovalov, S. 'Anglo-Russian Relations, 1617–1618', *OSP*, I (1950), pp. 64–103.

Konovalov, S. 'Anglo-Russian Relations, 1620–1624', *OSP*, IV (1953), pp. 71–131.

Konovalov, S. 'Twenty Russian Royal Letters', *OSP*, VIII (1958), pp. 117–56.

Konovalov, S. 'Seven Letters of Tsar Mikhail to Charles I, 1634–1638', *OSP*, IX (1960), pp. 32–63.

Konovalov, S. 'England and Russia: Three Embassies, 1662–5', *OSP*, X (1962), pp. 60–104.

Konovalov, S. 'Patrick Gordon's Dispatches from Russia, 1667', *OSP*, XI (1964), pp. 8–16.

Konovalov, S. 'England and Russia: Two Missions, 1666–1668', *OSP*, XIII (1967), pp. 47–71.

Konovalov, S. 'Sixteen Further Letters of General Patrick Gordon', *OSP*, XIII (1967), pp. 72–95.

Korb, Johann G. *The Diary of an Austrian Secretary of Legation at the Court of Czar Peter the Great*, trans. and ed. Count Macdonnell, 2 vols (London: Bradbury & Evans, 1863).

Kotkov, S. I. (ed.). *Vesti-kuranty, 1600–1639gg* (Moskva: Nauka, 1972).

Kotkov, S. I. (ed.). *Vesti-kuranty, 1645–1646, 1648gg* (Moskva: Nauka, 1980).

Kotkov, S. I. (ed.). *Vesti-kuranty, 1648–1650gg* (Moskva: Nauka, 1983).

Lambard, William. *Archaionomia, siue de priscis anglorum legibus libri sermone Anglico, vetustate antiquissimo, aliquot abhinc seculis conscripti, atq[ue] nunc demum, magno iurisperitorum, & amantium antiquitatis omnium commodo, tenebris in lucem vocati. Gulielmo Lambardo interprete. Regum qui has leges scripserunt nomenclationem, & quid pr erea accesserit, altera monstrabit pagina.* (Londini: ex officina Joannis Daij., An. 1568).

Lentin, Antony (ed. and trans.). *Peter the Great: His Law on the Imperial Succession in Russia, 1722: The Official Commentary* (Oxford: Headstart History, 1996).

Lettre des écossois a l'imperatrice de Russie (Edimbourg [i.e. Paris: s.n.], 1745).

Likhachev, D. S. (ed.). *Puteshestviia russkikh poslov XVI–XVIIvv.: Stateinye zapiski* (Moscow-Leningrad: Nauka, 1954).

Luttrell, N. *A Brief Historical Relation of State Affairs, 1678–1714.* 6 vols (Oxford: Oxford University Press, 1857).

Macfarlane, Alan (ed.). *The Diary of Ralph Josselin 1616–1683* (London: Oxford University Press, 1991).

Martynov, I.F. 'Prince Prozorovsky's Ambassadorial Speech to King Charles II', *OSP*, vol. 13, (1980), pp. 50–57.

Massa, Isaac. *A Short History of the Beginning and the Origins of these Present Wars in Moscow under the reigns of various Sovereigns down to the year 1610*, ed. and tranas. G. E. Orchard (Toronto: University of Toronto Press, 1982).

Milton, John. *Works of John Milton*, vol. 10 (New York: Columbia University Press, 1932).

Murdoch, Steve and Grosjean, Alexia (eds.). *Scotland, Scandinavia and Northern Europe, 1580–1707* (the *SSNE Database*): http://www.st andrews.ac.uk/history/ssne

O'Brien, C. B. (ed). 'Early Correspondence of a Muscovite Diplomat, 1642–1645', *CASS*, vol. 6, no. 4 (1962), pp. 606–619.

Olearius, Adam. *The Travels of Olearius in Seventeenth Century Russia*, ed. and trans. S.H. Barron (Stanford: Stanford University Press, 1967).

Passages from the Diary of General Patrick Gordon of Auchleuchries, A.D. 1635–A.D. 1699, ed. and intro. Joseph Robertson (Aberdeen: Spalding Club, 1859).

Pepys, Samuel. *The Diary of Samuel Pepys*, ed. J. H. Wheately (London: G. Bell and Sons, 1904–5).

Perry, John. *The State of Russia under the Present Tsar* (London: Tooke, 1716).

Pisma i bumagi Imperatora Petra Velikago. (S.-Peterburg: Gos. tip., 1887).

Purchas, Samuel. *Hakluytus Posthumus, or Purchas His Pilgrimes Contayning a History of the World in Sea Voyages and Lande Travells by Englishmen and Others* (Glasgow: J. MacLehose and Sons, 1905).

Register of the Privy Council of Scotland, Series 2: 1625–1660 (Edinburgh: H.M. General Register House, 1899–1908).

Roberts, Michael (trans. and ed.). *Swedish Diplomats at Cromwell's Court, 1655–1656: the Missions of Peter Julius Coyet and Christe Bonde* (London: University College London, 1988).

Sakharov, Ivan Petrovich. *Zapiskii russkikh liudei. Sobytiia vremen Petra Velikogo* (Sanktpeterburg: V tipografii Sakharova, 1841).

Samling utaf Kongl. Bref. Stadgar och förordningar &c. angående Sweriges rikes commerce, politie och oeconomie uti gemen: ifrån åhr 1523 in til gemen nårwarande tid: uppå Hans Kongl. Maj:ts nådigesta befallning. giord af And. Anton von Stiernman. (Stockholm: Tryckt uti Kongl. Tryckeriet, 1747–1775).

Selden, John. *Titles of Honor* (London: By William Stansby for Iohn Helme . . ., 1614).

Smith, Thomas. *Sir Thomas Smithes voiage and entertainment in Rushia. With the tragicall ends of two emperors, and one empresse, within one moneth during his being there: and the miraculous preseruation of the now raigning emperor, esteemed dead for 18. yeares* (London: [By W. White and W. Jaggard] for Nathanyell Butter, 1605).

Sobranie gosudarstvennykh gramot i dogovorov khraniashchikhsia v gosudarstvennoi kollegii inostrannykh del (Moskva: V Tip. N.S. Vsevolozhskago, 1813–1894).

Sochinenie Kil'burgera o russkoi torgovle v tsarstvovanie Alekseia Mikhailovicha, ed. B. G. Kurts (Kiev: Tipografiia I.I. Chokolova, 1915).

Sostoianie Rossii v 1650–1655 gg. po doneseniiam Rodesa. Chteniia v Imperatorskom obshchestve istorii i drevnostei pri Moskovskom universitete, CCLIII, ed. B. G. Kurts (Moscow: Sinodal'naia Tipografiia, 1915).

Spalding, John. *Memorialls of the Troubles in Scotland and in England, 1624–1645* (Aberdeen: Spalding Club, 1850).

Staden, Heinrich von. *The Land and Government of Muscovy: a sixteenth century account*, ed. and trans. Thomas Esper (Stanford: Stanford University Press, 1967).

Stuart, John (ed.). *Extracts from the Manuscript collection of the Rev. Robert Woodrow, 1605–1697*. Miscellany of the Spalding Club, 2 (Aberdeen, 1842).

Tabeller over Skibsfart og Varetransport gennem Øresund 1661–1783 og gennem Storebælt 1701–1748, vol. I, ed. Bang, Nina Ellinger (København: Gyldendal, Nordisk forlag, 1930).

Tagebuch des Generals Patrick Gordon, wahrend seiner Kriegsdienste unter den Schweden und Polen vom Jahre 1655 bis 1661, und seines Aufenthaltes in Russland vom Jahre 1661 bis 1699. ed. M. A. Obolenskii and M. C. Posselt, 3 vols (Moskau, Gedruckt in der Universitats-Buchdr, Leipzig, K.F. Kohler, 1849–1852).

Tamozhennye knigi moskovskogo gosudarstva XVII veka, I: Severnyi rechnoi put: Ustiug Velikii, Sol'vychegodsk, Tot'ma v 1633–1636gg. A. I. Iakovlev (ed.). (Moscow: Akademiia nauk SSSR, 1950).

Tanner, J. R. *Constitutional Documents of the Reign of James I, 1603–1625* (Cambridge: Cambridge University Press, 1961).

Theatrum Europoeum. see Abelin

Thurloe. see Birch
TKMG. See *Tamozhennye knigi* above.
Vinogradoff, Igor. 'Russian Missions to London, 1694–1687, Seven Accounts by the Master of Ceremonies', *OSP*, New Series, vol. 14 (1981), pp. 43–50.
Wicquefort, Abraham de. *The Embassador and his Functions.* Trans. John Digby (London: printed for Bernard Lintott, 1716).

Secondary Sources

Alekseev, M. P. *Angliia i Anglichane v pamiatnikakh moskovskoi pis'mennosti,* Uchenye zapiski Leningradskogo gosudarstvennogo universiteta, Seriia istoricheskikh nauk, vypusk 15 ([Leningrad]: Leningradskii gos. un-t, 1946).
Anderson, M. S. 'English Views of Russia in the Age of Peter the Great', *Slavic Review,* vol. 13 (1954), pp. 200–14.
Anderson, M. S. *Peter the Great* (London: Thames and Hudson, 1978).
Anderson, M. S. *The Rise of Modern Diplomacy, 1450–1919* (London: Longman, 1993).
Anderson, P. J. *Studies in the* History *and Development of the University of Aberdeen: A Quartercentenary Tribute Paid by Certain of Her Professors & of Her Devoted Sons.* Aberdeen University studies, no. 19 (Aberdeen: Aberdeen University Press, 1906).
Arel, Maria Salomon and Bogatyrev, Sergei. 'Anglichane (po dokumentam posol'stva T. Smita)', *Arkheograficheskii ezhegodnik za god 1997* (Moscow: Nauka, 1997), pp. 439–55.
Arel, Maria Salomon. 'The Muscovy Company in the First Half of the Seventeenth Century: Trade and Position in the Russian State – A Reassessment' (New Haven: Yale University PhD dissertation, 1996).
Arkhangel'skii, Sergei Ivanovich. 'Anglo-gollandskaia torgovlia s Moskvoi v XVII v.', *Istoricheskii sbornik,* V (1936), pp. 5–38.
Arkhangel'skii, Sergei Ivanovich. 'Diplomaticheskie agenty Kromvelia v peregovorakh s Moskvoi', *Istoricheskie zapiski,* V (1939), pp. 118–140.
Asch, Ronald G. *The Thirty Years' War: The Holy Roman Empire and Europe, 1618–1648* (Basingstoke, Hampshire: Macmillan, 1997).
Aston, Margaret. *The Fifteenth Century: The Prospect of Europe* (New York: Harcourt, Brace & World, Inc., 1968).
Aston, Trevor (ed.). *Crisis in Europe, 1560–1660: Essays from past and present* (London: Routledge and Kegan Paul 1965).
Åström, Sven Erik. *From Stockholm to St. Petersburg; commercial factors in the political relations between England and Sweden, 1675–1700* (Helsinki: Suomen Historiallinen Seura, 1962).
Åström, Sven Erik. *From cloth to iron; the Anglo-Baltic trade in the late seventeenth century* (Helsingfors: Societas Scientiarum Fennica, 1963–1965).
Åström, Sven Erik. 'The English navigation laws and the Baltic trade, 1600–1700', *Scandinavian Economic History Review,* vol. 8, no. 1 (1960).
Attman, Artur. *The Russian and Polish Markets in International Trade* (Göteborg: The Institute of Economic History of Gothenburg University, 1973).
Attman, Artur. *The Struggle for Baltic Markets. Powers in Conflict 1558–1618* (Göteborg: Kungl. Vetenskaps-och Vitter- hets-Samhället, 1979).
Aylmer, G.E. *The King's Servants. The Civil Service of Charles I, 1625–1642* (New York: Columbia University Press, 1961).
Babkine, A. 'Les Lettres de Russie du General Pierre Lefort'. *CASS,* vol. 10, no. 1 (1976), pp. 43–73.

Bakhrushin, S.V. 'Moskovskoe vosstanie 1648g', in *Nauchnye trudy*, vol. 2 (Moskva: Izd-vo Akademii nauk SSSR, 1954), pp. 46–90.

Bantysh-Kamenskii, N.N. *Obzor vneshnikh snoshenii Rossii* (Moskva: Izd. Kommissii pechataniia gos. gramot i dogovorov pri Moskovskom glavnom arkhivie Ministerstva inostrannykh diel, 1894–1902).

Barany, George. *The Anglo-Russian Entente Cordiale of 1697–1698, Peter I and William III at Utrecht* (New York: East European Monographs, 1986).

Barbour, V. 'Dutch and English Merchant Shipping in the Seventeenth Century', *English Historical Review*, vol. 2 (1930), pp. 261–90.

Barnhill, J. W. and P. Dukes. 'North-east Scots in Muscovy in the Seventeenth Century', *Northern Scotland*, vol. 1, no. 1 (1972), pp. 49–63.

Baron, S. H. 'Vasilli Shorin: Seventeenth-Century Russian Merchant Extraordinary', *CASS*, vol. 6, no. 4 (1972), pp. 503–48.

Bazilevich, K. V. 'Kollektivye chelobit'ia torgovykh liudei i bor'ba za russkii rynok v pervoi polovine XVII veka', *Izvestiia Akademii nauk SSSR. Otedelenie obshchestvennykh nauk. Bulletin de l'Académie des sciences de l'URSS. Classe des Sciences sociales.* (Moskva [etc.] Izd-vo Akademii nauk SSSR, 1932), no. 2, pp. 89–102, 109–17.

Beddard, Robert. 'Review: The Great Crisis of the British Monarchy, 1685–1730', *History Today*, vol. 56 (June 2006), p. 62.

Begunov, A. and Yu. K. ' "Opistanie vrat chestie . . .": a Seventeenth-Century Translation of William of Orange and the Glorious Revolution', *OSP*, New Series, vol. 20 (1987), pp. 60–93.

Benson, Sumner. 'The Role of Western Political Thought in Petrine Russia'. *CASS*, vol. 8, no. 2 (1974), pp. 254–73.

Bieganska, A. 'Scots involved in the War for Smolensk', unpublished paper.

Billington, J.H. *The Icon and the Axe: an interpretative history of Russian culture* (New York: Vintage Books, 1966).

The Birth of the European Press as reflected in the Newspaper Collection of the Royal Library, Stockholm [Folke Dahl] (Gothenburg: Rundqvists Boktryckeri, 1960).

Black, Jeremy. *War in European history, 1494–1660* (Washington, DC: Potomac Books, 2006).

Black, Jeremy. *Jacobitism and British foreign policy under the first two Georges 1714–1760* (Huntingdon: Royal Stuart Society, 1988)

Bol'shukhin, A. A. *Anglo-russkie otnosheniia v period krest'ianskoi voiny i pol'sko-shvedskoi interventsii v Rossii v nachale XVII* (Kandidatskaia dissertatsiia, Gor'kii: Gor'kovskii gosudarstvennyi pedagogicheskii institut im. A.M. Gor'kogo, 1949).

Borodin, A. V. *Inozemtsy: ratnye liudi na sluzhbe v moskovskom gosudarstve* (Petrograd: 1916).

Brenner, Robert. *Merchants and revolution: commercial change, political conflict, and London's overseas traders, 1550–1653* (Princeton: Princeton University Press, 1993).

Brown, Peter B. 'Tsar Aleksei Mikhailovich: Muscovite Military Command, Style and Legacy to Russian Military History', in Eric Lohr and Marshall Poe (eds), *The Military and Society in Russia, 1450–1921* (Leiden: E.J. Brill, 2002), pp. 119–45.

Bruce, Maurice. 'Jacobite Relations with Peter the Great', *SEER*, vol. 4 (1935–1936), pp. 343–62.

Budde, E. F. 'Poslanie shvedskogo polkovnika Aleksandra Lesli k Tsariu Mikhailu Fedorovichu iz Narvy o novouchrezhdennom rytsarskom polskom ordene v 1638-m godu', in E. F. Budde (ed.), *Pamiatniki drevnei pismennosti i iskusstva*, vol. CLXV ([S.-Peterburg]: Tip. I.N. Skorokhodova, 1906), pp. iii–vi, 20.

Burgess, Glenn. *Absolute Monarchy and the Stuart Constitution* (New Haven: Yale University Press, 1996).

Burns, J. H. *The True Law of Kingship: Concepts of Monarchy in Early Modern Scotland* (Oxford: Clarendon Press, 1996).

Bushkovitch, Paul. *Peter the Great: The Struggle for Power, 1671–1725* (Cambridge: Cambridge University Press, 2001).

Bushkovitch, Paul. *Religion and Society in Russia: The Sixteenth and Seventeenth Centuries* (Oxford: Oxford University Press, 1992).

Bussmann, Klaus and Schilling, Heinz (eds.). *1648: War and Peace in Europe*, vol. 1, *Politics, Religion, Law and Society*. (Münster-Osnabrück: 350 Jahre Westfälischer Friede mbh, 1998).

Cant, C. B. H. 'The Archpriest Avvakum and His Scottish Contemporaries', *SEER*, vol. 44 (1965–6), pp. 381–402.

Carswell, John. *The Descent on England. A Study of the English Revolution of 1688 and Its European Background* (New York: John Day Company, 1969).

Chakshov, V. N. 'Romanovy: kto oni?', *Otechestvennaia istoriia*, no. 1 (1998), pp. 167–76.

Childs, John. *The Army of James II and VII and the Glorious Revolution* (Manchester: Manchester University Press, 1980).

Christensen, Thorkild Lyby. 'Scots in Denmark in the sixteenth century', *Scottish Historical Review*, vol. 49 (1970), pp. 125–45.

Christiansen, E. *The Northern Crusades. The Baltic and the Catholic Frontier 1100–1525* (London and Basingstoke: Macmillan, 1980).

Christov, Theodore. 'Liberal Institutionalism Revisited: Grotius, Vattel, and the International Order of States', *The European Legacy*, vol. 10, no. 6 (2005), pp. 561–84.

Corp, Edward. *A Court in Exile: The Stuarts in France, 1689–1718*. With contributions by Edward Gregg, Howard Erskine Hill and Geoffrey Scott (Cambridge: Cambridge University Press, 2004).

Corvisier, A. *Armies and Societies in Europe, 1454–1789* (Bloomingdale: Indiana University Press, 1976).

Cracraft, James. *The Revolution of Peter the Great* (Cambridge MA: Harvard University Press, 2003).

Cross, Anthony G. 'Peter & Britain', in A. G. Cross, *Russia in the Reign of Peter the Great, Old and New Perspectives* (Cambridge: Study Group of Eighteenth Century Russia, 1998), pp. 25–39.

Crowhurst, P. *The Defence of British Trade, 1689–1815* (Folkstone: Dawson, 1977).

Cruickshanks, Eveline and Black, Jeremy (eds). *The Jacobite Challenge* (Edinburgh: John Donald, 1988).

Cruickshanks, Eveline. *Ideology and Conspiracy: Aspects of Jacobitism, 1689–1759* (Edinburgh: John Donald, 1982).

Crummey, Robert O. 'Crown Boiars under Feodor Ivanovich and Mikhail Romanov', *Canadian–American Slavic Studies*, vol. 6, no. 4 (1972), pp. 549–74.

Crummey, Robert O. 'Muscovy and the "General Crisis of the Seventeenth Century"', *Journal of Early Modern History*, vol. 2, no. 2 (1998), pp. 156–80.

Cust, Richard. 'News and Politics in Early Seventeenth-Century England', *Past and Present*, no. 112 (August, 1986), pp. 60–90.

Dalgård, Sune. *Det Petsoriske Kompagni af 1619* (København: Ejnar Munksgaard, 1955).

Daly, J. 'The Idea of Absolute Monarchy in Seventeenth Century England', *Historical Journal*, vol. 11, no. 2 (1978), pp. 227–50.

Davies, Brian. *State Power and Community in Early Modern Russia: The Case of Kozlov, 1635–1649* (London: Palgrave Macmillan, 2001).

Davies, Brian. 'The Second Chigirin Campaign (1678): Late Muscovite Military Power in Transition', in Eric Lohr and Marshall Poe (eds), *The Military and Society in Russia, 1450–1917* (Leiden: Brill, 2002), pp. 97–118.

Davis D. W. *A Primer of Dutch Seventeenth Century Overseas Trade* (The Hague: Martinius Nijhoff, 1961).

Demkin, A. V. 'Zapadnoevropeiskie kapitaly i proizvodstvo v Rossii v pervoi polovine XVIIv', in A.A. Preobrazhensii and A.V. Demkin (eds), *Obshchestvenno-politicheskoe razvitie feodal'noi Rossii: Sbornik statei* (Moscow: Akademiia nauk SSSR, 1985).

Demkin, A. V. *Zapadnoevropeiskoe kupechestvo* (Moskva: Institut rossiiskoi istorii RAN, 1994).

'The Diary of General Patrick Gordon', *Quarterly Review*, no. 180, vol. 90 (1852), pp. 314–32.

'The Diary of General Patrick Gordon', *Edinburgh Review*, no. 211, vol. 104 (1856), pp. 24–51.

Dooley, Brendan and Baron, Sabrina A. (eds). *The Politics of Information in Early Modern Europe* (London: Routledge, 2001).

Dow, J. *Ruthven's Army in Sweden and Estonia*. Historiskt Arkiv 13 (Stockholm, 1965).

Downing, Brian M. *The Military Revolution and Political Change: Origins of Democracy and Autocracy in Early Modern Europe* (Princeton: Princeton University Press, 1992).

Duffy, Christopher. *Russia's Military Way to the West: Origins and Nature of Russian Military Power, 1600–1800* (London and Boston: Routledge & Keegan Paul, 1981).

Dukes, Paul. *October and the World: Perspectives on the Russian Revolution* (London: Macmillan, 1979).

Dukes, Paul. 'Some Aberdonian Influences in the Early Russian Enlightenment', *CASS*, vol. 12, no. 4 (1977), pp. 436–51.

Dukes, Paul. 'Gordon and his Family Circle. Some Unpublished Letters', *Scottish Slavonic Review*, no. 10 (1988), pp. 44–67.

Dukes, Paul. 'How the Eighteenth Century Began for Russia and the West', in A.G. Cross (ed.), *Russia and the West in the Eighteenth Century* (Newtonville, MA: Oriental Studies Partners, 1983), pp. 2–19.

Dukes, Paul. 'The Leslie Family in the Swedish Period (1630–5) of the Thirty Years' War', *European Studies Review*, vol. 12, no. 4 (1982), pp. 401–24.

Dukes Paul. 'New Perspectives: Alexander Leslie and the Smolensk War, 1632–4', in Steve Murdoch (ed.). *Scotland and the Thirty Years' War, 1618–1648* (Leiden: Brill, 2001), pp. 173–89.

Dukes, Paul. 'Paul Menzies and his Mission from Muscovy to Rome, 1672–1674', *The Innes Review*, vol. 35 (Autumn 1984), pp. 88–95.

Dukes, Paul. 'The Thirty Years' War, the Smolensk War and the Modernization of International Relations in Europe', in Jarmo Kotilaine and Marshall Poe (eds), *Modernizing Muscovy: Reform and Social Change in Seventeenth-Century Russia.* (London: RoutledgeCurzon, 2004), pp. 203–22.

Dumschat, Sabine. *Ausländische Mediziner im Moskauer Russland* (Stuttgart: Franz Steiner Verlag, 2006).

Dunbar, A. M. *Scottish Kings: a revised chronology of Scottish history, 1005–1625, with notices of the principle events, tables of regnal years, pedigrees, calendars, etc* (Edinburgh: D. Douglas, 1906).

Dunning, C. S. L. 'A Letter to James I concerning the English Plan for Military Intervention in Russia', *SEER*, vol. 67, no. 1 (1989), pp. 94–8.

Dunning, Chester S. L. *Russia's First Civil War: The Time of Troubles and the Founding of the Romanov Dynasty* (University Park: Pennsylvania State University Press, 2001).

Edmundson, George. *Anglo-Dutch Rivalry during the first half of the seventeenth century, being the Ford lectures delivered at Oxford in 1910* (Oxford: Clarendon Press, 1911).

Eekman, Thomas. 'Muscovy's International Relations in Late Seventeenth Century, Johann Van Keller's Observations', *California Slavic Studies*, vol. 14 (1992), pp. 44–67.

Ehrman, John. *The Navy in the War of William III 1689–1697* (Cambridge: Cambridge University Press, 1953).

Elliott, John 'War and Peace in Europe, 1618–1648' in Klaus Bussmann and Heinz Schilling, (eds), *1648: War and Peace in Europe*, vol. 1, *Politics, Religion, Law and Society* (Münster-Osnabrück: 350 Jahre Westfälischer Friede mbh, 1998), pp. 23–39.

Elton, G. R. *England under the Tudors* (London: Putnam, 1956).

Erpenbeck, Dirk-Gerd. *Narva 1581–1721: Quellen zur Geschichte der Stadt in schwedischer Zeit* (Dortmund: Forschungsstelle Ostmitteleuropa, 1993).

Erpenbeck, Dirk-Gerd. *Narvaer Bürger- und Einwohnerbuch, 1581–1704* (Dortmund: Forschungsstelle Ostmitteleuropa, 2000).

Erpenbeck, Dirk-Gerd. 'Die Engländer in Narva zu schwedischer Zeit', *Zeitschrift für Ostforschung*, XXXVIII (1989) 4, pp. 481–97.

Erpenbeck, Dirk-Gerd. 'Die Bürgermeister Narvas im 17. Jahrhundert', *Ostdeutsche Familienkunde*, XXXI (1983), vol. 10, no. 2, pp. 33–40, *no. 3, pp. 83–7.

Esper, John. 'Russia and the Baltic, 1494–1558', *Slavic Review*, vol. 25, no. 3 (1966), pp. 458–74.

Esper, John. 'A Sixteenth-Century Anti-Russian Arms Embargo', *Jahrbücher für Geschichte Osteuropas*, n.s., vol. 15, no. 2 (1967), pp. 180–96.

Evans, Norman E. 'The Anglo-Russian Royal Marriage Negotiations of 1600–1603', *Slavonic Review*, vol. 61, no. 3 (1981), pp. 366–70.

Evans, Norman E. 'The Meeting of the Russian and Scottish Ambassadors in London in 1601', *SEER*, vol. 55, no. 4 (1977), pp. 517–28.

Fahlborg, Birger. *Sveriges yttre politik 1664–68* (Stockholm: Wahlström & Widstrand, 1949).

Fedorowicz, J.K. *England's Baltic trade in the early seventeenth century. A study in Anglo-Polish Commercial Diplomacy* (Cambridge: Cambridge University Press, 1986).

Fedosov, Dmitry and Nozdrin, Oleg. 'Lion Rampant to Double Eagle: Scots in Russia, 1600–1700', forthcoming.

Firth, C. H. *Oliver Cromwell and the Rule of the Puritans in England* (London: Putnam, 1938).

Fischer, Th. A. *Scots in Germany* (Edinburgh: O. Schulze & Co, 1902).

Fischer, Th. A. *Scots in Eastern and Western Prussia* (Edinburgh: O. Schulze & Co, 1907).

Fischer, Th. A. *Scots in Sweden* (Edinburgh: Otto Schulze & Co., 1907).

Floria, B. N. 'Torgovlia Rossii so stranami zapadnoi Evropy v Arkhangel'ske (konets XVI-nachalo XVII v.)', *Srednie veka*, XXXVI (1963), pp. 129–51.

Florinsky, Michael T. *Russia: a History in Two Volumes* (New York: Macmillan, 1953).

Frank, Joseph. *The Beginnings of the English Newspaper, 1620–1660* (Cambridge: Harvard University Press, 1961).

Franklin, Simon and Shephard, Jonathan, *The Emergence of Rus 750–1200* (London and New York: Longman, 1996).

Fraser, P. *The Intelligence of the Secretaries of State and the Monopoly of Licensed News, 1660–1688* (Cambridge: Cambridge University Press, 1956).

Frederiksen, O.J. 'Virginia Tobacco in Russia under Peter the Great', *SEER*, vol. 21 (1943), pp. 40–56.

Frost, Robert I. *The Northern Wars: War, State and Society in Northeastern Europe, 1558–1721* (Harlow: Longman, 2000).

Frost, Robert I. 'Scottish Soldiers, Poland-Lithuania and the Thirty Years' War', in Steve Murdoch (ed.), *Scotland and the Thirty Years' War, 1618–1648* (Leiden: Brill, 2001), pp. 209–12.

Gardiner, S.R. 'Britain under James I', *Cambridge Modern History*, vol. 3 (Cambridge: Cambridge University Press, 1907), pp. 549–78.

Gerson, Armand J. *The Organization and the Early History of the Muscovy Company* (New York: D. Appleton and Company, 1912).

Godziszewski, W. *Polska a Moskwa za Władysława IV* (Kraków: Nakł. Polskiej Akademji Umiejętności; skł. gl. w księg. Gebethnera i Wolffa, 1930).

Goldstone, Jack A. *Revolution and Rebellion in the Early Modern World* (Berkeley: University of California Press, 1991).

Grabar, V.E. *The History of International Law in Russia, 1647–1917: A Bio-Biographical Study*, ed. and trans. W.E. Butler (Oxford: Oxford University Press, 1990).

Grant, James. *The Scottish Soldiers of Fortune* (London: Heinemann 1890).

Gregg, Edward. 'The Politics of Paranoia', in Eveline Cruickshanks and Jeremy Black (eds). *The Jacobite Challenge* (Edinburgh: John Donald, 1988), pp. 42–56.

Grosjean, Alexeia. *An Unofficial Alliance: Scotland and Sweden, 1569–1654* (Leiden: Brill, 2003).

Gurliand, I.Ia. *Ivan Gebdon, kommissarius i rezident: materialy po istorii administratsii moskovskago gosudarstva vtoroi poloviny XVII veka.* (Iaroslavl': Tip. Gub. Pravleniia, 1903).

Halperin, Charles J. 'Muscovy as a Hypertrophic State: A Critique', in *Kritika: Explorations in Russian and Eurasian History*, vol. 3, no. 3 (2002), pp. 501–7.

Hamel, Josef. *England and Russia; comprising The Voyages of John Tradescant The Elder, Sir Hugh Willoughby, Richard Chancellor, Nelson and others, to the White Sea*, trans. John Study Leigh (London: Richard Bentley, 1854) (Translated by John Studdy Leigh)

Handover, P.M. *A History of the London Gazette* (London: HMSO, 1965).

Hansen, Heinrich Johann. 'Narvas Handel 1690–1722', *Das Inland: Eine Wochenschrift für Liv-, Est- und Kurlands Geschichte und Altertumskunde*, 25, 9 (1860).

Harris, Tim. *Politics under the Later Stuarts: Party Conflict in a Divided Society, 1660–1715* (London: Longman, 1993).

Hartley, Janet M. *The Study of Russian History from British Archival Sources* (London: Mansell, 1986).

Hartley, Janet. 'A Clash of Cultures? An Anglo-Russian Encounter in the Early Eighteenth Century', in Roger Bartlett and Lindsey Hughes (eds), *Russian Society and Culture and the Long Eighteenth Century: Essays in Honour of Anthony G. Cross* (Munster: Lit; New Brunswick, USA: Transaction Publishers, 2004), pp. 48–61.

Hartley, Janet M. *A Social History of the Russian Empire, 1650–1825* (London and New York: Longman, 1999).

Hellie, Richard. *Enserfment and Military Change in Muscovy* (Chicago: University of Chicago Press, 1971).

Hellie, Richard. 'The Stratification of Muscovite Society: The Townsmen', *Russian History*, 5, Part 2 (1978), pp. 119–75.

Hellie, Richard. *The Economic and Material Culture of Russia* (Chicago: The University of Chicago Press, 1999).

Herd, Graeme P. 'General Patrick Gordon of Auchleuchries: a Scot in 17th-century Russian mercenary service' (University of Aberdeen: Doctoral Thesis, 1994).

Herd, Graeme P. 'The London Gazette as a Source for Seventeenth Century Russian History', *Eighteenth Century Russian History Newsletter*, vol. 23 (1995), pp. 1–5.

Herd, Graeme P. and Alexander Nekrasov, 'Britanskii Istorik ob Azovskikh Pokhodakh Petra I', *Istoricheskii Arkhiv*, no. 3 (September 1997), pp. 195–205.

Herd, Graeme P. 'Fall of the House of Stuart and Rise of the Petrine Order: Gordon and the Jacobite Cause in Russia', in Murray Frame and Katherine Brennan (eds), *Russia and the World in Historical Perspective* (London: Macmillan, 2000), pp. 24–44.

Herd, Graeme P. 'Peter I and the Conquest of Azov, 1695–1696', in L. A. J. Hughes (ed. and introd.), *Peter the Great and the West: New Perspectives* (London: Palgrave, 2001), pp. 6–78.

Herd, Graeme P. 'Reformation, Rebellion and Russian Military Modernization', in Jarmo Kotilaine and Marshall Poe (eds), *Modernizing Muscovy: Reform and Social Change in Seventeenth Century Russia* (London: RoutledgeCurzon, 2004), pp. 263–90.

Horn, D.B. 'Scottish Diplomatists 1689–1789' (Historical Association Publication, 1944).

Hughes, Lindsey. 'V. T. Postnikov's 1687 Mission to London: Anglo-Russian Relations in the 1680s in British Sources', *SEER*, vol. 68, no. 3 (July, 1990), pp. 447–60.

Hughes, Lindsey. *Sophia, Regent of Russia* (New Haven, Conn.: Yale University Press, 1990).

Hughes, Lindsey. *Russia and the West, the Life of a Seventeenth Century Westernizer, Prince Vasily Vasil'evich Golitsyn (1643–1714)* (London: Yale University Press, 2003).

Hughes, Lindsey. *Russia in the Age of Peter the Great* (Cambridge: Harvard University Press, 2003).

Hunt, N. C. 'The Russia Company and the Government, 1730–42', *OSP*, vol. 7 (1957), pp. 27–65.

Israel, Jonathan I. *Dutch Primacy in World Trade, 1585–1740* (Oxford: Oxford University Press, 1989).

Iurasov, A. V. *Vneshniaia torgovlia Pskova v XVII v.*, Dissertatsiia na soiskanie stepeni kandidata istoricheskikh nauk (Moskva: Rossiiskaia akademiia nauk – Institut rossiiskoi istorii, 1998).

Iuzefovich, L. A. *Kak v posol'skikh obychaiakh vedetsia* (Moskva: Mezhdunarodnye otnosheniia, 1988).

Ivanov, A. N. *Anglo-gollandskoe torgovoe sopernichestvo na russkom rynke (1578–1633 gg.)* (Dissertatsiia na soiskanie uchenoi stepeni kandidata istoricheskikh nauk, Moskva: Moskovskii gosudarstvennyi pedagocheskii institut im. V.I. Lenina: Kafedra istorii drevnego mira i srednikh vekov, 1964).

Jackson, Clare. *Restoration Scotland, 1660–1690: Royalist Politics, Religion and Ideas* (Woodbridge, VA: Boydell Press, 2003).

Jasnowski, Josef. *England & Poland in the XVIth & XVIIth Centuries (Political Relations)*. Polish Science and Learning, VII (London: Oxford University Press, 1948).

Jones, H.G. *The Mainstream of Jacobitism* (Cambridge, MA: Harvard University Press, 1954).

Jones, J.R. *The Revolutions of 1688 in England* (New York: WW Norton, 1972).

Jones, J.R. *Britain and the World, 1649–1815* (Brighton: Harvester Press, 1980).

Jones, Raymond J. *The British Diplomatic Service, 1815–1914* (Waterloo, Ontario: Wilfrid Laurier University Press, 1983).

Kahan, Arcadius. 'Observations on Petrine Forteign trade', *CASS*, vol. 8 (1974), pp. 222–36.

Kazakova, N. A. 'A. A. Vinius i stateinyi spisok ego posol'stva v Angliiu, Frantsiiu ii Ispaniiu v 1672–1674', *Trudy otdela drevnerusskoi literatury*. vol. 39 (Leningrad: Akademiia nauk SSSR, 1985), pp. 348–64.

Keenan, Edward L. 'Muscovy and Kazan: Some Introductory Remarks on the Patterns of Steppe Diplomacy', *Slavic Review*, vol. 26, no. 4 (1967), pp. 548–58.

Keenan, Edward L. 'Muscovite Political Folkways', *The Russian Review*, vol. 45, no. 2 (1986), pp. 115–84.

Keep, John L. H. 'The Regime of Filaret, 1619–1633', *SEER*, vol. 38 (1959–1960), pp. 334–360.

Keep, John L. H. *Soldiers of the Tsar: Army and Society in Russia 1462–1874* (Oxford: Oxford University Press, 1985).

Kellenbenz, Hermann. 'La signification économique de la route d'Arkhangelsk (fin XVIe–fin XVIIIe)', in Michel Mollat (ed.), *Le Navire et l'Économie Maritime du Nord de l'Europe du Moyen-Age au XVIIIe siècle: Travaux du Troisième Colloque International d'histoire maritime tenu, les 30 et 31 mai 1958, à l'Académie de Marine* (Paris: SEVPEN, 1960).

Kenyon, John. *Stuart England* (Harmondsworth: Penguin, 1986).

Kenyon, John and Ohlmeyer, Jane (eds), *The Civil Wars: A Military History of England, Scotland, and Ireland 1638–1660* (Oxford: Oxford University Press 1998).

Kiernan, V. G. 'Foreign Mercenaries and Absolute Monarchy', *Past and Present*, vol. 11 (April, 1957), pp. 66–80.

Kirby, David. *Northern Europe in the early modern period: The Baltic World 1492–1722* (London and New York: Longman, 1990).

Kirchner, W. *The Rise of the Baltic Question* (Newark: University of Delaware Press, 1954).

Kirchner, W. *Commercial Relations Between Russia and Europe 1400–1800: Collected Essays* (Bloomington: Indiana University Press, 1966).

Kivelson, Valerie A., *Autocracy in the Provinces: The Muscovite Gentry and Political Culture in the Seventeenth Century* (Stanford: Stanford University Press, 1996).

Kivelson, Valerie A. *Cartographies of Tsardom: The Land and Its Meanings in Seventeenth-Century Russia* (Ithaca: Cornell University Press, 2006).

Kivelson, Valerie A. 'On Words, Sources, and Historical Method: Which Truth about Muscovy?', in *Kritika: Explorations in Russian and Eurasian History*, vol. 3, no. 3 (2002), pp. 487–99.

Kleimola, Ann M. 'Military Service and Elite Status in Muscovy in the Second Quarter of the Sixteenth Century', *Russian History*, vol. 7, Pts. 1–2 (1980), pp. 47–64.

Kobzareva, E. I. 'Vestfal'skaia mirnaia sistema i Rossiia', *Otechestvennaia istoriia*, no. 4 (1999), pp. 146–52.

Kobzareva, E.I. 'Zelo narod grub i protivo Korolevskogo Velichestva derzok', *Istochnik*, no. 5 (2002), pp. 24–9.

Kollman, Nancy. 'Ritual and social Drama at the Muscovite Court', *Slavic Review*, vol. 45, no. 3, (1986), pp. 486–502.

Kordt, V. 'Ocherk snoshenii moskovskogo gosudarstva s respublikoi Soedinennykh Niderlandov po 1631 god.' *Sbornik imperatorskogo russkogo istoricheskogo obshchesvta*, CXVI (St Petersburg, 1902).

Kotilaine, Jarmo. 'In Defense of the Realm: Russian Arms Trade in the Seventeenth and Early Eighteenth Century', in Eric Lohr and Marshall Poe (eds), *The Military and Society in Russia, 1450–1921* (Leiden: E.J. Brill, 2002), pp. 67–95.

Kotilaine, Jarmo. 'Jan Willem Veluwenkamp, Archangel: Nederlandse ondernemers in Rusland 1550–1785,' (Arkhangel'sk: Dutch Entrepeneurs in Russia, 1550–1785), *Kritika: Explorations in Russian and Eurasian History*, vol. 3, Part 4 (2002), pp. 715–22.

Kotilaine, Jarmo. 'Mercantilism in Pre-Petrine Russia', in J. T. Kotilaine and Marshall Poe (eds), *Modernizing Muscovy: Reform and Social Change in Seventeenth-Century Russia* (London: RoutledgeCurzon, 2004), pp. 143–73.

Kotilaine, Jarmo. *Russia's Foreign Trade and Economics Expansion in the Seventeenth Century: Windows on the World* (Leiden and Boston: Brill, 2005).

Kotilaine, Jarmo and Poe, Marshall (eds). *Modernizing Muscovy: Reform and Social Change in Seventeenth-Century Russia* (London: RoutledgeCurzon, 2004), pp. 143–73.

Kukanova, Nina. Grigor'evna *Ocherki po istorii russko-iranskikh torgovykh otnoshenii v XVII-pervoi polovine XIX veka: po materialam russkikh arkhivov* (Saransk: Mordovskoe knizhnoe izdatel'stvo, 1977).

Küng, Enn. *Rootsi majanduspoliitika Narva kaubanduse küsimuses 17. sajandi teisel poolel* (Tartu: Kirjastus Eesti Ajalooarhiiv, 2001).

Küng, Enn. 'Inglise kaubandus Narvas 17. sajandi II poolel', *Kleio: Ajaloo ajakiri*, 5/6 (1992), pp. 12–16.

Küng, Enn. 'Tubakakaubanduse riiklik reguleerimine 17. sajandil Narvas', *Kleio: Ajaloo ajakiri*, 9 (1994), pp. 3–11.

Lachs, Phyllis S. *The Diplomatic Corps Under Charles II and James II* (New Brunswick, N.J.: Rutgers Publishing, 1965).

Lane, Margery. 'The Diplomatic Service under William III', *Transactions of the Royal Historical Society*, 4th Series (1927), pp. 87–109.

Leitsch, W. 'Kliuchevskii's Study on the Reports of Foreign Travellers about Muscovy: a Belated Review', *Canadian-American Slavic Studies*, vol. 20, nos 3–4 (1986), pp. 299–308.

Lenman, Bruce P. 'Scottish Nobility and the Revolution', in R. Beddard (ed.), *The Revolutions of 1688* (Oxford: Clarendon Press, 1991), pp. 137–62

Letiche, John M. and Basil Dmytryshyn (eds), *Russian Statecraft: The Politika of Iurii Krizhanich* (London: Blackwell, 1985),

Lincoln, W. Bruce. *The Romanovs* (New York: Dial Press, 1981).

Likhachev, D. S. *Puteshestviia russkikh poslov XVI–XVII vv* (Moskva: Izd-vo Akademii nauk SSSR, 1954).

Lipson, Ephraim. *The Economic History of England*, 5th edn (London: Black, 1929),

Liubimenko, Inna. 'Torgovye snosheniia Rossii s Angliei i Gollandiei s 1553 po 1649 god', *Izvestiia Akademii Nauk SSSR, Otdelenie obshchestvevnnykh nauk*, 10 (1933), pp. 729–54

Lubimenko, I. 'A Project for the Acquisition of Russia by James I', *English Historical Society*, vol. 29 (1914), pp. 246–56.

Lubimenko, I. 'The Correspondence of the Early Stuarts with the First Romanovs', *Transactions of the Royal Historical Society*, 4th Series, vol. 1 (1918), pp. 77–91.

Lubimenko, I. 'The Struggle of the Early Dutch with the English for the Russian Markets in the Seventeenth Century', *Transactions of the Royal Historical Society*, 4th Series, vol. 7 (1924), pp. 27–51.

Lyubimenko, I. 'Les relations diplomatiques de l'Angleterre avec la Russie au XVIe siecle', *Revue Historique*, 121 (1916), pp. 48–82.

Lyubimenko, I. 'Letters Illustrating the Relations of England and Russia in the Seventeenth Century', *English Historical Review*, vol. 32 (1917), pp. 92–103.

Lyubimenko, I. 'Anglo-Russian Relations During the First English Revolution', *Transactions of the Royal Historical Society*, 4th Series, vol. 2 (1928), pp. 39–60.

Lyubimenko, I. *Les Relations Commerciales et Politiques de l'Angleterre avec la Russie avant Pierre le Grand* (Paris: Librarie ancienne Honoré Campion, 1933).

Loewenson, Leo. 'Did Russia Intervene after the Execution of Charles I?', *Bulletin of the Institute of Historical Research*, vol. 18 (1940–1941), pp. 70–85.

Loewenson, Leo. 'The Works of Robert Boyle and the Present State of Russia' by Samuel Collins (1671)', *SEER*, vol. 23 (1954–55), pp. 84–94.

Loewenson, Leo. 'The First Interviews between Peter I and William III in 1697: Some Neglected English Material', *SEER*, vol. 36 (1958), pp. 308–16.

Lohr, Eric and Poe, Marshall (eds). *The Military and Society in Russia, 1450–1917* (Leiden: Brill, 2002).

Longworth, Philip. *Alexis, Tsar of All the Russias* (London: Secker and Warburg, 1984).

Longworth, Philip. 'Russian-Venetian Relations in the Reign of Tsar Aleksey Mikhailovitch', *Slavonic Review*, vol. 64, no. 3 (1986), pp. 84–94.

Lossky, A. 'Dutch Diplomacy and the Franco-Russian Trade Negotiations of 1681', in R. Hatton and M. S. Anderson (eds), *Studies in Diplomatic History: Essays in Memory of David Bayne Horn* (London: Archon Books, 1970), pp. 32–46.

Macaulay, Lord. *History of England* (Albany: George D. Spoul, 1908).

McCabe, Ina Baghdiantz. *The Shah's Silk for Europe's Silver: The Eurasian Trade of the Julfa Armenians in Safavid Iran and India (1530–1750)* (Atlanta: Scholars Press, 1999).

Macinnes, Allan I. *The British Revolution*, 1629–1660 (London: Palgrave Macmillan, 2003).

McInnes, Angus. 'When was the English Revolution?', *History*, vol. 67 (October 1982), pp. 377–92.

McKay, Derek and Scott, H. M. *The Rise of the Great Powers, 1648–1815* (London: Longman, 1983).

McLynn, Frank. *The Jacobites* (London: Routledge & Kegan Paul, 1988).

Macquarrie, Alan. *Scotland and the Crusades, 1095–1560* (Edinburgh: John Donald, 1985).

Maier, Ingrid. 'Newspaper Translations in Seventeenth-Century Muscovy. About the Sources, Topics and Periodicity of *Kuranty* Made in Stockholm (1649)', *Explorare necesse est. Hyllningsskrift till Barbro Nilsson*. Acta Universitatis Stockholmiensis. Stockholm Slavic Studies 28 (Stockholm 2002), pp. 181–90

Maier, Ingrid and Pilger, Wouter. 'Second-hand translation for Tsar Aleksej Mixajlovič – A glimpse into the "newspaper workshop" at *posol'skii prikaz* (1648)', *Russian Linguistics*, vol. 25, no. 2 (2001), pp. 209–42.

Mallet, M. E. and Hale, J. R. *The Military Organization of A Renaissance State: Venice, c.1400 to 1617* (Cambridge: Cambridge University Press, 1984).

Malov, A. V. *Moskovskie vybornye polki soldatskogo stroia v nachal'nyi period svoei istorii 1656–1671gg* (Moscow: Drevnekhranilishche, 2006).

Marker, Gary. 'Russia and the "Printing Revolution": Notes and Observations', *Slavic Review*, vol. 41, no. 2 (Summer, 1982), pp. 266–83

Martens, F. F. *Rossiia i Angliia v Srednei Azii* (S.-Peterburg: Izd. E. Gart'e, 1880).

Martynov, I. F. 'Prince Prozorovsky's Ambassadorial Speech to King Charles II', *OSP*, vol. 13 (1980), pp. 50–7.

Matthee, Rudolph P. *The Politics of Trade in Safavid Iran: Silk for Silver, 1600–1730* (Cambridge: Cambridge University Press, 1999).

Matveev, Vladimir. 'Summit Diplomacy of the Seventeenth Century: William III and Peter I in Utrecht and London, 1687–1698', *Diplomacy & Statecraft*, vol. 11, no. 2 (November 2000), pp. 29–48.

Melville, James. *The autobiography and diary of Mr. James Melvill . . . with a continuation of the diary, ed. from manuscripts in the libraries of the Faculty of advocates and University of Edinburgh*, ed. Robert Pitcairn (Edinburgh: Printed for the Wodrow society, 1842).

Meyendorff, A. F. 'Anglo-Russian Trade in the Sixteenth Century', *SEER*, vol. 25 (1936–1937), pp. 109–21.

Miliukov, P. *History of Russia,* Vol. 1: *From the beginnings to the Empire of Peter the Great* (New York: Funk & Wagnalls, 1968).

Miller, John. *Popery and Politics in England, 1660–1688* (Cambridge, Cambridge University Press, 1973).

Miller, John. *The Jacobite Challenge* (Edinburgh: John Donald, 1988).

Miller, John. *James II and VII* (New Haven, Yale, 2000).

Miller, John. 'Proto-Jacobitism: The Tories and the Revolution of 1688–9', in Eveline Cruickshanks and Jeremy Black (eds), *The Jacobite Challenge.* (Edinburgh: John Donald, 1988), pp. 7–23.

Miller, John. *The Stuarts* (London: Palgrave Macmillan,2004).

Muddiman, J. G. *The King's Journalist 1659–1689: Studies in the Reign of Charles II* (London: John Lane, 1923).

Muliukin, A. S. *Ocherki po istorii iuridicheskago polozheniia inostrannykh kuptsov v Moskovskom gosudarstvie* (Odessa: Tip. 'Tekhnik', 1912).

Muller, Samuel. *Geschiedenis der Noordsche Compagnie door Mr. S. Muller Fz* (Utrecht: Gebr. Van der Post, 1874).

Murdoch, Steve. 'Soldiers, Sailors, Jacobite Spy: Russo-Jacobite Relations, 1688–1750', *Slavonica,* vol. 3, no. 1 (1996–7), pp. 7–27.

Murdoch, Steve. 'Diplomacy in Transition: Stuart-British Diplomacy in Northern Europe, 1603–1618', in Allan I. Macinnes, Thomas Riis and Frederik Pedersen (eds), *Ships, Guns and Bibles in the North Sea and Baltic States, c.1350–c.1700* (East Lothian: Tuckwell Press, 2000).

Murdoch, Steve (ed.). *Scotland and the Thirty Years' War, 1618–1648* (Leiden: Brill, 2001).

Murdoch, Steve and Grosjean, Alexia (eds). 'Scotland, Scandinavia and Northern Europe, 1580–1707' (the SSNE Database): http://www.st-andrews.ac.uk/history/ssne/about.php#fields

Murov, E. A. (ed.). *Istoriia gosudarstvennoi okhrany Rossii: Sobstvennaia Ego Imperatorskogo Velichestva okhrana, 1881–1917* (Moscow: Petronivs, 2006).

Novosel'skii, A. A. *Bor'ba Moskovskogo gosudarstva s Tatarami v pervoi polovine XVII veka* (Moskva: Izd-vo Akademii nauk SSSR, 1948).

O'Brien, C. Bickford. 'Muscovite Primal Administration of the Seventeenth Century, The Quality of Leadership', *Forshungen zur Osteuropäisschen Heschite,* vol. 24 (1954), pp. 223–35.

O'Brien, C. Bickford. *Muscovy and the Ukraine: From the Pereiaslavl Agreement to the Truce of Andrusovo, 1654–1667* (Berkley and Los Angeles: University of California Press, 1963).

Ouston, H. 'York in Edinburgh: James VII and the Patronage of Learning in Scotland, 1679–1688', in J. Dwyer, R. A. Mason and A. Murdoch (eds), *New Perspectives on the Popular Culture in Early Modern Scotland* (Edinburgh: John Donald, 1982), pp. 133–55.

Paeffgen, Thomas. *Englisch-russische Wirtschaftsbeziehungen im 16. und 17. Jahrhundert* (Heidelberg: Doctoral thesis, 1979).

Page, William Samuel. *The Russia Company from 1553 to 1660* (London: W. Brown and Co., 1911).

Parker, Geoffrey (ed.). *The Thirty Years' War* (London: Routledge and Kegan Paul, 1984).

Parker, Geoffrey (ed.). *The Military Revolution: Military Innovation and the Rise of the West* (Cambridge: Cambridge University Press, 1988).

Parker, Geoffrey and Smith, Lesley M. *The General Crisis of the Seventeenth Century,* 2nd edn (London: Routledge, 1997).

Pascal, Pierre. *Avvakum et les débuts du Raskol* (Paris: Mouton, 1963.)

Patterson, W. B. *King James VI and I and the Reunion of Christendom* (Cambridge: Cambridge University Press, 1997).

Pavlov, Andrei and Maureen Perrie. *Ivan the Terrible* (London: Pearson/Longman, 2003).

Peck, Linda (ed.). *The Mental World of the Jacobean Court* (Cambridge: Cambridge University Press, 1991).

Perjes, G. 'Army Provisioning, Logistics and Strategy in the Second Half of the Seventeenth Century', *Acta Historica Academiae Scientarium Hungaricae*. vol. 16, Budapest (1970), pp. 1–14.

Pernal, Andrew B. 'The London Gazette as a Primary Source for the Biography of General Patrick Gordon', *Canadian Journal of History*, vol. 38, no. 1 (April 2003), pp. 1–17.

Phipps, G. M. 'Britons in Seventeenth Century Russia: A Study of the Origins of Modernization' (University of Pennsylvania, Unpublished PhD Thesis, 1971).

Phipps, G. M. *Sir John Merrick, English Merchant-Diplomat in Seventeenth-Century Russia*. Russian Biography Series, 13 (Newtonville, Mass: Oriental Research Partners, 1983).

Phipps, G. M. 'The Study of Britons in Seventeenth Century Russia', in Janet M. Hartley (ed.), *The Study of Russian History from British Archival Sources* (London: Mansell Publishing, 1986), pp. 27–50.

Phipps, G. M. 'The Russian Embassy to London of 1645–46 and the Abrogation of the Muscovy Charter', *SEER*, vol. 68, no. 2 (1990), pp. 257–76.

Piirimäe, Helmut. *Kaubanduse küsimused vene-rootsi suhetes 1661–1700. a* (Tartu: Tartu Riiklik Ulikool, 1961).

Piirimäe, Helmut. 'Torgovye otnosheniia Rossii so Shvetsiei i drugimi stranami Evropy po materialam narvskogo vvoza v 1661–1700gg', *Skandinanvskii sbornik*, XI (1966), pp. 44–110.

Piirimäe, Helmut. 'Udel'nyi ves razlichnykh stran Zapadnoi Evropy v torgovle eston-skikh gorodov v XVII veke', *Skandinavskii sbornik*, XV (1970), pp. 7–22.

Piirimäe, Pärtel. 'Russia, The Turks and Europe: Legitimations of War and the Formation of European Identity in the Early Modern Period', *Journal of Early Modern History*, vol. 11, No. 1–2 (2007), pp. 63–86.

Pincus, Steven A. 'Popery, Trade and Universal Monarchy: The Ideological Context of the Outbreak of the Second Anglo-Dutch War', *EHR*, vol. 107 (1992), pp. 1–29.

Pincus, Steven A. *Protestantism and Patriotism: Ideologies and the Making of English Foreign Policy, 1650–1668* (Cambridge: Cambridge University Press, 1996).

Platonov, S. F. *Proshloe Russkogo Severa* (Berlin: Obelisk, 1924).

Platonov, S. F. *Moscow and the West*. Translated and edited by Joseph L. Wieczynski. Introduction by Serge A. Zenkovsky, Russian Series, Volume 9 (Harrisburg: Academic International, 1972).

Platonov, S. F. *The Time of Troubles: A Historical Study of the Internal Crisis and Social Struggle in Sixteenth-and Seventeenth-Century Muscovy*. ed. and trans. Alexander, J.T. (Lawrence, KS: University Press of Kansas, 1985).

Plokhy, S. *The Cossacks and religion in early modern Russia* (Oxford: Oxford University Press, 2001).

Poe, Marshall. 'The Consequences of the Military Revolution in Muscovy: A Comparative Perspective', *Comparative Studies in Society and History*, vol. 38, no. 4 (1996), pp. 603–18.

Poe, Marshall. *'A People Born to Slavery': Russia in Early Modern Ethnography, 1476–1748* (Ithaca and London: Cornell University Press, 2000).

Poe, Marshall. 'The Truth about Muscovy', *Kritika: Explorations in Russian and Eurasian History*, 3.3 (2002), pp. 473–86.

Poe, Marshall. *The Russian Elite in the Seventeenth Century.* 2 vols. (Helsinki: Annales Academiae Scientiarum Fennicae, 2004).

Pokrovskii, A. 'Iz istorii gazety v Rossii', *Vedomosti vremeni Petra Velikago: v pamiat dvukhsotlietiia pervoi russkoi gazety.* vypusk vtoroi, 1708–1709gg. (Moskva: Izd. Moskovskoi Sinodal'noi Tipografii, 1906), pp. 1–39.

Poli#aksensk#aay, Joseph. *Tragic Triangle: The Netherlands, Spain and Bohemia, 1617–1621* (Prague: Charles University, 1991).

Porshnev, B. F. 'Les rapports politiques de l'Europe occidentale et de l'Europe orientale à l'époque de la guerre de Trente Ans', *XIe. Congrès International des Sciences Historiques, Rapports IV, Histoire moderne* (Göteborg-Stockholm-Uppsala, 1960), pp. 136–63.

Porshnev, B. F. *Frantsiia, Angliiskaia revoliutsiia i evropeiskaia politika v seredine XVII v.* (Moskva: Nauka, 1970).

Porshnev, B. F. *Muscovy and Sweden in the Thirty Years' War*, ed. Paul Dukes, trans. Brian Pearce (Cambridge: Cambridge University Press, 1995).

Pozdeeva, I. V. 'Pervye Romanovy i tsaristskaia ideia (XVII vek)', *Voprosy istorii*, No. 1 (1996), pp. 41–52.

Price, Jacob M. *The Tobacco Adventure to Russia: Enterprise, politics, and diplomacy in the quest for a northern market for English colonial tobacco, 1676–1722* (Philadelphia: American Philosophical Society, 1961).

Rabb, Theodore K. *Enterprise & Empire: merchant and gentry investment in the expansion of England, 1575–1630* (Cambridge: Harvard University Press, 1967).

Raeff, Marc. *Origins of the Russian Intelligentsia: The Eighteenth Century Nobility* (New York: Harcourt, Brace & World, 1966).

Reger, William M. 'Baptizing Mars: The Conversion to Russian Orthodoxy of European Mercenaries during the Mid-Seventeenth Century', in Eric Lohr and Marshall Poe (eds), *The Military and Society in Russia, 1450–1917* (Leiden: Brill, 2002), pp. 389–412.

Reger, William M. 'European Mercenary Officers and the Reception of Military Reform in the Seventeenth-Century Russian Army', in Jarmo Kotilaine and Marshall Poe (eds), *Modernizing Muscovy: Reform and Social Change in Seventeenth-Century Russia* (London: RoutledgeCurzon, 2004), pp. 223–45.

Repin, N. N. 'Vneshniaia torgovlia cherez Arkahngel'sk i vnutrennyi rynok Rossii vo vtoroi polovine XVII – pervoi chetverti XVIII vv' (Kandidatskaia dissertatsiia, Moskovskii gosudarstvennyi universitet, 1970).

Riasanovsky, Nicholas V. *Russian Identities: A Historical Survey* (New York: Oxford University Press, 2005)

Robbins, Caroline, 'Carlisle and Marvell in Russia, Sweden and Denmark, 1663–1664', *History of Ideas Newsletter*, vol. 3 (1957), pp. 8–17.

Roberts, Michael. *The Military Revolution, 1560–1660* (Belfast: Queen's University of Belfast, 1956).

Roberts, M (trans. and ed.) *Swedish Diplomats at Cromwell's Court, 1655–1656: the Missions of Peter Julius Coyet and Christe Bonde* (Camden Society, 4th series, 36, London, 1988).

Rogers, James E. Thorold. *A History of Agriculture and Prices in England: from the year after the Oxford parliament (1259) to the commencement of the continental war (1793)* 7 vols in 8 (Oxford: Clarendon Press, 1866–1902).

Rogers, Nicholas. 'Riot and Popular Jacobitism in Early Hanovarian England', pp. 70–88, in Cruickshanks, E. (ed.) *Ideology and Conspiracy: Aspects of Jacobitism, 1688–1759* (Edinburgh: John Donald, 1982).

Roginskii, Z. I. *Poezdka gontsa Gerasima Semenovicha Dokhturova v Angliiu v 1645–1646 gg.; iz istorii anglo-russkikh otnoshenii v period angliiskoi revoliutsii XVII veka* (Iaroslavl: Iaroslavskiĭ gosudarstvennyĭ pedagogicheskiĭ institut imeni K.D. Ushinskogo, 1959).

Roginskii, Z. I. 'Missiia lorda Kolpepera v Moskvu (Iz istorii anglo-russkikh otnoshenii v period angliiskoi revoliutsii XVIIv.), in Liubomir Grigorevich Beskrovnyi and others, *Mezhdunarodnye sviazi Rossii v XVII-XVIII vv.: ekonomika, politika i kultura: sbornik stateĭ* (Moskva: Izd-vo 'Nauka', 1966), pp. 96–102.

Rogozhin, N. M. *U gosudarevykh del byt ukazano . . .* (Moskva: Izdatel'stvo Rossiiskoi Akademii Gosudarstvennogo Sluzhby, 2002).

Rothstein, Andrew. *Peter the Great and Marlborough: Politics and Diplomacy in Converging Wars* (New York: St Martin's Press, 1986).

Rukhmanova, E. D. 'Bor'ba Rossii za vykhod v Baltiiskoe more v 1656–1661 godakh' (Kandidatskaia dissertatsiia, Leningradskii gosudarstvennyi universitet, 1954).

Runciman, Steven. *The Great Church in Captivity: Study of the Patriarchate of Constantinople from the eve of the Turkish conquest to the Greek War of Independence* (London: Cambridge University Press, 1968).

Samling rörande Finlands historia I-V, ed. Johan Esaias Waaranen (Helsingfors: Finska Litteratur-Sällskapets tryckeri, 1863–1878).

Sashalmi, Endre. 'Sixteenth-Seventeenth Century Muscovite Ideology in European Perspective', in G. Szvák (ed.), *The Place of Russia in Europe* (Budapest: Magyar Ruszisztikai Intézet, 1999), pp. 166–72.

Sashalmi, Endre. 'Some Remarks on the Typology of Official Petrine Political Ideology', in G. Svák (ed.), *The Place of Russia in Eurásia* (Budapest: Magyar Ruszisztikai Intézet, 2001), pp. 233–243.

Schibli, R., *Die ältesten russischen Zeitungsübersetzungen (Vesti-Kuranty): Quellenkunde, Lehnwortschatz und Toponomastik.* Slavica Helvetica vol. 29 (Bern, New York: P. Lang, 1988).

Schmidt, H.D. 'The Establishment of 'Europe' as a Political Expression', *The Historical Journal*, vol. 9, no. 2 (1966), pp. 172–8.

Schwoerer, Lois G. 'Liberty and the Press and Public Opinion: 1660–1694', in J. R. Jones (ed.), *Liberty Secured? Britain Before and After 1688* (Stanford: Stanford University Press, 1992) pp. 199–230.

Scott, Jonathan. *England's Troubles: seventeenth-century English political instability in European context* (Cambridge: Cambridge University Press, 2000).

Scott, William Robert. *The Constitution and Finance of English, Scottish and Irish Joint-Stock Companies to 1720* (Cambridge: Cambridge University Press, 1910).

Seaward, Paul *The Restoration 1660–1688* (London and Basingstoke: Macmillan, 1991).

Seliga, Stanislaw and Koczy, Leon. *Scotland and Poland: A Chapter of Forgotten History* (Glasgow: Stanislaw Kostka Matwin, 1969).

Serech, Jurij, 'Stefan Yavorsky and the Conflict of Ideologies in the Age of Peter I', *SEER*, vol. 30 (1951–1952), pp. 40–62.

Sevcenko, Ihor 'Muscovy's Conquest of Kazan: Two Views Reconciled', *Slavic Review*, vol. 26, no. 4 (1967), pp. 541–7.

Sinclair, G.A. 'A Russo-Scottish General', *Aberdeen University Review*, vol. 10 (1922–1923), pp. 242–6.

Smirnov, Pavel P. *Ekonomicheskaia politika Moskovskago gosudarstva v XVII veke* (Kiev: Tipografiia T-va I.N. Kushnerev i Ko., 1912).

Smirnov, Pavel P. 'Novoe chelobit'e moskovskikh torgovykh liudei o vysulke inozemtsev v 1627g', *Chteniia v istoricheskom obshchesvte Nestora-letopistsa*, XXIII (1912).

Smout, T. C. (ed.). *Scotland and Europe* (Edinburgh: John Donald, 1986).

Snyder, H. L. 'The British Diplomatic Service During the Godolphin Ministry', in R. Hatton and M. S. Anderson (eds), *Studies in Diplomatic History* (London: Archon, Longman, 1970), pp. 47–68.

Soloviev, S. M. *History of Russia from Earliest Times in Fifty Volumes*, ed. and trans. G. E. Orchard, vol. 17; ed. and trans. Lindsey Hughes, Vol. 25 (Gulf Breeze, FL: Academic International Press, 1989, 1996).

Solov'ev, S. M. *Istoriia Rossii s drevneishikh vremen: v piatnadtsati knigakh* (Moskva: Izd-vo sotsialno-ekonomicheskoi lit-ry, 1959–66).

Somerville, J.P. 'James I and the divine right of kings: English politics and continental theory', in Linda Peck (ed.), *The Mental World of the Jacobean Court* (Cambridge: Cambridge University Press, 1991), pp. 55–70.

Speck, W.A. *Reluctant Revolutionaries: Englishmen and the Revolution of 1688* (Oxford: Oxford University Press, 1988).

Stashevskii, E. D. *Smolenskaia voina 1632–1634 gg. Organizatsiia i sostoianie Moskovskoi armii* (Kiev: Universitetskaia Tip. Akts. Ob-va pechat. i izd. diela, 1919).

Steiger, Heinhard. 'Concrete Peace and General Order: The Legal Meaning of the Treaties of 24 October 1648', in Klaus Bussmann and Heinz Schilling (eds), *1648: War and Peace in Europe*, vol. 1, *Politics, Religion, Law and Society* (Münster and Osnabrück: 350 Jahre Westfälischer Friede mbh, 1998), pp. 437–45.

Steuart, A. Francis. *Scottish Influences in Russian History from the end of the sixteenth century to the beginning of the nineteenth century* (Glasgow: Maclehose, 1913).

Stevens, Carol B. *Soldiers on the Steppe: Army Reform and Social Change in Early Modern Russia* (DeKalb: Illinois University Press, 1995).

Supple, B.E. *Commercial Crisis and Change in England 1600–1642* (Cambridge: Cambridge University Press, 1970).

Sutherland, John. *The Restoration Newspaper and its Development* (Cambridge: Cambridge University Press 1986).

Sutherland, N. M. 'The Origins of the Thirty Years' War and the Structure of European Politics', *English Historical Review*, vol. 107, no. 424 (1992), pp. 587–625.

Szechi, Daniel, 'The Jacobite Revolution Settlement, 1689–1696', *English Historical Review*, vol. 108 (1993), pp. 610–38.

Szechi, Daniel. *The Jacobites: Britain and Europe, 1688–1788* (Manchester: Manchester University Press, 1994).

Szeftel, Mark. 'The Title of the Muscovite Monarch up to the End of the Seventeenth Century', *Canadian-American Slavic Studies*, vol. 13, nos 1–2 (1979), pp. 59–81.

Tanner, J. R. *Constitutional Documents of the Reign of James I: A.D. 1603–1625* (Cambridge: Cambridge University Press, 1961).

Telegina, E.P. 'K voprosu o torgovo-predprinimatel'skoi deiatel'nosti anglichan v Rossi v 30–40-e gody XVII veka', *Uchenye zapiski Blagoveshchenskogo gosudarstvennogo pedagogicheskogo instituta imeni M.I. Kalinina*, IX (1958), pp. 179–311.

Terry, C.S. *The Life and Campaigns of Alexander Leslie, first earl of Leven* (London: Longmans, Green and Co., 1899).

Teschke, Benno. *The Myth of 1648: Class, Geopolitics and the Making of Modern International Relations* (London: Verso, 2003).

Thompson, John M. *Russia, Bolshevism, and the Versailles Peace* (Princeton: Princeton University Press, 1967).

Thomson, Mark A. *The Secretaries of State, 1681–1772* (London: Frank Cass, 1968).

Troebst, Stefan. 'Isfahan-Moskau-Amsterdam: Zur entstehungsgeschichte des moskauischen Transitprivilegs für die Armenische Handelskompanie in Persien (1667–1676)', *Jahrbücher für die Geschichte Osteuropas*, Neue Folge, XLI, 2 (1993), pp. 180–209.

Troebst, Stefan. *Handelskontrolle—'Derivation'—Eindämmung: Schwedische Moskaupolitik 1617–1661* (Wiesbaden: Harrassowitz Verlag, 1997).

Turnbull, G. H. *Hartlib, Dury and Comenius: Gleanings from Hartlib's Papers* (Liverpool: University Press of Liverpool, 1947).

Turner, Edward Raymond. 'Committees of the Privy Council, 1688–1760', *English Historical Review*, vol. 31, no. 124 (1916), pp. 545–72.

Turner, Edward Raymond. *The Privy Council of England in the Seventeenth and Eighteenth Centuries* (Baltimore: The Johns Hopkins Press, 1927–8)

Unkovskaya, M. V. 'Learning Foreign Mysteries: Russian Pupils of the Aptekarskii Prikaz, 1650–1700', *OSP*, New Series, vol. 30 (1997), pp. 1–20.

Uroff, Benjamin Phillip. 'Grigorii Karpovich Kotoshikhin, On Russia in the Reign of Alexis Mikhailovich: An Annotated Translation' (Columbia University, Unpublished PhD Thesis, 1970).

Ustrialov, N. *Istoriia tsarstvovaniia Petra Velikogo*. 5 vols (Sanktpeterburg: Tip. II-go otd-niia Sobstv. Ego Imp. Vel. Kantseliarii, 1858–1863).

Vainshtein, Osip L'vovich. *Rossiia i Tridtsatiletniaia Voina 1618–1648: Ocherki iz istorii vneshnei politiki Moskovskogo gosudarstva v pervoi polovine XVII v* (Leningrad: Gospolitizdat, 1947).

Varentsov, Vladimir. Alekseevich *Torgovlia i tamozhennoe upravlenie Novgoroda v XVI-XVII vekakh* (Novgorod: Novgorodskaia tamozhnia – Novgorodskii gosudarstvennyi universitet im. Iaroslava Mudrogo, 1996).

Veluwenkamp, Jan W. *Archangel: Nederlandse ondernemers in Rusland, 1580–1785* (Amsterdam: Balans, 2000).

Vernadsky, George. *The Tsardom of Muscovy, 1547–1682*. 2 vols (New Haven and London: Yale University Press, 1968).

Virginskii, V. 'Proekty prevrashcheniia Severovostochnoi Rossii v angliiskuiu koloniiu v XVII veke', *Istoricheskii zhurnal* (1940) 11, pp. 89–95.

Voskanian, Vazgen. Karapetovich *Armiano-russkie ekonomicheskie otnosheniia v XVII veke (Rol' armianskogo kupechestva v perdsidskoi torgovle Rossii)* (Dissertatsiia na soiskanie uchenoi stepeni kandidata istoricheskikh nauk, Erevan: Akademiia nauk Armianskoi SSR – Institut istorii, 1948).

Waugh, D. C. 'The Publication of Muscovite *Kuranty*', *Kritika: A Review of Current Soviet Books on Russian History*, vol. 9, no. 3 (1973), pp. 104–20.

Waugh, D. C (ed.). *Essays in Honor of A.A. Zimin* (Columbus, Ohio: Slavica, 1985).

Wedgwood, C. V. *The Trial of Charles I* (London: World Books, 1964).

Whittaker, Cynthia Hyla (ed., with Edward Kasinec and Robert H. Davis Jr). *Russia Engages the World, 1453–1825* (Cambridge, MA: Harvard University Press, 2003).

Wijnroks, Eric H. 'Mezhdunarodnaia konkurentsiia v torgovle mezhdu Rossiei i Zapadnoi Evropoi: 1560–1640 gg', in I. N. Bespiatykh (ed.), *Russkii Sever i Zapadniaia Evropa: Sbornik nauchnykh statei* (St Petersburg: Russko-Baltiiskii informatsionnyi tsentr BLITs, 1999), pp. 9–41.

Willan, T. S. 'Trade Between Russia in the second half of the sixteenth century', *English Historical Review*, vol. 63 (1948), pp. 307–21.

Willan, T. S. 'The Russia Company and Narva', *SEER*, vol. 31 (1952–1953), pp. 405–9.

Willan, T. S. *The Muscovy Merchants of 1555* (Manchester: Manchester University Press, 1555).

Willan, T. S. *The Early History of the Muscovy Company, 1553–1603* (Manchester: Manchester University Press, 1956)

Williams, Keith. *The English Newspaper: An Illustrated History to 1900* (London: Springwood Books, 1977).

Wills, Rebecca. *The Jacobites and Russia 1715–1750* (East Linton: Tuckwell Press, 2002).

Wirtschafter, Elise Kimerling. *Social Identity in Imperial Russia* (Dekalb, Illinois: Northern Illinois University Press, 1997).

Wormald, Jenny. 'James VI and I, Basilikon Doron and The Trew Law of Free Monarchies: the Scottish context and the English translation', in Linda Peck (ed.). *The Mental World of the Jacobean Court* (Cambridge: Cambridge University Press, 1991), pp. 36–54.

Worthington, David. *Scots in Habsburg Service, 1618–1648.* (Leiden: Brill, 2004).

Wretts-Smith, M. 'The English in Russia during the second half of the sixteenth century', *Transactions of the Royal Historical Society*, 4th Series, vol. 3 (1920), pp. 72–102.

Yakobson, S. 'Early Anglo-Russian Relations, 1553–1613', *SEER*, vol. 13 (1934–1935), pp. 597–610.

Zins, Henryk. *England and the Baltic in the Elizabethan Era* (Manchester: Manchester University Press, 1967).

Zordanija, G. 'Les premiers marchands et navigateurs français dans la region maritime de la Russie septentrionale. L'origine des relations commerciales et diplomatiques franco-russes', in F. Braudel et al. (eds), *La Russie et L'Europe, XVIe-XXe Siècles*. F. and others (Paris-Moscow: SEVPEN, 1970), pp. 7–30.

Index